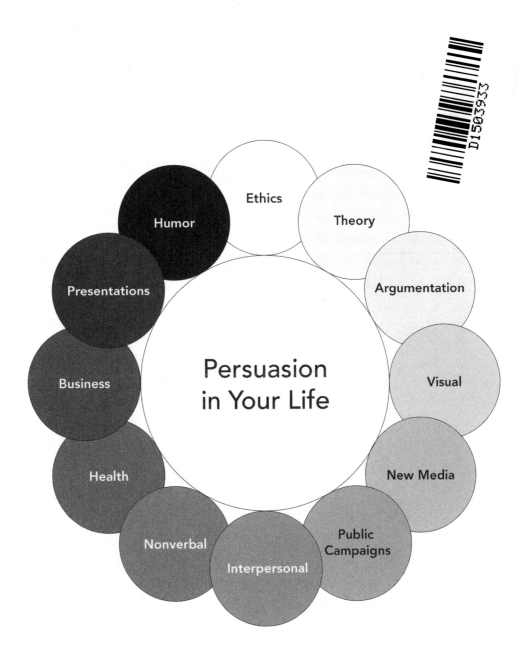

Persuasion
in Your Life

Ethics

Theory

Argumentation

Visual

New Media

Public Campaigns

Interpersonal

Nonverbal

Health

Business

Presentations

Humor

PERSUASION IN YOUR LIFE

Shawn T. Wahl
Missouri State University

Routledge
Taylor & Francis Group

LONDON AND NEW YORK

First published 2013 by Pearson Education, Inc.

Published 2016 by Routledge
2 Park Square, Milton Park, Abingdon, Oxon OX14 4RN
711 Third Avenue, New York, NY 10017, USA

Routledge is an imprint of the Taylor & Francis Group, an informa business

Credits and acknowledgments borrowed from other sources and reproduced, with permission, in this
textbook appear on page 343.

ISBN: 9780205741588 (pbk)

Library of Congress Cataloging-in-Publication Data
Wahl, Shawn T.
Persuasion in your life/Shawn T. Wahl.
    p. cm.
    ISBN 978-0-205-74158-8
    1. Persuasion (Rhetoric)   2. Persuasion (Rhetoric)—Social aspects.   3. Persuasion (Rhetoric)
in literature.   4. Persuasion (Psychology)—Social aspects.   I. Title.
    P301.5.P47W34 2013
    303.3'42—dc23   2012012389

Dedication

To Phyllis and Ron

Brief Contents

Detailed Contents

Preface

As instructors, we must explore many questions when planning a persuasion course. First, we must address the broader conceptual questions, such as: What do we want our students to learn? How can this information be applied to their current and future life? How can we make this material meaningful, useful, and interesting to students with a variety of life goals? How can all of the important information, skills, and competencies relevant to persuasion be covered in one term?

Next, we must address the critical questions that emerge about how to organize so much information and how to translate it in a way that students will understand. Instructors often grapple with questions such as: How many writing assignments should I require? Should I include a social media component? How much attention should be given to theory? How can this course be delivered online?

I considered many of the same questions and challenges as I made decisions about what content to cover in this text. My mission in writing this book was to focus on theory, research, and application of knowledge related to persuasion so that the subject can easily be covered in one term across delivery formats (e.g., traditional, online, hybrid). Further, I wanted to provide a book that speaks directly to the student by focusing on actual life experiences—from critically viewing persuasive public campaigns to making business and health care decisions. I also wanted to provide a text that is adaptable to a variety of instructional needs for my colleagues who may need the flexibility to emphasize, say, persuasive presentations and for others who may focus on persuasive campaigns, perhaps not include presentations at all, or deliver the course online. I recognize the diversity of needs from one college or university to the next.

In response to my goal of focusing directly on the individual student experience as it relates to the study of persuasion, I developed an organizing feature (the In Your Life feature described below), which I believe will help instructors guide students across life contexts. The In Your Life feature fosters the primary theme of this text—encouraging students to apply knowledge of persuasion theory and research in their lives.

I believe that one of the strengths of *Persuasion in Your Life* is that it streamlines the research base for persuasion. Coverage of this material by rhetorical/critical scholars and social scientists is extensive. While I understand that an in-depth research base is important to professors' adoptions of textbooks, I have taught persuasion and have worked with other teachers of the topic long enough to have discovered a common problem: Persuasion textbooks are divided; they force teachers into making a choice between critical and social scientific perspectives. This text is not driven by a particular methodological tradition. Rather, the goal of this text is to invite students to study persuasion as a part of their everyday lived experience.

As the various theories and ways of studying persuasion are covered, I work to constantly ground the material in what happens in everyday life. The book will reflect a balance of theory and skills or application. I want students to understand that persuasion is a legitimate area of study within the communication discipline, complete with research and theory. I also want to convey that there are many ways to study persuasion that contribute to helping students learn to be critical citizens in consumer culture and working professionals in a global market. Thus, there will be a balance between reading persuasive messages critically, studying their ethics, and recognizing how persuasive messages are applied to particular life contexts.

About the Author

Shawn T. Wahl, Ph.D., Professor and Head of the Department of Communication in the School of Communication Studies at Missouri State University, has been teaching at the college level for more than a decade with specializations in rhetoric and culture and instructional communication. He is coauthor of *Business and Professional Communication: KEYS for Workplace Excellence, The Communication Age: Connecting and Engaging,* and *The Nonverbal Self: Communication for a Lifetime* and has published articles in *Communication Education, Communication Research Reports, Communication Teacher, Journal of Family Communication,* and *Basic Communication Course Annual.* In addition to serving as a member of numerous editorial boards, Shawn has served as editor of the *Texas Speech Communication Journal* and is an active member of the National Communication Association and Central States Communication Association. Further, Shawn has worked across the nation as a corporate trainer, communication consultant, and leadership coach in a variety of industries. Outside his professional work, he enjoys spending time with his family and two Chinese pugs, Mia and Jake.

Organizing Feature: In Your Life

I believe that developing an organizing feature lends clarity to a textbook. The organizing feature running throughout this text is *In Your Life,* a feature that promotes students' application of persuasion theory and research to their lived experience.

The IN YOUR LIFE FEATURE appears as follows:

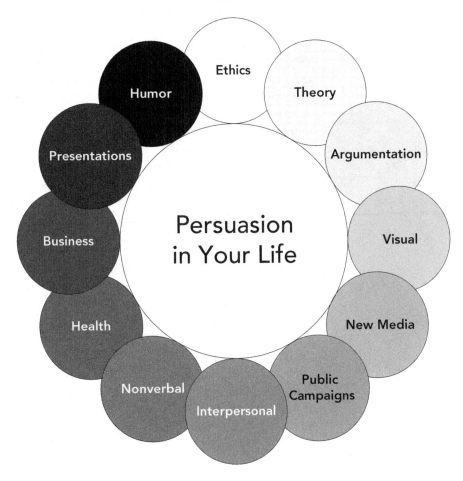

Overview of the Book

In this text, I provide 13 tightly focused chapters in which the best material—drawn from the research bases of communication, psychology, and other disciplines—is explored with relevance to the study of persuasion. This book doesn't attempt to cover the entire world of persuasion—I had to made difficult choices regarding the content, based on teaching communication in higher education, consulting with experts in the discipline, and experimenting with texts written by my friends and colleagues across the nation. What emerged is what represents the cutting-edge work in the field, combining rhetorical/critical and social scientist research on persuasion with applications to students' everyday lives to help them thoroughly understand, analyze, and use persuasion in their life and career—without overwhelming them.

Chapter 1, "Persuasion in Your Life," provides an introduction to the foundations and key concepts important to the study of persuasion, as well as a preview of the contexts explored in the text. Chapter 2, "Ethical Dimensions of Persuasion," connects the study of persuasion to ethics. Chapter 3, "Theories of Persuasion," helps students understand the basic functions of theory in their study of persuasion and covers the most common theories of persuasion.

The text then explores argumentation and the power of the visual as important topics in the study of persuasion in Chapter 4, "Argumentation," and Chapter 5, "Visual Persuasion." The following chapters explore new media and public campaigns, with Chapter 6 devoted to "Persuasion and New Media" and Chapter 7 to "Persuasive Public Campaigns." The next two chapters look at the persuasive dimensions of interpersonal and nonverbal communication. Chapter 8 delves into "Persuasion and Personal Relationships" and Chapter 9 examines "Persuasive Dimensions of Nonverbal Communication."

The next three chapters review persuasion in applied contexts such as in health, in business and professional situations, and in persuasive presentations. Chapter 10 explores "Persuasive Dimensions of Health Communication"; Chapter 11, "Persuasion in Business and Professional Contexts"; and Chapter 12, "Persuasive Presentations." The final chapter in the text, Chapter 13, "Persuasive Humor," includes cutting-edge research on the persuasive dimensions of humor that encourages students to focus on humor in personal life and popular culture, a topic not often covered in persuasion textbooks.

Pedagogical Features

This book includes 10 pedagogical features. Each chapter contains two opening features to help instructors deliver course content and enhance student learning. *Chapter Outlines* detail the organization of each chapter, while *Your Objectives* help students prioritize and personalize information so that they can learn more efficiently.

A *chapter opening vignette* connects students to the primary chapter content, providing a brief example to gain their attention as they move into a new topic. In all chapters, these vignettes represent actual events and real experiences intended to resonate with students. Themes from the vignettes appear throughout each chapter and are applied to and evaluated in the *In Your Life* feature that appears in each chapter. Another feature, called

Social Media in Your Life: Have You Seen This? appears throughout the text as marginal notes encouraging critical analysis of social media related to chapter content. Communication ethics is emphasized in all chapters with a feature called *Ethical Connection,* which connects the topic to an ethical perspective, because ethics should be the foundation of any study of persuasion. Chapters also contain a feature called *Engage: Take It to the Streets* designed to help students apply textbook material to real-life experiences.

Discussion Questions may be used by instructors as a means of generating class discussions about chapter content, as actual assignments, or as thought-provokers for students to consider on their own time. The *Persuasion Research Snapshot* feature appears across chapters, encouraging students to further explore peer-reviewed journal articles related to chapter content. Finally, complete *References* to the research base cited within the text appear at the end of the book and are organized by chapter. Students may find these references useful as they prepare assignments and/or conduct their own research projects. Instructors may use the *Persuasion Research Snapshots* and *References* to gather additional material for their own research or to supplement instruction.

Instructor Resources

Please visit the companion website at www.routledge.com/9780205741588

Acknowledgments

This project has been both exciting and challenging. Thus, there are many people I would like to acknowledge. I wish to thank the team at Pearson, with whom it's been a pleasure to work, including Assistant Editor Stephanie Chaisson and Karon Bowers, Editor-in-Chief, Communication, who offered great assistance, feedback, and encouragement.

I am grateful to my colleagues and friends in the field of communication whose advice and encouragement helped inform my decisions during the review process of this text. Reviewers include Lawrence A. Hosman, University of Southern Mississippi, Andrew Jacobs, SUNY Rockland Community College, Jennifer Robinette, Concord University, John Giertz, Bakersfield College, Ron Steffens, Green Mountain College, and Angela Jerome, Western Kentucky University.

Thanks also to my colleagues, friends, and students in the Department of Communication, Mass Media and Theatre, at Angelo State University and the Department of Communication and Theatre at Texas A&M University–Corpus Christi. I am especially grateful to Ashley Billig, Meagan Bryand, Sara Joe Chiles, Travis Covill, Kaitlyn Brosh, Nora Klie, Marissa Skye Gabaldon, Jayna Phinney, and Evan Richardson for their contributions to the research-gathering process, photographic selections, permissions, and assistance with instructional supplements.

Finally, I thank my family and friends for their support and belief in this book and my passion for teaching and studying communication. I thank my mother, Evelyn Wahl, who was always there to listen and provide support during the writing process; my brothers, Larkin Wahl and Shannon Wahl, for their confidence and support; and my dearest friends and mentors: Steve Beebe, Karla Bergen, Dawn O. Braithwaite, Chad Edwards, Autumn Edwards, Terry Lewis, Shad Tyra, Kelly M. Quintanilla, Phyllis Japp, Ronald Lee, Chad McBride, Scott Myers, K. David Roach, Kelly Russell, Bill Seiler, Virginia Wheeless, and David "Doc" Williams.

—Shawn T. Wahl

Contributing Authors

CHAD EDWARDS, PH.D., ASSOCIATE PROFESSOR OF COMMUNICATION
AT WESTERN MICHIGAN UNIVERSITY

Previously, Dr. Chad Edwards was a Hartel Fellow at Marietta College. Chad's research interests include communication in the teacher-student relationship, new media and student communication, and transformative communication practices. Recent publications include articles in *Communication Education, Communication Research Reports, Basic Communication Course Annual, Journal on Excellence in College Teaching,* and other communication and educational studies journals. He serves on numerous editorial boards including that of *Communication Education.* He has held offices at both national and regional communication conferences and is currently the 2nd Vice-President of the Central States Communication Association. In 2009, Chad received the Distinguished Teaching Award from Western Michigan University (the highest teaching award given by WMU). He also has been awarded teaching awards from the College of Arts and Sciences at Western Michigan University, University of Kansas, and Texas Tech University. Additionally, Chad has received several top paper awards for his research.

KATHERINE L. HATFIELD-EDSTROM, PH.D., PUBLIC INVOLVEMENT
COORDINATOR, HDR, INC., OMAHA, NEBRASKA

Dr. Katherine L. Hatfield-Edstrom specializes in rhetoric and public culture, visual and political communication, argumentation and public address. As a critical scholar, she is interested in the communicative nature of the visual. Her research has involved topics as varied as HIV/AIDS, terrorism, iconicity, public service campaigns, and health narratives. She has served as the Chair of the National Communication Association's Visual Communication Division. She happily resides in Omaha, Nebraska, with her husband Jason and son Sawyer.

ERIC JENKINS, PH.D., ASSISTANT PROFESSOR OF COMMUNICATION
AT THE UNIVERSITY OF CINCINNATI

Dr. Eric Jenkins studies visual media, culture, and critical theory, with an emphasis on the modes of perception accompanying various media and their impact on consumer culture. He has published works in *Critical Studies in Media Communication, Quarterly Journal of Film and Video,* and *Visual Communication Quarterly* as well as winning top paper awards at the Media

Ecology Association annual convention and the National Communication Association annual conference. He currently has a book under review with the University of Nebraska Press entitled *Consumer Dreams: Animation and the Translation of America*. The book traces early 20th-century animation's connections to consumer culture.

GEORGE PACHECO, JR., PH.D., GRADUATE DIRECTOR/ASSISTANT PROFESSOR OF COMMUNICATION AT ANGELO STATE UNIVERSITY

Dr. George Pacheco, Jr. joined the Department of Communication, Mass Media and Theatre, in 2007 after completing a Ph.D. in Communication Studies at The University of Southern Mississippi. George earned a Bachelor's and Master's Degree at West Texas A&M University. His research interests focus on the use of humor as a rhetorical device, Hispanic/Latino stereotypes/cultural identities, and first-generation studies. George is a member of the National Communication Association, Southern States Communication Association, and the Texas State Communication Association.

NARISSRA MARIA PUNYANUNT-CARTER, PH.D., ASSOCIATE PROFESSOR OF COMMUNICATION AT TEXAS TECH UNIVERSITY

Dr. Narissra Maria Punyanunt-Carter teaches the basic interpersonal and nonverbal communication course. She is a protégé of Drs. Rebecca Rubin and Alan Rubin, considered to be two of the most notable researchers in communication studies. Her research areas include mass media effects, father-daughter communication, mentoring, advisor-advisee relationships, family studies, religious communication, humor, and interpersonal communication. She has published over 30 articles that have appeared in several peer-reviewed journals, such as *Communication Research Reports, Southern Journal of Communication,* and *Journal of Intercultural Communication Research*. She has also published numerous instructional ancillaries and materials. Outside of her professional work, she enjoys spending time with her husband and her two boys, Ezra and Zavin.

MICHELLE MARESH, PH.D., ASSISTANT PROFESSOR OF COMMUNICATION AT TEXAS A&M UNIVERSITY, CORPUS CHRISTI

Dr. Michelle M. Maresh is an award-winning teacher who has taught undergraduate and graduate courses in public relations, crisis communication, media and society, communication theory, instructional communication, and research methods. Her research has appeared in *The Handbook of Crisis Communication* and *Designing and Conducting Mixed Methods Research*, and she has published articles in *Communication Education, Texas Speech Communication Journal,* and *American Communication Journal*.

Michelle is a regular presenter, reviewer, and active member of the National Communication Association, Central States Communication Association, and Texas Speech Communication Association. Michelle's involvement at TAMU-CC also includes being a member of the i-CERT campus emergency response team, serving as the Family Support Network Coordinator for the McNair Scholars Program, and being faculty advisor for the COMM Club and Lambda Pi Eta. Outside of work, Michelle enjoys being active in community service and regularly conducts training and development sessions for local organizations.

JOHN C. MEYER, PH.D., GRADUATE DIRECTOR/PROFESSOR OF COMMUNICATION STUDIES AT THE UNIVERSITY OF SOUTHERN MISSISSIPPI

Dr. John C. Meyer teaches courses in organizational communication, conflict management, and humor in communication. His current research involves developing a model of humor in human communication. Recently, his regional colleagues elected him Vice President Elect of the Southern States Communication Association, where he will succeed to the presidency in 3 years. He is author of the book *Kids Talking: Learning Relationships and Culture with Children* (Rowman & Littlefield, 2003) and articles including "Humor as a double-edged sword," *Communication Theory*, 2000.

JULIANN SCHOLL, PH.D., ASSOCIATE PROFESSOR OF COMMUNICATION AT TEXAS TECH UNIVERSITY

Much of Dr. Juliann Scholl's research emphasizes health care communication and crisis management. Some of her recent projects have looked at the use of hospice and diabetes care among rural populations and West Texas Latinos, the role of crisis communication centers in local communities, the use of humor in health care interactions, and developing a greater understanding of patient-centeredness. Juliann currently teaches undergraduate and graduate courses in leadership, organizational communication, business and professional communication, small group communication, health communication, and training and instruction. She has published in such journals as *Journal of Applied Communication Research, Health Communication, Qualitative Health Research, Communication Research Reports, Communication Quarterly, American Journal of Distance Education, Public Relations Review,* and *International Electronic Journal of Health Education*. In her spare time, Juliann enjoys traveling to New Mexico, reading, and endurance cycling.

Persuasion in Your Life

1

"
Did you see the new iPod? I really want to get one.... Maybe I'll just charge it to my Visa card.

I'm going to really dress up for the interview. Maybe they will hire me if I wear this cool red tie.

Health care really needs to be reformed. Stand up for change!

This new smoking ban is silly.

Who in the world would ever vote for Dick Cheney or Sarah Palin?
"

Persuasion in Your Life

What do these excerpts of conversation all have in common? They all refer to the power and presence of persuasion in your life. Think about some of the following questions related to persuasion: Why do you buy what you buy? What issues are most important to you? Did you vote for President Obama? John McCain? Are you satisfied with health care in the United States? Is smoking cigarettes *that* bad? Should it be illegal to text and drive? Is it okay to kiss on the first date? What are your values? You might be thinking, "Wow, these are some intense, personal questions. What do these questions have to do with this course?" While politics, health care, habits/behaviors (e.g., smoking, drinking beer, texting, voting), personal values, and the like may vary from person to person, it's important to understand what's at the core of so many attitudes, policies, behaviors, values, opinions, and judgments. In fact, persuasion is a fascinating topic that has received years of scholarly attention in a variety of academic disciplines such as communication, psychology, philosophy, criminal justice, business, and nursing. *Influence, motivate, sell, protest, market, advocate, increase,* and *change* are all words closely associated with policy, attitude, opinion, and behavior. Remember, persuasion is important in a variety of social, political, cultural, professional, and personal contexts.

So, welcome to the study of persuasion. This is a fascinating topic that is essential not only for students of communication, rhetoric and culture, and media studies, but a variety of other disciplines as well. I have been teaching persuasion for more than a decade and have been caught more than one time telling my students that persuasion is about pretty much everything. Let me introduce myself as your textbook author. My name is Shawn Wahl and I view myself as a tour guide and coach in the learning process. Connected to my passion for teaching in the college classroom and communication research is my passion for translating what can be rather dense or technical information into understandable words that students can apply to their personal and professional lives. I have collaborated with other communication scholars whom you will get to know in key chapters throughout the text. Our belief is that we can learn more about persuasion by grounding it in everyday experiences. That's why the title of this textbook, *Persuasion in Your*

Life—selected with you, the student of persuasion in mind—serves as a driving theme of every chapter. Throughout the book, you will notice references to everyday experiences, with attention given to a variety of face-to-face and mediated contexts where persuasion lives. Coupled with the driving theme of the book are important principles that encourage critical thinking, analysis, ethics, and application of knowledge related to the topic. You will also learn the importance of critical and ethical perspectives about persuasive messages, keeping in mind the need to apply persuasive techniques in personal, social, political, and professional contexts.

PERSUASION DEFINED

I often ask my persuasion students to locate and document messages that are, in their view, persuasive in nature. In class, we talk about what they notice in their everyday experiences that seems persuasive. To begin your study of this important topic, I believe it's important to define persuasion and coercion. The definition of **persuasion** I prefer is this: Persuasion is the process of attempting to change or reinforce attitudes, values, beliefs, or behavior. A term that is sometimes confused with persuasion is **coercion**— the use of force to get another person to think or behave as desired. I invite you to orient yourself to this course by thinking about your own definition of persuasion. I know that you'll soon find out what a huge topic this is to study, especially when you pay attention to your environment, both inside and outside, as you drive or walk to campus, whether you're online or off. Take a moment to think about messages that are persuasive to you. What statements make you want to change a behavior or attitude? What messages make you excited to buy a particular product (e.g., clothes, cars, vacations, smartphones)? What images or stories make you angry? Sad? What do your friends and family say to you that makes you feel loved and supported? Is it persuasive if you give someone a hug or pat on the back? These questions should lead you to understand that persuasive messages are connected to your role as a consumer, citizen, parent, advocate, teacher, friend, and more.

Persuasion in Your Life

One of the best places to locate examples of persuasion in your life is in popular culture. Think about the restaurants you eat in, the home you live in, what you purchase to decorate it, and what you use to personalize your surroundings. First, what does "popular culture" mean? Cultural studies scholar John Fiske (1989) explains that **popular culture** is created by the products of a culture that are owned and made by businesses for the purpose of generating a profit. Examples of popular culture include shopping malls, sporting events, movies, magazines, cell phones, vehicles, virtual communities, furniture, restaurants, amusement parks, and television sitcoms, to name a few. Popular culture persuades us to eat out at particular restaurants (e.g., TGI Fridays, Olive Garden, Red Lobster, Outback Steakhouse, McDonald's, Burger King), consume particular beverages (e.g., Starbucks coffee, Pepsi, Coke, Monster, Red Bull, Sprite, FIJI Water, Evian), and shop at particular stores (e.g., Macy's, Dillard's, JCPenney, The Gap, Eddie Bauer, Wal-Mart, Kohl's, Target). Further, popular culture provides consumers with a variety of products that shape everyday experiences, both personally and professionally. Can you think of some more examples of popular culture and connect them to persuasion?

Think of the last time you went for fast food and entered the restaurant (say, McDonald's, Burger King, or Taco Bell). Were you persuaded by the environment? Did the smell of burgers or the vivid images of burgers or tacos on the bright value menu make you hungry? Something as everyday and common as a fast-food restaurant serves as an example of intentional design driven by the need for customer turnover and corporate profits. The next time you visit a fast-food restaurant, pay attention to the design, seating, colors, lighting, smells, sounds, and temperature. You will likely find that the context in which you're eating serves as an awesome place to locate examples of persuasion. In fact, researchers have examined the persuasive features of restaurants to determine their influence on customers. What types of restaurants are you willing to spend more money on? Communication scholar Emily Langan (1999) investigated two theme restaurants—Hard Rock Cafe and Planet Hollywood—and found that the characteristics of entertaining theme restaurants persuade customers to spend more money, because they think they're getting an entertaining experience in addition to their food (see Photo 1.1). These theme

PHOTO 1.1 Why is the Hard Rock Cafe sign shown here persuasive?

PHOTO 1.2 Music diva Lady Gaga is viewed by some as a pop culture icon. It's no surprise, then, that popular performing artists like Lady Gaga play an important role in persuading fans to buy their music online, as well as T-shirts, posters, mugs, and more.

restaurants (e.g., Hooters, Rainforest Cafe) are usually built within commercial centers popular with tourists. In addition, restaurants like Hard Rock Cafe, Planet Hollywood, and Rainforest Cafe persuade their customers to purchase T-shirts, shot glasses, magnets, key chains, and stuffed animals, all located in convenient gift shops at the main entrance. You might also be tempted to consume products promoted by popular recording artists and athletes (see Photo 1.2).

In Your Life

Each chapter in this book will remind you to connect your study of persuasion to lived experience.

1.1 REMEMBER

persuasion	the process of attempting to change or reinforce attitudes, values, beliefs, or behavior
coercion	the use of force to get another person to think or behave as desired
popular culture	created by products of culture that are owned and made by businesses for the purpose of generating a profit

The Importance of Connecting and Engaging in Your Life

The process of studying persuasion is all about connecting and engaging. **Connection** refers to the power of communication to link and relate you to people, groups, communities, social institutions, and cultures (Edwards, Edwards, Wahl, & Myers, 2013). Modern technology and mobility seem to make connecting with others easier than ever though new social media. We communicate in a dynamic and intricate system of personal and social relationships, and each of us is linked to all the others by fewer degrees of separation than ever before. However, connecting alone is not enough to fully realize the potential of communication in transforming our identities, relationships, communities, and social realities (Edwards et al., 2013).

Your study of persuasion in the discipline of communication studies also requires engagement (Edwards et al., 2013). Simply "connecting" to the Internet or a social networking site fails to fully realize the possibilities of what we can achieve. You must also engage those you connect with. You must engage in your study of persuasion. **Engagement** refers to the act of sharing in the activities of the group. In other words, engaging is participating. It requires an orientation toward others that views them always as potential partners in the creation and negotiation of social reality (Edwards et al., 2013). In this way, being engaged in your study of persuasion is like being "engaged" in a close relationship. The idea of a promise to join and act together serves as an appropriate and uplifting metaphor for the attitude we can take when communicating with others (Edwards et al., 2013).

In almost every aspect of your life you're presented with both opportunities and challenges to connect and engage (see Photo 1.3). You're encouraged to be an engaged citizen, engaged community and group member, engaged member of a workforce, and engaged relationship partner (Edwards et al., 2013). One of the ways you can do so is by engaging in **communication activism**, or direct, energetic action in support of needed social change for individuals, groups, organizations, and communities (Frey & Carragee, 2007).

 ENGAGE: Take It to the Streets

Each chapter in this book contains a feature called Engage: Take It to the Streets that encourages you to connect and engage with your study of persuasion in real-life situations. The goal of this feature is to promote application of knowledge and to address important social issues by asking the question, "What would you do?"

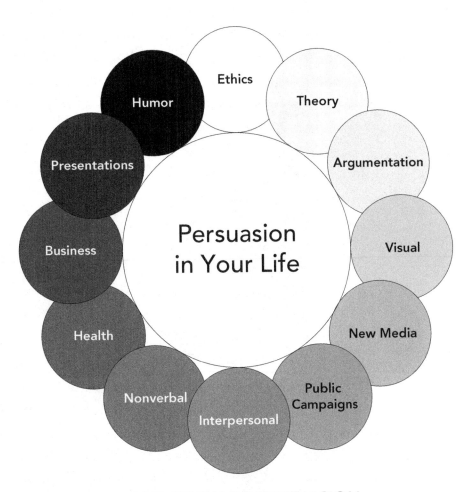

OVERVIEW: YOUR STUDY OF PERSUASION

Before you begin your journey with this important topic, it's important to understand the concepts that receive specific attention in this book. Your study of persuasion will explore the following: ethics, theories of persuasion, argumentation, visual communication, new media, persuasive public campaigns, nonverbal communication, interpersonal communication, health communication, business and professional communication, persuasive presentations, and humor. These topics are all important to the study of persuasion in your life. Let's take a look at each in more detail.

Ethics

Chapter 2, "Ethical Dimensions of Persuasion," connects your study of persuasion to an ethical perspective. **Ethics** is the general term for the discussion, determination, and deliberation processes that attempt to decide

PHOTO 1.3 As this photo of naked PETA (People for the Ethical Treatment of Animals) protesters suggests, there are a variety of ways to advocate for what you believe in.

what is right or wrong, what others should or should not do, and what is considered appropriate in our individual, communal, and professional lives (Japp, Meister, & Japp, 2005; Johannesen, Valde, & Whedbee, 2008). What considerations or factors help shape your ethical decisions when you're persuading others or evaluating persuasive messages? **Ethical considerations** are the variety of factors important for you to consider across communication contexts (Japp et al., 2005). Ethical considerations vary from person to person and are not always as simple as right or wrong. For example, you may experience **ethical dilemmas**; situations that do not seem to present clear choices between right and wrong, or good or evil. Our increasingly technological, global, and multicultural society requires us to be ever more sensitive to the impact of the words we choose, the images we portray, and the stereotypes we may hold.

So, what counts as ethical communication? How do we determine whether or not our communication conduct respects self, other, and surroundings? Communication philosopher and ethicist Jurgen Habermas (1979) maintains that ethical communication is that which promotes **autonomy** (freedom) and **responsibility**. To be ethical, communication

Ethical Connection

Each chapter in this book will connect persuasion to an ethical perspective, because it's the foundation of evaluating persuasion in your life.

1.2 REMEMBER

connection	the power of communication to link and relate us to people, groups, communities, social institutions, and cultures
engagement	the act of sharing in the activities of the group. Engagement is about participation that requires an orientation towards others that views them always as potential partners in the creation and negotiation of social reality
communication activism	direct, energetic action in support of needed social change for individuals, groups, organizations, and communities
ethics	general term for the discussion, determination, and deliberation processes that attempt to decide what is right or wrong, what others should or should not do, and what is considered appropriate in our individual, communal, and professional lives
ethical considerations	the variety of factors important to consider across communication contexts
ethical dilemmas	situations that do not seem to present clear choices between right and wrong or good and evil
autonomy	freedom to make individual choices
responsibility	being accountable for choices that impact others and our communities

should provide a sense of choice and empowerment, while simultaneously acknowledging and encouraging a sense of social responsibility. Communication that limits the free will and self-determination of our selves or others, or strips people of their power, is not ethical. Likewise, communication without regard for our shared responsibility to each other and our communities is not ethical.

Theories of Persuasion

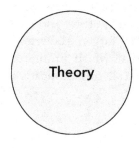

Chapter 3 surveys the most common theories of persuasion. Theories are also always evolving and are constantly under review by other scholars—new data is found and theories are modified and updated over time. The ancient Greeks referred to the making and doing functions of communication as **poesis** and **praxis**. Historically, most scholars and everyday people have paid more attention to communication praxis, or how communication can be used as an instrument to accomplish things. Recently, however, the creative (poesis) aspect of communication has received greater appreciation. This chapter will help you understand the basic functions of theory in your study of persuasion—that is, the making and doing functions of persuasion. When does persuasion work? When does it not work? What new creative (poesis) techniques of persuasion promote social change (changes in attitude, mood, opinion, behavior)? Studying theories of persuasion will also promote your understanding of how to persuade and how to judge the goodness (ethics) of persuasion.

Argumentation

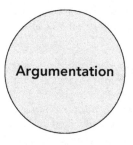

Chapter 4 treats argumentation as a topic that's central to your study of persuasion. A persuasion book would be incomplete without adequate coverage of **argumentation**, the presentation of reasoned evidence as a form of persuasion. Argumentation crosses many different fields and takes place in many different arenas of our lives. Across public and private communication contexts, argumentation plays an important role. In this chapter, we will explore the basic principles and standards of argumentation across all of these fields. There is very little persuasion that takes place without argumentation, so learning these principles will help you become more persuasive and also help you make better decisions when faced with a persuasive appeal.

Visual Persuasion

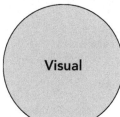

Chapter 5 explores the persuasive power of the visual. What is visual communication? **Visual communication** refers to the ways in which the images that humans interact with, such as signs, symbols, pictures, photographs, and art, either intentionally or unintentionally create meaning in their lives. As human beings we create, use, and interpret symbols to help us make sense of the world around us and our experiences in that world. Many of these symbols are visual. Think about visual images that influence your own behaviors. What's persuasive about particular images that come to mind? What images are memorable? What images evoke emotional responses? Can images tell a story? The communicative power of the visual is an important part of studying persuasion in your life.

Persuasion and New Media

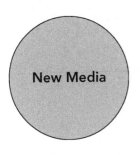

Chapter 6 connects your study of persuasion to **media**—the variety of message delivery formats such as print news, radio, television, and the Internet that have evolved over time. In fact, it's not uncommon to hear references to new media or the information age as ways of talking about and understanding the powerful and persuasive presence of media in your life. People across the globe are now able to connect with a simple click of a mouse or by retrieving information using smartphone technology (via, for example, an iPhone or BlackBerry). The term **media convergence**—the blending or collapse of print, radio, electronic, and digital formats as one dominant medium—is important to your study of persuasion. Today, **hypermedia** allow the sender and receiver to interact in real time with new media technologies such as chat, text, videoconferencing, etc. President Obama's address to Congress during the heart of the health care reform debate in September of 2009 reached the public in a variety of media formats (print, radio, television, and the Internet). Media give power to those trying to persuade public opinion or influence attitude, perception, behavior, and the like. Popular culture and media are the locations of persuasive statements about what products to buy and the types of clothes to wear. Bloggers can post arguments for or against issues such as health care reform, abortion, social security, education, global warming, military funding, political candidates, and more. As you dig deeper in your study of persuasion in this course, challenge yourself to locate examples of persuasion in popular culture and media.

Persuasive Public Campaigns

Chapter 7 considers the ways that **public relations (PR)**—the ongoing use of two-way communication to develop, maintain, and sustain positive relationships with the public—functions as a persuasive element in our society. Specifically, we will consider the definition, history, and various types of persuasive public campaigns. You will also learn about the persuasive strategies used in PR efforts to influence the public. As we explore

Social Media in Your Life: Have You Seen This?

Each chapter will invite you to engage in social media as one way to study persuasion via popular culture and social media. The Social Media In Your Life: Have You Seen This? feature will provide key words and/or links to view media clips via YouTube.

Go to YouTube and enter the following keywords: public service announcement, PSA.

After viewing a form of a public service announcement (PSA), how did this persuade you to take part in the movement? Did the PSA alter your perception of the issue at hand?

1.3 REMEMBER

poesis	the term used by the ancient Greeks to refer to creative aspects of communication
praxis	how communication can be used to accomplish things
argumentation	the presentation of reasoned evidence as a form of persuasion
visual communication	the ways in which images that humans interact with, such as signs, symbols, pictures, photographs, and art, either intentionally or unintentionally create meaning in their lives
media	the variety of message delivery formats such as print news, radio, television, and the Internet that have evolved over time
media convergence	the blending or collapse of print, radio, electronic, and digital formats as one dominant medium
hypermedia	allow the sender and receiver to interact in real time with new media technologies
public relations (PR)	the ongoing use of two-way communication to develop, maintain, and sustain positive relationships with the public

the topic of PR and persuasive campaigns, we will continue to apply the BP oil spill to the various concepts along with other recent examples of PR to enhance your understanding of these concepts. As you will learn in Chapter 7, PR is an ongoing process that affects each of us daily, whether we realize it or not. Because of this, it is important for us to understand the ways that we are influenced by these messages. Upon reading this chapter, you will be well equipped to recognize both subtle and explicit attempts at persuasion and PR in your life.

Persuasion in Interpersonal Relationships

Interpersonal

Chapter 8 connects your study of persuasion to **interpersonal relationships**—your relations and interactions with another person. For instance, Mark and Rosalee have been married for two years and have bought their first house. They have an agreement to talk openly about each of their design preferences for the new house. Rosalee likes modern, streamlined furnishings in neutral tones. Mark likes bold colors and comfortable furniture like recliners. Rosalee tries to convince Mark that her design ideas are the best way for them to go for the future. For Rosalee and Mark, something as simple as home decorating illustrates the use of persuasion in relationships. How do you use persuasion in your own relationships? What are the topics? What are your techniques?

Nonverbal Communication

Ever thought about how **nonverbal communication**—all the ways you communicate without using words—is persuasive? As you focus on the persuasive dimensions of nonverbal communication, keep the following questions in mind: How can nonverbal cues persuade others? What counts as nonverbal communication and how can that impact persuasion and influence? What are the specific codes (categories) of nonverbal communication connected to the study of persuasion? Chapter 9 explores nonverbal persuasive messages that are communicated through nonverbal codes (e.g., your environments and surroundings; use of space, physical appearance, body movements, and gestures; facial and eye expressions; touch).

Health Communication

Health communication is (a) the construction and sharing of meanings about the provision of health care delivery and (b) the promotion of public health through mediated channels. Chapter 10 focuses on how persuasion plays out in your health and the health care system in which you take part, as well as how you talk about your health with others close to you. As you probably have already learned, persuasion—both subtle and large scale—is **ubiquitous** (a term meaning that it is everywhere in your life), and one of its most influential roles is in matters of your health. Health communication scholars particularly interested in persuasion might look at the motivations people have for adopting positive or harmful health behaviors, as well as the influence social networks have on our daily health-related practices. These connections will be made as you study the persuasive dimensions of health.

Business and Professional Communication

Chapter 11 explores persuasion that occurs in the business and professional settings you'll encounter in life, such as organizations and companies where persuasion is important in getting and succeeding in a job. This chapter covers both direct and indirection persuasion in business and professional contexts. **Direct persuasion** refers to what you do during a live interview with a hiring committee, manager, or business owner, whether it's accomplished through face-to-face interaction, telephone communication, or perhaps even an online interview that might occur via a webcam. In contrast, **indirect persuasion** refers to those job interviewing decisions or actions that tend not to occur face to face. Put simply, indirect persuasion comes before or after the actual interview, but it's just as important as direct persuasion.

Persuasive Presentations

Chapter 12 reviews the importance of persuasive presentations in your life. Presenting information and ideas through connecting and engaging with others is important. Whether you're discussing a state environmental issue or speaking in favor of civil unions, you're engaged in the possibility of making a persuasive case. With the emergence of video-conferences, Skype, and the like, no longer can you expect a persuasive presentation to reach only those seated in front of you. Instead, your persuasive presentations can be disseminated globally using new media. Therefore, you need to prepare for future careers and know how to make persuasive presentations in your life to be able to persuade larger audiences. This chapter will address how you can create organized and effective persuasive presentations as well as be familiar with the different types of argument used in persuasion. It will help you support your claims and arguments as well as learn how to organize your information in order to persuade others.

Persuasive Humor

The last chapter focuses on the communicative aspects of humor; more specifically, its persuasive aspects. Humor as a communicated message has the power to persuade. Message creators use humor in a variety of different situations and in very specific ways. Advertisers, public relations firms, politicians, educators, and salespersons all use humor as a method of establishing a rapport with their audience and persuading via their messages. By making sense of these humorous devices, the audience begins to understand the message and develop a more critical view of it. With such a wide range of vehicles carrying humorous messages to audiences, it's important to understand the powerful messages communicated within humor.

1.4 REMEMBER

interpersonal relationships	your relations and interactions with another person
nonverbal communication	all the ways we communicate without using words
health communication	the construction and sharing of meanings about the provision of health care delivery and the promotion of public health through mediated channels
ubiquitous	everywhere in your life
direct persuasion	what you do during a live interview with a hiring committee, manager, or business owner, whether it's accomplished through face-to-face interaction, telephone communication, or perhaps even an online interview via Skype
indirect persuasion	refers to those job interviewing decisions or actions that tend not to occur face to face. Put simply, indirect persuasion comes before or after the actual interview, but it's just as important as direct persuasion

SUMMARY

In this chapter, you reviewed fundamental information to begin the study of persuasion in your life. Remember the definition of persuasion: the process of attempting to change or reinforce attitudes, values, beliefs, or behavior. Further, an important distinction was made between persuasion and coercion—the use of force to get another person to think or behave as desired.

Next, your topic of study was situated within your lived everyday experience. The driving theme of this book, persuasion in your life, serves as a reminder for you to identify and evaluate everyday messages. The following were listed as key topics to study: ethics, theories of persuasion, argumentation, visual communication, new media, persuasive public campaigns, nonverbal communication, interpersonal communication, health communication, business and professional communication, persuasive presentations, and humor. These topics are all important to the study of persuasion in your life.

This introductory chapter has provided you with an understanding of some of the basic terminology and the importance of persuasion in your life. In the second chapter, you'll explore ethics as a core component in your study of persuasion.

DISCUSSION QUESTIONS

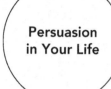

Persuasion in Your Life

1. What is the difference between persuasion and coercion?
2. Why is it important to study persuasion?
3. How does popular culture connect to your study of persuasion?
4. Identify a topic provided in the overview of your study of persuasion that you find interesting (e.g., ethics, nonverbal communication, visual communication).
5. Write down your own definition of persuasion and compare it to the one in the chapter. Do you think all communication is persuasion?

Ethical Dimensions
of Persuasion

2

Pro-choice voters are immoral!

Pro-life voters value life and family!

BP is the most unethical oil company in the world!

The public is unethical for not voting Bristol Palin off *Dancing with the Stars* sooner!

Ethics

What do the above statements all have in common? The correct answer can be articulated in one word: *ethics*. Each of you encounters ethics and ethical choices in your life. Your values, beliefs, and morals help develop your understanding of ethics. Many ethics, or codes of ethics, are universal while others are strictly meant for particular individuals or groups. However, you may encounter particular situations where you're forced to confront your own ethics. Think about it: Where do your ethics come from?

Let's face it. Understanding ethics is complicated. However, ethics is critical to your study of persuasion, so it's an important topic to study. This chapter explores the connection between persuasion and ethics. Each day you're faced with situations in which you have ethical decisions to make about how you persuade others and how you allow them to persuade you. Should you say hello to your boss this morning? Can you wait until tomorrow to feed the dog? Should you file a grievance against your supervisor for gender discrimination or keep your mouth shut?

In order to study the presence of persuasion in your life, it's important to place ethics at the core of your critical evaluation process. The process of critically evaluating persuasive messages is connected to ethical perspectives. You can think about ethical perspectives as a unique set of lenses that you may want to use to critically evaluate persuasive messages. There are many different lenses available, and each one that you put on will allow you to see the world of persuasion from different points of view. Similarly, each of the lenses covered in this chapter will encourage you to evaluate persuasive messages from different ethical points of view. Think about ethics as a set of lenses you can use to evaluate persuasive messages in your life. Let's get more familiar with the term as connected to your study of persuasion.

DEFINING ETHICS

When you hear the word *ethics*, what comes to mind? Words such as *right*, *wrong*, *values*, and *principles* may come to mind. Put simply, **ethics** is a system of accepted principles that make up an individual's or group's values and judgments as to what's right and wrong. These principles can change from culture to culture or group to group. Maybe you've heard of a **code of ethics** before. These are all different sets of principles that people hold themselves to or that are held by organizations or groups. Take a moment to review the code of ethics held by the National Communication Association (NCA). This code establishes the importance of ethics in the study of communication across contexts (see Figure 2.1).

Think for a moment about something that you're a part of, perhaps a group or an organization. For example, maybe you have a religious affiliation or belong to a fraternity, sorority, sports team, or academic institution that provides a daily code of ethics for you. There are two abilities that you must have to properly understand ethics. The first is the ability to **distinguish**. In order to distinguish, you need to be able to decide what's right and wrong. The second ability that you must have is **dedication**. Dedication is the ability to commit to doing what is right no matter the situation.

Think about this scenario: You're supposed to meet with your professor to make up an exam due to an absence. You arrive at her office just a

In Your Life

Think about the number of times each day that you make ethical decisions. What factors drive your personal ethics? Make a list of the things that inform your own system of ethics.

National Communication Association Credo for Ethical Communication

(Approved by the NCA Legislative Council in 1999)

Questions of right and wrong arise whenever people communicate. Ethical communication is fundamental to responsible thinking, decision making, and the development of relationships and communities within and across contexts, cultures, channels, and media. Moreover, ethical communication enhances human worth and dignity by fostering truthfulness, fairness, responsibility, personal integrity, and respect for self and others. We believe that unethical communication threatens the quality of all communication and consequently the well-being of individuals and the society in which we live. Therefore we, the members of the National Communication Association, endorse and are committed to practicing the following principles of ethical communication:

- We advocate truthfulness, accuracy, honesty, and reason as essential to the integrity of communication.
- We endorse freedom of expression, diversity of perspective, and tolerance of dissent to achieve the informed and responsible decision making fundamental to a civil society.
- We strive to understand and respect other communicators before evaluating and responding to their messages.
- We promote access to communication resources and opportunities as necessary to fulfill human potential and contribute to the well-being of families, communities, and society.
- We promote communication climates of caring and mutual understanding that respect the unique needs and characteristics of individual communicators.
- We condemn communication that degrades individuals and humanity through distortion, intimidation, coercion, and violence, and through the expression of intolerance and hatred.
- We are committed to the courageous expression of personal convictions in pursuit of fairness and justice.
- We advocate sharing information, opinions, and feelings when facing significant choices while also respecting privacy and confidentiality.
- We accept responsibility for the short- and long-term consequences for our own communication and expect the same of others.

FIGURE 2.1

Source: http://www.natcom.org

bit early, and the answer key is lying on the desk. Perhaps you're part of a church or religious organization that provides you with a code of ethics that assists you in choosing the right option. Maybe you signed an agreement with the university to obey its academic honesty policies. Regardless of the ethical code or codes you decide to honor or reject, ethics plays a role

ethics	a system of accepted principles that make up an individ-ual's or group's values and judgments as to what is right and what is wrong
code of ethics	different sets of principles that people hold themselves to, or are held, to in multiple organizations or groups
distinguish	to decide what is right and what is wrong
dedication	the ability to commit to do what is right no matter the situation
values	beliefs and attitudes we have that can conflict with our ethical decisions

in almost every decision you make throughout the day. In assessing this situation, you must use the two abilities that we just discussed. In your mind, you must distinguish between what is right and what is wrong, and then decide to commit to the ethical decision or to reject it.

The definition of ethics includes the word *values*. **Values** are beliefs and attitudes we have that can actually conflict with our ethical decisions. For instance, in the previous example, you may have not been prepared for the test, and perhaps a low grade would cause you to fail the class or drop below the GPA required by the graduate school you hope to attend. One of your values may be success, and a low grade on this exam could cause you to be unsuccessful. Thus, you may choose to violate your code of ethics to honor your values.

Now that you have a general understanding of ethics, let's not forget to connect this term to persuasion. What comes to your mind when you think of persuasion? How do you go about getting what you want from others, and where do you draw the line? What ethical criteria do you use when evaluating persuasive messages? Do you consider ethics when you're crafting a persuasive message? Would you consider yourself to be an **ethical persuader** or an **unethical persuader**? Ethical persuaders value truthful information. They want to help others make the best choice based on fair and accurate information. Unethical persuaders will cover up the truth in order to receive a benefit from others who will accept false or modified information.

Lying simply undermines persuasion and communication. However, lying can sometimes be more than just not telling the truth. When people testify in a court of law, not only do they swear to tell the truth, but they swear to tell the whole truth. If we don't provide those that we're trying to

In Your Life

Perhaps you've had a friend who was convinced to buy a used car. Chances are the salesman told him that the car was in perfect running condition. However, after signing his name on the dotted line and driving the car off the lot, your friend realized that he had been deceived.

Ethical Connection

What persuasive messages can you think of that you've noticed in your life that you view as unethical? Why?

2.2 REMEMBER

ethical persuader	a person who wishes to help others make the best choice based upon truthful information
unethical persuader	a person who will cover up the truth in order to receive a benefit from others who will accept false or modified information
lying	simply undermining the truth, refusing to tell the truth as a whole
truth	the accurate and honest word of another person
reliability	the degree to which others can depend on us
motives	the true reasons for our actions when we have something to lose or gain as a result

persuade with the whole truth, we are still lying. Any time we intentionally or unintentionally leave out information or fail to disclose our motives, we are lying. Now that we have talked about lying, let's talk about the **truth** and the characteristics of the truth. Telling the truth is not only telling someone what you know, but it's also being up-front about the things that you don't know. You want to make sure that your facts are truly facts. You want to make honesty a priority in your personal policy. This will lead to a very important outcome, which is reliability. When people view you as being reliable, you must maintain this view by being consistent. **Reliability**, like reputation, can take a lifetime to build and only seconds to destroy. Another term that's important to your study of the ethical dimensions of persuasion is **motives**. Anytime that you're trying to persuade someone, or someone is persuading you, you should question your motives as well as the motives of others. What is it that you're hoping to gain by persuading others? Do you desire money, such as a commission, or are you just trying to promote good? If you examine motives, you can immediately grade yourself and others on an ethical scale.

THE IMPORTANCE OF ETHICS

The February 23, 1987, edition of *U.S. News and World Report* had a headline reading, "A Nation of Liars?" Many times throughout U.S. history, primarily in reference to politics, people have felt that our leaders have lied to us. This headline is just one example that may encourage us to believe others have deceived us. However, it is more than two decades old. Do you feel today that those who run our nation, states, or cities are lying to us? What about you? Have you ever lied on a resume, cheated on a test, or told a white lie? What are some things that we do on a daily basis that are unethical? Some people believe that a society without ethics would be in big trouble. Do you think ethics are important? Ethics can often give us a broad set of principles that keep everyone accountable. However, the broad set of principles are open to individual interpretation that can lead to ethical violations. Many people are likely to remain ethical until it comes to the loss of their job or until they have a chance to gain money or favor. This might make us wonder, what good is an ethical system anyway? Philosopher Carl Wellman (1988) states:

> An ethical system does not solve all one's practical problems, but one cannot choose and act rationally without some explicit or implicit ethical system. An ethical theory does not tell a person what to do in any given situation, but neither is it completely silent; it tells one what to consider in making up one's mind what to do. The practical function of an ethical system is primarily to direct our attention to the relevant considerations, the reasons that determine the rightness or wrongness of any act.

The United States is known for its value of freedom; therefore, it's important that we respect the rights of all citizens. If we're all so diverse in our religious perspectives or values, then we must have a common code of how to conduct ourselves that is tied, not directly to one religion or doctrine, but instead to human decency. Therefore, a code or a system of ethics is crucial to our survival, as philosopher Jack Odell reminds us. No doubt, ethics has a presence at your college or university. Think about your student handbook and review the current syllabus for this course. What statements can you find that address cheating and plagiarism? Take a look at the Persuasion Research Snapshot, which connects plagiarism to your study of persuasion.

 ## PERSUASION RESEARCH SNAPSHOT

Students are expected to abide by college and university conduct codes. Yet, research has shown that many students continue to plagiarize. The syllabi that professors distribute commonly discourage plagiarism and promote academic honesty, but are they not persuasive enough?

Medical research proposes a method of inoculation in which you inject a small amount of the illness into patients so that they don't get the full-blown sickness. In the same manner, communication scholars Josh Compton and Michael Pfau studied the process of inoculating students with a small dose of anti-plagiarism policy and guilt to prevent them from plagiarizing in future instances.

Their research study looked at students' attitudes and how inoculation can serve as a means of resistance to plagiarism. The researchers proposed the use of messages using this strategy to persuade students not to commit plagiarism. The source of the message plays a major role in influencing attitudinal behavior. To better relate to this notion, think back to Aristotle's concept of ethos (character/credibility). Does the credibility of an advertisement influence your belief in its persuasive message? To understand participants' feelings, the researchers conducted three phases of scale-based questionnaires. Between stages two and three, messages using fear and guilt were used as forms of inoculation.

To their disappointment, results showed that inoculation strategies did not succeed in persuading students to change their opinions about and willingness to commit plagiarism, although fear-based inoculation messages proved to be somewhat effective. In this tactic, persuaders manipulated the message to produce the fear in students that if they participated in plagiarism, they would get caught and get into serious trouble. But overall, the use of inoculation and of fear and guilt messages did not prevent students from plagiarizing or change their attitudes about plagiarism.

How is this study applicable to your everyday life? Students are constantly tempted to take the easy way out and take other people's ideas without giving them recognition. Inoculation, in fact, may not be the "cure" for plagiarism and academic dishonesty on college campuses. If you were hit over the head with a message that used scare tactics to try to convince you not to cheat, would you cheat anyway or avoid the behavior?

Do you want to know more about this study? If so, read: Compton, J., & Pfau, M. (2008). Inoculating against pro-plagiarism justifications: Rational and affective strategies. *Journal of Applied Communication Research, 36,* 98–119.

ETHICAL CONSIDERATIONS

Many of you are probably thinking by now that you have a pretty good sense of ethical perspective. You probably understand the groundwork and many of the components of ethics. To expand your understanding of ethics, take a look at a few considerations and apply these to your life (see Figure 2.2).

The list of ethical considerations in this figure can help walk you through a process of what to ask yourself when you're trying to persuade someone, or when you feel as though you are being persuaded. You must always consider your motives, attitudes, integrity, and the like. You probably feel as though you're a fairly ethical person. Perhaps you don't cheat, steal, or lie. However, the interesting thing about persuasion is that many times you don't recognize when you're engaging in it or it's being done to you. Therefore, the only thing that you can do in order to stay on top of ethics is to educate yourself on what you are doing and when you are doing it. Think about every conversation that you've had in the past 24 hours. What questions were asked? Did you withhold information? Did you gossip? Did you

Ethical Considerations

Communication ethics is central to the study of persuasion in your life.

Lying:	Are you telling the truth?
Secrets:	Are you respecting the boundary placed around information by avoiding disclosure to others?
Integrity:	Are you discerning right from wrong and explaining your reasoning for your decision? In other words, are you vocal about the ethics driving your decision (e.g., care and love, financial considerations, respect for individual rights, equality for all)?
Aggressive Communication:	Are you communicating with others without resorting to power abuse and aggression? Are you communicating with others in a dignified and respectful manner? Are you communicating with mutual respect and open dialogue?
Plagiarism (Cheating):	Are you communicating information that is authentic and not plagiarized? Is the source of information being credited appropriately?

FIGURE 2.2

tell the truth? At some point during the day, many of you probably used an unethical tactic to get something from someone else (it can be as simple as exaggerating when telling a story).

Ethical guidelines can save you time and stress. You might want to write down the considerations in Figure 2.2 and keep them with you at all times. Think about these key ethical elements at the beginning and end of each day. Hold yourself accountable regarding ethics. Check each conversation against this chart until you are able to achieve ethical conversations and persuasion; you'll be surprised at the level of respect that others will have for you when you consider their feelings and needs by holding yourself accountable for doing what's right.

The Ethics of Electronic Communication

Think about your electronic communication choices. How can electronic communication be used to persuade others? What forms of electronic communication persuade you? The preceding questions can be explored by evaluating the presence of electronic communication in your life. Look at Figure 2.3 and fill in the blanks as you read the questions.

Think back to when you read the ethical considerations in Figure 2.2. Many of you probably just considered your face-to-face conversations.

In the past 24 hours, how many times have you ...

Had a face-to-face conversation? _____

Made a phone call? _____

Sent a text message? _____

Sent an email? _____

Total: _____

FIGURE 2.3

However, given our strong reliance on technology today, it's important to apply the same ethical principles to electronic communication. Consider the following scenario concerning Travis and Alex.

> Travis was having a bad day. One of his coworkers, Alex, whom he had been dating for several years, had broken up with him via text message! Needless to say, Travis was angry—he couldn't believe that Alex had used such an impersonal and cold way to break up with him. They both worked in an accounting office at a large oil refinery and socialized with a nice group of coworkers on Friday nights—there was clearly a social network that existed outside of work. In order to get back at Alex, Travis wanted to make a statement. To put it mildly, the breakup got dirty. He decided not to use a text message to respond to Alex and also didn't want to confront her face-to-face at work. Instead, he used the workplace email list (the same list used to organize the Friday night gatherings) to go on the attack. Travis used Reply All to reply to one of Alex's old email messages and told the entire story about the text message breakup. Not only that, but he continued to write about Alex, using obscene language and spreading rumors that she had a sexually transmitted disease (STD). As you can see, this is an example of someone using email to attack another person.

Electronic communication allows people like Travis the opportunity to sit behind their computer screen or other digital device and promote confrontation. While Travis's motivation to behave the way he did was personal, it could just as easily have been professional. People across social contexts take topics in need of discussion, or that are controversial, and place them in electronic formats often termed **email dialogues**—exchanges of messages about a particular topic using email, blog spaces, and other electronic tools to encourage participation that will hopefully lead to new ideas, planning, and sound decision making. These electronic forums are supposed to promote rational arguments for or against policies, proposals, and the like; as such they can be useful and should not be avoided. However, there's a drawback to email dialogues that many of you have already experienced. The dark side of these electronic exchanges is **electronic aggression**—a form of aggressive communication in which people interact about topics filled with emotionality (Quintanilla & Wahl, 2011). Exchanges that begin in an appropriate spirit can get nasty when people don't agree with the direction of the discussion or use offensive language to disagree about a program or ideas others support. People engaged in electronic aggression think their responses are persuasive. Unfortunately, these electronic exchanges filled with emotionality serve as daunting examples of incivility and unethical communication today.

The great thing about advances in new media is that you can send messages now and communicate at faster and faster rates each day. The downfall is that people often don't take the time to think before they "speak" or hit Send. If you take some time to cool down during a heated conversation or electronic debate, you'll establish rational discussion rather than aggression. However, you probably have heard of situations where hurtful or inappropriate electronic messages are forwarded to hundreds or even thousands of people in order to make a statement. If Travis had taken some time to cool off before constructing a hurtful message to embarrass Alex, perhaps he would not have been fired. It's important to be mindful when speaking to or about others in an electronic mediated message because once you say it or type it, it doesn't go away.

How do you use electronic communication as persuasion in your life? Have you ever experienced a situation like the one between Travis and Alex? Think about how people use their cell phones or emails to persuade others. Perhaps you've sent your significant other or friends text messages, hoping to initiate some sort of response. Maybe you've called someone and hidden your number. People often use technology to communicate with others when they want things their way. For instance, you might try to convince your boss that you're sick through a text message or perhaps message others during a test to persuade them to send you the answers. Whatever the motivation, new media are often used in disturbing ways. It's important that before you press the Send button on any message, you apply the same ethical considerations as you do in face-to-face communication. Take a moment to evaluate your electronic communication (e.g., text messages and messages using Gmail, Facebook, and Twitter) from an ethical perspective. Ask yourself if you're honest with people when you use electronic communication. Think about your communication motives. Does anything need to change? Perhaps these ethical considerations could save you and others some grief and hurt. Each time you pick up your cell phone or turn on your computer, be mindful of how you go about getting your way when using electronic communication.

Social Media in Your Life: Have You Seen This?

Go to YouTube and enter the following keyword: email etiquette

email dialogues	exchanges of messages about a particular topic using email, professional blog space, and other electronic tools to encourage participation that will hopefully lead to new ideas, strategic planning, and sound decision making
electronic aggression	a form of aggressive communication in which people interact on topics filled with emotionality

ETHICAL RESPONSIBILITY

Now that we've covered the basics of ethics, let's focus on ethical responsibility. According to communication ethics scholar Richard L. Johannesen and his colleagues, **responsibility** includes the elements of fulfilling duties and obligations, of being accountable to other individuals and groups, of adhering to agreed-upon standards, and of being accountable to one's own conscience (Johannesen, Valde, & Whedbee, 2008). In every social situation that you encounter in life, there's at least one sender and receiver. While we have reviewed many responsibilities of the message sender, do you think that the receiver of the message has ethical responsibilities too?

From the point you are the receiver of a message, it is your ethical responsibility to check the credibility of the sender. From that point on, it is your ethical responsibility as a receiver to check the credibility of the sender. If at any point you do not agree with the sender or you know that he is being unethical, you also have an ethical responsibility to take appropriate action. On the other hand, you might contend that, in argumentative and persuasive situations, communicators have an ethical obligation to double-check the soundness of their evidence and reasoning before they present it to others; sloppy preparation is no excuse for ethical lapses (Johannesen et al., 2008).

Ethical Responsibility in Politics

When you think of people who are allegedly of questionable character, politicians might come to mind. Many of you have probably heard several jokes or quotes comparing politicians to used car salesmen or lawyers. In general, politicians aren't viewed as the most honest individuals in today's society. From Watergate to the Clinton sex scandal, Americans have seen their share of "dirty" politicians. However, instead of focusing on the individual, focus on the ethical process of politics. One of the many political processes is campaigning. A political figure such as Barack Obama didn't become the president of the United States on his own. It took a team of people

In Your Life

Think about this: Let's say that you bought a cleaning product from a sales consultant because you took his word that this product would do everything he said it would do. On your way home, you run into a friend and you tell her that she needs to buy the product too because it works better than anything you've ever tried. However, when you get home, you try the cleaner, and it doesn't work at all. What would you do?

representing him and constantly working on his portrayal to the public to get him into the White House. Sadly, many Americans never really know what's going on in a campaign; they only see the production put together by the team, which of course makes every attempt to avoid any imperfections. Campaigns are normally run through commercials that point out flaws in opposing candidates. Indeed, the media have usually been a major factor when candidates find themselves in office after election time.

With so many types of communication and with so many communicators in a campaign, it is almost impossible to monitor campaign ethics. Outside of the media, think of all of the people involved with a campaign team: the candidate, representatives, consultants, reporters, editors, and more. Each should be held responsible for following a strict code of ethics. However, many of them are also responsible for portraying the candidate's image in an appealing manner in hopes of winning the election, which can sometimes encourage them to cover up or blur the truth. The difficulty of enforcing ethics within politics or campaigns is further complicated by special interest and political action committees (e.g., Swift Boat Veterans for Truth, Human Rights Campaign, National Rifle Association), known for funding negative political campaign ads.

Adapting to the Audience

Many of you taking this course will probably by now have taken public speaking. Think back to the stereotypical speeches that some of your peers may have given. Maybe some of the guys talked about sports; some of the women might have talked about fashion trends. Many times when people speak to an audience, they take into consideration only their own personal opinions or values. At the opposite end of this spectrum, some people will try to please everyone in the audience. Questions about how far persuaders should go in adapting their message to particular audiences should also be associated with ethical responsibility (Johannesen et al., 2008).

Many politicians and business professionals face criticism associated with ethics (see Photo 2.1). Sometimes you may have to step on a few toes or fall short of some people's expectations in order to remain ethically responsible in front of an audience. Some degree of adaptation for specific audiences in language choice, evidence, value appeals, organization, and communication medium is a crucial part of successful and ethical persuasion. As a communicator, always be mindful of others' spiritual perspectives (if any), values, personal experiences, families, and the like. You've probably seen speakers who are completely unmindful of their audiences as well as speakers who are willing to say anything to win their audience's favor. Both of these extremes are unethical and irresponsible.

PHOTO 2.1 Former New York Congressman Anthony Weiner is seen here leading the New York City Gay Pride Parade in 2010. While Weiner was successful politically in regard to a variety of issues, he faced ethical criticism of his personal life.

SOME ETHICAL PERSPECTIVES

To get more familiar with ethics and its connection to your study of persuasion, let's review a few different perspectives concerning ethics. These perspectives can be used alone or in combination to help seek out the best ethical solution in certain situations. Think of these perspectives as a shelf full of eyeglasses at an optometrist's office. Each different pair that you try on causes you to see things around you a bit differently. As you read through these perspectives, try to see things with a different point of view.

Religious Perspective

At one time or another, we have all channel surfed or hunted through a newspaper to find a show or article that appealed to our beliefs. Many religious leaders have reputations of appealing to people's psychological needs in hopes to gain money or power. The **religious perspective** examines the relationship between us as humans and a higher power. Throughout the history of religion and media, there have been instances where leaders stated that God would take their lives or those of other people if they were not able to raise a certain amount of money. Trinity Broadcasting Network (TBN) televangelist Steve Munsey was seen recently in a televised broadcast urging people to send him their tax refund checks so that they would receive blessings.

Many times in life we have to question the ethics of those who are attempting to persuade us. Does this pastor really need our money? What are his motives? To assess Munsey's appeal from an ethical perspective, let's consider Emory Griffin's ethics for Christian evangelism, established in 1976. To what degree could Munsey's persuasion be criticized as that of a "rhetorical rapist" who uses psychological coercion to force a decision to give (Johannesen et al., 2008)? This is not to say that we should reject our religious views or values. However, in every situation, we have an ethical responsibility as senders and receivers. Therefore, we must be sure to notice when others may appeal to our emotional needs in hopes of deceiving us. Are there other ethical standards of religious doctrine that you may be able to utilize in an instance like this to evaluate Munsey's plea for your tax refund check?

Human Nature Perspective

What makes us human? This is a question that many people often ponder. Perhaps you've heard someone use the phrase "I'm only human." What does this mean? Most often when people use this phrase, they are stating that they are prone to make mistakes and declaring their imperfection. However, often as humans we are held accountable for our mistakes. We are judged or we

In Your Life

What are some of the first lessons you remember being taught by someone that may have shaped your values or morals at an early age?

face consequences. Other mammals do not face trial or risk going to prison, so what is it about the human race that sets us apart? The **human nature perspective** states that we have an ability to judge, to reason, and to comprehend that far exceeds that of any other species. Therefore, we hold ourselves accountable to make good judgments and decisions. This is where our ethics come into play. You often hear parents say to their children that they are old enough to know right from wrong. It's at this point that the parents feel they have taught their children the ability to distinguish what's good and what's bad; they expect them to make the right judgment calls in the future.

Throughout the last decade we have seen leaders of our country and of the world commit unethical acts or fail to make ethical decisions. Perhaps such things were going on all along, or perhaps social media such as Facebook and YouTube have made it more convenient to access footage and descriptions of events minutes after they happen. However, we've experienced the acts of 9/11, the hanging of Saddam Hussein, and even the throwing of a shoe at President Bush during a press conference. We've seen companies shut down for discrepancies in the way they've handled their money and the way they've lied to customers about their money. We've seen the FCC tell musicians that their music cannot be played on the radio due to explicit and vulgar content. In each of these situations, humans have failed to make ethical decisions. The human nature perspective is both a gift and a curse. More than any other species, we are liable for our mistakes and misjudgments as humans.

Dialogical Perspective

Dialogical perspectives emerge from current scholarship on the nature of communication as dialogue rather than as monologue (Johannesen et al., 2008). **Monologue** is normally looked at as a performance or speech of a single person. **Dialogue**, on the other hand, is a conversation that occurs between two people. Think about the way that you handle yourself in a conversation with someone you like. You may be very attentive and interested, even if the subject matter doesn't necessarily pertain to you; you still have a general interest because you care about this person. Now think of a person that maybe you aren't so fond of and your last conversation with him or her. How did you handle yourself in this conversation? In the dialogical perspective, we think of communication as a dialogue by considering the different attitudes that we display towards others in a conversation. These attitudes can include hatred, prejudice, jealousy, inequality, and manipulation. On the other hand, they may be a bit more charitable, such as tenderness, compassion, interest, or love. Although we've just examined a few extreme ends of the spectrum, we encounter many different attitudes in each dialogue that we engage in throughout each and every day. These dialogues are important because we must consider how to treat others ethically. In each social situation that we encounter, we must consider our audience, even if it is an audience of one. This consideration of others and their feelings will help us remain ethical as we engage in conversations.

Let's take this same idea of communication as dialogue and apply it now to persuasion. If we engage in a conversation with others and have hidden motives, we are being unethical. People who have a hidden agenda or a desire to initiate a reaction through persuasion are also acting unethically. It is important that, as we attempt to persuade others in our dialogues, we do so by letting them know the choice that we wish they would make and why we think it would be the best choice for them. This act of persuasion is not manipulative, unlike hiding or disguising our true intention.

Situational Perspective

The **situational perspective** examines every situation that we encounter related to persuasion. Oftentimes when we think of scenarios where persuasion is involved, we think of car dealerships, clothing stores, jewelry shops, or perhaps politics. However, think about what you do when you want something. How far are you willing to go to get it? Do you think you ever violate any ethical codes? Consider the concrete contextual factors in order to make a purely situational ethical evaluation (see Figure 2.4).

Each aspect of persuasion must be identifiable before any decision should be made. These contextual factors were designed to help people make the best ethical decisions whether they are on the listening or speaking side of persuasion.

- The role or function of the persuader for receivers
- Expectations held by receivers concerning such matters as appropriateness and reasonableness
- The degree of receivers' awareness of the persuader's techniques
- Goals and values held by receivers
- The degree of urgency for implementing the persuader's proposal
- Ethical standards for communication held by receivers

FIGURE 2.4 Contexual Factors to Consider

Source: Johannesen, R. L., Valde, K. S., & Whedbee, K. E. (2008). *Ethics in Human Communication* (6th ed.). Prospect Heights, IL: Waveland Press.

responsibility	the ability to be held accountable for our actions or to be trustworthy
religious perspective	examines the relationship between us as humans and a higher power
human nature perspective	states that we have an ability to judge, to reason, and to comprehend that far exceeds that of any other species
dialogical perspective	examines communication as dialogue between two people by studying the attitudes and motives of each party
monologue	a performance or speech of a single person
dialogue	a conversation that occurs between two people
situational perspective	examines every situation that we encounter where persuasion is involved

 ENGAGE: Take It to the Streets

Remember: You can use your knowledge of persuasion to engage real-life situations. Consider the scenario below and think about what you would do as you apply your study of the ethical dimensions of persuasion in your life.

You're taking a class with a person you are attracted to. The professor assigns you to a group for a project, and soon you find that this person is in your group. Throughout the two weeks of group meetings, you decide to take your attraction to the next level, a date. As you sit in the coffee shop trading stories and getting to know one another, the night begins to draw to an end. You are very interested in this person although you both have different religious values and tend to disagree on many political issues as well. As you walk to the door, you ask about a second date, to which the response is, "I feel as though we may be too different. I don't think it is a good idea—it would never work." You decide that you're going to persuade this person to see you again for a second date. How do you do this in an ethical fashion that would not cause either of you to compromise your values? What would you do?

SUMMARY

This chapter has connected ethics to your study of persuasion and emphasized how large a role ethics plays when you're attempting to persuade others, or when others are attempting to persuade you. Different perspectives, or lenses, can be utilized to help you see the good and bad in each persuasive situation. Ethics is the driving force of each of these lenses used to help you evaluate persuasive messages in your life. After reading this chapter, you should become mindful of how to evaluate your methods of persuasion and consider others as you encounter each social situation. No matter if you're communicating with your phone or computer or in face-to-face conversations, you're always persuading or being persuaded. Consider everything that you'll learn in this course as you evaluate information and make communication choices in your life.

DISCUSSION QUESTIONS

1. Which ethical perspective discussed in the chapter do you think you would use most often and why?

2. What current situations in the world around you are due to either good or bad ethical decisions?

3. When speaking to others, what ethical responsibilities do you have as a speaker?

4. When listening to others, what ethical responsibilities do you have as a listener?

5. What ethical perspective in this chapter resonates with you as you observe and evaluate persuasive messages in your life?

Theories of Persuasion

3

YOUR OBJECTIVES

After studying this chapter, you should be able to:

1. Explain what theory is and its connection to your study of persuasion.
2. Have a basic understanding of popular theories of persuasion.
3. Identify the aspects of Aristotelian theory that are the foundations for current persuasive theory.
4. Examine how theories are used in your study of persuasion.
5. Apply theories of persuasion in your life.

CHAPTER OUTLINE

> Am I going to go to class today? Should I wear sweatpants or jeans?
>
> *Good morning, Roomie.*
>
> Should I make pancakes or grab a protein bar for breakfast? Walk or ride my bike to class? I wonder if those two are dating.
>
> *Hi, Gina, how was the movie last night? Maybe I'll see you later at Mark's.*
>
> Should I sit beside Marcus or Sam today?
>
> *Good morning, Dr. Lawrence.*
>
> I hope she didn't grade the last quiz too harshly.

Theory

Each morning you start the day by making decisions. There is a reason that you make one decision instead of the other, and it has to do with persuasion. When you interact with different people in your life, such as roommates and professors, you make decisions about how you will communicate with them. You choose how to address them, what words to use, the tone to say them in, and the like. Each of these decisions is part of how you persuade others. You can better understand how and why this happens by learning about theories of persuasion.

WHAT IS THEORY?

Before you get started learning about the important theories involved with persuasive communication, it's important to first understand what theory is. **Communication theory** is about understanding and explaining human interaction. As you learned in Chapter 1, theories are also always evolving and are constantly under review by other scholars—new data is found and theories are modified and updated over time. This chapter will help you understand the basic functions of theory in your study of persuasion. When does persuasion work? When does it not work? What new creative techniques of persuasion promote social change (e.g., changes in attitude, mood, opinion, or behavior)?

To jump-start your study of persuasion theory, let's consider a basic example. Say you notice that when you eat a peanut butter and banana sandwich for breakfast, your stomach doesn't growl during your 11:00 class, but it does if you eat cereal. You could theorize that "peanut butter and banana sandwiches are a more filling breakfast than cereal." The next week you test your theory. You eat cereal Monday and Tuesday and the sandwich Wednesday and Thursday and record whether or not your stomach is growling during class. You have just created and tested your own theory. This is similar to the process scholars go through when they are developing theories. They find a phenomenon or occurrence that interests them, make a hypothesis or assumption, observe the phenomenon under specific conditions, and record their observations and analyze them. This process is repeated many times before a theory is developed from the findings.

Students often make the mistake of believing that theories have rules that must be followed or that all theories must be correct all the time. Theories don't have rules that have to be followed, but they may contain principles, or guidelines, to refer to and compare phenomena to. This analysis will either support or contradict the theory. Theories are also always evolving and are constantly under review by other scholars, and as new data is found, theories are modified and updated over time.

The theories explained in this chapter are the ones most commonly used in the study of persuasion. As you continue to study persuasion in this course, you can reflect on these basic theories to help you better understand how persuasion works. As the driving theme of this text suggests, it's important to explain and understand the presence of persuasion in your life.

EARLY THEORIES

The early theories provide a foundation for the study of persuasion. The section that follows explains three early theories of persuasion: (1) Aristotelian theory, (2) Rank's model, and (3) the narrative paradigm.

Aristotelian Theory

The study of communication is said to be the first field of study, dating back to Aristotle and his book, *Rhetoric,* which is still seen as the most important book in the study of public speaking. Aristotle also created the first theory on persuasion, which has been used to build theories in modern times. His idea is that there are **artistic proofs** that can be manipulated by the persuader to create a reaction in the person being persuaded. **Inartistic proofs** are things that help to persuade but can't be controlled by the persuader, such as environment or physical attractiveness of the speaker. The three main artistic proofs are *ethos, pathos,* and *logos.*

Ethos is the charisma and credibility of a speaker. Before the speaker has the opportunity to speak, the audience has evaluated his or her credibility by taking cues from physical characteristics including the speaker's stature or posture, clothing, age, and many other nonverbal cues. This is the first layer of ethos that the audience gathers from the speaker. If the speaker is already known and has a reputation, this will also be part of the first layer.

The second layer of ethos is developed when the speaker begins to talk. Vocal quality, volume, choice of words, energy in speaking, sincerity, and eye contact are a few of the things that can have either a negative or positive effect on total credibility. During the 2008 presidential election campaign, then senator Barack Obama was often described as a charismatic speaker who was very intelligent and sincere. These characteristics helped to build his ethos, and voters found him to have high credibility. Occasionally, though, one piece of the ethos can be important enough to obscure flaws in other areas. Although Obama was considered a great speaker and intelligent, his opponent, Senator John McCain, had more credibility in discussions about military efforts. McCain had a long history of military involvement, was nicknamed "Maverick," and the stories of his heroic actions in battle were widely publicized. These points, along with his age and stature, persuaded the audience that McCain was a credible speaker when discussing military issues. His personal experience was more relevant than his presentation style and skill. As you can see, a person's ethos can change quickly and frequently depending on the situation, audience, topic, and many other factors. It's important to realize that even though it may change frequently, it's still a very important aspect of influence in persuasion.

ENGAGE: Take It to the Streets

Remember: You can use your knowledge of persuasion to engage real-life situations. Consider the scenario below and think about what you would do as you apply your study of the artistic proofs. Try to connect pathos (emotional appeal) to the situation below.

You finally got your first check from your new job. You are so tired of your current living situation that you head out to see a few properties that you could possibly afford. The landlord tells you that the properties listed are no longer available but there are a few others you may want to consider. As you walk into two of the houses you notice that they are higher priced than those advertised and do not look nearly as good. The landlord begins pointing out all of the good qualities of the spaces and you feel as though he is trying to create a diversion and may be hiding something. Although you feel as though you aren't being told the whole truth, you know that you can't afford anything else and you are tired of your current living situation. How could you use persuasion and theory to resolve this situation with the landlord so that you get a fair deal without engaging in unethical tactics such as those being used by the landlord? What would you do?

Pathos is the second of Aristotle's artistic proofs. These are passions, or things people connect to with emotional responses. Aristotle outlined several values he found to be universal including justice, prudence, generosity, courage, temperance, magnanimity, magnificence, and wisdom, which are further explained in Figure 3.1. Persuaders can gauge what issues their audience will have an emotional connection to and formulate messages to influence them.

For example, Michael's friend Tyler is taking the same English class Michael had last semester but with a different professor. Tyler wants Michael to sell him a paper he wrote. Tyler tells Michael, "No one will ever know." Tyler is trying to reach out to what Aristotle would consider Michael's value of justice. Both students know that they should not share papers like this, but Tyler uses an emotional appeal to convince Michael no one will get in trouble.

Aristotle's third proof is called **logos**, which refers to appeals to logic. Logical appeals assume that humans are rational beings who think through facts before making a decision. The use of logical appeals also requires that the audience is capable of understanding and processing the information in the way the presenter intends them to. Syllogisms were the first logical appeals described by Aristotle and other scholars. A syllogism depends on a major premise, which is related to a minor premise that ends in a conclusion. Figure 3.2 provides an example.

Examples of logical appeals can easily be found in our daily lives. Statistics are often used by persuaders to convince the audience that there is significant reasoning for their argument. By using percentages, graphs, and tables, they are supporting their argument with numbers. People are

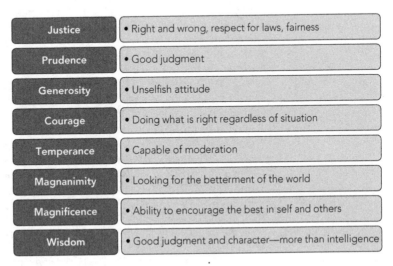

FIGURE 3.1 These are the values that Aristotle found to be universally important.

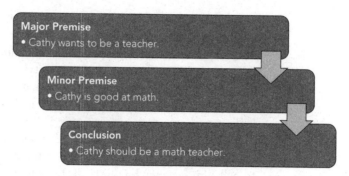

FIGURE 3.2 This is an example of a syllogism.

taught from a young age that numbers are very consistent (2 + 2 always equals 4), and this makes them seem reliable in persuasive messages.

Aristotle began the study of persuasion in ancient Greece and his ideas have held true for many years and are still the basis of much of the persuasion research done today. His explanation of ethos (credibility), pathos (emotional appeals), and logos (appeals to logic) has helped us to better understand what influences an audience and how you can persuade them. If you're wondering how Aristotelian theory might influence the study of persuasion today, take a moment to read the Persuasion Research Snapshot.

PERSUASION RESEARCH SNAPSHOT

From his election into office as president of the United States in 2000 to the end of his second term following the 2004 election, President Bush had both fans and nonsupporters. So how is it that he stayed in office for an extra term if there were constituents who did not agree with his actions? Scholars Roderick P. Hart and Jay P. Childers performed a rhetorical analysis of Bush's discourse towards the public from these two elections. Hart and Childers used a program called DICTION, which is a computerized method of analyzing text. For this study, they took Bush's speeches, transcribed them into text, and then ran them through this software. The three main aspects that DICTION sought were the amount of words spoken, how common the dialogue was in comparison to recent speeches, and location of words that were related to news or entertainment. By looking at these three factors, Hart and Childers found that over the course of time Bush went from being cautious, clear, and concerned with everyday problems to being solely concerned with support of the war in Iraq.

In 2000, Bush's campaign urged the necessity to address each aspect of life that impacted Americans. When he addressed a topic, he was sure to provide clarity as to how he would achieve improvements through precise plans of action. The 2004 election, however, was a response to the terrorist attacks of September 11, 2001. His style of address had changed from emphasizing the strong need for action to telling stories. Bush would tell the story of the al Qaeda terrorist group. He used phrases like "because we acted" and "before September the 11th of 2001," referring to past events. The nation perceived his messages as a form of storytelling that kept us tuning in for next week's episode. Through repetition of these stories, President Bush sustained approval from much of the public, which kept him in office. Were you aware of the entertainment you received from President Bush? Did his messages make you feel comforted and familiar with the situation? Or did you feel angered that the president was patronizing you by using a child-like form of conversation?

This study notes that through the use of a changing oratory style, Bush kept public opinion in his favor. The way in which our political leaders communicate to us greatly affects how we feel about them. Does a simple vocabulary speak to you because you easily understand it? Or do eloquent words catch your attention and add credibility to the persuader? In times of turmoil, do our needs change? Current and future leaders will continue to pave the way for new, innovative styles of address. Which one will best suit you?

Do you want to know more about this study? If so, read: Hart, R., & Childers, J. (2005). The evolution of Candidate Bush: A rhetorical analysis. *American Behavioral Scientist, 49,* 180–197.

In Your Life

What type of appeals do you use when persuading your parents? How would your appeals change if you were trying to persuade your siblings, professor, roommate, or boss? Does the topic of discussion influence the type of appeal you might use to persuade them?

3.1 REMEMBER

communication theory	understanding and explaining human interaction
artistic proofs	features of a persuasive message that can be manipulated by the persuader
inartistic proofs	things that help to persuade but can't be controlled by the persuader
ethos	charisma and credibility of a speaker
pathos	passions, things that evoke emotional responses
logos	appeals to logic

Rank's Model of Persuasion

There are two basic ways that persuaders attempt to change the opinion of the audience. Hugh Rank outlined these two strategies with the intensify/ downplay schema. The concept explains that persuaders either intensify or downplay specific features of the product, issue, or candidate to influence attitude change. The purpose is to highlight the aspects that will positively influence opinion and camouflage aspects that might produce negative opinions. This is done by

1. Intensifying positives of self
2. Intensifying negatives of other
3. Downplaying negatives of self
4. Downplaying positives of other

As Figure 3.3 shows, there are three main ways in which characteristics are intensified and three ways they are downplayed.

Intensification refers to the process of presenting information in such a way that the audience will pay more attention to it. To invoke positive attitudes toward a product, candidate, or issue you support, you might choose to draw more attention to, or intensify, the positive aspects of your side or intensify the negative aspects of the opposition. According to Rank's model, this is done through *repetition*, *association*, and *composition*.

Repetition is done by presenting the same idea over and over. Imagine you are looking to buy a new house. The agent shows you a property that is

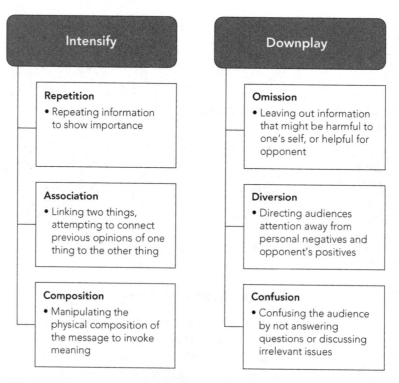

FIGURE 3.3 The Intensify/Downplay Schema outlines the ways in which a persuader might intensify or downplay specific information to make a message more persuasive.

more expensive than you wanted but is in a very popular neighborhood with a park nearby and a shopping area with several restaurants within walking distance. She also shows you a property much more affordable but farther from entertainment areas. You really like both homes, and the real estate agent says "location, location, location." Chances are that you have heard this phrase before. The repetition of the word *location* helps to intensify how important real estate agents believe location is, and the fact that you have heard the phrase multiple times also is a form of repetition reinforcing how important location is in buying real estate. By using this phrase, the real estate agent is trying to persuade you to buy the more expensive house by intensifying its good location as well as intensifying the bad location of the other house.

Repetition is also frequently used in advertising. Companies will use the same slogan for long periods of time and will use it in all of their advertising in magazines, flyers, coupons, TV commercials, radio ads, and in any materials that they may give to their customers. This form of repetition works to make you remember the company as well as provide a positive image to persuade you to buy or use its product.

Another intensification strategy that is often used in advertising is **association**. Association requires that the product, issue, or candidate is linked to something the audience already has an opinion about (see Photo 3.1). This allows for the previously held opinions to be projected onto

PHOTO 3.1 This image draws an association between being a clean-shaven man and getting the attention of a woman.

the product, issue, or candidate of interest. When companies choose to use a spokesperson to promote their product, they are hoping that the positive feelings and opinions people have about that person will be transferred to their product. Makeup companies often use a popular female celebrity in their advertisements to associate the celebrity's beauty with the makeup.

Association might also be accomplished by using representations of "real" people who would use the products, such as athletes swallowing sports drinks, clean-cut men using shaving cream, or moms putting bandages on their children as in Photos 3.2 and 3.3. In product advertising, associations are usually obvious, but subtle associations can be distinguished, too. You can look at these subtle associations in conjunction with the third intensification strategy, composition.

Composition is the manipulation of the physical structure of the message to evoke a desired opinion. It's used when choosing graphics, music, words, pictures, colors, fonts, and placement within the message. Together, these parts compose the desired message. Consider Photo 3.3.

The creator made several specific choices to produce a detailed message. The banner in the background is a bright blue. Blue hues lower the blood pressure and have a calming effect on the viewer; the subtle association here would

PHOTO 3.2 If this image were used for a bandage ad, the association would be between the specific brand of bandage and the happiness of the mother and daughter. What other associations might be drawn from Photos 3.1 and 3.2?

PHOTO 3.3 Examine the compositional elements of this image.

be that the candidate is a calm and secure person. The words placed on the poster in front of Obama are very simple. "Change" was the platform used by the candidate, so using all capital letters emphasizes this message, while "We can believe in" connotates that the supporters (1) want something to believe in and (2) have found it in this candidate. Choosing to use white for "Change" reiterates the importance of this word because of its strong contrast with the poster's blue background.

The picture of the candidate also has components that add to the composition of this image. The photographer shot the photograph from below, looking up at Obama. Using this angle gives the viewer the perception, or creates an association, that this is a person who should be looked up to. Again the color white, in his shirt and tie, is used for contrast against the background.

As you can see in this example, composition and association work closely together in intensification. We've heavily discussed these strategies in relation to visual messages. It's important to remember that each of these strategies can also be used within **auditory messages**, messages that are only heard, as well. A radio ad trying to achieve the same reaction as Photo 3.3 might air a portion of a live speech from the candidate with a cheering audience. There might be an instrumental version of "Proud to be an American" playing in the background, and ending with a simple voiceover of "Change we can believe in" followed by a few more seconds of music and "Paid for by the Obama-Biden Campaign," voiced over the end of the message. Auditory messages are composed and carry associations through tone of voice, choice of words, emphasis, and background noise. Alone, visual or auditory messages can be strong, but messages that carry both visual and auditory cues are the strongest. This is one reason advertisers choose to use commercials or web ads. They allow them to use visual and auditory associations, connecting them together to make the message

In Your Life

Think about some of your favorite sitcoms. Can you think of an episode where a point of omission was the turning point, or the center of the humor? Does this episode reflect a real moment in your life when omission was used in a persuasive message?

more persuasive. This is true of a single individual presenting a message as well. Individuals not only use vocal quality, choice of words, and speech pattern to create messages, they use physical movement as well. While some nonverbal gestures and movements may be unconscious, they still contribute to the composition of the message and therefore the associations that are created.

The alternative to intensification is **downplaying**. Downplaying occurs when the persuaders attempt to minimize the importance of certain characteristics. To increase positive opinion about their side, persuaders can downplay the negatives of their own product, issue, or candidate or the positives of the opponent's. As with intensification, there are three basic strategies used to downplay characteristics: omission, diversion, and confusion.

Omission is the act of purposely leaving out information. A persuader would choose to omit points that could be harmful to his or her own stance or those that might increase support of the opposition. Omission can have some ethical repercussions because some people view omission as lying. "It was not a lie, it just was not the whole truth," is the rationalization often used to minimize ethical obligations. The repercussions of omitting information are generally related to the amount of damage that could occur because of the omission.

The second downplaying strategy is **diversion**. This is the process of shifting attention away from a particular event, issue, or characteristic. Returning back to the house-buying example, the seller might put new countertops and floors in the kitchen to divert the potential buyer from realizing how old the cabinets are. Diverting is also very common in political campaigns. Rather than strictly discussing issues important to the voters, opponents begin to attack each other. This is done by revealing something from the opponent's history, the way that he or she raises money for the campaign, or any other personal issues. Doing this might shift media coverage from a vulnerable portion of one candidate's platform to examination of the personal merits of the opponent. Once this happens, it can be difficult to turn the discussion away from personal details back to the political issues.

Confusion is the third downplaying strategy. This is an attempt to leave the audience with uncertainty. It can be done by using terminology unfamiliar to the audience or by changing the topic. When people confidently use a lot of technical jargon, others tend to believe that they know what they are talking about. Persuaders can use this to their advantage. When talking to an audience unfamiliar with the product, issue, or candidate they can use this terminology to explain why theirs is the best choice. Since they sound like they know what they are talking about, the audience is likely to agree with them.

A large problem with confusion as a downplaying strategy is that the audience members generally know that they've been confused. If audience members feel that they've been insulted, there may be an opposite effect

REMEMBER

intensification	presenting information in a way that will make the audience pay more attention to it
repetition	presenting the same idea about something over and over
association	connecting previously held opinions to new situations
composition	manipulation of the physical structure of the message to evoke a desired opinion
auditory messages	messages that are only heard
downplaying	minimizing the importance of certain characteristics
omission	purposely leaving out information
diversion	shifting attention away from a particular event, issue, or characteristic
confusion	leaving the audience with uncertainty

from what the persuader wanted. If they feel the persuader did not make a genuine attempt to explain the concepts, they may decide the persuader was being condescending or trying to trick them.

Narrative Paradigm

The narrative paradigm is based on a theory presented by Walter Fisher in 1984. Fisher believes that stories and narratives are the most powerful and persuasive tools that humans possess. This is why stories have been told all around the world since the beginning of human civilization. The earliest use of stories as oral histories not only allowed people to record and pass down the history of their people, but also served to persuade and teach new generations.

Fisher assumes that (1) we are essentially storytellers; (2) we make decisions on the basis of good reasons; (3) history, biography, culture, and character determine what we consider to be good reasons; (4) narrative rationality is determined by coherence and fidelity of the story; and (5) the world is a set of stories from which we choose, and thus constantly recreate our lives. Figures 3.4 and 3.5 show his narrative paradigm in comparison to the rational-world paradigm, which is the set of beliefs regarding human behaviors that is more widely held.

The narrative paradigm is used to analyze the narrative rationality based on narrative probability and narrative fidelity. This seems very complicated

Rational World Paradigm

People are essentially rational.

We make decisions on the basis of arguments.

The type of speaking situation (legal, scientific, legislative) determines the course of our argument.

Rationality is determind by how much we know and how well we argue.

The world is a set of logical puzzles that we can solve through rational analysis.

FIGURE 3.4 These are the commonly held beliefs about human behavior.

Narrative Paradigm

People are essentially story tellers.

We make decisions on the basis of good reasons, which vary depending on the communication situation, media, and genre (Philosophical, technical, rhetorical, or artistic).

History, biography, culture, and character determine what we consider good reasons.

Narrative rationality is determined by the coherence and fidelity of our stories.

The world is a set of stories from which we choose, and thus constantly recreate our lives.

FIGURE 3.5 These are Fisher's beliefs about human behavior.

but makes a lot of sense once you break down the terminology. Narrative probability, or **coherence**, questions whether or not the story hangs together and is free of contradictions. Narrative **fidelity** refers to the reliability or truthfulness of the story. It addresses the Logic of Reasons (soundness of reason according to standards of formal and informal logic) and the Logic of Good Reasons (relevance, consistency, values). The narrative paradigm is also used to look at multiple stories within a complete piece to see if the entire text has the same relevance as each of the individual stories.

It's important to remember that Fisher believes that all messages and situations can be viewed through this narrative frame as long as you are able to figure out: (1) who the characters are, (2) the setting (where and when it takes place), (3) what happens or is said, (4) why it is done or said, and (5) what results from it. This includes individual print ads, commercials, and conversations with friends, as well as the entirety of a politician's campaign.

SOCIAL THEORIES

Social theories are theories that are based on some premise arising from social interaction. As you will see, each of the following theories assumes that we take cues from the social world around us and that these cues contribute to how we are persuaded and how we persuade others. The section that follows explains three social theories of persuasion: (1) attribution theory, (2) social judgment theory, (3) the elaboration likelihood model, and (4) social learning theory.

Attribution Theory

The basic premise of attribution theory comes from Fritz Heider's book, *The Psychology of Interpersonal Relations*. It refers to figuring out how we determine the reasons that we do things. First he found it important to examine how people make inferences about behavior and the world around them. An **attribution** is an inference made about why something happened, why someone did or said something, or why you acted or responded in a particular way (Petty & Cacioppo, 1996). We make these inferences throughout the day about our friends, professors, parents, the guy next to us in class, and strangers we've never met. Any time that we ask ourselves "I wonder why she said (or did) that?" we will answer our own question with an inference or assumption. This also applies to understanding why we ourselves do and say things. Heider created a system to classify the different types of causal attributes. The main two classifications are *personal* and *external* attributes. When you attribute something to **personal causes**, you assume that the behavior occurs because of specific characteristics or personality traits of that particular person, or yourself. If the causes are assumed to be due to factors outside of the decision maker, then they are **external causes**. The more specific classifications are effort, desire, sentiment, belonging, obligation, and permission, which are outlined in Figure 3.6.

For example, imagine that your roommate tweets that he bought a car. This roommate is notoriously behind on paying the bills, constantly comes

Causal Attributions

Effort	Desire	Sentiment	Obligation	Permission
• Trying to do something	• Wanting to do something	• Feeling like doing something	• Ought to do something	• Allowed to do something

FIGURE 3.6 The more specific inferences, or attributes, that may be made.

home late at night, and rarely goes to class. If you were to think to yourself, "He just wants to be the center of attention," you would be attributing the purchase of the new car to a *personal* cause, a personality trait. If you were to think, "He works really long hours and still lives paycheck to paycheck, so his car must have completely broken down this time," you would be attributing the purchase to *external* causes, something outside of his control. These are only two possibilities that you might come up with out of a multitude of reasons why your friend might have bought a new car. We sort through these possibilities and decide which one we feel fits the situation best. This sorting of information is another factor that Heider chose to examine.

Heider wanted to understand how "laypeople," those unfamiliar with the traditional scientific process, produced these inferences. He found that they do use logical information processing and analytical reasoning to reach conclusions. Even so, he found that the attributions were affected by the perceiver's own frame of reference. These inferences are made based on interactions we've had in the past; how these interactions affected us can have an impact on the type of causal inferences we make.

Heider refers to this as **perceptual styles**, or individual patterns of perception. Perceptual styles can be affected by a person's inclination to be pessimistic versus optimistic, religious and cultural beliefs and values, as well as age and exposure to different types of behavior. This means we make inferences about other people based on our personal experiences. It's important to remember that these are just inferences, not definitive answers. Knowing the real motivations behind some actions can be very difficult. How, then, do attributions actually work? Although people are capable of making logical inferences, they are often actually biased and illogical in their processing of cues when making attributions. This imbalance between Heider's finding of logical information processing and research findings of biased processing leads to the **fundamental attribution error**, which refers to how people make assumptions based on personality characteristics. This also includes the idea that people are responsible for what happens to them. The bias is obvious when you consider that people are much more considerate of situational factors when making inferences about their own behavior. For example, if a friend forgot your birthday, you

coherence	being free of contradictions
fidelity	reliability or truthfulness of a story
attribution	inference made about why something happened, why someone did or said something, or why you acted or responded in a particular way
personal causes	specific characteristics or personality traits
external causes	factors outside the person
perceptual styles	individual patterns of perception
fundamental attribution error	the idea that people make assumptions based on personality characteristics

might infer that she is inconsiderate and doesn't value your relationship, but if you were to forget a friend's birthday, you would more likely consider that you have been really busy or haven't seen a calendar and were not even sure what day it was. You might sincerely apologize to your friend, but you will still try to justify the mistake in your own mind. This type of behavior would be true of most face-saving situations.

Attribution theory is one of many theories that focus on how people acquire and process information. Trying to understand how people make assumptions and how attitudes are created is very important in understanding how persuasion works. Once there is an understanding of how attitudes are created, it's easier to produce messages that will create the attitude desired by the persuader. Social judgment theory relates to how we make judgments about statements that are presented to us.

Social Judgment Theory

Psychologist Muzafer Sherif developed an analysis of attitudes which he called the social judgment-involvement approach, most commonly called the social judgment theory. This theory works to develop predictions about what types of messages will persuade an individual. The theory assumes that people arrange information cogitatively into an important order (biggest to smallest, tallest to shortest, most enjoyable to least enjoyable) that is useful in processing information. This sorting of information is done by comparing new data to other information that is already possessed.

Previous beliefs or attitudes are called **anchors**. These anchors are what we compare all other opinions, beliefs, and information to. Surrounding these anchors are areas into which all other information can be categorized. These categories describe the level of probability that an individual will accept a new concept or idea.

The **latitude of acceptance (LOA)** is the range in which someone is most likely to accept the new idea. This would be the area closest to an anchor point. The **latitude of rejection (LOR)** is the range in which ideas won't be accepted. These issues would fall the greatest distance from the anchor point. The third range is for ideas that don't have a definite positive or negative correlation. The **latitude of noncommitment (LON)** is comprised of the range in which further consideration would occur before making a judgment, or in which no positive or negative commitment is made. The latitude of noncommitment is centered between the latitudes of acceptance and rejection.

Below is a list of 10 statements regarding texting and driving. Review these statements and circle the ones you completely agree with. Now reread all of the statements and place an X on the ones you disagree with.

1. Drivers caught texting while driving should be punished as severely as drunk drivers.
2. Texting while driving is no worse than eating, applying makeup, or smoking while driving, so it shouldn't be regulated.
3. Texting should be banned in all school zones.
4. Everyone is impaired when he or she texts and drives.
5. Stricter laws on texting and driving should be passed.
6. There should be no regulations on texting while driving.
7. The ability to text and drive depends on the texting skill of the driver.
8. Public transportation employees should not be allowed to have cell phones while on duty.
9. Teens are the most dangerous texting drivers.
10. Texting does not impair a driver.

Are there any that you didn't mark with a circle or an X? You have just outlined your LOA with circles and your LOR with Xs. Your LON is the unmarked statements, those you don't have a strong negative or positive opinion about.

Figure 3.7 shows an example of what the ranges for a hypothetical responder might look like if graphed. This diagram also includes the anchor, which is the main belief this person had that all other ideas were compared to. For the persuader, it's important to understand the audience's ranges in order to present arguments that will most likely move their anchors, or initially held opinions. Sherif says that this can be done by gauging an individual's ego-involvement.

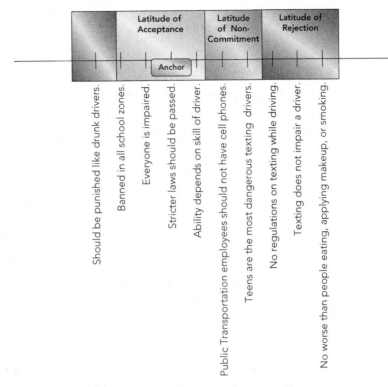

FIGURE 3.7 This is an example of what a person's LOA, LON, and LOR might look like in regard to the texting and driving statements provided.

Ego-involvement is how important an issue is in a person's life. High ego-involvement means that the issue is very important in defining who we are and is related to our values and beliefs. With high ego-involvement there is a very small latitude of acceptance and a large latitude of rejection. Messages that fall on the very edge of the latitude of acceptance would be the most effective at persuading these people. This means that very few opinions will be acceptable and persuading these people to change their attitude will be very difficult.

When there is low ego-involvement, there is a large area of noncommitment and smaller areas of acceptance and rejection. This is because low ego-involvement issues don't threaten our values or our opinion of ourselves. Persuading someone with low ego-involvement to change an opinion would be easy since he or she doesn't have a strong negative or positive feeling about the issue. This also means that the attitude created may be easily changed again in the future.

When you relate this to the texting and driving example, you see that some people will have high ego-involvement because they feel unsafe drivers

anchor	belief or attitude that previously existed
latitude of acceptance (LOA)	range in which someone is likely to accept a new idea
latitude of rejection (LOR)	range in which someone is likely to not accept a new idea
latitude of noncommitment (LON)	range in which further consideration would be needed before making a judgment
ego-involvement	how important an issue is in a person's life

threaten their safety. Some people who text while driving may be defensive about their driving ability and also have high ego-involvement because they don't want anyone regulating their activities. Others, like those who don't drive, don't have a cell phone, or don't think texting impairs a driver, may not believe the topic affects them.

In short, Sherif suggests that persuasion is more about the distance between the new message and a person's current attitude than how the message is presented. Messages that are very far from the anchor will be rejected quickly and messages similar to the anchor will be quickly accepted. Finding the right latitude in which to introduce a new message can be difficult but is important in making a successful persuasive argument.

Elaboration Likelihood Model

You are going shopping with a list. On this list is toothpaste, 2% milk, a new remote control for your entertainment center, and a case of bottled water. Where will you spend the most time while you are shopping? Which purchase will require more in-depth thought? The elaboration likelihood model explains how these decisions are made.

When presented with ideas or concepts, individuals compare these ideas to their previously held beliefs. According to Richard Petty and John Cacioppo (1996), the depth in which we consider ideas depends on which route they travel, peripheral or central. The route that is used depends on how much message elaboration happens while processing the message. **Message elaboration** is how much a person has to think about a particular argument in a persuasive message. The **central route** is used when concepts and ideas relevant to the issue at hand are thought through more carefully. The **peripheral route** is used when cues are not relevant to the issue and very

Ethical Connection

Should companies that sell health products be allowed to advertise using an actor portraying a doctor, even if there is fine print saying "Not a real doctor" on the advertisement? Why might this practice be considered unethical? What other persuasive tactics have you encountered that you felt were ethically questionable?

little thought is used to process the message. The route that the persuasive message follows affects how much a person is persuaded and the strength of the attitude acquired. Enduring attitudes, attitudes that won't change easily, are the result of deeper consideration of issue-related information (the central route). Attitude changes that are not enduring, or are easily changed, come from non-issue-related stimuli (the peripheral route). The most obvious cues that will lead to peripheral processing and, in return, a quick decision, are tangible rewards. These can include money, social acceptance, time, safety, and comfort. Peripheral cues also include speaker credibility. When a persuasive message is presented by a person or a company we feel is credible or that we like, it's assumed by the elaboration likelihood model that the message will be accepted. This is why advertisers often use celebrities to promote their product. They hope that using someone popular to whom the target audience can relate will win approval through the peripheral route. This is also why advertising for medical products often includes confirmation of the product by health experts (e.g., doctors, researchers).

Returning to your shopping list, your purchase of 2% milk will most likely result from information processed through your peripheral route. Generally there are only two options available for 2% milk, the store brand or the name brand. Your decision will most likely be persuaded by either a cheaper price or a loyalty to one brand or the other. Both are a result of peripheral processing. If you were persuaded by the cheaper price, your reward would be the money you saved. If you chose the more expensive one, you are probably more comfortable with that brand or you feel safer with that decision.

Now you're in the toothpaste aisle. How will you choose which toothpaste to buy? This purchase will require a little more thought. One box advertises that it tastes the best, but the one beside it offers germ-fighting protection for 12 hours longer, and the next is specially formulated for sensitive teeth. You must now think about your personal preferences and relate them to the different toothpastes offered. For a few more dollars you can purchase one formulated for sensitive teeth that tastes great (according to the advertising), has whitening power, and fights germs longer. Peripheral cues may eliminate the more expensive one or, after deeper thought (the central route), you may decide that the all-inclusive product is worth more money. While thinking through the decision, you would have compared the product offerings to the things you have learned about personal hygiene (fighting germs keeps cavities away) or from personal experience (some toothpastes taste bad). Some people may not care about the taste but are concerned with germ fighting, so they may decide that they don't need to spend the extra money on something they don't feel is relevant for them. This decision was made by processing information through the central route.

As you can tell from the toothpaste example, messages don't strictly pass through one route alone. Some decisions rely on processing separate pieces of the message through each route. The routes rely heavily on each other for successful attitude change. If arguments are weak but presented by someone with a lot of charisma, the speaker will only be able to persuade the audience to listen, not necessarily accept, his or her ideas. If the presentation of information is weak but the arguments are strong, there is a risk that the audience won't even attend to what is being said. The persuader's job is to provide the most compelling arguments while also presenting them in a way the audience will accept peripherally.

Social Learning Theory

Some scholars believe that persuasion is a specialized way in which we learn. Albert Bandura's (1977) social learning theory is based on the belief that humans respond to the continuous interaction between their internal state and the social reinforcements that follow from their behaviors with others. Assuming this to be true, we accept that we interpret responses from others to learn whether or not our behavior is socially acceptable. For example, role models can be considered a generally important element of social learning theory. Consider the following comment: "The reason she behaves that way is because she has never had a positive role model." Put simply, the reactions we get from others persuade us to believe or act in a certain way. We gauge our behaviors, observing whether they are socially rewarding or we are punished for our behavior in some way.

Our interpretation of what is acceptable and what is not is affected by two reinforcers, external information and internal systems. External reinforcements come directly from the experience and internal systems include our self-concept and value and belief systems.

This can often be seen in people who belong to gangs. Although they are punished for their behavior (fighting, possessing drugs, threatening and harming others), they value their power or social status (internal reinforcement) more than they fear the negative reactions and punishments (external reinforcement). It's possible that over time, with repeated negative reinforcement, internal attitudes can be changed, but this can often be a long process.

Self-esteem can also be a major factor in what will influence a person's internal systems and reinforcement. People with low self-esteem are going to have very little internal reinforcement. They will assume that what other people think of them is true and will be strongly influenced by external reinforcements. People with high self-esteem will be more likely to have strong internal reinforcement and less likely to be affected by external reinforcements.

TENSION REDUCTION THEORIES

Tension reduction theories are based on the human desire to minimize tension, stress, or anxiety. These theories explain how tension affects us, how we try to minimize the tension, and the role persuasion plays in tension reduction. The section that follows explains three tension reduction theories of persuasion: (1) cognitive dissonance, (2) balance theory, and (3) uses and gratifications.

Cognitive Dissonance

In cognitive dissonance, which is receiver based, the receiver's interpretation of messages creates cognitions and the receiver evaluates their relationships to other cognitions. A **cognition** is a belief, thought, idea, or piece of knowledge that an individual has. Cognitive dissonance is created when an individual possesses two cognitions that don't fit together and make the individual feel psychologically uncomfortable. This uncomfortable feeling is the result of *dissonance*. People are generally motivated to change uncomfortable situations so that they feel better. This is done by using modification behaviors, which will be outlined below.

Let's take a look at an example of cognitive dissonance: Judy really wants to eat a banana split after dinner, but she also has a goal to lose 10 pounds this month. Knowing that the dessert is unhealthy and won't help her achieve her goal creates dissonance, or makes her uncomfortable. According to the theory of cognitive dissonance, Judy has three options to relieve the anxiety created by choosing to eat a banana split. First, Judy tells herself she will work out an extra hour at the gym tomorrow. She has rationalized a response to modify her feelings. By presenting the idea that she will intensify her workout, she *introduces a consonant cognition to the situation.* **Consonant cognitions** are two ideas that are consistent with one another. By devising her plan to work out harder, she has inserted a consonant cognition into the equation, making her feel better about her decision to eat the banana split.

The second way to adjust cognitive dissonance is *the modification of one or both cognitions* to make them agreeable. Judy might rationalize that because of the bananas, the dessert is not really unhealthy. She has changed the cognition, or belief, that the dessert is unhealthy. Since she now believes that the banana split is a healthy dessert option, she has removed the cognitive dissonance.

Changing the importance of the cognitions is the third alternative for resolving cognitive dissonance. If Judy were to suggest to herself that she'd had a bad day and the banana split will make her feel better, she would be saying that her happiness (eating the dessert) is more important than the weight-loss goal. By decreasing the importance of the goal, she is able to be more comfortable with her unhealthy decision.

Social Media in Your Life: Have You Seen This?

Go to YouTube and enter the following keyword: This is your brain on drugs

The Partnership for a Drug Free America has produced a series of public service announcements as part of an anti-drug campaign. How can cognitive dissonance theory be used to understand the persuasion dimensions of these clips?

Understanding cognitive dissonance is important to the study of persuasion because of its fundamental role as a negative motivator. If Judy had refused the dessert and her friend Kim had suggested to her that the potassium in the bananas would actually benefit her more than the sugar from the ice cream harmed her, Kim would have helped Judy modify her dissonant feelings and persuaded her to have the dessert.

If persuaders can decipher previous beliefs and predict what types of messages will create cognitive dissonance for individuals, they can also provide one of the modifications to increase the probability that the individuals will be persuaded. This is evident in many advertising campaigns of cleaning products. The commercials might show people doing normal activities with dramatized "magnified" scenes showing where germs and bacteria are likely to be, usually in places the advertisers believe you will think don't need to be disinfected. This creates dissonance because you most likely have the belief that these items are clean but the advertiser is telling you otherwise. This is where the advertiser solves the dissonance for you by introducing a consonant cognition, the use of their product.

The desire to feel better motivates us to resolve dissonant feelings. By using one of the methods of modification, we find a way to resolve the negative feelings and feel better. Persuaders can use this knowledge to their benefit by offering modifications that resolve our dissonance. Figure 3.8 reminds us of the three methods of modification.

Balance Theory

Preceding the cognitive dissonance theory was balance theory, which was presented by Fritz Heider (1946, 1958) and later elaborated on by Theodore Newcomb (1953). This theory was the first to deal with the phenomenon of psychic tension reduction. Like the cognitive dissonance theory you just reviewed, it's based on the idea that people want to reduce negative feelings created by possessing opposing ideas. Balance theory also focuses on the interaction between two individuals discussing one topic.

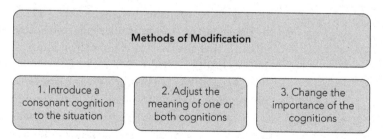

FIGURE 3.8 The three ways in which you might modify information to reduce cognitive dissonance.

In Your Life

Make a list of the most common persuasive messages used to promote dissonance. One example would be associating cigarette smoke with cancer. In this case, the outcome of cancer is supposed to promote dissonance. What other examples come to mind?

3.5 REMEMBER

message elaboration	how much a person has to think about a particular argument in a persuasive message
central route	used when concepts and ideas relevant to the issue at hand are thought through more carefully
peripheral route	used when cues are not relevant to the issue and very little thought is used to process the message
cognition	a belief, thought, idea, or piece of knowledge that an individual has
consonant cognitions	two ideas that are consistent with one another

Three interactions occur during this exchange: the feelings between people, the feeling Person 1 has about the topic, and the feeling Person 2 has about the topic. There are three ways that the exchange can be balanced, or comfortable:

1. Both people like each other and both like the topic.
2. Both people like each other and dislike the topic.
3. They dislike each other and share differing opinions on the topic.

For an imbalanced exchange, there are also three possibilities:

1. Both people like each other, but they have differing opinions on the topic.
2. They dislike each other and both like the topic.
3. They dislike each other and both dislike the topic.

The last two imbalances that occur when both people dislike each other can be easily explained by saying that we don't want to share the same opinion with someone we dislike. If you dislike someone, you don't want to consider that you might have something in common because that would make you more like your opposition. Figure 3.9 visually depicts these balances.

Uses and Gratifications

Uses and gratifications theory is a major theory involving the influence of mass media. Before the introduction of uses and gratifications theory, it was assumed that audience members were sponges that absorbed the messages directed to them. This theory is based on the assumption that people have specific needs that need to be filled, ranging from low-level, basic

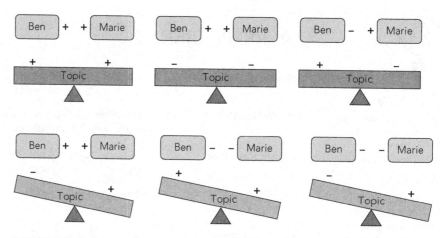

FIGURE 3.9 Illustration of the combinations of possibilities that result in balanced and imbalanced cognitions.

needs such as food and water to high-level, complex needs. These needs can be fulfilled in many ways, but often the mass media are an option for fulfilling these needs, although they may be competing with other nonmediated possibilities. Jay Blumler (1979) presents four kinds of needs that people are motivated to fulfill by using media: surveillance, curiosity, diversion, and personal identity.

Surveillance refers to the need to understand what is going on in our environment. This can encompass the need to know how the economy is doing, what the weather will be like for the rest of the week, or what popular TV show your coworkers will be talking about tomorrow.

Curiosity is the need for previously unknown information. When a coworker who wasn't known to have a serious boyfriend receives flowers at work, others in the office are likely to want to know who sent them. Even if they don't really care about her dating life, there is a pull of curiosity to know where the flowers came from. How do you choose which piece of mail to open first? Would you open the greeting card with no return address or the one with "Bill Enclosed" stamped below your cable company's return address?

We are often looking for a **diversion** from our routine. The diversion allows us to escape from responsibilities and things that have to be done to something that we are more interested in. This need does not have to be met through mediated methods, but the highly technological world in which we live makes it easy to be diverted from responsibilities. Smartphones, widely available Internet, social networking, personal music devices, and portable reading devices such as the Kindle create constant diversion possibilities.

The last of Blumler's defined needs was **personal identity**. The idea of personal identity as a need that can be met refers to the possibility that people look to the behavior of other people to define themselves.

In Your Life

What types of media do you utilize in your daily life? Which of Blumler's four motivational needs might you be trying to satisfy?

3.6 REMEMBER

surveillance	the need to understand what is going on in our environment
curiosity	the need for previously unknown information
diversion	allows escape from responsibilities and things that have to be done to something that we are more interested in
personal identity	the possibility that people look to the behavior of other people to define themselves

It has been found that people who are sure of their own identity are less likely to turn to mediated means to reinforce it. People who are unsure about their identity are more likely to turn to mediated means such as TV to better understand themselves or as a substitute for social interaction.

Understanding how people choose to gratify their needs is important for persuaders so that they can place their messages, or advertisements, in a media format that will have the largest impact on their preferred audience.

SUMMARY

Communication is arguably one of the oldest academic disciplines, and even the very first scholars could see the importance of persuasion. Aristotle provided an understanding of the basic persuasive qualities that has been used and expanded on to further develop the persuasive theories informing the study of communication for many years. Communication theory allows scholars to study how and why communication happens. In this particular chapter, you've reviewed some of the most important theories of persuasion. It's important to remember that there are other theories of persuasion, but these basic ones will serve as a foundation for your future studies. Figure 3.10 on the next page provides a brief review of the most common theories of persuasion studied in this course.

DISCUSSION QUESTIONS

Theory

1. What is theory and how does it connect to your study of persuasion?
2. What information might a political figure try to intensify during a campaign? What information might he or she want to downplay?
3. What process do people experience when making attributions about the behaviors of others? How does this differ when they are making attributions about their own behaviors?

4 What types of information are processed through the central route? The peripheral route?

5 Can you identify a recent time in which you experienced cognitive dissonance?

Theory	Author	Description
Aristotelian	Aristotle	Outlines the three components of persuasion: ethos, pathos, and logos.
Rank's Model	Hugh Rank	The intensify/downplay schema explains the ways in which a persuader might intensify or downplay specific information.
Narrative Paradigm	Walter Fisher	Explains how persuasive messages can be analyzed as narratives to understand persuasive ability.
Attribution Theory	Fritz Heider	Examines how you make attributions about the behaviors of self and others.
Social Judgment Theory	Muzafer Sherif	Describes how messages are compared to prior beliefs and fall into our latitude of acceptance, latitude of noncommitment, or latitude of rejection.
Elaboration Likelihood Model	Richard Petty & John Cacioppo	Demonstrates that different types of persuasive messages are processed through either the central or peripheral route and how each route produces different strengths of persuasion.
Social Learning Theory	Albert Bandura	People learn to, or are persuaded to, behave in certain ways because of previous experience and social feedback.
Cognitive Dissonance	Leon Festinger	Dissonance is created when you hold contradicting beliefs and you engage in behaviors that will eliminate the tension.
Balance Model	Fritz Heider, elaborated on by Theodore Newcomb	Outlines the possible combinations in an interaction between two people that will result in either a balanced or imbalanced cognition about the interaction.
Uses and Gratifications Theory	Jay Blumler	There are specific needs that humans need to fulfill, and they choose what type of medium is most sufficient to gratify these needs.

FIGURE 3.10 In Review: Theories of Persuasion

Argumentation

Eric Jenkins

4

YOUR OBJECTIVES

After studying this chapter, you should be able to:

1. Understand the role argumentation plays in persuasion.
2. Know the difference between argumentation and arguing or fighting.
3. Explain the basic elements of any argument.
4. Explain the importance of warrants for argumentation.

We shouldn't go to eat Chinese food tonight because I ate it last night.

I shouldn't buy this new shirt because I don't have the money.

Kids shouldn't play video games because they promote violence.

Freedom is America's most valuable contribution to the world because freedom reduces suffering.

Our business shouldn't make this investment because it is too risky.

You shouldn't vote for Rand Paul because he lacks experience in Washington.

Voting is an obligation for all citizens because democracies depend on citizen input.

Stem cell research is necessary to cure disease because it allows us to develop new medicines.

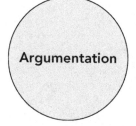

Argumentation

What on earth could all of these statements possibly have to do with each other? How can stem cell research and Rand Paul, Chinese food and freedom, investments and video games, shopping and voting be related? At first glance, you might think that this is simply a random list, but these statements are examples of **argumentation**, the presentation of reasoned evidence as a form of persuasion. Argumentation crosses many different fields and takes place in many different arenas in your life. From the personal to the political, from the world of science to the world of business, from entertainment to morality, argumentation plays a crucial role. This chapter explores the basic principles of argumentation across all of these fields. (More information about types of arguments is covered in Chapter 12.) Very little persuasion takes place without argumentation, so learning these principles will help you become more persuasive and also help you make better decisions when faced with a persuasive appeal.

ARGUMENTATION, NOT ARGUING

Despite the importance and necessity of argumentation in all areas of your life, the term *argument* has a negative connotation to some. Instead of arguing, they ask, can't we all just get along? Some students who decide to take an argumentation class figure they would be good at it since they argue with their parents or their girlfriends or boyfriends all the time. Their interpretation of argument is very different from the one presented in this chapter. Their interpretation is similar to Dictionary.com's first definition of argument: "an oral disagreement; verbal opposition; contention; altercation: a violent argument." In contrast, the interpretation of argument presented here does not require an altercation and certainly does not advocate violence. In fact, this chapter's interpretation features arguments where the participants respectfully present reasons and may even in the end come to a consensual agreement. This interpretation is closer to the other definitions of argument on Dictionary.com, which include "a discussion involving differing points of view," "a process of reasoning; series of reasons," "a statement, reason, or fact for or against a point," and, most importantly, "an address or composition intended to convince or persuade." Argument in this sense has to do with reason, logic, and evidence, not bickering and shouting. We might distinguish these two interpretations by saying that the first is about *arguing* while the second is about *argumentation*.

A Culture of Argument?

Despite the differences between arguing and argumentation, the negative associations with the term *argument* persist. Even some scholarly accounts dismiss argumentation as a bad practice that encourages disagreement and conflict rather than collaboration and cooperation. These accounts are understandable because the most prominent examples of argument in our culture seem to conflate argumentation and arguing. If you turn on television news shows, it seems like the *Crossfire* style is the most popular format, where representatives from the "right" and the "left" debate current events by yelling at each other, cutting the other side off, and frequently engaging in name-calling. These shows have contributed to a political atmosphere that appears extremely polarized and divided. In response, it is understandable that some critics would desire more cooperation and less arguing. In fact, this is precisely the stance of Deborah Tannen in her book *The Argument Culture: Stopping America's War of Words*. For Tannen (1998), American culture has become saturated with too much arguing. As she states in the opening paragraphs, "The argument culture urges us to approach the world—and the people in it—in an adversarial frame of mind. It rests on the assumption that opposition is the best way to get anything done" (p. 3).

Tannen's criticism is well taken since cooperation is necessary to address both personal and political issues. Yet both cooperation *and* conflict depend on argumentation in the sense presented in this chapter. Without the presentation of reasoned evidence, we would have little reason to agree or disagree.

Reasoning and evidence help us make decisions in every arena of our lives, from business to family, from entertainment to ethics, from science to art. Argumentation through reasoning is especially crucial for democracy since democracy subscribes to a belief that the best government is one ruled by the people employing free speech to influence decision-making, rather than by a ruler with a monopoly on power using force to rule. Whether you agree or disagree with any of the statements that open this chapter, presenting these arguments is the necessary first step to agreement or disagreement. Without an argument, how could we know where we might stand? Ultimately even Tannen (1998) agrees, stating, "Public discourse requires *making* an argument for a point of view, not *having* an argument—as in having a fight" (p. 4).

Tannen's quotation introduces another distinction between the first and second interpretation of argument. Her distinction is between making an argument and having an argument. My distinction was between argumentation and arguing. Whichever distinction makes more sense to you, the basic point is that making an argument (argumentation) is different from having an argument (arguing). A truly persuasive argument need not and often can not resort to fighting, name-calling, and mudslinging. Such tactics often undermine persuasion by angering or turning off your audience. This is not to say that all conflict is bad but simply to insist that argumentation is a necessary element for conflict and cooperation alike. Without the presentation of reasoned evidence, persuasion becomes much more difficult, if not impossible.

Ethical Arguing

What is really at stake in the distinction between argumentation and arguing is a difference in argumentative style. Some arguers may take on a style closer to fighting, attempting to persuade by brute force. Others may take on a more democratic style, attempting to persuade through the power of their reasons. In this chapter, we will focus on this second style, learning how to present and evaluate reasons in a logical manner. Before proceeding, however, let's spend a little more time clarifying these styles to help you see the ethical value of argumentation and counter some of the negative assumptions about arguing many people hold.

What does the ethical value of argumentation mean? We are not talking about whether you find a particular argument ethical or not. We are talking about the process of argumentation. Certain styles of arguing can be ethical, where other styles seek to manipulate or coerce their audience into consent. In our "argument culture," it seems that these styles of manipulation and coercion are the most prevalent, at least on the airwaves. Yelling, fighting, and name-calling tend to bring in the ratings, so we see

Ethical Connection

Think of a time you might have used unethical tactics to get your way during a discussion. Were there negative consequences for your actions? Looking back, what ethical tactics could you have used to reach a better outcome for all people involved?

these styles promoted. Wayne Brockeride (1972) explains the aggressive style, where the arguer does not seek mutual agreement about reasonable claims but instead seeks to coerce consent out of opponents. The arguer sees others as inferior objects ripe for their own exploitation. Through intimidation and the brute force of yelling or humiliation, these arguers seek personal gain at the cost of the other's pain. Obviously, such an approach may occasionally persuade, but it does so by sacrificing any claim to being ethical.

There is another style outlined by Brockeride with similarly questionable ethics. In this style, Brockeride compares the arguer to a seducer. Seducers use charm, deceit, or beguilement to persuade (see Photo 4.1).

PHOTO 4.1 Advertisers often use the strategy of seduction rather than argumentation to entice you to buy their products.

They often use strategies of fallacious argument (discussed more below), such as appealing to prejudice in order to persuade their audience. Once again, the end goal matters more to the seducer than the means of persuasion used to achieve the goal. So lying, distraction, and exaggeration are frequently practiced without regard for the audience. The seducer manipulates the audience for personal gain.

An ethical approach to argument rejects the style of the aggressor and the seducer. In its place, Brockeride contends, the arguer should see himself or herself as a lover. Lovers view themselves as part of an equal relationship with their audience. They respect the other and present their arguments in order to win willing consent. The lover is willing to risk losing the argument rather than pursuing any means whatsoever for victory. In other words, the lover makes an argument rather than having an argument. Even if the conflict becomes heated, the lover always respects the right of the other to disagree. The lover listens, compromises, and is willing to adapt when necessary. Such a style of argumentation may not always be persuasive, but it ensures that the reasons behind any decision are as true, tested, and solid as possible. That is, the lover is more able to correct mistakes than either the aggressor or the seducer because the lover is willing to be wrong, willing to be persuaded otherwise. Due to the importance of credibility for persuasion, in the long run the lover will generally be more persuasive because the audience will learn to trust such a person. Thus the lover's style has the dual advantage of being a more effective and a more ethical approach to argument. The rest of this chapter will address how to best perfect the lover's style of argumentation.

LOCATING EXAMPLES OF ARGUMENTATION

Now that you have examined the difference between argumentation and arguing, consider some instances in your life where argumentation plays an important role. The esteemed argumentation scholar Thomas Goodnight (1982) has distinguished between three different spheres of argumentation. He calls these the private, the technical, and the public spheres, and they indicate different arenas of our lives where argumentation takes place. The **private sphere** is the sphere of our personal relationships in day-to-day life. The **technical sphere** is where arguments based on a technical form of knowledge take place, such as arguments based in science, engineering, or administrative procedures. Finally, the **public sphere** is the arena of arguments with a broad public concern, such as the arguments made in political discussions or commercial advertising. It is important to note that these spheres are not so much physical locations as they are types of argumentation. You might have a political argument in your living room or design a science experiment in your backyard, two areas that are usually considered private space. Yet a political argument in your living room is still, for Goodnight, considered a public sphere argument and a science experiment in your backyard is still considered a technical sphere argument. What distinguishes the spheres is the type of reasoning used in making the argument. As Goodnight (1982) explains, "Sphere denotes branches of activity—the grounds upon which arguments are built and the authorities to which arguers appeal. Differences among the three spheres are plausibly illustrated if we consider the differences between the standards for arguments among friends versus those for judgments of academic arguments versus those for judging political disputes" (p. 216). Let's discuss some examples from each of these spheres.

Argumentation in the Private Sphere

Argumentation in the private sphere has its own unique grounds upon which to build. The argumentative ground is private; the decision is justified based on personal concerns. The reasons are usually those identified with common sense, the practical and everyday forms of reason we all engage in. Thus private sphere argumentation can be distinguished as intrapersonal and interpersonal argumentation. Intrapersonal argumentation is the process of presenting reasoned claims to ourselves. For instance, sometimes when we have to make a major life decision such as whether to move, to take a new job, or to date someone new, we make arguments for either side of the decision. Although we do not always list the arguments on a sheet of paper, we do something similar to listing the pros and cons when we make arguments in our head. Maybe we consider the longer commute to work as a negative argument against that new job, but on the other hand we are really attracted to the higher salary. Or perhaps we do not want to get into a relationship because we just ended a long-term one. Yet, the time we spend with this new love interest is always fun and meaningful.

We are all familiar with such kinds of intrapersonal arguments, but it is always good to distinguish them from other forms of intrapersonal communication to be sure we can locate argumentation in our lives. Intrapersonal argumentation, like all argumentation, requires the presentation of reasoned evidence. So intrapersonal argumentation is different from intrapersonal arguing and from making decisions without reasons or evidence. Calling ourselves names or degrading ourselves with negative thinking ("I am such an idiot!") is intrapersonal arguing, not argumentation. Likewise, if we make a decision without thinking it through or without a real reason, this is also not intrapersonal argumentation. If I make a decision based on a feeling, or a hunch, or out of habit, or without being aware of my other choices, then this too is not intrapersonal argumentation.

Interpersonal argumentation is very similar to intrapersonal except that interpersonal takes place between two or more people rather than simply with oneself. If you and your partner are deciding whether to move, to have children, to buy a house, or to make an investment, you are usually engaging in interpersonal argumentation. If you try to persuade your parents to buy you a new car or to extend your curfew hours, then the presentation of reasoned evidence will also represent interpersonal argumentation. If the discussion breaks down into you exclaiming that your parents do not love you and your parents retorting, "We brought you into this world, so you will do what we say," then we have again a case of arguing rather than argumentation. In this example, the children are acting like Brockeride's seducers, trying to manipulate their way into a favorable decision. The parents are acting more like Brockeride's aggressor, using the power of authority to forcefully resolve a dispute. As these examples make clear, argumentation plays a significant role in everyday persuasion, from the intrapersonal to the interpersonal. Can you think of other examples of intra- and interpersonal argumentation? In what other arenas might argumentation take place?

Argumentation in the Technical Sphere

Sometimes arguments take place in spheres where technical knowledge is required. Technical sphere arguments are less common and more specialized than private sphere arguments. They require a formalized type of reasoning whose standards are defined by a community of experts. In Goodnight's (1982) terms, the argumentation is "created in such a way as to narrow the range of permissible subject matter while requiring more specialized forms of reasoning" (p. 220). For instance, scientists run experiments and develop hypotheses based on previously existing theories and established procedures. Engineers might make arguments about the best way to design a new technology, or architects might make arguments about how to best construct a building for energy efficiency. Scholars make arguments based on a certain statistical methodology or theoretical vocabulary that is more technical and less accessible to the general public. These arguments are usually aimed at a small group of experts, taking place according to the standards and vocabulary of that expert community.

Argumentation in the Public Sphere

One way to think about Goodnight's spheres is that they designate the type of audience for which the argument is intended. Private sphere arguments are intended for a private audience of yourself and your

In Your Life

When you participate in a class discussion, consider which sphere the style of argumentation is in. Is it technical because the students are all experts on the material that is being discussed, or is it in the public sphere because the discussion is being held to reach a better understanding for all students in the class?

acquaintances. Technical sphere arguments are intended for a small group of experts. The public sphere represents the arguments intended for a broad public audience. Common examples include the arguments we might find in political campaigns, a legislative debate in Congress, or advertising. Public sphere arguments use forms of reasoning that are not quite as informal and fluid as in the private sphere but not as formal and restricted as in the technical sphere. Public sphere arguments are about the broader public good and are based on the shared values, beliefs, and reasons of the community or society. In this way, public sphere argumentation is crucial to the functioning of a democratic form of government. When politicians or citizens argue over, for instance, the best direction for health care reform, this is public sphere argumentation. Such arguments are not based on what is best for an individual's personal interest ("We should pass health care reform because I can make a lot of money"). They are also not based on purely technical standards like those a doctor might use to diagnose your illness. Instead, public sphere arguments are grounded in what is good for the society or the public at large ("Health care reform is crucial to keep the outrageous costs of health insurance under control").

Politicians or other public figures are not the only people who make public sphere arguments, however. Any time you engage in a discussion with fellow citizens about what policies or candidates to support, you are engaging in a public sphere argument. Again, these arguments can take place anywhere, from a very "public" location like the steps of your town hall, to a very "private" location such as your living room, to more of a hybrid location such as the local coffee shop (see Photo 4.2). What distinguishes the public sphere is that the arguments are grounded in the public good. That is, the arguments are based on what is good for the general public or society. As such, these arguments are not always about politics in the traditional sense either. Businesses often engage in public sphere arguments when they launch public relations campaigns about the good work they are doing in the community. Sometimes, advertisements are also based on public sphere arguments, such as when businesses contend that you should buy their product because it is produced in an environmentally friendly manner or because your purchase will trigger a donation to a good cause. Here, the business uses a public sphere argument (our product is good for the larger public) to advance its private interests (to sell products).

In short, it is the presentation of reasoned evidence that defines argumentation, and the various types of reasoned evidence help us to distinguish the spheres of argument. Personal reasons represent the private sphere. Technical or expert-based reasoning designates the technical

PHOTO 4.2 In much scholarship on the public sphere, the coffee shop is identified as one of the early places where citizens began engaging in political discussions.

4.1 REMEMBER

argumentation	the presentation of reasoned evidence as a form of persuasion
private sphere	the sphere of our personal relationships in day-to-day life
technical sphere	where arguments based on a technical form of knowledge take place
public sphere	arena of arguments with broad public concern

PERSUASION RESEARCH SNAPSHOT

Campaigns use numerous arguments in order to keep their voters' loyalty. Arguments are used to mobilize support for particular political issues. Ever attended a school rally in which a local congressperson came to speak to your campus? Did the issues he or she covered include educational costs (tuition), employment after graduation, or the current economic situation (cost of living)? If so, you participated in mobilization on the audience end. These persuaders knew exactly what you cared about and what you wanted to learn more about before they took a stance in those areas. This technique assures receivers that their concerns are the concerns of the candidates. But does this method always work?

In fact, scholars John Sides and Andrew Karch sought to specifically target senior citizens, veterans, and parents to see if specific mobilization attempts were triumphant. For senior citizens, they wanted to see if messages about social security increased the receivers' liking of the politician. Messages about veterans towards veterans were also measured. In the final section, the study looked at messages about child care and education that targeted parents of children under the age of 18. The researchers pointed out that relationships between audiences and campaign messages are especially important for two reasons: to prove whether campaigns have an impact on voter behavior and to look at responsiveness to American democracy as a whole. The two scholars examined data about advertising in the 1998, 2000, and 2002 elections as well as from other media markets. Campaign messages were evaluated through these surveys about how and why participants voted.

The study provided no consistent evidence that campaign messages about Medicare and social security had an impact on senior citizens' voting turnout. There was also no direct correlation between veterans' choices to vote and campaign messages about veterans. Minimal support was provided by the education and child care group relating their approval of a politician or voter turnout to the messages that were aimed at this group. Sides and Karch proposed that mobilization would be more established if the targeted audiences were less active in the campaign participatory process and the amount of advertising was enormous. In such cases, voters are not aware of the technique being used on them and are not aware of a better candidate, and so the advertisements are sure to be seen. Next time you hear a candidate speak or view an advertisement about that individual, how will you perceive his or her message?

Different forms of media as well as direct speeches will continue to thrive as forms of persuasion in American democracy. We must consider what matters most to us and what is best for our community. Will a photograph of Barack Obama giving a pro-choice speech at the University of Texas enhance your decision to keep him in office? Does a print ad showing a presidential candidate standing in Antarctica with drowning baby seals make you yearn to support his decision to eradicate global warming? Next time you view a

(continued)

campaign message, be aware of where the candidate stands on that particular matter. Do the advertisements have an actual impact on you or are they merely a form of entertainment?

Do you want to know more about this study? If so, read: Sides, J., & Karch, A. (2008). Messages that mobilize? Issue publics and the content of campaign advertising. *The Journal of Politics, 70*, 466–476.

sphere. Reasons related to the general society represent the public sphere. One advantage of describing these different spheres of argument is recognizing the significant role argumentation plays in all aspects of our daily lives. Whether our arguments are private, technical, or public, everyone engages in argumentation. Now that we know the basics of what makes an argument and the importance of argument in all aspects of our lives, we can attempt to break arguments down into their composite parts.

DEFINING ARGUMENTATION

Earlier in the chapter argumentation was defined as the presentation of reasoned evidence. Although this description is accurate, an elaboration on the definition will be helpful as you proceed to identify the parts and types of arguments. Argumentation scholar David Zarefsky (1994) provides just such an elaboration, defining *argumentation* as the "practices of justifying decisions under conditions of uncertainty" (p. 17). Zarefsky's definition contains four parts. To go in reverse order, argumentation takes place under conditions of uncertainty. This aspect of the definition simply indicates that we do not argue about things that are certain. The time of the day, the name of a person, the existence of gravity, and the fact that the sun rises in the east are just a few of many facts that we take as certain. There is no room or reason to argue over certainties; argumentation, like persuasion, only takes place when there is something uncertain to be decided. This leads into the next element of the definition: that argumentation is about making decisions. Again, as with persuasion, we engage in argumentation when there are choices to be made and legitimate options from which to choose. Look back at the arguments that started this chapter; each implies a choice, usually through the term *should*. Should we eat Chinese or should we eat something else? If Chinese is the only option, then there would be no argument. The same is true for voting for Sarah Palin, pursuing stem cell research, or picking a business investment. In all instances, we decide amongst an array of choices such as to vote for Palin or someone else, to fund stem cell research or other research, to invest in the stock market or bonds.

In Your Life

Can you think of a situation where the principles of argumentation would be important in your life?

The third part of Zarefsky's definition really gets to the heart of argumentation. This third part is the essential element of the original definition, the presentation of reasoned evidence. Zarefsky describes this part as justifying. Argumentation is a practice of justifying, or, in other words, supporting your decision with what are considered good reasons. We justify our arguments with reasons and evidence. For instance, we might decide to censor what video games our children play because we believe that video games promote violence. Or we might vote for another candidate because we believe Palin lacks the necessary experience. In a moment, we will explore the parts of an argument, and we will see that it is these reasons, or what scholars call the grounds or data, that turn any claim into a full argument. Finally, the last part of Zarefsky's definition is that argumentation is a practice. As with persuasion, argumentation is something that people *do*. Argumentation is a social activity where people justify and make decisions under conditions of uncertainty. This emphasis on practice ensures that we examine argumentation in a concrete context with specific people making particular decisions.

Logicians, Formal Argument, and the Syllogism

The practice part of Zarefsky's definition might seem like an unnecessary addition since it seems so obvious that argumentation is something that people do. Yet there is a long history of studying argumentation in isolation from the people who argue and the specific context of the argument. Logicians study arguments by examining the reasons without considering the practice of argumentation. They will take an argument (for instance, "Voting is an obligation for all citizens") and try to determine whether the argument is universally true, in every instance. An argument proposition that passes various tests of rationality and logical proof is deemed valid; one that fails these tests is deemed invalid. In the logician's approach, arguments are static propositions that can be evaluated as true or false. Arguments are not the practices of people but instead are the propositions themselves.

In the logician's tradition, arguments are typically made of a three-part structure called a **syllogism**. A syllogism is an argument in which the conclusion is inferred from two other premises, often called the major premise and the minor premise. One famous syllogism is represented in Figure 4.1. The major premise is "All humans are mortal." The minor premise is "Socrates is a human." If the major premise and the minor premise are both true, we can infer the conclusion that "Socrates is mortal." Such syllogisms are the prime representatives of what is often called **deductive reasoning**. Deductive reasoning begins with general claims in order to draw specific, narrower inferences. That is, the syllogism in Figure 4.1 begins from the general claim "All humans are mortal" in order to draw the specific conclusion that "Socrates is mortal."

Major Premise:
All humans are mortal

Minor Premise:
Socrates is human

Conclusion:
Therefore Socrates is mortal

FIGURE 4.1 The Syllogism

Logicians have developed many different types of syllogisms and numerous tests for the validity of a syllogism. In fact, this approach to the study of logical argumentation remained dominant in Western education until the Enlightenment, when it was criticized by Francis Bacon, one of the forefathers of modern science. Bacon preferred inductive reasoning over deductive reasoning, contending that careful observation of specifics would better allow thinkers to draw broad conclusions. **Inductive reasoning** works from the observation of specifics to draw general conclusions. In effect, inductive reasoning is the reverse of deductive reasoning. You can see why inductive reasoning is the preferred method of modern science. Science works by observation and experimentation in order to test and prove general hypotheses. For instance, beginning with the observation of an apple falling from a tree, Galileo reasoned that all things that go up must come down. From this, he developed the theory of gravity. Inductive reasoning starts with the specific (the apple) and moves to the more general (gravity). Bacon's criticism of deductive reasoning did not end the formal, logician-based approach to argumentation. On the contrary, sparked by the faith in science, logicians continued to depict argumentation as a universally testable form of reason or logic. They developed more refined standards for both deductive and inductive reasoning. Like the scientist, they attempted to observe and define the universal principles or laws for a logical argument. Arguments that violated these principles were deemed invalid. Those which met the principles were deemed valid. Such an approach has some merit, but it takes us further away from an understanding of argumentation as a practice and as a form of persuasion. Indeed, even someone without a textbook understanding of persuasion can readily recognize that false or invalid claims can sometimes persuade more than true or valid ones. Propositions that meet all of the standards for validity may still result in silly conclusions or even harmful choices. Furthermore, many arguments cannot be 100% true or 100% false. More often in our everyday lives, we deal with arguments that contain an element of truth and an element of falsity, with probabilities and uncertainties, with shades of gray rather than blacks and whites. A perspective on argumentation as persuasion must follow another perspective, a perspective that views argumentation as a practice and has an equally long and impressive intellectual history.

Argumentation, Aristotle, and Logos

The history of viewing argumentation as a practice extends back to one of the first great ancient Greek thinkers, Aristotle. Writing in the 4th century BCE, Aristotle mostly addresses argumentation in his work entitled *Rhetoric*. For Aristotle, rhetoric was an art. The art of rhetoric was the ability to observe in any given situation the available means of persuasion. In other words, rhetoric was considered the art of persuasion. Aristotle divided the means of persuasion into three broad categories. The terms Aristotle used for these three categories are *ethos, pathos,* and *logos.* **Ethos** is defined by Aristotle as good moral character and goodwill. *Ethos* is often taken to mean the credibility or believability of the arguer, not the argument. Good moral character and goodwill towards the audience will result in a strong *ethos* or credibility for the arguer. **Pathos** designates an appeal to the passions or the emotions. An appeal to pathos attempts to incite an emotional state in the audience (such as fear or anger) to make the argument more persuasive. Finally, **logos** is generally considered to be the use of reasoning to construct an argument, using either inductive or deductive reasoning.

For logicians, argumentation is only about logos. They even label the "appeal to emotion" as one of many types of logical fallacies. The logician's exclusion of ethos and pathos from logic results from their perspective. They see an argument as a logical proposition, not as a practice of people. This was not the case for Aristotle, who was concerned with the art of persuasion. Persuasion often depends on the credibility of the arguer (ethos) as well as the emotions of the audience (pathos). So, for Aristotle and for us in this chapter, argumentation is a practice of persuasion that is dependent on the situation, including the specific speakers and audiences. We, like Aristotle, are concerned with how different people at different times find different arguments to be persuasive. We are not concerned with the universal truths and logical proofs of the logician. Persuasion is a much more uncertain and much messier practice than the logician's take on argument.

Although the logician's approach to the study of argument dominated for centuries, our persuasion-based approach to argumentation has an equally long history, stretching back to before the days of Aristotle. Unfortunately, this approach was put on the back burner for many years, until it finally experienced a resurgence in the 20th century. Zarefsky is one of many scholars who helped advance this movement towards studying argumentation as a persuasive practice. Before Zarfesky, Chaim Perelman and Lucy Olbrechts-Tyteca called for a similar turn away from formal logic into a renewed emphasis on practical persuasion in their book *The New Rhetoric: A Treatise on Argumentation* (1969). Perelman and Olbrechts-Tyteca were very influential in the United States, and their work continues to draw interest today.

Perhaps the most influential scholar in the revaluation of argument as a practice was the British philosopher Stephen Toulmin. In Toulmin's work *The Uses of Argument* (1958), he develops a critique of the formal logician's approach to argumentation that faulted them for absolutism. In other words, he criticized the belief in absolute truths that were universally applicable regardless of the context or situation. These absolute principles are almost always irrelevant to the actual situations encountered by humans in their daily lives. (Just imagine trying to make a decision based solely on the logical principle of the logician, ignoring values and emotions, beliefs and credibility.) Instead, Toulmin contends, most arguments are "field-dependent." That is, an argument's persuasive value depends upon a certain field or context. What makes sense in one context might be completely irrational in another. For example, doctors generally recommend 15 minutes of sun exposure daily for good health. Yet, for someone with an allergy to the sun, 15 minutes of exposure can be life-threatening. Toulmin directs us, instead, to focus on argumentation as a practice, one which includes human beings and varies from field to field. In developing his practical study of

4.2 REMEMBER

syllogism	an argument in which the conclusion is inferred from two other premises, often called the major premise and the minor premise
deductive reasoning	reasoning that begins with general claims in order to draw specific, narrower inferences
inductive reasoning	the observation of specifics to draw general conclusions
ethos	the credibility or believability of the arguer, not the argument
pathos	designates an appeal to the passions or the emotions
logos	the use of reasoning to construct an argument

argumentation, Toulmin formulated a model of argument that helps explain how we argue in our everyday lives. The components of this model will be crucial for our understanding of argumentation throughout the rest of this chapter.

The Toulmin Model

Today, the Toulmin model is the most common way to describe the parts of an argument, and is used everywhere from public speaking classes to debate tournaments to common speech about argumentation. Learning the parts of the model will help you to understand what makes up an argument as well as recognize the strengths and weaknesses of a particular argument. First, we must outline the basics of the model. Many of these basics have already been implied throughout this chapter. For instance, we defined argumentation as a practice or presentation. This implies the first part of the Toulmin model, seen in Figure 4.2. The first part is called the **claim.** Arguers present a claim. The claim is the part of the argument to be defended. It spells out the general conclusion of the argument in clear and straightforward terms. Arguers present the claim for evaluation, as something factually true or false, as something morally right or wrong, as a direction that should or should not be followed. The claim is usually the first stated part of an argumentative proposition, followed by the reasons. Look again at the arguments that opened this chapter. The claims included "We shouldn't

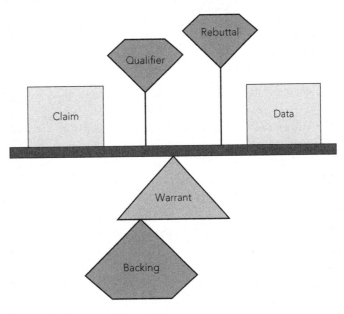

FIGURE 4.2 The Toulmin Model

go to eat Chinese food tonight," "I shouldn't buy this new shirt," "Kids shouldn't play video games," "Freedom is America's most valuable contribution to the world," "Our business shouldn't make this investment," "Voting is an obligation for all citizens," and "Stem cell research is necessary to cure disease." The claim is the primary and most basic part of an argument. The arguer attempts to persuade the audience to accept his or her claim.

Yet, a claim alone does not fully constitute an argument because it lacks the reasoned evidence or the justification part of our definition. This second part of the Toulmin model, called the data, is thus also implied in our definition of argument. An argument is not just a presented claim but a claim backed by reasons or **data**. The data is the evidence or reasons that supports the claim. The data usually comes after the claim, following the "because" in a complex sentence. So, in the examples from the introduction and in Figure 4.3, the data for why I shouldn't buy a new shirt is that I do not have the money. The data for not making a business investment is because it is too risky. The data supporting stem cell research is that the research helps develop new medicines. Together, the data and the claim represent the fundamental elements of any argument we encounter in our everyday lives. Whenever we engage in argumentation, the propositions will be composed of a claim and supporting data.

Claim	Data	Warrant
1. I shouldn't buy this new shirt.	I don't have the money.	Buying things when you don't have the money is a bad practice.
2. We shouldn't go to eat Chinese food tonight.	I ate it last night.	Eating things two nights in a row is undesirable.
3. Kids shouldn't play video games.	Video games promote violence.	Kids learn behaviors from the games they play.
4. Freedom is America's most valuable contribution to the world.	Freedom reduces suffering.	Reducing suffering is a valuable contribution to the world.
5. Our business shouldn't make this investment.	It is too risky.	Risky investments are bad for business.
6. Stem cell research is necessary to cure disease.	The research discovers new medicines.	New medicines are the key to curing diseases.
7. You shouldn't vote for Sarah Palin.	She lacks experience.	Experience is a necessary characteristic of a presidential candidate.
8. Voting is an obligation.	Democracies depend on citizen input.	Voting is a good means of providing citizen input.

FIGURE 4.3 Identifying Warrants

There is a third element of extreme importance in Toulmin's model, called the warrant. The **warrant** is the part of the argument that links the data and the claim. The warrant authorizes or makes possible the movement from the data to the claim. Thus, like the data and the claim, all arguments will also contain a warrant. Yet, unlike the data and the claim, warrants are frequently implied rather than explicitly stated. Warrants are frequently implied because when we argue in our everyday lives, we often use a type of argument that Aristotle called the enthymeme. An **enthymeme** is an argument with an unstated assumption that is supplied by the audience. So, for instance, when I say "You should quit smoking," you might supply the data that "smoking is bad for my health." More often, however, enthymemes leave out the warrant of the argument. For instance, in the argument, "You shouldn't vote for Sarah Palin because she lacks experience," what is left out is the premise that experience is a necessary characteristic of a presidential candidate. The audience supplies the connecting warrant about experience being a necessary characteristic. In the argument, "Voting is an obligation for all citizens because democracies depend on citizen input," the implied warrant is that voting is a productive means of giving a citizen's input. Nothing guarantees that the warrant will be accepted or viewed as persuasive by the audience. The audience might contest the assumptions in the enthymeme or accept them, but either way, the warrant is present whether it is explicitly stated or simply implied.

Figure 4.3 spells out the warrants for all of the arguments that started this chapter. If you look closely at these warrants, it might appear that the warrant often takes parts of the claim and parts of the data and combines them into one sentence. For instance, in the argument "Dogs are the best pets because they are so loyal," the warrant takes the best pets part of the claim and the loyalty part of the data and combines them into "The best pets are the most loyal." This is not true for all warrants, especially when parts of the data or the claim are implied. Yet many warrants can be discovered by simply combining elements of the data and claim into one sentence. This combination can take place because, as stated before, the warrant is the part of the argument that links the data and the claim. The warrant moves the argument from data to claim. The warrant, in other words, is the glue that holds the other major parts of the argument together.

As the glue linking claim and data, the warrant is frequently the most important part of an argument. Even when the warrant is implied, the warrant says a lot about the assumptions upon which the arguer builds an argument and the assumptions the arguer believes the audience shares with him or her. Without data, there can't be an argument in the sense of our definition here. Yet the same data can be used to justify completely opposite claims. For instance, the data that the United States spends

In Your Life

Where would you go to retrieve research, data, and supporting information to support an argument you're trying to make in a real situation?

$500 million a year on aid to Africa can be used to support the claim that "the United States spends too much on foreign aid" (since $500 million seems like a lot to most people) or to support the claim that "the United States doesn't spend enough on foreign aid" (since $500 million is a drop in the bucket, less than 1% of the total federal budget). Therefore, the warrant says much more about the argument than the data alone. The warrant points us to the assumptions behind the argument and the process of thinking that links the claim and data. The warrant is where argument as a practice is truly located.

Before you move into reviewing types of warrants and what they say about the arguers and their situations, three final elements of Toulmin's model should be covered. Although these elements are not always present like the claim, data, and warrant, they are present frequently enough to deserve mention. The first element is called the **backing**. Sometimes, a warrant itself needs further data or support. The backing is the further support for the warrant. For instance, the warrant that voting is a good means of citizen input might need further support. After all, most of us can think of instances where politicians do not seem to follow the will of the people or when we vote for a candidate despite disagreeing with her on some issues. Voting seems like a very limited form of input since we only get to do it once every few years and we do not get to specify anything about particular issues on our ballot. We just vote for a name and then seem to get no other say. So, the warrant that voting is a good means of citizen input needs more backing. Perhaps we could argue, for a backing, that voting keeps politicians attuned to polls and other forms of citizen input so they can win the vote the next time around. Even if voting is limited as a direct form of input, it may have positive indirect effects that encourage our politicians to pay attention to citizen input. As in this example, backing is most necessary when the warrants themselves are weak, in doubt, or contested.

The final two elements of the Toulmin model also address arguments that may be contested or in doubt. These elements are called the *rebuttal* and the *qualifier*. The **rebuttal** is a counter to arguments made against the claim. For example, the argument "Kids shouldn't play video games because they promote violence" might be answered by the response, "The violence is not real; people know it is just a game." The rebuttal might respond, "Children, especially young children, have a hard time distinguishing between real and virtual violence." Here is a response to an objection to the original claim. This is an instance of a rebuttal. A **qualifier** does what it sounds like, qualifies the extent or degree of the claim. Words like "usually," "mostly," "probably," "possibly," "presumably," "often," "in many cases," and so on all qualify the claim. In the example, "Kids should not play most video games except the nonviolent ones," the qualifier is represented by the

4.3 REMEMBER

claim	the part of the argument to be defended
data	the evidence or reasons that supports a claim
warrant	part of the argument that links the data and the claim
enthymeme	an argument with an unstated assumption that is supplied by the audience
backing	further support for the warrant
rebuttal	counter to arguments made against the claim
qualifier	statement that qualifies the extent or degree of the claim

term "most" and the exception of nonviolent games. The qualifier signals the degree of strength of the claim. Let's not qualify our way out of further discussing the importance of warrants, however. Without qualification, warrants represent the most important element of an argument.

WARRANTS: THE HEART OF ARGUMENT

Warrants are the heart of arguments because they represent the assumptions upon which the argument depends, and they indicate the type of thinking that links the data and the claim. As such, warrants say a lot about argumentation as a practice. They provide insights into the arguer, the situation, and the presumed audience of the argument. Because of this insight, some scholars have even called warrants the psychology of an argument. Psychology is the study of mental states and processes, and it is warrants that provide the most direct insight into the mental states and processes of reasoning of both the arguer and the audience. Much of the psychological insight of warrants depends on three factors: the types of warrants, the extent to which warrants are implied or explicit, and how much backing is provided for the warrant. You will read about these factors momentarily. But first, let's explore further the importance of warrants as the heart of an argument.

Importance of Warrants

Warrants connect the claim and the data. By providing this connecting glue, warrants become the assumption or premise on which our arguments rest. If the assumptions and premises of the warrant are believed to be strong, then the argument is generally strong and will typically evoke audience agreement. If the assumptions and premises of the warrant are believed to be weak or questionable, then the argument is generally weak and will have a more difficult time garnering audience agreement. Let us look at some of the warrants in our original arguments (refer again to Figure 4.3) and see if we can determine the strength of the arguments. For brevity's sake, I will refer to the arguments by their number assigned in Figure 4.3. Which warrants seem to you to be particularly strong and hard to argue against? I think the warrants in arguments #1, #4, and #6 seem very strong. "Buying things when you don't have the money is a bad practice," "Reducing suffering is a valuable contribution to the world," and "New medicines are the key to curing diseases" are all warrants that most people would have a hard time arguing against. They are assumptions that most of us share. There may be room for disagreement with a few instances of these warrants, but generally speaking, these are widely agreed upon premises. An argument with a strong warrant—a warrant that most people agree with—will likely be the most persuasive type of argument.

Now which warrants in Figure 4.3 seem mostly true but might have a little more room for disagreement? Your answers may vary from mine, but to me it seems like argument #2, #5, and #7 are mostly true but might be disputed by some people in some instances. For instance, most people find it undesirable to eat the same food night after night, but I had friends in high school who ate at Taco Bell every day or would have loved to eat pizza for dinner every night. Or, most people would say risky investments are bad for business, but some businesses make a lot of money making the risky investments that others will not make. With high risk often comes high reward. Finally, most people probably agree that experience is a good characteristic for a presidential candidate. However, part of Palin's appeal is that she is not a Washington insider. So, her lack of experience, to some, can be an advantage because she has not been corrupted by the Washington political game. These arguments have solid warrants but not ones that are quite as universally agreed upon as the arguments in the above paragraph. Most people will find them persuasive, but some might not. The arguer then might have to engage in rebuttal or provide more backing for the warrant to become persuasive.

Finally, which warrants in Figure 4.3 seem the most questionable? Obviously, it is the warrants that are left over, # 3 and #8. We have already discussed why the warrant, "Voting is a good means of citizen input," might need more backing. There are plenty of reasons to doubt how effective voting is at actually conveying the desires and beliefs of the people to their politicians. In fact, these doubts have sparked an extended debate over the value of representative democracy (where citizen input is limited to voting) and participatory democracy (where citizens get more direct say on policies, such as ballot referendums). By looking at this warrant, we can see that the argument is not very strong as presented because it rests upon a questionable premise. The same is true with argument #3. The idea that "kids learn behaviors from the games they play" has been disputed by many people. Some people claim that children know video games are just games. Plus, many children play violent video games without being violent in their real lives. Still other critics of this argument contend that the violence in games is good because it provides an outlet for children who might otherwise turn violent in their real lives. In other words, violent video games work like a pressure valve that lets children blow off steam. The point is not to reject this particular argument but to show that the warrant faces many counterarguments. Once again, these counterarguments have provoked a whole host of debates over video games, with each side offering more backing for its warrants.

You can see that weak warrants can provoke a whole debate over their quality, with much more data advanced simply to support an original warrant. Strong warrants, on the other hand, provoke little further debate because the argument rests upon an assumption on which most people agree. This is why I have called warrants the heart of arguments. Their strength or weakness often determines the strength or weakness of the overall argument. If you can identify the warrant, you can quickly determine whether this is a generally strong or weak argument. Identifying the warrant can also help point out the assumptions that you share and do not share with your audience Doing so might advance the cause of persuasion by pointing out shared premises on which the arguers can build for further agreement. Another important benefit of identifying the warrant is that it can help you understand what type of thinking the arguer relies upon.

Types of Warrants and Types of Thinking

Scholars have typically outlined three primary types of warrants which, as we shall see, parallel three different types of thinking upon which an arguer might base his or her arguments. The three types of warrants are frequently called substantive, motivational, and authoritative. **Substantive warrants** are warrants that draw upon the substance of an argument, rather than on the arguer or the audience. These warrants are another substantive claim that grounds the original claim and data. Substantive warrants are the most common form of warrant. Over one-half of the arguments in Figure 4.3, for instance, are based on substantive warrants. The substantive warrants are in arguments #3, #5, #6, #7, and #8. Argument #3 relies on the substance that children learn from games. Argument #5 relies on the substance that risky investments are bad business. Argument #6 rests on the substance that new medicines will cure disease. Argument #7 rests on the substance that experience is a good characteristic for candidates. Finally, argument #8 depends upon the substance that voting is a good form of citizen input. These are arguments whose warrants draw on substances such as learning, investments, business, medicine, disease, experience, candidates, voting, and citizen input. These are all concrete entities—substances—upon which the warrants are based.

Motivational warrants, in contrast, are based upon values or needs of the arguer or the audience. These warrants rest upon less concrete and more abstract things like needs, desires, values, and beliefs. Terms such as *freedom, equality, security, self-confidence, family values, honor, respect, fear, anger, greed, belonging,* and *love* are frequently found in motivational warrants. They are called motivational because there is a principle, need, or value that motivates the argument and the arguers. So an arguer's commitment to equality might mean that a warrant based on the value of equality is particularly persuasive or motivational. Arguments #1, #2, and #4 in Figure 4.3 represent the motivational warrants. Argument #1 is based on the principle that spending money you do not have is a bad practice. It is addressing the needs of the arguer (the need to not go into debt, to effectively manage money). Argument #2 is based on desires, saying it is undesirable to eat something two nights in a row. Although food might be a substance, this argument has a motivational warrant because it is about the motivation and desires of the arguer (who does not want to eat the same thing again). Finally, argument #4 is based on the values of freedom and the reduction of suffering. It has the term *valuable* right in the warrant, so this one might be easy to spot. However, this is an argument about a value (freedom) that bases itself on another value (the reduction of suffering). It is motivational in the sense that it encourages continued American support for the value of freedom and the reduction of suffering. Another example of a value-based motivational warrant is contained in the following argument: "Americans should spend less time shopping and more time with their families because research shows we spend a majority of our leisure time consuming." The warrant here is that family should be a value priority over shopping. It is based on a comparison of the value of family time versus the value of shopping. It attempts to motivate the audience to reevaluate its priorities.

Authoritative warrants are the final type. Authoritative warrants are based in the credibility, or ethos, of the data. Although there are no examples in Figure 4.3, authoritative warrants are common any time someone cites an authority or a source to ground a claim. When a person argues, "Global warming is real because a consensus of climate scientists say so," the warrant here is authoritative. The warrant reads something

Social Media in Your Life: Have You Seen This?

Go to YouTube and enter the following keywords: PETA, humane society

As a result of viewing these clips, are you motivated to support animal rights?

like, "Climate scientists are a credible or authoritative source when it comes to global warming." Another example is the argument made above about doctors and exposure to the sun. In the argument "Doctors recommend 15 minutes of sun exposure a day for good health because it provides vitamin D," the warrant is once again authoritative. The warrant reads: "Doctors are trustworthy sources on how to maintain good health." Any time someone makes an argument using data based on testimony or evidence from another source or expert, you can expect that the warrant is an authoritative one. In fact, if an argument follows the basic structure of "X is true" because "so-and-so said so," then the warrant will always be authoritative.

Now that you understand the types of warrants, you should be able to recognize the types of thinking that each one represents. An authoritative warrant represents a type of thinking based in the expert, the source, or the authority. It values research and sources more than commonsense reasoning. This type of thinker might ask for your sources for any statistic or data you offer. Such people tend to defer to authorities or experts, allowing the opinions of those they trust to shape their own opinion. For this type of thinker, the biggest factor in the reliability of the argument is the ethos of the source. A motivational warrant represents a type of abstract, principled form of thinking. This thinking is based in needs, desires, and values, and views them as the fundamental motivating factors for making decisions. These types of thinkers might place beliefs or values above credibility or substance. If an argument or an expert does not mesh with their beliefs or values, they are likely to defer to the values over the substance or the quality of the source. For this type of thinker, the biggest factor in the reliability of the argument is its pathos. Finally, a substantive warrant represents the type of thinker who relies mostly on concrete reasons and substances to make decisions. This kind of thinking values logic, the measurable, the concrete, and the quantifiable. This type of thinker might reject an expert source or an esteemed value because of expediency or pragmatic reasons. If the source or value lacks a concrete benefit or observable logic, the substantive thinker will often be suspicious. For this type of thinker, the biggest factor in the reliability of the argument is its logos.

Of course, we all use every type of warrant and each type of thinking from time to time. These categories are not mutually exclusive. Yet, identifying the most frequently used types of warrants can provide a general clue into how the arguer thinks. When it comes to persuasion, having an insight into how the other person thinks can be invaluable. In the following section, we will discuss further what warrants say about the arguer and his or her practice of arguing.

In Your Life

Advertising surrounds you each day, and most ads use a warrant to help persuade you that their product will be useful for you. Think of an advertisement you have seen or heard recently. Which type of warrant did it use to persuade? Examine the ads you see as you check your email and watch TV. Can you pick out what kinds of warrants are used most?

What Do the Warrants Say about the Argument?

Warrants indicate the primary form of thinking taking place. Likewise, the number, frequency, and explicitness of the warrants also say a lot about the arguer's perception of the argument. The number, frequency, and explicitness of the warrants can tell us about the perceived relationship between the audience and arguer, the tone of the argument, and the situation of the argument. Let's start first with the number of warrants. If an argument contains a high number of warrants, then the arguer is offering many different reasons to support her major claim. This might tell us about the relationship between the audience and the arguer. In an instance with many different reasons and, subsequently, many different warrants, the arguer assumes that the audience may be difficult to persuade. The audience may be reluctant to accept the major claim; therefore the arguer provides many different reasons and warrants to back her claims. In contrast, an arguer who believes that the audience generally agrees with her argument will provide fewer warrants. If the arguer thinks that the audience will quickly assent to the argument, then there is less need to provide a large number of warrants and data to back the claim. Additionally, an argument with numerous warrants also tells us about the situation of the argument. Obviously, if the arguer takes the time to provide numerous warrants, she must feel that the decision is an important one. When deciding what movie to watch, we might give only one piece of data and one warrant because the decision is not going to permanently change our lives. On the other hand, when deciding what candidate to vote for or what investment to make, the decision has far-reaching consequences for our lives, so we might consider many pieces of data and hence many warrants. In short, the sheer number of warrants can provide some insight into the seriousness of the argumentative situation. A casual decision will typically feature few warrants and less data; a more serious decision will usually feature more warrants and data.

The frequency of the warrants also tells us a lot about the audience-arguer relationship. An arguer who frequently returns to the same warrant probably believes that the audience shares this argumentative assumption. If, for instance, in evaluating the various candidates for president, an arguer repeatedly relies on the warrant "Experience is a necessary characteristic of a presidential candidate," then he must either know or assume that the audience agrees with this warrant. If the audience challenges this warrant, and the arguer frequently repeats it nevertheless, the argument will not be very persuasive. In contrast, an arguer may offer many warrants but without any frequency. He might only rely on each warrant a single time. This might tell us that the audience-arguer relationship is unsure or unfamiliar. The arguer is uncertain what assumptions are shared with the audience, so he offers many warrants, hoping to hit the persuasive mark.

The frequency of the warrant can indicate another insight related to the tone of the argument. An oft-repeated warrant in an argument may give the whole of the speech an insistent or stubborn tone. The speaker's continual repetition of the warrant signals to the audience that she is quite married to this particular argumentative assumption. An argument featuring numerous, infrequent warrants might give the speech a frantic or flippant tone. In this instance, the speaker seems to shift from one argumentative assumption to another rapidly, conveying a much different tone from the insistent or stubborn tone of the first example. Many times, we recognize these differences in tone due to the differences in warrant frequency in our everyday conversations. We might tell someone to calm down or remind him that a second ago his argument was different when he continues to shift between a large number of infrequent warrants. Or, we might tell him he is being too stubborn when we question a warrant and he continues to invoke it nevertheless.

Tone can also be discerned through the explicitness of the warrants. When a speaker implies most of his warrants rather than spelling them out, we might hear the tone as one of boldness. Here, the arguer asserts claims and provides data but continually assumes that the audience shares his warrants (his assumptions). The arguer may be correct or incorrect, but this is a bold assumption nevertheless. The argument's tone is simultaneously bold and presumptuous. For instance, an argument that reads, "Taxes are bad because they are a waste of money" relies on an assumed warrant that the government is inefficient and ineffective at spending money. Implying this warrant allows the arguer to take a bold stance against all forms of government programs. However, to some audience members who believe the government is effective at such things as building roads, maintaining police forces, and providing public education, this warrant may seem presumptuous and even a little bit arrogant. In contrast, an arguer who explicitly states warrants often conveys a more measured or patient tone. He takes the time to spell out each warrant independently, conveying a sense that he is carefully considering every assumption in his argument. Stating each warrant explicitly slows down the overall pace of the argument, conveying a more measured and deliberate tone than when an arguer quickly moves from data to claim without explicitly stating her warrants.

The explicitness of the warrant often tells us quite a bit about the audience-arguer relationship and the situation of the argument as well. Roderick Hart (1970) contrasts the speaker-audience relationship in "doctrinal" and 'hostile" rhetoric. In doctrinal rhetoric, speakers are addressing an audience who accepts the doctrine of the speaker, such as a preacher speaking to a congregation. In such instances, the speakers rarely provide explicit warrants because they can presume that their listeners share the same assumptions (they subscribe to the same doctrine). In contrast, hostile rhetoric occurs when the audience is hostile to the speaker or the speaker's position. Here, the arguer will often explicitly provide the warrants in an attempt to overcome the hostility by illustrating that she does indeed share assumptions with her audience. In general, the casualness and friendliness of the argumentative situation is signaled by the explicitness of the warrant. In a casual and friendly situation, arguers rarely provide explicit warrants because they can assume the audience will grant them the assumptions. So, when I make the argument to a friend that "Dogs are the best pets because they are the most loyal," I do not feel the need to supply the warrant that "Loyalty makes the best pets." I can assume my friend will give me the benefit of the doubt and supply the warrant for me. In a hostile or less friendly situation, I might need to provide explicit warrants. If my audience is against me from the get-go, providing warrants spells out my arguments in more detail in an attempt to overcome their hostility or resistance. I cannot expect that they will fill in the missing warrants since they do not want to agree with me.

The same is true for the seriousness of a situation. In a congressional debate or a legal proceeding, providing explicit warrants indicates that the decision is quite serious and not to be taken casually. The arguer cannot assume that the audience will fill in the missing assumptions and may wish to convey the argument in its full details because of the gravity of the situation. Congressional debate, for instance, is often called *deliberation*. The term comes from the deliberate nature of the discussion. Congressional representatives often deliberately provide explicit warrants, slowing down the pace of argumentation and conveying the seriousness of the decision and the situation.

In review, warrants are the heart of arguments because they designate the assumptions upon which an argument rests. The warrant authorizes the movement from the data to the claim, indicating to you how the practice of arguing is moving along. By examining the warrant, you can

4.4 REMEMBER

substantive warrants	warrants that draw upon the substance of an argument, rather than the arguer or the audience
motivational warrants	warrants based upon values or needs of the arguer or the audience
authoritative warrants	warrants based on the credibility, or ethos, of the data

Remember: You can use your knowledge of persuasion to engage real-life situations. Consider the scenario below and think about what you would do as you apply your study of argumentation. Apply information from this chapter to the situation below.

It's the holiday season, and you are thinking of gift ideas for your friends. Your best friend had a flat-screen television stolen from her apartment and you decide that you are going to get her a new one. As you head to the stores, you realize that there are hardly any flat-screens left. You find one for a great price, and you put it in your shopping cart when you realize that you just took the last one. You turn around to look at a few different movies and, after reading a couple of titles, you turn and see a person walking off with the television that you had in your cart. As you attempt to confront him, he gets angry, stating that your cart was unattended and the television was fair game. Using persuasion and argumentation, how would you handle this situation in an ethical manner?

determine the true strength of the argument, seeing whether the assumption is one most people would agree with or questionable and in need of further support. Furthermore, the number, frequency, and explicitness of warrants tell us a lot about the audience-arguer relationship, the situation, and the tone of the argument. Few, frequent, implicit warrants signal a close audience-arguer relationship, a more casual situation, or a bold and assertive tone. Many, infrequent, explicit warrants signal a more distanced audience-arguer relationship, a more serious situation, or a more careful and concerned tone. Warrants thus provide us insights into the practice of arguing by pointing to the relationship between the audience and the arguer, the situation of the argument, the tone of the argument, the assumptions behind the arguments, and the style of thinking on which the argument depends. Recognizing these factors can assist you greatly in both shaping a more persuasive argument and considering the persuasiveness of someone else's argument.

SUMMARY

In this chapter, you have learned the difference between having an argument and making an argument, or between arguing and presenting reasoned evidence. The definition of argumentation as the practice of justifying decisions under conditions of uncertainty was discussed. You saw how argumentation plays a crucial role in many spheres of life, from the personal to the technical to the public. Following the Toulmin model, you reviewed the various components of arguments including the claim, data, and warrants. In so doing, you discovered the significant importance of warrants, which are the hearts or assumptions of our arguments. You should also know how the various classes of warrants—authoritative, substantive, and motivational—can tell you about the tone and the reasoning process engaged in by the arguer. Understanding the argumentation should help assist you in offering more persuasive arguments and in evaluating the arguments you encounter in your life.

DISCUSSION QUESTIONS

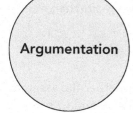

1 What is the definition of argumentation, and why is each part of the definition important?

2 Can you come up with your own examples of arguments in the private, technical, and public sphere? Which spheres of argument do you encounter most often in your daily life? Which ones seem the most important? Why do we need to distinguish between these spheres?

3 Can you identify which question might be the best to raise about each of your examples?

4 Find a short letter to the editor from a newspaper. Dissect the text according to the Toulmin model, identifying the claims, data, and warrants. Is this a strong argument? What does the Toulmin analysis tell you about the genre of letters to the editor in relation to types of argument, the audience-arguer relationship, and the tone?

5 What are some ways that you go about identifying credible sources in your private life? In the public sphere?

Visual Persuasion

Katherine Hatfield

5

YOUR OBJECTIVES

After studying this chapter, you should be able to:

1. Understand the role the visual plays in persuasion.
2. Know the properties of a visual argument.
3. Explain the nature of visual culture.
4. Explain the concept of witnessing.
5. Describe how campaigns use visual communication to help draw an audience and support.

CHAPTER OUTLINE

Twin Towers Burning

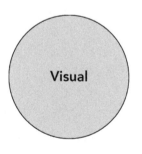

Visual

What is this a picture of? Do you remember when you first saw the photographs of this event? What were you doing? How did you react? Did it provoke an emotional response? Prior to witnessing these images, what did you think of when you heard the word *terrorism*? Was it the Oklahoma City bombing? Columbine High School attacks? What did terrorism look like to you? What does it look like now? For many Americans, terrorism now looks like or is visually communicated through the representation of the attacks on the World Trade Center on September 11, 2001. These images have emerged as visual points of reference when we talk about or think about terrorism. Thus, they themselves have the power to influence the way we think, act, and communicate about terrorism. Put simply, all images have persuasive power. In the very meeting of viewer and image, the viewer is influenced by what she is witnessing. This chapter explores the persuasive nature of the visual. It allows you to study the ways human beings interact with, use, and make sense of the persuasive images that we all encounter in our lives.

VISUAL COMMUNICATION DEFINED

Think about it: You are constantly interacting with images—signs, pictures, symbols, and the like. Essentially all things are visual—they communicate in very persuasive ways. From the road signs and symbols that help direct us through traffic to the influence of famous works of art or advertisements on our lives, the visual is powerful. Images rhetorically interact with people. Rhetoric is the art of using signs and symbols to persuade. While Aristotle taught about the art of persuasion from a more linguistic perspective, modern-day scholars have come to agree that rhetoric involves more than words. Thus, when you fail to understand or pay attention to the ways in which visual images impact your life, you're missing an important aspect of persuasion.

Visual communication refers to the ways in which the images that humans interact with either intentionally or unintentionally, such as signs, symbols, pictures, photographs, and art, create meaning in their lives. As human beings we create, use, and interpret symbols to help us make sense of the world around us and our experiences in that world. Many of these symbols are visual. Think about the stop sign you encounter when you approach an intersection. What does it look like? How is it memorable? How do you react when you see this sign? Do you stop? Hopefully, you do! Ultimately what this involves is that the stop sign visually represents a suggestion of what you should do. It has persuasive power. It tells you that you should stop and that if you do not, the implications could be negative.

Too often we fail to recognize the communicative power of the visual, prioritizing the discursive, or what is spoken or written, as being more important. Sonja Foss (2004) argues that ignorance of the visual is ignorance of much of the world. It is important that you pay attention to and attempt to understand the power of the visual in your life.

VISUAL CULTURE

In the world of competitive speech and debate, the standard organizational pattern for a persuasive speech is Problem-Cause-Solution. When a speaker strays from that normative choice, the reaction from judges and the audience can be resistance. However, Maeve, a competitive persuasive speaking student, knew that the normative organizational pattern just would not work as well for the topic she had chosen to speak about as another choice. For Maeve, the organizational pattern needed to be Monroe's Motivated Sequence. The Motivated Sequence asks the audience to visually imagine what the world would be like if the problem either continued to exist and worsen or if the world was free of the problem. Maeve's speech was about environmental apathy. It was easy to describe the behaviors and symptoms of an environmentally apathetic public and to suggest specific strategies that would allow audience members to change their own behavior, but with an apathetic audience the problem is just that—they are apathetic. They know the problem exists, but they don't seem to see it as something that directly affects them and are not motivated to act. Thus, it became necessary for Maeve to fully, richly, and in great detail describe what exactly will happen if the audience members do not take immediate action. The **visualization** step of Monroe's Sequence provides just the right opportunity for this visual imagery. While Maeve's speech didn't actually create a physical image for the audience to *see,* it created an image in their mind's eye that allowed them to see the world and their place in it differently. Monroe's Sequence employs the idea that the visual is just as powerful, if not more so in some cases, as the linguistic. For Maeve, it certainly was.

In Your Life

Is there a particular image that comes to mind as powerful? What statement did it make? What impact did it have on you?

Indeed, we are a visual culture. In fact, images have **cultural salience**—what is visual helps to frame or construct culture. Symbolically, images have the power to disrupt and challenge the ways we have traditionally thought about those cultures because they serve as a powerful reminder of specific cultural events and experiences. Images have the power to alter people's perceptions and reactions to those experiences. When you capture a moment, experience, or event on film, it's not only captured for the sake of remembrance. Rather, it reminds you of the impact of that moment in your life. You turn to these images to remind you of the power of that moment, to help frame your way of knowing your reality, and to guide your future behavior. This means that images have the power to change your life.

Witnessing

Ever driven down the road and seen an accident? Did you feel compelled to look? Did you find yourself drawn to the spectacle of what was going on? John Durham Peters (2001) argues that the act of **witnessing** has two faces, "one of seeing" and "one of saying" (p. 709). The first is a passive act; the second is active. By witnessing what has taken place, the witness passively observes the world around him. He becomes the possessor of knowledge. Peters contends "what one has seen authorizes what one says: an active witness first must have been a passive one. Herein lies the fragility of witnessing: the difficult juncture between experience and discourse" (pp. 709–710).

On September 11, 2001, when Mayor Giuliani banned the taking of amateur photographs and disallowed citizens from coming to the place where the Twin Towers had fallen, the world was left to witness the events of 9/11 through the lenses of those who did have access. For millions of Americans across the country and billions of people across the world, the experience of 9/11 began in the meeting of person and image. The images (whether amateur or professional) provided the world with access to the experience. Those who were not physically present were able to experience the day.

Some have related this act of capturing the experience in a more permanent state as similar to a tourist behavior. Just as a family would pose for a picture outside a national monument or theme park to help preserve and remember the event, during moments of tragedy and disaster it is part of human nature to capture the event and allow others to also witness it. Act of tourism or not, their active witnessing of 9/11 allowed the American people to come to terms with terror as it impacted so many lives. Just as each person in New York City experienced the events in a unique way, as viewers from afar, all Americans lived the experience uniquely as well. In the same way, monuments are built in honor of our collective past as a way to commemorate the experience of those who were there to experience an event firsthand and also for those who will come to know the event in its aftermath.

Traditionally a great deal of time passes between the event to be commemorated and the building of a monument to serve as a physical and visual reminder to the public. However, it may be argued that as a possible outgrowth of the American desire to remember these events, there was faster motion toward a consensus on the need for and even the design of a 9/11 memorial. At one point in time, people waited a considerable number of years to acknowledge events such as World War II, the Korean War, or the Vietnam War. The 9/11 memorial is perhaps considered an act of closure that functions simultaneously as an act of renewal. In fact, within two years of the attacks, a design for "One World Trade Center" was chosen to serve as a permanent memorial of the attacks on 9/11. The rapid desire to develop and build a memorial does indeed underscore the strength of this image and the need to memorialize the event and the lives lost.

In Your Life

Visual images of natural disasters (e.g., hurricanes, tornadoes) and acts of war or terrorism (9/11 attacks, Oklahoma City bombing) can be extremely emotional. What images from the 9/11 attacks stand out in your mind? What images of 9/11 resonate with you the most?

5.1 REMEMBER

visual communication	the ways in which the images humans interact with either intentionally or unintentionally, such as signs, symbols, pictures, photographs, and art, create meaning in their lives
visualization	step of Monroe's Motivated Sequence that emphasizes the power of the visual in helping the audience to see or imagine
cultural salience	concept that visual images help to frame or construct culture
witnessing	two-step process of passively observing and then acting on what one sees in the world after becoming the possessor of knowledge

DOES THE VISUAL ARGUE?

In the 1990s, scholars in communication studies initiated a theoretical discussion about whether or not we can include what is visual as an argument. Ultimately, the question was asked, "Can the visual or an image make an argument?" Those who argued against the question did so based on two major premises. First, argumentation scholars noted that visual images are naturally ambiguous in nature and, as a result, it is very difficult to determine their intention or meaning. The second premise is that all arguments must be propositional. This means that an argument will propose that something must be done. Argumentation scholars wondered whether or not an image, something that is not inherently linguistic, could make such a proposition.

Anthony Blair (1996) argued that the visual could indeed make an argument. His theory suggests that there are five basic properties of an argument. First, a claim must be present. Second, there should be a reason, or reasons, for that claim to be made. Third, the reason for the claim should be able to be expressed. Fourth, the claim should be able to be explained. Finally, there should be an attempt to communicate what the claim is and what its reason for existence is. Blair's original thesis in the 1990s was that these principles could apply to both arguments built from language, that are discursively articulated, *and* the visual.

Images undeniably play a significant role in persuasion. But do images make arguments, and can a person engage in argumentation through visual representation alone? On this question, there is some reasonable dispute. Following the Toulmin model explained in Chapter 4, if you consider an argument as only a two-part proposition containing a claim supported by data, then it seems that images can't meet this standard. As David Fleming (1996) contends, images do not offer claims supported by data; these must be inferred by the audience. The main reason for an image's inability to provide the two-part structure of an argument has to do with the differences between language and image. Language allows people to reason linearly and analytically, breaking down a proposition into its requisite two parts (claim and data). Images, on the other hand, are perceived as a whole, without differentiation between the claim and the data. In Fleming's (1996) terms, "(A) picture typically functions as a simultaneous whole rather than a sequence of bits. It lacks, in other words, the internal linear arrangement that characterizes verbal discourse" (p. 14). Here, Fleming is making an argument by definition against the idea that there are visual arguments. His syllogism runs something like this: (1) Arguments are defined as the two-part structure of claim-data. (2) Images do not have this two-part structure. (3) Therefore, images cannot be arguments.

As far as it goes, Fleming's argument is reasonable. Yet, many other scholars contend that images play a crucial role in argumentation and therefore the definition Fleming relies upon is too limited. In both popular and scholarly discourse, there is a long history of recognizing the persuasive power of images. In fact, many critics fear that images detract from rational argumentation by substituting heavily emotional, inflammatory, or misleading thoughts for carefully considered deliberation over the issues. See Photo 5.1 (an Obama/Joker image). This image has circulated widely in U.S. culture, provoking heated responses from people of different political beliefs. Conservatives often see it as a perfect expression of their fears of the Obama presidency, while liberals view the image as inflammatory and potentially racist.

The image is undeniably powerful at first glance. Yet, what we have here is an example of arguing rather than argumentation, fighting rather than reasoning. The image uses a villain from popular culture (the Joker from the Batman movie *The Dark Knight*) in order to drum up fear over the Obama presidency. It seems to offer a claim (Obama is a socialist), but offers no evidence for this claim (what does the Joker or Obama have to do with socialism?). In fact, the claim itself represents arguing rather than argumentation since it is based in what Richard Weaver (1953) calls a **devil term.** Weaver describes devil terms as terms that the culture generally regards as evil or wrong, terms such as *tyranny, terrorism, fascism,* and, here, *socialism.* Opposed to devil terms are **god terms,** terms typically revered in a culture, such as *freedom, rights,* or *democracy.* The image is designed to invoke fear through the devil term *socialism* and the association with the evil Joker rather than make a reasoned argument. It is an example of arguing rather than argumentation. Predictably, the image sparked a fight rather than reasoned deliberation.

PHOTO 5.1 Obama-Joker Image

Images can often be used for arguing rather than argumentation, and they have an emotional, persuasive effect on the audience regardless of whether they really offer a reasoned argument. Perhaps this power to distract and mislead is why critics such as Fleming want to exclude images from the realm of argument. Yet such a move is too drastic because images continue to be used for argumentation as well as arguing. Perhaps images cannot provide the two-part structure of an argument, but they can be used either to assert claims or as a form of data. That is why you are studying the use of images in argumentation in this section. There is, indeed, a long history in the realms of science and the law of using images as data to support a hypothesis or case. Scientists use microscopic images as data for arguments about the structure and behavior of cells or atoms, and they rely upon telescopic images of the stars to hypothesize about the galaxy. Prosecutors and defense attorneys alike submit pictures of the crime scene or, occasionally as in the Rodney King case, of the crime itself as evidence for their claims. Indeed, some data such as the spatial relationships between objects (say, two cars in an accident) or features such as color or size are best illustrated through images.

Images can also assert claims, sometimes with the help of language. There is a long history of cartoons that make political claims. Such cartoons typically work like an enthymeme, making an argumentative claim and requiring that the audience supply the missing data or warrants. For instance, consider a political cartoon that makes an argument about the 2010 health care reform issue. Its basic assertion is that the reform is a tangled morass, similar to a ball of Christmas lights. It might light up but it is not a thing of beauty or even very functional. The claim is presented in the cartoon, but the data must be supplied by the audience. An audience that is aware of the messy negotiations and compromises that it took to get the health care reform passed, as well as the seemingly piecemeal array of regulations that resulted from the reform, will understand the argument. The image makes a claim, and the audience supplies this missing data. Although this lack of data might seem to confirm that the image is not an argument, many language-based arguments in your life are also enthymemes and equally require that the audience supply the missing elements.

Arguments by image are a unique case as well, because they can be any of the types of arguments outlined above. For instance, many arguments by image are actually arguments by analogy. Picture this: an image of a child and a mule yelling at each other, with the text below the image reading "Internet Argument." This image makes an argument by analogy, claiming that debates on the Internet are like arguments between a child and a mule. They are often immature and irrational, like a child, and stubborn like a mule. Arguments by image can also be arguments by cause (i.e., smoking causes cancer). Thus, when evaluating arguments by image, you can use the standards and questions outlined for the various other types of argument. Once again, you can always question the relevance and the sufficiency of the data supporting an argument by image.

Besides these typical questions, you should be aware of three other factors when it comes to arguments by image. First, be on guard against the persuasive power of images. Images can speak a thousand words, but oftentimes we as communicators respond to images based on emotion rather than logical considerations. Perhaps you've seen the Joe Chemo image that's powerful because of the horror of the camel's emaciated body in a hospital bed. The image packs much more of a punch than simply saying "Smoking causes cancer," and this is why persuaders of all stripes frequently rely on images. Images cause an emotional response that often short-circuits our logical responses. In the case of Joe Chemo, this image adds persuasive power to a very reasonable and logical claim ("Smoking causes cancer"), but in many instances, such as the Obama/Joker example, the image can undermine logical thinking in favor of an emotional response. Second, never assume that an image alone is absolute proof. The meaning of images often depends on the viewer and her cultural and social *ways of seeing*. Different people at different times can see different things in the same image. For instance, in the Rodney King case, the video seemed to show police officers abusing a helpless and non-threatening King. However, when the video was shown in court, the jury apparently saw it differently, concluding that the police were justified in subduing a resisting criminal. This is a tragic example because the jury's verdict sparked a wave of riots in Los Angeles. Many African American viewers saw the video as absolute proof of police abuse, so they responded with anger when the jury decided to see the video differently. Images rarely prove something absolutely because so much of what the image argues is up to the interpretation of the audience. Especially today, with widespread ability to alter images through photo-editing software, you should always be skeptical of images when they are presented as proof.

Finally, always be wary of the credibility of images. Because of the persuasive power of images, many biased sources will create images in order to support their interests. They will attempt to use images to bypass your logical thinking. So always ask who made the image and what interest it serves. For instance, the Obama/Joker image was made by an anonymous person who has refused to admit to creating it. This anonymity is a sign that the image was intended either as a joke or to deliberately inflame the public. The creator of the image was not willing to put his or her own credibility behind it; therefore, we should be suspicious of its claims. In fact, as you will see in the next section, credibility is a crucial aspect of any type of argument you encounter.

In Your Life

How, if at all, have you used visual images to make an argument in your life?

UNICEF Belgium and the Smurfs: An Example of Visual Argument

In 2005 the United Nations Children's Fund (UNICEF) of Belgium created an advertising and public service campaign commercial that specifically challenged the notion that an argument has to be linguistically bound. The commercial offers a unique site of investigation for visual rhetoric scholars in that it challenges traditional ways of theorizing that argumentation must be linguistically bound. UNICEF's traditional method of soliciting donations is by showing starving children in war-torn areas while a spokesperson narrates the request for financial support. Belgium's approach was much different. Instead of using real images of war and devastation coupled with a linguistic narrative, it turned to animation employing some of the most popular characters on children's shows—the Smurfs.

The scene is set with a gleeful display of Smurf village, Smurfs frolicking throughout, and familiar Smurf humming and singing. Within moments the Smurf village is bombed and destroyed, leaving dead Smurfs in the wake and a crying, helpless baby Smurf among the wreckage. In a matter of moments, a carefree Smurf community is completely destroyed. For the viewer, the scene is very compelling because the Smurfs are childhood friends.

If you apply Blair's five properties of an argument (see Figure 5.1) to the Smurf example, you can demonstrate how the commercial argues visually. First, the claim: War leaves children without a support network. Second, the reason for the claim: War is real. Third, the expression of the claim: War can impact anyone—even the seemingly happy Smurfs in Smurf village. Fourth, UNICEF is able to express the claim by the creation of the commercial, providing an immediately understandable context for the argument. Finally, the fifth property is that there must be a reason for the claim. The commercial is clear: Here we come to understand UNICEF's purpose. The commercial argues that the viewer needs to donate funds to help support child victims in war-torn countries. Visually, the commercial is successful in persuading the audience member to think about war in a different way.

Social Media in Your Life: Have You Seen This?

Go to YouTube and enter the following keywords: unicef smurfs

1. There is a claim.
2. There is a reason(s) for the claim.
3. There is an expression of the claim.
4. There is an ability for the claim to be expressed.
5. There is a reason for the claim's existence.

FIGURE 5.1 Five Properties of an Argument

Now that you have studied the connection between visual persuasion and argumentation, the next section explores how visuals are used to tell stories.

THE VISUAL NARRATIVE

Walter Fisher (1984), known for his scholarship on the power of narrative, once said that human beings are storytelling creatures. By our very nature we navigate through our lives by telling the stories of our experiences. We have individual narratives, but we also have cultural or collective narratives. The narratives that emerge from cultures transcend both time and space, meaning that they will carry over from generation to generation and across varying cultural boundaries. These narratives continue to evolve as new symbols are formed, based on the evolution of beliefs and values. **Visual narratives** are not necessarily all "told" through the use of language, but also through the sharing of signs and symbols or, for our purposes, images. As preferences towards certain ways of thinking evolve, so too will the symbolic artifacts used to create and express ideological perspectives change. Edwards and Winkler (1997) note that cultures are compelled by images. They draw your attention, construct a story, and guide your behaviors. People not only remember an event based on what they were doing at that moment, but also based on the things that they saw.

One of the most widely accepted, yet later proven incorrect, myths in political communication is the listener-viewer disagreement of the Kennedy-Nixon 1960 presidential debate. Prior to the 1960 presidential debates, candidates debated over the radio. However, in 1960, network television featured the debating candidates for the first time. Reportedly, members of the public who had only auditory access to the debates through radio broadcast thought that Richard Nixon was the hands-down winner of the debate. The narrative that was constructed following the debate, often still recounted in political punditry, is that those who witnessed the debates on television thought that John F. Kennedy was clearly the winner. The narrative recounts how Kennedy's visual appearance was calm, attractive, youthful, and energetic. Further, it was suggested that Nixon's appearance communicated quite the opposite. While it was reported that Nixon's discursive arguments were stronger than Kennedy's, his visual appearance communicated weakness, which was why the viewing public thought Kennedy was the stronger candidate.

The visual appeal of Kennedy and the strong argumentation of Nixon created a *myth of viewer-listener disagreement*. This myth, however, is just that, and in 1987, Vancil and Pendell debunked the myth, suggesting that there was little evidence to support such a claim. However, in 2010, the 50th anniversary of the Kennedy-Nixon debates still had pundits reliving the spirit of the myth, this time focusing less on who won the debate than on the power that image has in presidential politics.

Even today, political candidates build teams around themselves to provide insight and guidance about what to wear and how they should present themselves to the public. The candidate's image is an incredibly important component of a campaign. From the way the candidate cuts her hair to the choice of suit color, the way that a candidate visually constructs her image will help to determine how the public perceives her. Ultimately, candidates are visually constructing a story or narrative of how they want the public to see them.

The Twin Towers of 9/11: An Example of Visual Narrative

The events of September 11, 2001, left a remarkable imprint on the American public. The images of 9/11 serve as a visceral reminder of the tragedy that took place that day. Each image, while only a snapshot of a particular moment that day, helps to commemorate the entire day as a significant historical event in American history. The photographs function as a space of public deliberation, where members of a public are able to publicly memorialize and debate the events of 9/11 and, ultimately, their experiences as members of a culture of victims.

We have been left with a history captured in images. The images will serve as tools by which we communicators can retell the story for generations to come. Even now, a decade later, people continue to discuss the design of the memorial constructed to commemorate the Twin Towers and the tragedy of 9/11. Yet, the National September 11 Memorial and Museum was dedicated on September 11, 2011, and the memorial opened to the public the next day. The museum is due to open on September 11, 2012. The National September 11 Memorial and Museum is one part of the new World Trade Center complex. The complex also includes One World Trade Center (the lead office building to be completed in 2013) and three other hi-rise office buildings.

The hope is, as in the case of the Vietnam Veterans Memorial, that it will replace the images of loss and terror with a symbol of remembrance, one that encompasses the tragedy while not dwelling on its more poignant, sadder moments. Thus, the 9/11 memorial built at Ground Zero will ideally reinforce the values Americans cherish as well as serve as a symbol of renewal of the national spirit. The design of the memorial and of the One World Trade Center building may seem to reject the original spirit of the Twin Towers' design, suggesting in their place a stronger, taller, possibly less vulnerable and more symbolic representation of the experience. Viewers may witness in the completion of the memorial a symbol of unity, strength, and freedom. In a sense, the memorial further continues the narrative by providing a symbolic referent for how the American public achieves a level of healing, honoring those who were lost, and looking towards the future. Further, it can be argued that the design of the memorial competes with the pre-9/11 and post-attack images of the Twin Towers. The pre-9/11 images are indicative of power, elitism, global economic leadership, fortitude, and strength. The post-attack images communicate terror and destruction.

VISUAL PERSUASION IN ADVERTISING

It is impossible to think about the impact of the visual without acknowledging the fact that consumers are in undated with the visual through advertisements. Advertisements that appear on television, websites, and billboards and in magazines, newspapers, and the like rely on their ability to display and persuade the consumer to buy the product. Have you noticed that the sexual content of advertising has become increasingly more explicit to distinguish between competing soft drink, perfume, and other brands? Consider how much more sexual content is relied upon in advertisements selling hotel and casino experiences in Las Vegas in competition with the other area hotels and casinos.

For decades now, scholars in communication and advertising have suggested that the images used in advertising have a strong impact on those who engage with them. For instance, when advertisers use certain types of models to sell their clothes, they choose models that will inspire consumerism. The hope is that the consumer sees what the model looks like and begins to envision looking the same way. Put simply, you can call this the power of visual appeal or visual suggestion. This is visual persuasion at work. Advertisers are in the business of visual persuasion. One of their primary responsibilities is to show potential buyers what they can have and make it appear so visually appealing that buyers decide to buy.

One study examined content from three Hard Rock Hotel Casino billboards in the Las Vegas area between 2001 and 2003 to determine how the casino used sexual appeals in its advertising. One of the billboards, placed near McCarran International Airport, displayed a same-sex-themed advertisement. In it, two youthful, scantily clad women have their arms around each other. The ad's text has a suggestive double meaning. The 2002 billboard, located in the connector between the airport and the car rental area, shows a topless young woman holding a pair of dice in a strategic location. The 2003 billboard's message was aimed directly at the annual

National Finals Rodeo audience. The rodeo is held on the University of Nevada, Las Vegas, campus near the Hard Rock Hotel Casino. The billboard conveyed a blatant message about the sexual activity one could expect at the Hard Rock Hotel Casino. The billboards, and other print ads over time, offended a lot of people.

The research showed that the use of sex to advertise in an already sexually heightened environment invites the use of overtly explicit sexual ad messages that will offend local residents, parents, the news media, and regulatory agencies. The study found that for more than a year the local press engaged in an argument over the "unacceptable images" in the Hard Rock Hotel Casino's advertising content. Also, the Nevada Gaming Commission and Gaming Control Board fined the Hard Rock Hotel Casino $100,000 for its sexually suggestive content. Notably, somewhere between 200 and 300 people attended the commission's hearing to support its complaint against the Hard Rock's explicit advertising. Although sex sold the Hard Rock experience, ethically and morally, the Hard Rock Hotel Casino used tactics that the local residents found offensive.

Think about the last time you went shopping for clothing. Did you go to a certain store because you saw an advertisement? If so, what did you like about what you saw in the advertisement? Was it the way that the clothing seemed to fit on the model? Was it the colors or the styles of the season? Was it the way the advertisers visually created a storyline that was suggestive of happiness and contentment? Advertisers find ways to compel a response to the image that they are selling. Absent the visual, an advertiser's success rate would most likely decrease. Some advertisers push this persuasive strategy to the edge, illustrating the extreme nature of human experience in advertising in order to evoke a powerful reaction to the message.

Ethical Connection

Your study of the persuasive dimensions of visual communication is important to connect to an ethical perspective. Other than the examples provided in this chapter, what are some visual images that you view as unethical? Why?

 PERSUASION RESEARCH SNAPSHOT

This chapter examines the persuasive power of the visual. It's easy to notice the persuasive impact of a large billboard or racy commercial, but have you ever wondered how websites use visual communication to persuade you? From the colors used on the website to its graphics, font, and logos, many different factors are used by advertisers to influence you to purchase something on their site. In fact, online advertising can be very creative. Think about this: What company comes to mind when you think about a gecko?

The Geico gecko is just one example of many corporate mascots that dot the advertising landscape. Mascots have the ability to help consumers

(continued)

draw connections between everyday things and corporate products. For example, it's hard not to think of Tony the Tiger when talking about Kellogg's Frosted Flakes or Mickey Mouse when thinking about Disney. These mascots have become almost inseparable from the products they endorse. In the online environment, there is a different name for these mascots: They are called avatars. Much like mascots, an online avatar can create a sense of recognition and build rapport with a consumer. Having the Geico gecko walk you through the process of buying insurance online is one example of an avatar at work. Do you think an avatar might influence you to use a product or service?

Recently, researchers Natalie Wood, Michael Solomon, and Basil Englis have examined the role these avatars have in online persuasion at e-commerce sites. Avatars can range from fanciful animated characters to literal photographic depictions of the web surfer. When used correctly, avatars can help aid consumers in recognizing brand names and positively affect product sales. The researchers focused on one important question for this study: Can avatars influence decision-making for apparel products and consumers' overall evaluation of a website? This is an important question to ask because personalized websites using online avatars are generally much more expensive than comparable dynamic websites. Participants were allowed to access four hypothetical avatar-assisted shopping scenarios from their home computer. Each scenario involved a different apparel product (lingerie, dress, raincoat, bathrobe) with separate avatars to choose from. Ten days later, the participants logged in again and were randomly assigned to two different groups: (1) one with their preferred avatar or (2) one with no avatar (control group). The website was not changed in any way.

The study yielded mixed results. When participants considered buying lingerie or a dress, the use of an avatar increased both purchases online and overall purchase satisfaction. There was no significant difference in results when participants were shopping for raincoats or bathrobes. Still, most participants reported overall increased satisfaction with the website when avatars were used.

Understanding how to reach and persuade consumers in the information age is a great challenge for students and businesses in today's world. This study serves as a prime example of how complex this process can be. How important do you think online persuasion and advertising are today? How do websites personalize their content and cater to your unique profile or avatar?

Do you want to know more about this study? If so, read: Wood, N. T., Solomon, M. R., & Englis, B. G. (2006). Personalization of the web interface: The impact of web avatars on users' responses to e-commerce sites. *Journal of Website Promotion, 2,* 53–69.

Sexual Appeals in Advertising: Does Sex Sell?

Does the image of a beautiful woman using a product have more persuasive power than an image of an "ordinary" or average-looking woman using the same product? Could the average Joe sell a power drink with as much ease

PHOTO 5.2 Sex in Advertising—Calvin Klein

In Your Life

As you think of unethical visual images or those that you take issue with in your own life, how do you usually respond? Do you boycott the product? Do you engage in other forms of social activism or protest to make a statement? Can you think of hot topics that you're willing to advocate for or against?

as an athletic, muscular, attractive male? Sex is used in obvious ways in some advertising and in more complex, suggestive ways in others.

Beautiful women seemingly experiencing sexual arousal from the use of particular shampoos and conditioners are used to elicit a heightened emotional response to convince the viewer that she too will enjoy a similar experience if she buys these products. Sex is compelling. It is evocative and can create a response with relative ease when the message or image is presented in a way that suggests the use of this product can make you feel good, too.

Many have argued that these images have a potentially strong detrimental or negative impact on a people's psyches. Advertisers have used unrealistic images of men and women to sell their products. To promote discussion about the sex appeals advertising, we have included Photo 5.2. Discuss this Calvin Klein ad with other students in class, friends, family, and your instructor. What do you think?

VISUAL CAMPAIGNING

In the early 2000s, the state of Montana found itself faced with a serious methamphetamine problem. Montana's meth use had hit a record high, and Tom Siebel, founder of the Siebel Foundation, decided that something aggressive needed to be done. So he founded the Montana Meth Project. The project developed a research-based messaging campaign to visually demonstrate the impact of meth use. The project's goal was to show the devastating effects of meth use on the individual and the collateral damage on the user's family and friends. The campaign, still operating today, reaches 70% to 90% of Montana teens on a weekly basis. The billboards, commercials, posters, and television advertisements display the consequences of an addict's life. One particular billboard shows an addict's mother who is the victim of violence associated with meth use (see Photo 5.3). The caption reads, "My mom knows I'd never hurt her. Then she got in the way."

Kim Witte's (1992) **extended parallel process model (EPPM)** provides a theoretical underpinning for understanding some of the meth campaign's communicative strategies. EPPM is a theory of fear appeals. In its most basic sense, EPPM suggests that fear can influence a person's attitudes towards something in different ways. It specifically contends that there are two different ways by which fear can influence an attitude: threat and efficacy. First, a person must sense a threat from the message, suggesting that the person is in the way of danger. The second, efficacy, allows for the ability of the person to respond to the danger or threat. Witte theorizes that for a fear appeal to work as a persuasive strategy,

PHOTO 5.3 Billboard from Montana Meth Project

both elements must be present. In a sense, this suggests a basic problem-solution way of thinking about fear appeals.

Let's consider EPPM as a way to help explain what the developers of the Montana Meth Project were aiming for. Clearly, the visual displays used help communicate a grave sense of fear about the use of meth. Not only does the campaign use visual images that are compelling and definitely communicate a threat, it provides the efficacy, or solution to the fear, by suggesting that stopping or simply not starting the use of meth will result in an opposite outcome.

The developers of the Montana Meth Project or other advertising, social movement, or public service campaigns depend on the persuasive strategies discussed in this book. Just as importantly, they employ the power of the visual to help garner support and change behaviors and/or attitudes about their cause, issue, or product. Think about advertising, for example. Imagine watching a television commercial that showed only a black screen or snowy static. The only thing such an advertisement does is provide 30 seconds of an announcer telling you about the product. You never see the product, the impact the product has on your life, how it works, or what it looks like. How compelling would such an ad be? Would it make you want to run out and buy the product? You are probably more likely to change the channel! The advertisement would be rendered ineffective because the visual appeal is missing.

Public service campaigns have tried to use the visual in provocative and exciting ways in order to present their traditional arguments in new ways. For instance, in the PETA advertisement shown in Photo 5.4, the image is sexy and compelling. But more importantly, its juxtaposition against the simplicity of the word "VEGETARIAN" asks the viewer to

5.2 REMEMBER

devil terms	terms that the culture generally regards as evil or wrong (e.g., *tyranny, terrorism, fascism, socialism*)
god terms	terms typically revered in a culture (e.g., *freedom, rights, democracy*)
visual narratives	stories told not only through the use of language, but also through the sharing of signs, symbols, and images
extended parallel process model (EPPM)	provides the theoretical underpinning for understanding campaigns' communicative strategies; a theory of fear appeals

Remember: You can use your knowledge of persuasion to engage real-life situations. Consider the scenario below and think about what you would do as you apply your study of visual persuasion. Try to apply the information you learned in this chapter.

You are on a design team at a reputable business in Los Angeles, California. You have been waiting for your opportunity to shine. A company contacts your design team and says that it is interested in a design to help sell its new exercise equipment. Your coworkers are busy with other designs that have deadlines coming up very soon, and they ask you to take charge on this offer. How could you use persuasion and all that you've learned about visual communication to help this company achieve its goals through your design? (This could be an image, video, logo, etc.) What would you do?

cognitively grapple with PETA's argument. Is Alicia Silverstone's naked body an argument for the vegetarian cause of raw cooking? Or is PETA using sex to compel the viewer, suggesting that a vegetarian lifestyle is sexy? What do you think?

PHOTO 5.4 PETA Vegan Alicia Silverstone

SUMMARY

This chapter explored visual communication and its connection to persuasion in your life. You examined the idea of witnessing and studied how the act of witnessing allows you the opportunity to experience and be influenced by what is happening. You also learned about visual narratives and how the visual tells the story of what is and what should be. In addition, you reviewed Anthony Blair's five properties of an argument and how the visual can also argue, applying Blair's properties to a commercial that relied primarily on the visual image to make an argument. You also explored advertising and the role of sex in visual persuasion. Finally, you learned about the power of the visual in campaigns, such as public service campaigns, and about Kim Witte's theory on fear appeals, the extended parallel process model.

As you study persuasion and begin to understand that all communication is inherently persuasive, you also need to consider visual communication. Although visual communication is a relatively new area of scholarly inquiry in the discipline of communication studies, it is an important part of your study of persuasion in your life.

DISCUSSION QUESTIONS

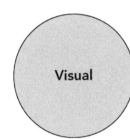

1. Define visual communication and explain why it is important that we study it from a persuasive perspective.

2. List several examples that support the idea that we live in a visual culture.

3. How does the visual tell stories?

4. Choose a public service campaign with which you are familiar and discuss how it uses images to help communicate its cause. Are the images successful in persuading you?

5. Explain how sex is used to visually construct an ideal product and to persuade an audience of consumers.

Persuasion and New Media

6

Michelle Maresh

YOUR OBJECTIVES

After studying this chapter, you should be able to:

1. Understand how persuasion has changed among the various stages of technological development.
2. Differentiate between the six elements of mass persuasion.
3. Understand and explain how power and privacy function in social networking.
4. Identify the new media strategies that businesses use to persuade us to action.
5. Apply your experiences with social networking to the various elements of persuasion.

ava_tx78414: Bridgette! How was your date with Liam last night? I've been dying to hear the details!

surfer_gurl21: Oh, Ava, it was so disappointing. He wasn't at all like what I thought he'd be!

ava_tx78414: What do you mean?

surfer_gurl21: Well, first of all, his Facebook said that he "liked" the Beatles, Rolling Stones, and Elton John, but when I made a reference to an Elton John song, he didn't even know what I was talking about! If that wasn't bad enough, he looked nothing like his default picture! I didn't even recognize him when I walked into the restaurant.

ava_tx78414: That's crazy! I've heard about using flattering photos online and I can understand that, but I just don't understand why someone would "like" fan pages for bands they have never listened to. What's the point?

surfer_gurl21: I have no idea, but I think it's safe to say that I won't be seeing Liam again.

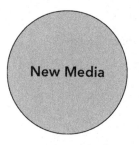

New Media

Consider the conversation above. It is probably safe to say that many of us have experienced a scenario similar to Bridgette and Liam's in the past. While the characters, context, and details may differ, the general notion remains the same: **New media**—the convergence of traditional media (such as film, music, language, images, and text) with the interactive ability of computer technology—have shifted the way that we experience persuasion in our everyday lives. New media have permeated many facets of our lives and will continue to play a role in how we view ourselves, others, entertainment, consumerism, and politics for many years to come. In this chapter, you will explore the difference between traditional media and new media. You will learn the various ways that new media have influenced and been influenced by persuasion, as well as the ways that people manage their identities using new media. Additionally, you will consider surveillance and filtering as they pertain to the public and private nature of new media technologies. With U.S. culture becoming more reliant on social networking and other technologies, it is important to understand the ways that people persuade and are persuaded by others in this context. Doing so will help you become more persuasive and also help you make better decisions when confronted by implicit persuasion.

TRADITIONS OF TECHNOLOGICAL DEVELOPMENT

To understand the impact that new media have had on your ability to persuade and be persuaded by others, you must first understand the difference between traditional media and new media. To make these connections, let's turn to Walter Ong's important works on the technologization of verbal communication. Ong was primarily concerned with the shift from orality to literacy and the impact that this shift would have on culture and education (1982). Since then, many scholars have followed Ong's lead in giving attention to the ways that technology impacts culture. This development in thought has extended Ong's attention to oral and print culture to include electronic culture and, more recently, the culture of new media. Let's briefly consider each of these aspects of communication technology.

Oral Tradition

The **oral tradition,** also referred to as *oral culture* or *oral age*, consists of cultural messages or traditions verbally transmitted across generations (Vansina, 1985).The oral tradition can be classified as **primary orality,** which is a culture that has no knowledge of technology beyond the spoken word, or as **secondary orality,** which is when verbal communication is sustained through other technologies, such as the telephone or Internet (Ong, 1982). Consider, for example, the earliest form of human communication, where individuals transmitted messages to one another through stories, chats, songs, and folklore. Today, it is difficult to conceive of any cultures that are strictly primarily oral, but it is easy to imagine how secondary orality allows us to transmit knowledge through technologies such as the BlackBerry, Chatroulette, and YouTube.

Written/Print Tradition

There has been much debate about the tradition that follows the oral tradition. Some scholars believe that the **written tradition,** which refers to early forms of written communication such as hieroglyphics, immediately follows the oral tradition; whereas other scholars (such as Ong) believe that the development of the alphabet must precede the written tradition. For the latter, the **print tradition,** which embodies the creation and dissemination of printed text, is the next identifiable period of technological development. Nevertheless, the print tradition is largely viewed as having begun around the year 1440 as a result of the development of Johannes Gutenberg's **printing press,** a mechanical device that applies

new media	the convergence of traditional media (such as film, music, language, images, and text) with the interactive ability of computer technology
oral tradition	cultural messages or traditions verbally transmitted across generations
primary orality	a culture that has no knowledge of technology beyond the spoken word
secondary orality	a culture in which verbal communication is sustained through other technologies
written tradition	refers to early forms of written communication such as hieroglyphics
print tradition	embodies the creation and dissemination of printed text
printing press	a mechanical device that applies pressure from an inked surface to a print medium

pressure from an inked surface to a print medium (Eisenstein, 1980). The advent of this device allowed for the first mass production of books (McLuhan, 1962). Essentially, the development of the written/print tradition allowed for the expansion of literacy and the ability to produce and share information with the masses, rather than having communication limited by verbal communication and geographic location. As Ong believes, educating people in writing causes individuation and adaptation to occur (1982).

Electronic Tradition

The **electronic tradition,** also referred to as the *electronic age* or *electronic media*, are media that require users to make use of electronics to access content. Where some media are considered static because they do not require the audience to use electronics (newspapers, for example), the electronic tradition focuses on media such as audio/visual recordings, radio, telegraph, and television. Using this definition, many scholars believe that the advent of the Internet should also be considered part of this tradition; however, because the Internet allows the consumer to also become the producer, many others believe that the Internet is part of a different tradition of technology known as *new media*.

In Your Life

Can you give examples
of how all three traditions
are currently melded and
used together? Do you
feel that this allows for
a more complete and
successful communication
experience?

Digital/New Media Tradition

Consider the traditions of technology we have already mentioned: oral, written/print, and electronic. Given the definitions and characteristics of these traditions, it appears that all existing media can fit into these categories. Take, for instance, the smartphone. A smartphone, such as a BlackBerry or iPhone, allows us to talk to our loved ones (oral technology) via the cell phone (electronic technology), while surfing the Internet (electronic technology), reading an e-book (print technology), and downloading applications (electronic technology again). Thus, various facets of the smartphone allow us to tap into multiple traditions at the same time, rather than having to purchase five separate devices to accomplish our complicated communication goals. Because of the multifunctionality of many new media devices, such as the smartphone, researchers created a new classification for technological advancements of this type: the digital tradition, also referred to as **new media tradition,** *mash-up culture, information age,* and *attention age.*

Traditional Media versus New Media

As mentioned above, the development of technology that shifts the consumer into the role of producer has changed the way that you view media. Traditional media (commonly referred to as "old media") has become **mashed up,** or converged into new media technologies. Where traditional media formats (oral, print, electronic) limit the audience to more passive, one-dimensional roles, new media allow for an increased quantity of media and media storage, quick delivery of information across temporal and spatial dimensions, unrestricted on-demand access to content, interactive feedback, and the democratization of production and consumption of media content (Manovich, 2003). Similarly, the focus on social networking and active participation illustrates the difference between old and new media. Thus, viewing *Despicable Me* on a Blu-ray DVD player is an example of using traditional media, whereas using the Tag Reader application on a cell phone to take a photo of a cardboard advertisement for *Despicable Me* at a movie theater with the purpose of viewing additional scenes from the movie is an example of using new media.

As previously mentioned, considering the difference between traditional and new media allows us to understand the impact that these technologies have on our ability to persuade and be persuaded by others. For example, in oral culture, persuasion is mostly a function of our ability to craft a logical (using logos), credible (using ethos), and emotional (using pathos) narrative—as Aristotle prescribed in *The Rhetoric*. As Walter Fisher's (1984) narrative paradigm theory contends, as long as a story has **fidelity,** or matches our own beliefs and experiences, and **coherence,** appears to hold together and make sense, we are likely to be persuaded by it, regardless of its truthfulness. Essentially, the oral, written/print, and electronic cultures position audience members as passive consumers, where the producers of texts are transmitting polarized, persuasive material to the audience and the audience is accepting it. New media, however, tout the democratization of the media through an emphasis on nonconformity and active individualism. Where the audience is a consumer in old media, they now become a producer in new media. This gives the audience **agency,** or the ability to generate change in a culture's thought, beliefs, and actions and, thus, persuade others while simultaneously being persuaded by them.

In October 2009, *The Tonight Show with Conan O'Brien* aired a parody of Michelle Obama's visit to the television show *Sesame Street*. In the original episode of *Sesame Street*, Michelle Obama visited popular characters Elmo, Big Bird, and the Basket Bunch to discuss healthy eating habits for children. However, the *Tonight Show* parody featured Big Bird questioning the authenticity of President Barack Obama's birth certificate and heckling Michelle Obama about President Obama's health care agenda. In its traditional, electronic media format, this TV episode presented an argument that may have resonated with critics of President Obama's health care reform proposal. In this sense, it was true to the reality of these individuals and made sense to them; in other words, it had fidelity and coherence.

With traditional media, this is where the persuasion occurs—individuals view something on TV, for instance, and may trust it and accept it. With new

 PERSUASION RESEARCH SNAPSHOT

This chapter focuses on new media as they relate to your study of persuasion. Chances are any time you open your email, you can see this in action. Have you ever opened a message to find a company trying to sell you a product or service? Maybe you have even taken a part in new media persuasion by liking your favorite TV show or music group on Facebook. Do you think the use of online campaigns affects your attitudes or buying preferences? Chances are you have at least once in your life used new media to purchase something, but how much does online campaigning influence your decisions? Can it even affect the way you feel about political candidates?

Use of the Internet as a persuasive tool has not had a very long history. The first major national campaign to make use of the Internet was the 1992 presidential campaign. Since that time, however, the Internet has exploded with different forms of persuasive communication. How people react to this new medium is still under contention. While email campaigns and social networking have been shown to have an influence on people's perceptions, there is little agreement as to the nature or importance of that influence. With almost all different media converging onto single platforms (laptops, smartphones, touchpads, etc.), the effectiveness of online campaigning is something important for researchers to study.

Researchers Kevin Wagner and Jason Gainous looked at the growing use of the Internet to campaign in elections across the United States. Because of the relative lack of previous research on this subject, the authors created a theoretical framework to understand the effect of the Internet on modern campaigning. Basically, while the Internet offers a dynamic change in campaigning technology, it does not change the underlying premises behind why people vote and campaign. Since voter motivation is still largely driven by individual-level costs and economic considerations, this theory posits that the relative inexpensiveness of online campaigning will allow candidates to reach a greater number of potential voters. The researchers used the 2006 U.S. congressional elections as the sample for their study. Any races deemed competitive by Congressional Quarterly, Inc., were examined and were also cross-referenced with the website PageRank, which estimates different candidates' web presence. In the individual congressional races, candidates were compared to one another based on who had a greater web presence.

The study found that Democrats generally had a higher web presence than their respective counterparts, and Senate races had a greater web presence than House races. Researchers also found that for every respective point of web presence (measured as an average on a scale of 0–3), each candidate received roughly 279,000 more votes. With Democrats taking the majority of 2006 congressional seats, the authors concluded that their greater web presence played a large part in their victory.

Knowing how new media influence us on a personal, social, and governmental level is critical to our understanding of persuasion in the information age. Next time you log in on your Facebook page, take a look at the different types of advertisements that pop up. Do they feature products or services that appeal to you? Or at the very least, do they stick in your mind more than similar products or services?

Do you want to know more about this study? Is so, read: Wagner, K. M., & Gainous, J. (2009). Electronic grassroots: Does online campaigning work? *Journal of Legislative Studies, 15*(4), 502–520.

media, however, individuals are encouraged to seek additional sources, give feedback, and have dialogue with others about what they have seen. A simple YouTube search will reveal a video clip from the Michelle Obama *Sesame Street* parody featured on *The Tonight Show*. However, rather than being restricted to viewing this video and moving on, the audience is asked to post comments about the video, post video responses, and engage in discussion or debate with others about the authenticity of the arguments presented in the video. For instance, some of the comments on this YouTube video denounce

For	Against	Neutral
The Basket Bunch is perceptive. Too bad vegetables are not constitutionally able to run for Congress. Though, come to think of it, Bawney Fwank is a fruit.	How about...obama has continued w/ the bush genocide/torture regime. is that funny? can we all laugh at that sesame street?	This video is hilarious and am so glad that liberals have a sense of humor about the Obamas being made fun of just like the conservatives were supposed grin and bear it when both President Bush and Sarah Palin were mocked over and over again :D
Finally! Big bird has the courage to say what the other media elites are afraid to!! Obama will probably try to disparage him by saying he acted "stupidly" haha ha.	lmao....lol......I love when people remind me of the adoration i have for our President Obama...and how horrible that makes some people fell inside that he is in office..... Victory is so sweet.... year by year	The birth announcement newspaper articles from 1961 do not say that Barack was born in Honolulu or mention any hospital's name. They merely say that Barack Sr. and his wife Stanley Anne now have a son and the address listed for their residence was actually the home of Barack's white grandparents. The mystery may never be solved.

FIGURE 6.1 YouTube user comments about the October 2009 Michelle Obama *Sesame Street* parody featured on *The Tonight Show with Conan O'Brien*.

this video, while others applaud it and find examples that would seem to point to its accuracy (see Figure 6.1). In this sense, the audience has now been given the agency to persuade other audience members rather than solely being a target of persuasion.

6.2 REMEMBER

electronic tradition	media that require users to make use of electronics to access content
new media tradition	mash-up culture, information age, and attention age
mashed up	converged into new media technologies
fidelity	the quality of matching our own beliefs and experiences
coherence	the quality of appearing to hold together and make sense
agency	the ability to generate change in a culture's thought, beliefs, and actions

SOCIAL NETWORKING

To date, no form of new media has had as much of an impact on our everyday lives as **social networking,** website networks specifically created to allow users to create and exchange content of mutual interest and communicate directly with one another. In fact, the use of social networking has risen 230% since 2007, with two-thirds of Americans now using Facebook, Twitter, MySpace, and other social networking websites each day and women having become the heaviest users of social networking (Diana, 2010; Smith, 2009). In order from most popular to least popular, people have cited the following reasons as to why they engage in social networking: keep in touch with friends; for fun; keep in touch with family; reconnect with people; express themselves and views; meet new friends; communicate with like-minded people; find information relevant to them; get recommendations; keep in touch with professional contacts; for political reasons; make new professional contacts; for professional development; and because it's part of their job (Experian Simmons, 2010). As can be inferred from this list, social networking has found its way into businesses, with 69% of people having become a fan or friend of a product, service, or company on a social networking site in 2010, compared with 57% in 2009 (Experian Simmons, 2010). Given its growing user base, along with the reasons cited above, it is no wonder that social networking is changing persuasion as we know it. One of the ways that persuasion functions in social networking is via a concept known as *mass interpersonal persuasion.*

Mass Interpersonal Persuasion

Many scholars believe that a new form of persuasion emerged in 2007 due to advances made in social networking. Dubbed **mass interpersonal persuasion (MIP),** or the ability of individuals to change attitudes and behaviors on a mass scale, social networking is viewed as joining "the power of interpersonal persuasion with the reach of mass media" to create "the most significant advance in persuasion since radio was invented in the 1890s" (Fogg, 2008, p. 1). Fogg argues that mass interpersonal persuasion occurs through six components: persuasive experience, automated structure, social distribution, rapid cycle, huge social graph, and measured impact. Prior to Facebook, each element of MIP existed independently, but with the launch of Facebook all six of the elements came together in one system making people—from ordinary individuals to corporate structures—better able to reach and persuade the masses (Fogg, 2008). While Facebook was the beginning of this phenomenon, other social networks have now begun to use this form of persuasion to their advantage. To illustrate the capability of MIP, Fogg taught a 10-week course on the Psychology of Facebook in the

In Your Life

Could you be one of the 16 million people who installed an application in the 2007 study? What might have persuaded you to use the application? Consider this question after you read each of the following sections concerning mass interpersonal persuasion (MIP).

computer science department at Stanford University. One of the course requirements was that students create applications for Facebook and attempt to get others to install their applications. By the time the course had ended in December 2007, Fogg's students had persuaded over 16 million people to install their applications, and about 1 million people used the student-created applications each day (Fogg, 2008). To further understand each of the elements of mass interpersonal persuasion, let's consider these elements as they apply to the social networking tool that changed the way we experience persuasion in our lives: Facebook.

Persuasive Experience

The **persuasive experience** is an experience that is created specifically with the goal of persuasion—changing attitudes, beliefs, behaviors, or values. One of the most implicit forms of persuasion on Facebook deals with **identity management,** or the representation of the self as socially desirable. Think for just a moment about the time and careful attention that you or your friends have put into creating a Facebook profile. Many different elements of the profile contribute to our view of that person. First, the default photo that is used can communicate a great deal to others. Many individuals on Facebook choose to use a recent photo of themselves to "prove" that they are "who they really say they are," while others choose to post a photo where they are with friends to show that they are fun and socially desirable. But let's return to the scenario at the beginning of this chapter for just a moment. What happens when someone like Liam posts a deceptive photo? Individuals such as Bridgette then form a false impression of what Liam looks like. This false impression is created as a result of persuasion.

Photos are not the only persuasive elements found on a Facebook profile. Status updates, "fan pages," "About Me" sections, interests, activities, pieces of flair, bumper stickers, and other applications exist with the purpose of persuading others to form a certain desired image of our identity. A young man who wishes to portray that he is a strong Christian may include Bible quotes or images of crosses in his profile and may post status updates stating that he "just got home from church." Similarly, a female student who is interested in politics may include links to political articles and videos in her profile, as well as bumper stickers showing her preference in political candidates and parties.

Automated Structure

Automated structure deals with the view that digital technology serves as the structure for the persuasive experience. In this sense, mass interpersonal persuasion on Facebook takes place through the automation of computer technology, such as the delivery of email, requests, and links promoting ideas or events (Fogg, 2008). For example, a student organized a walk/run to benefit a young girl suffering from a life-threatening illness. She created a Facebook event for this walk/run and posted a link to it on her own profile. Without even formally inviting a single Facebook friend to this event, she drew almost 200 participants to her event page!

Much of the persuasive power of Facebook is inherent in the simplicity of automation. The ability to click a link and complete the task of accepting an invitation or inviting a friend to an event makes it easy for us to take part in the persuasive process, as both the persuader and the person being persuaded. As Fogg says, "simplicity is important in persuasion ... if a task seems simple to us—like clicking the mouse once or twice—we are likely to do the task right away. When tasks are complex or have multiple steps, we are more likely to avoid the task or procrastinate" (p. 6).

Social Distribution

In **social distribution,** the persuasive experience is shared between friends. While it is important to persuade one person to agree with you, use your product, or donate money to a cause, it is even better to persuade many people to do the same. Mass persuasion easily occurs through social networking tools like Facebook due to the ease and peer pressure involved in maintaining a specific image. For example, when a worker died in an accident at a British Petroleum plant in Texas City, Texas, his daughter invited relatives to join a "cause" on Facebook titled "The United Support and Memorial for Workplace Fatalities (USMWF)." The site supports those who have lost loved ones to workplace accidents, and it grows in membership as new members send a link to their own friends. At the time of this writing, the USMWF cause had achieved $1,585 in donations from Facebook members. Through this process, the Causes application has been quickly shared between friends, friends of friends, and so on.

Rapid Cycle

When the persuasive experience is distributed quickly among persons, **rapid cycle** occurs. Rapid cycle refers to the time that occurs between actions between individuals. Consider the development of new applications, like those created by the students in Fogg's class, and the way that many of them appear to spread quickly. Similarly, think of Liam in the scenario presented at the beginning of this chapter. He may have "liked" the Beatles, Rolling Stones, and Elton John's pages because it was easy to do or because his friends had done so, not because he actually enjoyed their music. Another example that comes to mind is Farm Town, a Facebook application

REMEMBER

social networking	use of website networks specifically created to allow users to create and exchange content of mutual interest and communicate directly with one another
mass interpersonal persuasion (MIP)	the ability of individuals to change attitudes and behaviors on a mass scale
persuasive experience	an experience that is created specifically with the goal of persuasion—changing attitudes, beliefs, behaviors, or values
identity management	the representation of the self as socially desirable
automated structure	the view that digital technology serves as the structure for the persuasive experience
social distribution	sharing of the persuasive experience among friends
rapid cycle	the rapid distribution of the persuasive experience among persons

that allows users to build a farm, hire other users to harvest the farm, use profits to purchase other items for the farm, and eventually expand the farm. This particular application automatically posts status messages with requests for friends to help water the farm, which includes a link to join Farm Town. Thus, others can see that you are playing Farm Town through your wall and/or their NewsFeeds and decide to click the link and join Farm Town as well. The rapid cycle of Farm Town is evident in the fact that there were 5.7 million players at the time that this chapter was written.

Huge Social Graph

A **huge social graph** refers to the ability of a persuasive experience to reach millions of people through a network. Facebook, which was created in February 2004, is believed to have a huge social graph, as it boasted a total of 400 million active users across the world in February 2010, a steep rise from the 30 million reported in July 2007 (Zuckerberg, 2010). Now, the potential for growth in this social graph is stronger than ever, as Facebook has added a "like" feature that allows users to surf the web and "like" pages, such as other social networks. Thus, the users of Facebook may migrate to other social networks or tools, contributing to the growth of those social graphs as well. At any rate, any time 300 million-plus users are being exposed to a wide range of individually created content, persuasion occurs, and its influence has the potential to spread like wild fire.

Measured Impact

Of course, no persuasive attempt is complete without **measured impact,** or the ability to observe and measure its effects. By having the ability to see how many people have become a fan of a page, joined an event, installed an application, or "liked" a website, we are able to measure the successes of the persuasive attempts on Facebook. Recently, entertainment TV show *Showbiz Tonight* reported on the popularity of pop singer Lady Gaga as she became the first person to reach more than 10 million fans on Facebook (at the time this chapter was written, she had reached over 13 million)—more than any other living celebrity, including the president of the United States, and only surpassed by Michael Jackson (16+ million). According to Fogg (2008), developers of Facebook applications "know how long people spend on each screen, what buttons get clicked, how many invitations get sent by new users, and so on. This gives creators a clear view of how people use their app and how modifications affect adoption and use" (p. 9).

THE INHERENT PERSUASIVENESS OF SOCIAL NETWORKING

So far, you have looked at many individual elements of social networking via a discussion of Facebook. However, by considering social networking websites in their totality, you can see how they are inherently persuasive in their construction and function. Let us consider Twitter—a website that appears to have been spawned by Facebook status messages. The main purpose of Twitter is to answer the question, "What's happening?" This is considered a *tweet*. Another significant aspect of Twitter is the "Trending Topics," or a list of which topics are being tweeted about the most. Unlike Facebook, Twitter is mostly concerned with written text and is less concerned with photos and applications, although users are allowed to customize the background shown in their profile, their default photo, and post pictures through third-party websites such as TwitPic. Regardless, the ability to reach a mass audience with your individual thoughts is inherently persuasive. Similarly, the ability to retweet material (or spread persuasive messages) to wide audiences and view what is important to others (Trending Topics) is also persuasive in nature.

Facebook is similarly persuasive via its features, including profiles, status messages, photos, boxes, applications, causes, and links. At this point, you may be wondering how some of these elements are persuasive.

In Your Life

Have you ever modified
a social media profile
to change perceptions
about you? Did you add
information? Hide or omit
information? Why did you
feel it was necessary to
change the information?

The answer to this question should help you understand just how pervasive persuasion is in your life. Indeed, persuasion is occurring even when we do not realize it. In this case, the mere existence of features like applications and status updates is persuading us to believe that certain parts of our lives are more important to reveal than others. Recall the earliest form of Facebook, which merely had an "About Me" section, a default photo, and a wall. There were no applications, photo albums, links, or status messages. With each evolution of Facebook, we are persuaded to reveal more personal information about ourselves to others, changing the way that we value privacy and exclusivity.

With every piece of content or post that you use to customize your social networking profiles, you are persuading people to believe, feel, or do something. Whether you are trying to create an identity for yourself or convince someone to accept your "friend" requests, persuasion is inevitable in social networking. The posts made on these websites are persuading people to become involved in areas of society that they may not have cared about before. One example of the prevalence of this type of persuasion includes the recent advertisements for Haiti earthquake relief that were posted on Facebook and Twitter asking users to text "HAITI" to 90999 to donate $10 to Red Cross relief efforts, as well as the tweets and retweets alerting others to this fundraising ef-fort. Another example is the number of "Save the Gulf of Mexico" groups (approximately 180) that have appeared on Facebook following the British Petroleum oil spill. Who wants to be the one friend who does not accept an invitation to support the cleanup of the Gulf of Mexico? This pressure for conformity is a hallmark of Facebook, where feelings become hurt if someone does not accept a request from a "friend." With conformity, however, comes control—a topic that will be discussed in the followingsection.

Power and Control

Cultural studies scholars, such as Stuart Hall, have long considered the impact that media have on our view of class. In fact, **cultural studies theory** argues that the media are powerful tools of the elite and serve to keep powerful people in control. This view of the media was developed by a group of neo-Marxist German American scholars known as the Frankfurt School. This group of theorists believed that the working class is oppressed because the media are owned by large corporations and, thus, driven by profit. Consequently, cultural studies theory argues that ideology is created in such a way that one social group dominates another, a concept otherwise referred to as **hegemony.** Hegemony is sustained based on two main ideas: **false consciousness,** or the idea that individuals are unknowingly exploited by a social system that they support, and **out-of-control bodies,** or the representation of lower-class individuals as out of control and dangerous (Fiske, 1989). An understanding of hegemony can be achieved by examining the representations of class for users of MySpace and Facebook.

Digital Divide: MySpace versus Facebook

Before there was Facebook, there was MySpace. MySpace launched in August 2003 and was considered the most popular social networking site in the United States in 2006. While Facebook and Twitter have successfully created new features in order to attract and maintain users, MySpace has experienced declines in membership (Goldman, 2009). By June 2009, MySpace had laid off 30% of its employees, a sign that the social networking empire was struggling to stay afloat (Goldman, 2009). While it appears that Facebook has beaten MySpace to the punch, so to speak, in the development of new ideas, another significant reason for the decline of MySpace has been cited: digital divide.

Many scholars believe that the shift from MySpace to Facebook can be blamed on an increasing digital divide that has caused teens to segregate themselves, racially, from one another. Specifically, many teens now refer to MySpace as "ghetto," which is a term derived from "a set of tastes that emerged as poor people of color developed fashion and cultural artifacts that proudly expressed their identity" (Boyd, in press). When reflecting on the history of MySpace and Facebook, it is evident that elements of class were built into these networks from the beginning. MySpace began as a site for hip-hop bands to showcase their music, while Facebook targeted college students, beginning with Harvard, then moving on to Ivy League campuses, top-tier campuses, and other colleges before becoming open to high schools, companies, and, later, the public.

Social Media in Your Life: Have You Seen This?

Go to YouTube and enter the following keywords: did you know, facebook.

Facebook has grown to be a very popular form of social media. How do you feel about social media after viewing this clip?

6.4 REMEMBER

huge social graph	the ability of a persuasive experience to reach millions of people through a network
measured impact	the ability to observe and measure the effects of a persuasive attempt
cultural studies theory	idea that the media are powerful tools of the elite and serve to keep powerful people in control
hegemony	domination of one social group over another
false consciousness	idea that individuals are unknowingly exploited by a social system that they support
out-of-control bodies	the representation of lower-class individuals as out of control and dangerous

As both MySpace and Facebook moved toward the ability to customize individual profiles, Caucasian students and affluent or college-educated individuals increasingly began to flock to Facebook, whereas African American and Hispanic students appeared to be drawn to MySpace. As Boyd found, "teens' aesthetics shaped their attitudes towards each site. In essence, the 'glitter' produced by those who 'pimp out' their MySpaces is seen by some in a positive light while others see it as 'gaudy,' 'tacky' and 'cluttered.' While Facebook fans loved the site's aesthetic minimalism, others viewed this tone as 'boring,' 'lame,' and 'elitist'" (pp. 22–23).

As evidenced by this phenomenon, our use of specific social networking sites is a result of persuasion. First, an ideology of what it means to be a user of Facebook or MySpace is created. This ideology is largely informed by dominant, elite individuals as a power structure that is created by describing MySpace as "ghetto," and Facebook as "elite." People are persuaded by the belief that MySpace users are viewed as out-of-control bodies, "pimping out" their pages with "bling" and images of gang culture, such as marijuana leaves and handguns. Furthermore, since Facebook "turns off" many individuals who enjoy colorful pages, animated graphics, and music, these individuals turn to MySpace, further perpetuating the idea that MySpace is for the lower-class individual. Through this creation of ideology, the elite stay elite and the nonelite remain unknowingly represented as low class. Thus, hegemony is sustained and persuasion has occurred without many of us realizing it has happened.

Public versus Private

Another aspect of persuasion occurring in new media, specifically social networking, deals with the handling of personal information. For just a moment, think about the type of information that you have shared on your personal Facebook, Twitter, MySpace, or other social networking website. Have you posted, or been tagged in, photos that you may not want certain people to see? Have you created a note, wall post, or status message about a private matter, such as infidelity, dislike of a professor, or your skipping school? Have you accepted an invitation for a public event? At this point in time, many of us may be able to answer a resounding "yes" to these questions. Users of social networks are increasingly revealing more private information to each other than ever before. As stated earlier in this chapter, this is partly due to the fact that we as communicators are being persuaded that we must reveal more information to each other; however, it is also due to the fact that we are being persuaded to believe that our information is secure because of the increasing emphasis placed on "privacy controls" and other matters of security.

Because of the ability to customize privacy controls, many people believe that they have complete control over the information they post on their social networking profiles. Facebook users, for example, are given opportunities to create custom lists that allow only certain people to view portions of a profile. Similarly, Twitter users are allowed to secure their tweets so they can only be viewed by people that they have accepted as friends. This seems safe, doesn't it? Unfortunately, this is a false sense of safety and should be a major concern for individuals who are persuaded to reveal private information about themselves to their social networking alliances. While many of us view social networking as a relatively private space, we must understand that privacy controls fail; once our information has been posted in a public space like Facebook, it no longer belongs to only us. One popular example in the media is that of Casey Marie Anthony, who was indicted by a grand jury on charges of the first-degree murder of her 2-year-old daughter Caylee. Upon being implicated in this murder, Anthony saw many popular television shows, websites, and blogs reveal personal photos she had posted to her MySpace and Photobucket accounts. The majority of the photos taken from her personal sites depicted her in less than favorable conditions—urinating in a parking lot, vomiting in a toilet, passed out in the passenger seat of a car, exposing her buttocks to other partygoers, and having her breasts fondled by a male friend. These once-private personal photos—likely used as identity management to show friends that she was a "cool" young mom—were distributed in mass form for public viewing and deliberation. To this day, several websites still exist with the sole purpose of "exposing" the mother that Casey Anthony was—based on the photographs released by the media.

At this point, you may be thinking: "I know who has access to my information. My privacy settings are updated and my profile is practically as secure as my diary. This doesn't apply to me." What you may not know is the degree to which your private profile information is actually public. To illustrate, let's consider the creation of Openbook. In May 2010, following a rather debatable update to Facebook's privacy settings, a trio of San Francisco–based software engineers and developers created a website called Openbook as a critique of Facebook's privacy settings. Openbook is essentially a search engine that allows people to search for specific words and phrases on the walls of Facebook users. You do not have to be a registered Facebook user to use the search engine and view the information and photos of the poster. Furthermore, many of the Facebook users whose posts are being retrieved by this search engine have unknowingly allowed their information to be available to others—some by their own mistake and others due to Facebook's flawed privacy settings. Consequently, Openbook developers argue that Facebook causes an erosion of privacy based on a failure to educate users on their privacy choices and how their

information will be stored, and by changing privacy rules so frequ
they generate confusion rather than understanding (Heussner, 2010).

At first glance, Openbook appears identical to Facebook; however, upon further inspection, Openbook includes a few witty "digs" at Facebook. For example, where Facebook states that it "helps you connect and share with people in your life," Openbook adds another line—"Whether you want to or not." The "Learn More" link has been renamed to "Learn why this is bad!" Openbook visitors are also greeted with a list of recent searches, revealing keywords such as: "hate my life," "hate my boss," "cheated on my boyfriend," "one night stand," "my DUI," and "just found out HIV." Only two weeks after being launched, Openbook reportedly received approximately 6 million page views from people in over 200 countries. Following the apparent success of Openbook, other sites, such as Lurkbook, have attempted to explore Facebook's privacy flaws by mimicking the format and function of Openbook.

While sites such as Openbook and Lurkbook highlight the flaws within Facebook's privacy settings, the problem is our vulnerability to persuasion from all social networking sites. As illustrated by the example above, we are persuaded to view ourselves as having control over the information that we share on social networks. We are, in turn, persuaded to believe that our shared information is mostly private. Nevertheless, social networks are not private—even when they claim to be. After all, social networking sites merely persuade us to believe that certain information *should be* shared, but do not explicitly tell us to share this information. We make this choice based on false perceptions of security and control. In this sense, it is arguable that social networking is more likely to serve the purpose of voyeurism and surveillance rather than privacy.

VOYEURISM AND SURVEILLANCE

While there is something to be said about the importance of maintaining privacy when using new media technology, many take a different stance on this topic. For these individuals, there is a deep-seated desire to uninhibitedly share private details with anyone and everyone who will view them. Hal Niedzviecki, author of "The Peep Diaries," refers to this as **peep culture,** or "entertainment derived from peeping into the real lives of others" (p. 6). According to Niedzviecki (2009), "Peep emerges, at least in part, from our increasing and ongoing desire to adopt the mantle of celebrity and try out life lived in front of and for an audience.... Meanwhile, the more we're encouraged to reveal ourselves, the more we're becoming used to being observed constantly and perpetually" (p. 17). As he argues, this culture of surveillance is rooted in persuasion—specifically, as the

Ethical Connection

When does peeping
become more serious and
ethically questionable?
Does celebrity status give
reporters the right to
expose a person's private
life? Whose ethics are
more questionable: the
celebrity news companies
and tabloids publishing
the information or the
people who consume
the media in which it
is published? Are the
producers or consumers
responsible for unethical
persuasion?

functions available to us with new media technologies encourage us to reveal more about ourselves to others, while our revelations encourage others to share more about themselves with us.

One of the earliest forms of media that facilitated peep culture was reality television. Television shows such as MTV's *Real World* created a desire for peeping at our neighbors' lives—everything from telephone conversations to fistfights and make-out sessions. This led to the development of celebrity "news" sites such as TMZ and PerezHilton that solely function to peep at celebrities' tumultuous lives. The success of reality television and celebrity gossip sites has further driven peep culture, as people now turn to their real-life neighbors, friends, and family to feed this desire for voyeurism. Websites and applications such as Spokeo, which allows you to find out information about a person's home and email addresses, property value, income, and interests; Foursquare, which allows you to tag your physical location on a map so that others can see where you are at any given moment; Seesmic, which encourages users to post short video conversations with each other; and Grouphug, which prompts users to post anonymous confessions, all facilitate the ease of voyeurism and surveillance.

While many who embrace "peeping" do so for self-fulfilling reasons—to feel like a popular celebrity, or feel better about their lives by viewing another person's problems—others put themselves on display because of a sense of security. In our culture, we have been persuaded to believe that we are safer when we are under surveillance. Consider the ways that surveillance has been traditionally used—to monitor our assets, catch thieves, and guard prisoners. In fact, in 1791 philosopher Jeremy Bentham proposed the panopticon, an architectural design that would increase the safety of prisons by including circular cells with a central observation tower where guards could watch all cells while remaining anonymous.

The idea of the panopticon is closely linked to Big Brother, a fictional character in George Orwell's book, *1984* (1961). "Big Brother" referred to keeping track of every person's actions with complete video surveillance. Today, many media researchers have transferred the ideas of the panopticon and Big Brother to the media; specifically, they argue that the media serve as a form of surveillance (often dubbed the "virtual panopticon"), where all eyes are always on us. Throughout Orwell's novel, the phrase "Big Brother is watching you" was used to remind us of the power of this all-encompassing surveillance. As a matter of fact, you have probably heard this phrase in your lifetime as a means of instilling fear of the government's impeding the civil liberties of its citizens (i.e., through wiretapping). With the influence of new media, such as Facebook, the idea of surveillance has become increasingly normalized and is often welcomed by users. In essence, the idea that "Big Brother is watching you" no longer instills a fear of the reduction of civil liberties. Big Brother is now embraced. For one, Big Brother has come to be seen as a means to safety—after all, how can something bad happen to you if your friends constantly know where you are and what you are doing? Big Brother also becomes a means to having your personal preferences fulfilled—if you set your marital status to "Engaged" on Facebook, you will see a variety of advertisements for discounted items, such as a recent advertisement for "Steve Madden Bridal," which exclaims, "Get 15% off Steve Madden wedding shoes! Become a fan for an instant coupon."

Accordingly, "the notion that we are somehow safer when under surveillance...that there's little or no downside to helping corporations and governments serve us better by allowing them to store and analyze our preferences and personal details" has contributed to a rise in peep culture (Niedzviecki, 2009, p. 17). While peep culture promises us the freedom to be ourselves and still be liked, there is also a downfall: Peep culture presents a life of constant surveillance, where our every move is on public display and may be used by others however they wish.

BUSINESS AND INFLUENCE

As Niedzviecki pointed out, one way that our personal information and desires have been used is by corporations. Corporate use of our personal information typically presents itself as a colonization of private space (Wahl, 2003). Consider this: you are invited to sign up for a rewards card at a clothing store. The sales associate promises you monthly discounts, including a birthday "gift" each year. Eagerly, you sign up and end up being bombarded with email about related stores and products, along with the promised discounts. This type of surveillance does not happen by chance; rather, corporations—typically via advertisers, public relations practitioners, and marketers—have studied the use of persuasion extensively and know how to use the surveillance afforded by new media to their advantage.

One tool for understanding how persuasion occurs in the business context is *Influence: The Psychology of Persuasion*, written by Dr. Robert Cialdini. In his book, Cialdini (2007) explains his theory of the psychology of influence that resulted from three years of going "undercover" at car dealerships, fundraising organizations, and other businesses. Ultimately, Cialdini argues that there are six fundamental principles of ethical influence that we cannot help but respond to during social interaction: reciprocation, commitment and consistency, social proof, liking, authority, and scarcity. Although this book was written before new media emerged, each of these principles is applicable to the methods used for persuasion in new media technology. Learning these principles of influence is helpful in aiding your understanding of the ways that you experience persuasion in your life.

Reciprocation

The first principle of influence that Cialdini discusses is **reciprocation**. As humans, we are naturally inclined to reciprocate, or return a kindness that another has provided to us. Thus, corporations can tap into this natural inclination by first giving something to us, in order to prompt us to return the favor. Facebook fan pages serve as an example of reciprocation, as many businesses have offered discounts or free products to individuals who become fans of their Facebook page. After receiving a discount, users are likely to return the favor by recommending the fan page to their friends and visiting the business multiple times. Similarly, if we feel that we have received good service at a business, we may tag it in our status messages or tweets to say thank you, which, in turn, serves as a free advertisement for that company.

Commitment and Consistency

Another principle of influence is **commitment and consistency,** or feeling obligated to act in ways that are reliable and constant. Fundamentally, Cialdini argues that people feel pressured, internally and externally, to remain committed and consistent in their choices. This idea can be applied to new media, with the abundance of groups, fan pages, and events sent to users daily. If a friend sends a request for you to "friend" his band, it can be difficult to deny that request. Essentially, denying this request may be seen as not being committed and consistent in your friendship. Now apply this to the business context. If you "like" or accept a company as a friend, you would not feel comfortable denying its wishes to try a new product or to refer a friend to its site.

Social Proof

In Your Life

Have you ever done research using social media to find out more information about a company? Did the company have its own social media profile? Were any of your friends associated with this company through their profiles? Where there any special offers for "liking" the company? How did your research affect your feelings about the company?

Cialdini also argues that **social proof** is a powerful form of influence. This principle argues that determining whether a behavior is acceptable occurs by observing others to find out how they feel about the behavior. This easily explains why so many people "like" businesses that they have never visited before on Facebook upon seeing that a trusted friend "liked" that business. For instance, Jana became interested in rekindling her love for dance and noticed that several of her friends "liked" the fan pages for a new dance studio that had opened up in town. As a result, she also "liked" the fan page and began attending classes at the studio about 2 weeks later. Had she not seen her friends "like" this particular page on Facebook, she probably would not have given the studio a chance. Luckily, she had a great experience, even though she later found out that her friends had never been to the studio either—they merely "liked" it because they enjoyed the music featured on the studio's profile!

Liking

Similarly, **liking** also explains how many businesses persuade us to action. The principle of liking, according to Cialdini, explains that we prefer to say yes to people that we enjoy or feel are similar to us. We determine our affinity, or liking, for another person based on several factors, such as physical attractiveness, homophily ("love of the same"), and familiarity. In following the liking principle, it makes sense for a company to have an attractive website or product. For instance, a July 2010 advertisement for the Barnes & Noble Nook e-reader boasts that it allows "over one million titles," "a better reading experience," and "endless shelf space." Each of these large textual elements is in a different, bright color and is followed by a brief paragraph. Below the explanatory paragraphs are clear images that illustrate the amount of space that can be saved by purchasing a Nook. Immediately after these product features are presented, Barnes & Noble provides images of colorful designer covers that can be used to personalize the appearance of the Nook. In this sense, Barnes & Noble provided an attractive advertisement for a seemingly attractive product. People who liked this advertisement and felt that it resonated with their desires would have been likely to purchase the product.

Authority

A fifth principle of influence is that of **authority.** Authority is essentially the testimonial form of persuasion, whereby a person is persuaded by a famous or well-respected person's endorsement. In one Media and Society class, the professor witnessed the power of persuasion as it pertains to authority. At the beginning of the semester, the professorstated that one of the course requirements would be to maintain a Twitter page. This resulted in excitement from some students and dreadful looks from others. Around midterm, the MTV Music Video Awards were taking place and MTV, using the "Twitter Visualization" tool created by Stamen and Radian6, tracked over 2,000 tweets following the Taylor Swift/Kanye West incident and approximately 1.75 million tweets about the show by the end of the second airing. After MTV's focus on Twitter, the professor noticed a sudden participation from some of the students who dreaded Twitter. A few of these students later mentioned that, if their favorite celebrities were using Twitter, it must not be such a bad site.

Scarcity

Scarcity, or limiting the availability of a product, offer, or membership, is a final tool of influence. In terms of new media, scarcity often occurs in the form of a "limited offer" or contest. However, new media are

6.5 REMEMBER

peep culture	idea that people derive entertainment from peeping into the real lives of others
reciprocation	the return of a kindness that another has provided to us
commitment and consistency	feeling obligated to act in ways that are reliable and constant
social proof	concept that we determine whether a behavior is acceptable by observing others to find out how they feel about the behavior
liking	concept that we prefer to say yes to people we enjoy or feel are similar to us
authority	idea that a person is persuaded by a famous or well-respected person's endorsement
scarcity	limiting the availability of a product, offer, or membership

 ENGAGE: Take It to the Streets

Remember: You can use your knowledge of persuasion to engage real-life situations. Consider the scenario below and think about what you would do as you apply your study of new media and persuasion to your life.

You create a group on a social networking site in hopes of gaining support for American soldiers who have fought in combat. On this site you allow people to post memories of their experiences or of loved ones who have gone before. A classmate hears of this group that you've created and decides to join your group. Upon accepting her request, you read her initial post:

"War is pointless, and each life taken by war is pointless. What business do we have to go into other countries and tell them how to run their lives? We have enough troubles of our own in this country and no soldier with a gun can help anything."

Your initial reaction is to delete this post and remove the person from the group. Then you remember that she is a classmate of yours and you will have to see her every day. How might you use persuasion and what you've learned in this chapter to confront this person in an online setting without deleting her post or membership? What would you do?

often inherently scarce in that, while advertised as tools that everyone can enjoy—take the iPad, for example—many individuals cannot afford them. The exclusivity of ownership of the iPad results in a status image that creates an even stronger desire for those who cannot own it. As such, people often turn to more contests and offers (e.g., filling out online surveys) to try to obtain the product at a free or reduced price. This circular scarcity perpetuates constant persuasion.

It is important to remember that Cialdini's principles of influence were written to expose the characteristics of human nature often targeted by persuaders. While they can be used in an abusive manner, they can also be used for positive purposes such as in the example of gaining participants for the benefit walk/run described earlier in the chapter.

SUMMARY

To conclude your study of persuasion in new media, remember that the techniques and functions of persuasion change as technology changes. Just as persuasion primarily took place in the form of a one-sided verbal argument in oral culture, it has shifted to an active, dialogic form with the development of new media technologies such as Facebook, Twitter, YouTube, and the iPad. Along with this shift to new media, persuasion has become a tool of the masses more than ever before. Social networking, for example, was created with the sole purpose of persuasion—it is automated, which makes persuasion easier; it allows persuasion to be shared among friends and thus quickly distributed among persons in a network; it has the ability to reach millions of people; and its successes or failures are easily measurable. With the bombardment of persuasion in new media, persuasion is occurring even without our knowledge. The mere existence of features such as status updates or applications persuades us that certain actions are more important than others and that certain aspects of our lives should be revealed. This, of course, has important implications for our privacy.

While you are being persuaded to reveal increasing amounts of personal information to your networks, you are also being persuaded to believe that this information is private and exclusive to your networks. As evidenced by the privacy debates concerning Facebook and other sites, your information is not as secure as you would hope. Once your information is posted to a public space, it belongs to the network and is no longer exclusive to you. This abundance of free information, while certainly democratic in nature, also drives you to believe that surveillance is important and should be embraced. While people once loathed the idea of having Big Brother constantly watching them, they now feel safer having the world view their every move. People welcome surveillance because they have been persuaded to believe that it is designed to protect them and satisfy their desires. They now believe that being watched is to their advantage, even though being watched can be used against them.

While much of the information discussed in this chapter highlights the dangers of the inherent persuasion that occurs in social networking, it is important to understand that not all persuasion occurs to deceive or harm us. Many businesses do use persuasion to satisfy our desires and, as humans, we are constantly persuading each other to like us. As you are learning in this book, persuasion does not have to be a negative experience. What matters most is that you are able to identify persuasion as you experience it in your life, so that you will know when you are encountering it. When you are able to see persuasion occurring, it becomes much easier to protect yourself from those instances that are negative and embrace those that are positive.

DISCUSSION QUESTIONS

New Media

1. Create a list of the media technologies that you use on a daily basis (e.g., Nook, smartphone, TV, Facebook) and consider the various features of these technologies. From which technological traditions do these features appear to have developed?

2. What are some elements of mass interpersonal persuasion that you have witnessed in other forms of new media? Is mass interpersonal persuasion possible in traditional media?

3. What recent examples of persuasion have you witnessed on a social networking website?

4. Do you agree that a digital divide is occurring in social networking? Explain and justify your answer.

5. How have you experienced conflicts with privacy and/or surveillance in your life?

Persuasive Public Campaigns

7

Michelle Maresh

YOUR OBJECTIVES

After studying this chapter, you should be able to:

1. Articulate the difference between advertising and public relations campaigns.
2. Differentiate between the three types of advertising campaigns.
3. Identify the elements of persuasion within the Yale five-stage developmental model.
4. Recognize the ways that persuasion is embedded in the PIE model of public relations.
5. Identify the way that new media have changed the use of persuasion in public campaigns.

CHAPTER OUTLINE

Riley: Dude, have you seen this commercial? You'd think British Petroleum would have figured out by now that we don't believe a word that they say!

Bill: Are you talking about the commercial where they say that many of their employees are from the Gulf so they feel the impact of the oil spill and are going to do everything they can to make sure it doesn't happen again?

Riley: That's the one! I just find it hard to believe that they are going to do everything they can when obviously they didn't do it in the first place or this wouldn't have happened.

Bill: Yeah, man, I don't think anyone believes a word they say anymore. I just can't believe they are wasting their money on PR rather than cleaning up the spill and protecting their workers.

Riley: I couldn't agree with you more! Maybe I would believe them if I knew that they cared before an accident, rather than starting to care after the fact. After all, this isn't the first time they've launched a PR campaign after a major incident at one of their locations.

Public Campaigns

The above interaction between Bill and Riley was an actual conversation following the April 20, 2010, British Petroleum (BP) Deepwater Horizon drilling rig explosion. With this explosion, BP became responsible for the deaths of 11 workers, injuries to 17 other individuals, and the release of approximately 4.9 million barrels of crude oil into the Gulf of Mexico—the largest marine oil spill in the history of the petroleum industry (Robertson & Krauss, 2010; Welch & Joyner, 2010). As Bill and Riley's conversation suggests, criticism concerning the BP missteps that ultimately caused the oil spill was plentiful, but an even larger focus was placed on its efforts at **public relations,** or the ongoing use of two-way communication to develop, maintain, and sustain positive relationships with the public.

In this chapter, you will consider the ways that public campaigns—namely, advertising and public relations campaigns—function as a persuasive element in society. Specifically, you will consider the definitions, elements, processes, and types of advertising and public relations campaigns. You will also learn about the persuasive strategies used in both types of campaigns to influence the public. As you explore the topic of persuasive campaigns, you will continue to apply the BP oil spill along with other recent events, such as Barack Obama's 2008 campaign for president of the United States, to enhance your understanding of these concepts. As you will learn in the following chapter, persuasion is an ongoing process that affects each of us daily, whether we realize it or not. That is why it is important for us to understand the ways that we are influenced by the messages presented in persuasive advertising and public relations campaigns. Upon reading this chapter, you will be well equipped to recognize both subtle and explicit attempts at persuasion in your everyday life.

FOUNDATIONS OF PERSUASIVE PUBLIC CAMPAIGNS

In Your Life

What does public relations mean to you? Think of some persuasive examples of public relations in your own life.

Public persuasion is not a new art. Forms of persuasive public campaigns have been in existence for centuries. As Aristotle argued in *Rhetoric* over 2,000 years ago, the successful persuader must utilize **logos** (logic), **ethos** (credibility), and **pathos** (emotion) to gather the support of the public. Aristotle's vision holds true today as a variety of public campaigns, aiming to persuade us to change our attitudes and behaviors, are created and presented to us on a daily basis. Public persuasive campaigns expose us to human-interest issues, politics, reforms, new products, and organizational practices and are an essential aspect of American culture. This is because, as Russian philosopher Mikhail Bakhtin (1982) argued, to create **democracy,** or a well-informed public, all communication about an issue must be **dialogic,** or take the form of a dialogue. Public persuasive campaigns allow the public to become part of a larger dialogue about the issues at the heart of the campaigns. For the remainder of this chapter, you will explore two main types of public persuasive campaigns: (1) advertising campaigns and (2) public relations campaigns.

ADVERTISING AS PERSUASION

In 1937, Disney opened the doors to an advertising revolution when it became the first studio to sell items to promote a movie (*Snow White and the Seven Dwarfs*). Since then, advertising has rapidly become the most pervasive form of persuasion in American culture. An **advertising campaign** is a paid form of impersonal communication, concerned with selling specific products, services, brands, images, and lifestyles to the public, and the typical American consumer is no stranger to its influence.

To understand the influence of advertising campaigns, briefly reflect on your day thus far and list all the forms of advertisement that you have seen, heard, or read from the time you woke up today until now. Once you have completed your list, count all of the advertisements you have been exposed to today. In one class, students were given1 minute to compile a list of all the advertisements they could remember seeing that day. One student was able to recall at least 20 advertisements, and these were just the advertisements he had time to write down and could remember actually taking a moment to look at (see Figure 7.1). As you consider this advertising bombardment, it is easy to see that, by the age of 65, each of you will have been exposed to more than 140 million advertising campaigns (Owen, 1981). This is of particular importance as you attempt to discover the role of persuasion in your life. If you are constantly vulnerable to the messages delivered through public persuasive campaigns, you need to be able to understand the messages you are receiving and the influence that they have on your attitudes, beliefs, and values. To begin this exploration, we must consider the definition and characteristics of an advertising campaign.

Below is a description of advertisements written by a student enrolled in a Communication Theory course:

"Woke up. First advertisements I saw were the Groupon and Living Social coupons emailed to me early in the morning. Believe they were for tanning and resume help. Then I turned on Wheel of Fortune. That whole show is an advertisement for the various products, including groceries, vehicles, trips to places, etc. Then on my way to a meeting, I saw a couple billboards. All the fast food restaurants had specials on their signs. When I went into Subway, there were advertisements for their $5 footlongs and featured footlongs, etc. Then, of course, commercials on TV. Lots of them. Of course there's always advertisements on the websites. I threw away a whole load of paper advertisements from the mail. People's shirts had advertisements on them. Coke, local construction sites. Vehicles on the road, especially for local business owners. I saw a vehicle with the local hockey team on it, local fried chicken shack. Neon signs in the window of businesses trying to draw you in. The Quiznos on the corner of a major intersection had a strobe light to draw attention to it. I saw a political sign for a man running for local office. When I logged into Facebook, I saw some ads on the side asking me to like a certain page. I saw some product placement in a movie I watched. I saw some flyers at the coffee shop. I received some e-blasts from organizational newsletters I subscribe to. I saw a blurb on the side of my coffee cup. That's all I have time to write."

FIGURE 7.1 What advertisements have you seen today?

Definition

As stated earlier in this chapter, an advertising campaign is a paid form of impersonal communication, concerned with selling specific products, services, brands, images, and lifestyles to the public. Author, speaker, and filmmaker Jean Kilbourne (1999) once likened advertising to a cattle auction, claiming that, just as cattle are rounded up and sold without a choice, the public are sold to advertisers by the media they consume. Her analogy makes perfect sense when we consider what an advertising campaign is and how frequently our consumption of such advertising is beyond our control. Consider, for example, the small ad placed on the right-hand side of our Facebook profile, urging us to "Buy bunk beds and loft beds and create more space!" or to "LIKE G4tv for Mortal Kombat News Now!" Regardless of our desire to receive such a message, those ads were paid for by companies or individuals who, without speaking to us directly to learn our preferences, have tried to persuade us to buy a particular product, service, brand, image, or lifestyle. While the obvious form of persuasion in this scenario is that we may actually purchase a product or service after viewing the advertisement, the more subtle form of persuasion that occurs is the most dangerous. Regardless of whether we purchase or agree with the message(s) presented in an advertising campaign, our mere exposure to the campaign will inform us about and influence how we view society. Thus, in the following section, you will learn about the various persuasive elements used in advertising campaigns. By understanding the definition and elements of advertising campaigns, you will be able to recognize their presence and influence on your life.

Elements of Advertising

There is no more powerful source for gaining information about the meaning of objects than advertising (Leiss, Kline, Jhally, & Botterill, 2005). In advertising, much time is spent on one-way communication, or developing an image that will sell a product, service, brand, image, or lifestyle, without much feedback from the audience. Advertising is effective, regardless of its lack of attention to public feedback, because it taps into the core of our human needs. If we situate an advertisement in its historical period, we can see how the values of a time period influence the strategies used in the advertisement. In other words, our purchasing habits have evolved from buying things considered necessities (such as soap), to buying things that we want (such as perfume), to buying things that make us stand out in a crowd (maybe an iPad). Because of this evolution, advertising has shifted its focus from persuading us to purchase a product for what it can do (perhaps it cures a cold) or what it signifies (it's refreshing) to what it says about us (it's cutting edge, meaning we are, too). To understand the persuasion that occurs within the advertising campaign, you must return to Aristotle's three persuasive proofs: logos, ethos, and pathos. Each of these appeals is discussed in the sections that follow.

Emotion Advertisers often use emotional appeals, such as fear, humor, and guilt to stimulate the public. Positive emotions, such as humor or joy, can cause viewers to feel attached to a product, service, brand, image, or lifestyle. One example is the Dove Campaign for Real Beauty, which was launched in 2004 to celebrate "real" women of different shapes and sizes. This campaign delivered a series of online short films, including one titled *Onslaught* that featured an image of a young red-haired girl followed by a bombardment of images illustrating the standards of beauty in our media. Words such as "younger, smaller, whiter, fuller, tighter, thinner, softer" were spoken alongside images of women eating and gaining weight, throwing up and losing weight, and having cosmetic procedures done to their bodies. The advertisement ends with the young girl walking to school with her friends while the phrase "Talk to your daughter before the beauty industry does" appears on the screen. This advertisement elicited a positive feeling in viewers, as it reminded them to appreciate and embrace their natural looks. This positive appeal to emotion resonated so well with the public that "normal" women are now being referred to as "Dove Beauties."

While positive appeals to emotion can have lasting effects, consumers are most likely to remember advertising campaigns that use fear appeals. However, advertisers must beware of using too strong a fear appeal, which can cause a person to ignore the message. In 2009, one advertising campaign illustrating the dangers of texting while driving caused an uproar in the United States due to its unprecedented level of explicitly gory imagery. In the public service announcement (PSA), we as viewers see two girls laughing about a text message they are sending while driving when the driver has a head-on collision with another car. We then see the girls exchange glances as a third vehicle crashes into the passenger side of the vehicle. The driver then sees her friend lying dead next to her, and the viewer sees a young child in one of the other vehicles asking why her parents will not wake up. Only time will tell if this campaign will be effective in the United States; however, the level of fear caused by this advertisement may be detrimental to its message.

Logic Another strategy that advertisers use to sell a product, service, brand, image, or lifestyle is appealing to logic, or providing sensible reasons as to why an individual should buy or agree with something. By focusing on logic, the advertising campaign tells us what is important or not important, good or bad, in or out, right or wrong, and it raises the public's awareness of a particular message. One advertisement famed for its appeals to logic is the 18-month campaign launched in June 2008 by the Corn Refiners Association with the goal of improving the public's perception of high fructose corn syrup (HFCS). This $30 million advertising campaign argued that HFCS has the same natural sweeteners as table sugar and honey and, as a result, is no more fattening than sugar. This campaign faced a difficult task head-on, as the public has been told, in numerous mediated messages, that the nation's growing problem with obesity and diabetes is linked to their consumption of sweetened beverages. With HFCS being the main sweetener used in many of these beverages, the Corn Refiners Association had to create a more logical argument than the one posed by its opposition. The result was a set of TV spots and full-page newspaper advertisements arguing that HFCS has "had its name dragged through the media" and that HFCS is made from corn, has no artificial ingredients, has the same amount of calories as sugar, and is acceptable when consumed in moderation; therefore, HFCS is no more dangerous to the public than sugar.

Credibility   The final strategy is to appeal to credibility and show how the organization or individual selling the product, service, brand, image, or lifestyle is credible and how buying or approving of it will help us to become more credible as well. Consider the ongoing NOH8 campaign, which began in November 2008 as a photographic silent protest created by celebrity photographer Adam Bouska and partner Jeff Pashley in response to the passing of Proposition 8 in California, banning same-sex marriage. Photos in this campaign are aimed at symbolizing the silencing of voices due to Proposition 8 legislation. The 8,000-plus individuals featured in the campaign range from celebrities to politicians to artists to everyday people. These individuals are depicted with duct tape over their mouths and "NOH8" painted on their cheeks. Through the use of credible individuals, the campaign has garnered much support from the public.

By understanding and recognizing the persuasive appeals used in advertising campaigns, you will become more aware of the way that advertisers create a position in the public's mind concerning topics ranging from what to consume to what social behaviors to accept. However, the campaign process is not as simple as finding a strong appeal to emotion, logic, and/or credibility. Each advertising campaign must pass through a series of stages. Understanding this process is necessary to become a more critical and informed member of the public. Thus, the following section details the five steps of the advertising process.

THE ADVERTISING PROCESS

The advertising process typically requires one or more of the stages included in a model developed by researchers at Yale University, referred to as the Yale five-stage developmental model (Binder, 1971). This model has been applied to many advertising campaigns to illustrate how the campaigns persuade the public to action. Specifically, the steps of this model include identification, legitimacy, participation, penetration, and distribution. Each of these steps is discussed in some depth in the following sections, using Barack Obama's 2008 campaign for president as an example.

Identification

The first stage of this model is identification. **Identification** is defined as becoming known in the mind of the public. In this stage, the advertising campaign seeks to establish a position in the mind of the public. It employs tactics, such as logos and slogans, to deliver a persuasive message about the ideals that the product, candidate, or organization stands for. According to this step, people will only join your campaign if they can identify with, or relate to, it. For this reason, the campaign should have a distinct visual and symbolic identity that distinguishes it from other campaigns. One example of creating identification can be found in the logo used in Barack Obama's 2008 presidential campaign. This logo is a blue "O" that consists of a circle in the center and red and white stripes draped across the bottom. At first glance, it appears to be a white sun in a clear sky rising over a field comprised of the American flag. This logo was designed specifically to evoke a particular feeling in the audience. One of the creators of this logo was quoted as saying, "the sun rising over the horizon was intended to evoke a new sense of hope" (Yue & Glenn, 2007).

Another symbol used in this campaign to create identification is the use of the slogan *sí se puede*, which is Spanish for "Yes, it can be done." This slogan was used specifically to gain support from the Latino voters who relate to this phrase as a symbol of their culture. Cesar Chavez actually created this slogan as the motto for the United Farm Workers in 1972. Barack Obama used it in campaign signage, speeches, and YouTube videos to promote the ideology of his campaign platform, which was to create change and hope for America (see Photo 7.1).

Legitimacy

The next stage of the advertising campaign is to establish **legitimacy,** or to become known as trustworthy and believable. In the political realm, gaining legitimacy includes winning primaries, becoming endorsed, appearing

PHOTO 7.1 Obama campaign signs seen here featured a phrase, "Si Se Puede," that appealed to Latino voters.

with well-known supporters, and having a visible presence through the use of symbols, ads, and media coverage. Legitimacy is a necessary step in the process because it allows the public to take the campaign seriously and it secures the campaign from the persuasive messages of the opposition. One of the ways that Barack Obama gained legitimacy in his campaign was through the use of social media. His campaign website reportedly received more Internet traffic than any other website in the 2008 campaign (Dorausch, 2007). He was also the first candidate to use Facebook and Twitter, social media websites targeted to college students. According to Blue State Digital, the agency responsible for creating BarackObama.com, the website is "to date, the most effective campaign website in the history of electoral politics anywhere in the world" (n.d.). According to the agency's website, BarackObama.com allowed the campaign to garner 6.5 million donations totaling $500 million; gather 13 million email addresses; send more than 2 billion emails to supporters; create more than 2 million user profiles with the capabilities of blogging, event postings, and volunteer group creation; make more than 3 million phone calls prior to Election Day; and gain 50 million video views and 1.2 billion minutes of view time (Blue State Digital, n.d.).

Participation

The next step of the advertising campaign process is **participation,** or the involvement of individuals who were not committed at the beginning of the campaign. This involvement can range from showing support symbolically—such as putting a campaign sign up in the front yard—to achieving the ultimate desired behavior, such as voting for the candidate. In this phase of the process, individuals are recruited to the campaign by being given opportunities to become involved, which makes them feel committed to the individual, organization, or product. In his campaign for the presidency, Barack Obama invited individuals to participate in the campaign process in many ways. He had approximately 3.3 million Facebook friends, 1 million MySpace friends, and 137,000 followers on Twitter. There was also an application for the iPhone called "Obama '08" that featured links such as a countdown to Election Day, a tab to donate to the campaign, and areas for calling friends, getting involved, receiving updates, and finding local campaign events. Much like the many American Cancer Society Relay for Life campaigns, Barack Obama's campaign included an element of personalization, which allowed individuals to have their own personal fundraising page with a goal for contributions and donations.

Penetration

When a campaign becomes noticed and unavoidable, it has achieved the **penetration** stage. As the campaign builds momentum, the person, product, or service being sold no longer has to work as hard to recruit supporters. Instead, the campaign works to continue being visible to persuade those who are not supporters to join or face being left behind. In the political process, this not only refers to gaining the support of the previously unsupportive public, but it also refers to gaining the support of competitors. Following the Montana and South Dakota primaries in June 2008, Barack Obama was able to secure enough delegates to have his remaining opponent, Hillary Rodham Clinton, concede defeat at the Democratic National Convention. At this convention, Clinton urged her supporters to give their support to Obama. Obama's campaign remained visible and popular in the opinion polls and, ultimately, led to his being elected president of the United States.

Distribution

The final phase of the campaign is **distribution,** or the success of the campaign in rewarding supporters. At this point, the owners of the campaign attempt to show that they have staying power and can live up to promises that they have made in their advertising campaign. It is important to note, however, that not all individuals and/or organizations live up to their promises. In many advertising campaigns, products (such as popular weight-loss drugs and devices) are shown to not work, and individuals change their perspectives once they take office. In the case of Barack Obama, there have been several instances where onetime supporters have grown frustrated with his policies. In December 2009, Obama's increase of troops in the war in Afghanistan caused a backlash from many of his supporters. According to MacAskill (2009), this reaction "mirrors a wider liberal backlash against Obama that has been growing for the last few months over the watering down of the health bill, the failure to make a significant move on climate change and, above all else, the deployment of more U.S. troops to Afghanistan…". The anger did not stop here; in December 2010 a group of students at UCLA held up banners and signs that read, "Obama, you let us down!" in reference to his approval of tax cut extensions for everyone, regardless of their socioeconomic status (Carter, 2010). Most recently, Obama has become the target of criticism concerning his intervention in the Libyan civil war, as he said he didn't need congressional authorization because the Senate had unanimously approved a resolution to impose a no-fly zone over Libya (Boyd, 2011). This series of noted disappointments will become increasingly important to President Obama's 2012 campaign for re-election. In following this advertising campaign process, Obama will need to focus his efforts on the second stage of the process, to work toward gaining legitimacy once again.

 PERSUASION RESEARCH SNAPSHOT

This chapter explores advertising campaigns and the persuasive influence they can have on consumers. However, it is important to realize that not all advertising campaigns are designed to persuade you to buy something. Sometimes, advertising campaigns are focused on changing people's perceptions about a product or company. Think back to the tragic oil spill in the Gulf of Mexico a few years ago. The company responsible for the disaster, British Petroleum (BP), suffered a huge backlash of public criticism for its perceived negligence on its oil rigs. BP responded by creating one of the largest image repair campaigns in the history of advertising. How effective do you think this strategy was?

Indeed, persuasion and advertising go hand in hand. From every commercial, billboard, or magazine ad to every Internet pop-up, advertising is there to influence you to buy something. Can an advertisement persuade you to buy an image? This is an important question to ask, because a tarnished reputation can turn consumers away from a product just as quickly

(continued)

as faulty merchandise or high costs. BP is not the first company to attempt image repair, nor will it be the last. From the press releases and television commercials you have seen, would you place your trust in British Petroleum?

In a recent study, researchers William Harlow, Brian Brantley, and Rachel Harlow examined the BP image repair campaign to evaluate how effective the company was in its efforts. The researchers applied image repair theory to their study to better understand their findings. This theory analyzes different damage control strategies and how they are used (or not used) to correct negative public perceptions. The researchers wanted to ask: Were the strategies that BP used initially after the Gulf disaster effective in improving public perception of the company? Initial damage control is the most widely publicized, so BP used some improvization for some of its early press announcements. BP created a prominent "Gulf of Mexico response" section on its website, detailing the company's response to the disaster and how it planned to correct things and compensate the victims of the disaster. The researchers examined all the press releases, video clips, still photos, and contact information BP released for the first 2 months after the disaster, then evaluated the intended effects of the messages.

The research findings showed that BP used two key strategies in this initial campaign: First, BP publicly described how it planned to correct the problem. Second, the company focused on how it would compensate the victims. BP did not, however, either admit responsibility or shift blame to another company. The researchers were careful to mention that there was no "ideal" strategy for the company, only several different ways in which BP could handle the disaster.

It's difficult to call BP's initial attempt at image repair successful. President Obama publicly condemned the company and demanded BP take responsibility, and public pressure forced the company to create a $20 billion repair fund. A long-term study is really needed to see how effective BP has been in its image repair campaign. How have its press releases and public announcements affected your opinion of the company? Has the company convinced you that it is doing everything possible to make this disaster right? One important to thing to realize as a communication student in this age is that the power of persuasion in the professional world cannot be overstated. BP's response to this public relations nightmare had the potential to make or break the company, and you may find yourself working in a company one day with a similar crisis on your hands.

Do you want to know more about this study? If so, read: Harlow, W., Brantley, B. C., & Harlow, R. (2011). BP initial image repair strategies after the Deepwater Horizon spill. *Public Relations Review, 37*(1), 80–83.

TYPES OF ADVERTISING

A final step in understanding the influence of advertising campaigns is to be able to identify the type of advertising you are exposed to. There are three basic types of persuasive advertising campaigns: product-oriented, person-oriented, and idea-oriented campaigns. Each type of campaign is specifically designed to deliver a variety of persuasive messages that get the public's attention; create a position (e.g., like versus dislike) in the public's mind about the product, person, or idea; and call the public to action (e.g., to vote for or against it).

Product-Oriented Advertising

The focus of most advertisers is the promotion of products and services. Thus, the goal of **product-oriented advertising** is to promote a specific product and service to a target audience. This type of advertising may range from sharing information about what a product does to a more explicitly persuasive form of advertising that is aimed at getting consumers to make a purchase. Burger King is known for its variety of product-oriented advertising, which includes the giveaway of free paper birthday crowns and several viral advertising campaigns. One of these campaigns is the "Creepy King," a medieval king with a large, smiling plastic head. The "Creepy King" turns up in unexpected places and has inspired an *Internet meme*, or a concept that has spread via the Internet. In these memes (rhymes with "dreams"), the King is Photoshopped into odd settings. Another campaign is "The Subservient Chicken," used in 2004 to raise awareness of the new TenderCrisp chicken sandwich. In these ads, a man is seen telling a person in a chicken suit to behave however he wishes. This is followed by the slogan, "chicken the way you like it." The persuasive appeal of each of these product advertisements is evidenced by the number of parodies found on popular websites, such as YouTube.

Person-Oriented Advertising

Another focus of advertising campaigns is the promotion of a person or candidate, or **person-oriented advertising**. This type of advertising is most common to political campaigns, as it focuses on raising the public's awareness about a particular person in hopes that they will either support or not support the person. One of the most popular forms of person-oriented advertising occurred in 1964 in a television ad often referred to as the "daisy ad." In this advertisement, an innocent little girl stands in a field of daisies counting the petals on a daisy she is holding in her hands. Suddenly, a countdown from 10 to 1 begins, the camera zooms in to her eyes, and a mushroom cloud explodes in their reflection. We then hear a voiceover: "These are the stakes. To make a world in which all of God's children can live. Or to go into the dark. We must either love each other or we must die." We are then told to "Vote for President (Lyndon B.) Johnson on November third" because "the stakes are too high for you to stay home." In this powerful advertising campaign, we are persuaded to vote for Lyndon Johnson to save our children and avoid a nuclear war.

Idea-Oriented Advertising

A final category of advertising campaigns is **idea-oriented advertising** campaigns, or those focused on gathering support for a particular message or cause. These campaigns can take the form of image campaigns or the promotion of a nonprofit organization, interest, or social advocacy. An idea-oriented campaign, for example, can be a series of paid advertisements to raise money to be used for cancer research and treatment. This type of campaign can also be used during a political election to allow interest groups to campaign for their issues. It can also be used in the form of a public service announcement. In 2008, an advertising campaign titled "Think Before You Speak" sponsored by the Ad Council, ThinkB4YouSpeak.com, and Gay Lesbian and Straight Education Network (GLSEN), was run to address the homophobic phrase, "That's so gay," popularly used among young Americans. The campaign was designed to discourage use of this slur. The advertisements feature people in various situations stating that something they do not like is "so gay." Then a popular celebrity, such as Wanda Sykes or Hilary Duff, walks out and tells the speaker not to use the word "gay" to describe something that he or she does not like. Each advertisement ends with text and a voiceover saying, "When you say 'that's so gay,' do you realize what you say? Knock it off." This campaign won the Ad Council's top award for "Best Public Service Advertising Campaign" and received much attention across the nation.

While advertising campaigns are a popular and pervasive form of persuasion, they are not the only attempts at persuasion in the public sphere. Public relations (PR) campaigns are another form of persuasion that we are exposed to on a daily basis. However, unlike with advertisements, people are rarely aware of the influence that public relations campaigns have on their daily lives. The process of PR is much more implicit. It is embedded into our daily rituals, such as the way we are treated by our employers and the way we learn about a crisis. Hence, the remainder of this chapter is dedicated to investigating the role of persuasion in public relations campaigns.

PUBLIC RELATIONS AS PERSUASION

Before you study each individual element of the definition of PR, let's begin by thinking about the many interpretations that we have of what PR is and is not. In the margins of this page (or on the piece of paper that you used earlier), write down a list of words that come to mind when you hear the words "public relations." When you are finished, compare your list with the list in Figure 7.2. As you can see, people use many words to describe the act of PR, though many of these words are inaccurate and negative. To help us

Below is a list of words generated by undergraduate students enrolled in a Public Relations course:

Negative	Neutral	Positive
Crisis	Promotion	Informing Public
Story Manipulation	Self-Interest	Public Opinion
Spin	Advertising	Interaction
Stunt	Strategies	Relationships
Damage Control	Campaigning	Open
Deception	Image	Informing
Sleazy	Reputation	Loyalty
Negative News	Media	Customer Satisfaction

FIGURE 7.2 What words come to mind when you think of public relations?

understand the true purpose of PR, a definition is provided and explained in the following section. Understanding this definition will make clear that persuasion is at the forefront of this form of communication.

Definition

PR is inherently persuasive—its primary function is to influence audiences to change their beliefs, attitudes, or behavior. This emphasis on changing an audience's opinion often leads us to assume that PR is merely a publicity stunt that requires deception, spin, negative news, or story manipulation. In turn, this emphasis on negativity assumes that PR is strictly **reactive,** or occurring after a company's or individual's image has been damaged by a negative event or crisis. What many people do not realize, however, is that the field of PR is not negative at all—it actually exists to build relationships between a company, organization, or individual (hereafter referred to as "organization") and its public **proactively,** before an organization's image is compromised. Thus, as mentioned in the opening section of this chapter, **public relations** may be defined as the ongoing use of two-way communication to develop, maintain, and sustain positive relationships with the public. Let's break this definition down further.

As mentioned before, PR exists to build a positive image before a negative event occurs. Because of this, PR is ongoing. In other words, it should begin before an organization becomes part of the public eye, and it should not end. Because of its ongoing nature, we must remember that we are constantly targets of persuasive PR messages. As we will see in the section covering the various types of PR, we are exposed to these messages in many areas of our everyday lives—from working for a company to purchasing products and surfing the Internet.

This definition of PR also emphasizes **two-way communication,** or the communication between the organization and its public. This is an important step that sets PR apart from the fields of marketing and advertising. With marketing or advertising, much time is spent developing an image that will sell a product or service with little regard to the way that people feel about the company or organization in the long term. Consider the Mac versus PC computer debate. While many of today's youth become persuaded by the images used in the Mac versus PC commercials, such as nerdy-uptight PC versus casual-cool Mac, Mac does little by way of developing a relationship with its users. In this advertising campaign, Apple does not ask for feedback about Mac, nor does it follow up on the purchases made by the public. Rather, these advertisements are focused on selling Macs and beating the competition that PC provides. On the other hand, Domino's Pizza launched a successful PR campaign in which it responded to customer complaints about its pizza tasting like cardboard by holding focus groups. During this campaign, Domino's lowered the price of its pizza, changed the recipe, followed up with the customers who had complained, and posted the results on YouTube, Twitter, its website, and in TV commercials. This form of two-way communication is exactly what PR is about—a mutual benefit between the organization and its public.

The last segment of this definition emphasizes the importance of developing, maintaining, and sustaining positive relationships with the public. If we return to the idea of PR being proactive and reactive, we can see that a proactive approach allows an organization to develop a relationship with its public before a negative event occurs. Once this positive relationship has been developed, PR professionals seek to maintain it with various strategies. Then, if a negative event does occur, these positive relationships are strong enough that the relationship between the organization and its public can be sustained. This allows for longevity and a more solid reputation than advertising or marketing can provide alone. In order to understand how this definition was crafted, you must first become familiar with the history of PR.

History

There has been much contention surrounding the history of PR. Some have argued that PR has been with us since biblical times, while others trace it back to the early Greeks, who focused on σημαντκός (*semantikos*, or **semantics**), which refers to the use of symbols to create meaning. Loosely translated, many have argued that *semantikos* was primarily used to persuade people to believe certain things and act in certain ways. While this seems like a plausible beginning, others believe that PR began with the Boston Tea Party, in which colonists dumped hundreds of pounds of tea into Boston Harbor to protest an import tax. In addition, some believe that P.T. Barnum of the Barnum & Bailey Circus was the first to employ PR, as he often manipulated audiences to promote his events. However, this is not an example of PR as we know it today, as Barnum focused on manipulation and deception rather than on building positive relationships with the public.

Still others believe that PR did not actually exist until 1905, when Ivy Lee founded one of the United States' first consulting firms, Parker and Lee (Bobbitt & Sullivan, 2009). Not only did Ivy Lee advise a famous client—John D. Rockefeller—on how to improve his public and media image, but he was also one of the first practitioners to abide by a code of ethics (Bobbitt & Sullivan, 2009). Lee referred to this code of ethics as a declaration of principles, which included the need for being open with the public, being accurate in information-giving, and supplying the press and the public with prompt information about items of interest to them (Turney, 2000). As a result, Ivy Lee has been credited with shaping PR into a practice that focuses on building positive relationships between companies, organizations, individuals, and the public.

Following Ivy Lee, another former journalist further developed the field of PR. Edward Bernays, the nephew of Sigmund Freud, began working for the U.S. government during World War I in an effort to gain public support for the war. After the war, he opened an office in New York and is credited with developing the term *public relations* to describe the services that he provided. Bernays's approach to PR stemmed largely from Freud's theories on the unconscious motives that drive human behavior. As such, he decided to take the idea of wartime propaganda and use it in a positive manner. In addition to his linguistic and theoretical contribution to PR, Bernays has also been cited as having made three additional contributions to the study of PR. According to Bobbitt and Sullivan (2009), he was the first to teach PR at a university, he was one of the earliest advocates for professional PR ethics, and he was one of the first practitioners to take a scientific approach to researching public opinion for the purpose of PR (p. 6).

Today, a vast majority of PR practitioners still strive for the ideals set by Lee and Bernays over a century ago. As a result, the practice of PR has seen many positive changes, such as growth, respect as a field of study and profession, and a vast increase in published literature and theory. Now, with the rise in new media, PR is continuing to develop and become an increasingly influential persuasive factor in our everyday lives. As you will read in the forthcoming section titled "New Media and Persuasive Public Campaigns," this technological trend has contributed to new PR strategies that allow the PR process to be more effective than ever before.

7.1 REMEMBER

public relations	ongoing use of two-way communication to develop, maintain, and sustain positive relationships with the public
logos	logic
ethos	credibility
pathos	emotion
democracy	a well-informed public
dialogic	taking the form of a dialogue
advertising campaign	a paid form of impersonal communication, concerned with selling specific products, services, brands, images, and lifestyles to the public
identification	becoming known in the mind of the public
legitimacy	becoming known as trustworthy and believable
participation	the involvement of individuals who were not committed at the beginning of the campaign
penetration	when a campaign becomes noticed and unavoidable
distribution	the success of the campaign in rewarding supporters
product-oriented advertising	advertising that promotes a specific product and service to a target audience
person-oriented advertising	advertising that promotes a person or candidate
idea-oriented advertising	advertising focused on gathering support for a particular message or cause
reactive	occurring after a company or individual's image has been damaged by a negative event or crisis
proactive	paying attention to an organization's image before it is compromised
two-way communication	the communication between the organization and its public
semantikos **(semantics)**	the use of symbols to create meaning

THE PUBLIC RELATIONS PROCESS

The PR process almost always includes the following elements: a client, an agency, a team of practitioners, and a formula for persuasion. In attempting to persuade target audiences to alter their behaviors or opinions, PR practitioners must carefully construct and present key messages and themes in a repetitive fashion so that audiences will remember the messages and identify the messages as belonging to the organization. This process has been labeled in various ways over the years; specifically: RACE (or research, action, communication, and evaluation), ROPE (or research, objectives, programming, evaluation), and PIE (planning, implementation, and evaluation). Regardless of the acronym, the process is ultimately the same, with an intense focus on researching public opinion (as Ivy Lee advocated), implementing a program to accomplish the goals determined from research, and evaluating the program's effectiveness. This model is often favored because of its simplification and nonlinear emphasis. In other words, each step can be repeated and the model does not have to be completed in succession. The PIE model, as identified by Bobbitt and Sullivan (2009), will be explained in some detail in the following section.

Planning

The **planning** phase of the PR model consists of primary and secondary research about a client, identifying the target audiences for the campaign, proposing channels of communication and strategies to be used in the campaign, and constructing goals, objectives, messages, and themes (Bobbitt & Sullivan, 2009). This is one of the most important steps, if not the most important, for launching a successful persuasive effort. Research allows the PR team to identify the needs of the organization by consulting public opinion. This is persuasive in two ways: (1) The public's opinion shapes the way that PR practitioners approach the campaign, ultimately allowing public opinion to impact the organization, and (2) the PR practitioner, in turn, uses public opinion to craft specific messages and themes to persuade people to think, act, or behave in certain ways.

If you refer back to the dialogue between Riley and Bill that opened this chapter, the importance of the planning stage becomes obvious. In the time leading up to British Petroleum's full-page newspaper advertisement and series of television commercials, public opinion of the company was negative. It was reported that the results of a poll found that 76% of the American public disapproved of the way that British Petroleum was handling the oil spill (Terkel, 2010). Furthermore, over one dozen organized protests took place in major cities during Memorial Day weekend alone, such as in Clearwater, Florida, where protestors stood in front of

PHOTO 7.2 BP protests like this were seen outside of the United States, making it a global issue, as the placards in this image illustrate.

a British Petroleum gas station holding protest signs (Collette, 2010). Protests were also seen in the United Kingdom (see Photo 7.2). The negative perceptions held by the public prompted British Petroleum to launch a PR campaign in an effort to gain public support and restore its image. This is a wonderful example of the persuasive power of public opinion and how it is used in the planning stages of a PR campaign. Upon gathering research about public opinion and determining strategies to meet their goals, practitioners move into the next stage of the PR process: implementation.

Implementation

The **implementation** phase of the PR process consists of making decisions about which strategies and tactics will be used to respond to the goals of the organization and executing those strategies and tactics (Bobbitt & Sullivan, 2009). In this phase, considerations concerning budget, timelines, and feasibility are discussed thoroughly and the campaign plan is executed. This stage is where the most obvious attempts at persuasion occur, as organizations turn to social media, press releases, advertising, documents, events, and personal testimony to achieve their goals of changing public opinion.

If you return to the British Petroleum example, you can see how BP used the planning phase to identify the negative feelings held by the public and used this knowledge to execute a multimillion-dollar campaign in hopes of relieving tension and addressing the public's concerns. It was reported in Bloomberg Businessweek that British Petroleum spent at least $93.4 million in its PR campaign, which largely focused on advertising, including daily full-page ads in the *Washington Post, New York Times, Wall Street Journal*, and *USA Today* and smaller daily ads in local newspapers along the Gulf states, along with various commercials that were aired nationally (Bush, 2010; Plungis, 2010). Many of these advertisements, such as those featured in the *Washington Post* on May 25, 2010, and the *New York Times* on June 2, 2010, include an image of the Gulf cleanup efforts, along with copy that bolsters the cleanup unit and claims full responsibility for the oil spill. This example should help you understand how our daily lives are bombarded with persuasive messages delivered to us by companies, organizations, and individuals hoping to change our attitudes about something. While it is nice to think that British Petroleum would have responded this way even if the public had not held a negative opinion of its initial crisis response efforts, the fact is that BP did not launch this campaign before the public outcry. Unfortunately, this type of persuasion can have negative repercussions if the planning phase was not successful. The outcomes can be measured in the evaluation step of the process.

Evaluation

The final stage of the PR campaign process is the evaluation phase. In the **evaluation** phase, practitioners can measure the success of the campaign in persuading the public to change their attitudes and can identify the level of effectiveness of each of the strategies. This stage does not necessarily mark the end of a campaign, as practitioners should continue researching public opinion and implementing ideas long after the initial campaign has been executed. In doing so, they ensure that the campaign remains effective and that constant relationship management between the public and the organization occurs. This phase involves few attempts at persuasion from the organization, as it primarily evaluates whether the organization's attempts at persuasion worked. However, the persuasive value in this phase occurs if an organization realizes that its PR attempts were unsuccessful and moves back into the planning and implementation stages of the campaign.

Following British Petroleum's PR campaign, public opinion remained negative. Some would even argue that people's perceptions of British Petroleum worsened as they compared the company's past incidents and initial communication about the oil spill with the communication that occurred via the campaign. YouTube and Twitter parodies were created with the purpose of mocking British Petroleum's crisis response, specifically the use of then-CEO Tony Hayward's image, and others chose to express their frustration in any forum that they could. Further, a variety of social media (e.g., blogs, tweets, videos, etc.) were utilized by concerned citizens to argue for BP to take responsibility for the clean up of the oil damaged Gulf Coast. While BP attempted to work on corporate image and persuade the public of their genuine concern for solving the problem, You Tube, Twitter, and other forms of social media helped to foster and disseminate criticism of the BP crisis response. One particular criticism was the amount of money BP spent taking out large ads in national newspapers and popular magazines. Citizens argued that the substantial amounts of money spent on crisis response advertising should have instead been used to clean up the disaster area and support small business owners, fishermen, and coastal communities impacted by the spill.

What do you remember about the BP oil spill media coverage? Is there a particular image or story that specifically reminds you of the event? Consider the images of the spill as well as criticism of BP's response shared globally through the use of social media. What are the qualities of social media that allow people to protest or hold large companies like BP accountable? Beyond the BP example, think of other topics or events important to you. If you needed to argue for a particular cause (e.g., animal rights, free speech, civil rights, environmental issues), what aspects of social media would you use as a persuasive tool? Perhaps you would share video clips or links to images with the intention of persuading others to support your cause. Indeed, BP faced intense criticism from blogs, tweets, shared videos of the spill, and more, which exemplifies how social media can be used to persuade.

At the time this chapter was written, the PR efforts of British Petroleum were still under way. Only time will tell how the power of persuasion will pan out in this case, but understanding the way that a PR campaign functions will be beneficial in identifying the persuasive messages that you receive from other types of PR campaigns in your everyday life.

In Your Life

Take a moment to think about disasters like the BP oil spill or airline crashes. What persuasive strategies come to mind when you think about disasters? Can you think of some examples of persuasion that stand out in your mind?

7.2 REMEMBER

planning	primary and secondary research about a client, identifying the target audiences for the campaign, proposing channels of communication and strategies to be used in the campaign, and constructing goals, objectives, messages, and themes
implementation	making decisions about which strategies and tactics will be used to respond to the goals of the organization and executing those strategies and tactics
evaluation	when practitioners measure the success of the campaign in persuading the public to change their attitudes and can identify the level of effectiveness of each of the strategies

TYPES OF PERSUASIVE PUBLIC RELATIONS CAMPAIGNS

Now that you have a basic understanding of the definition and history of PR and the process by which persuasive PR campaigns are developed, you can fully understand how the public is influenced by various types of persuasive campaigns. As shown earlier in this chapter, when people think of PR campaigns, they often think of crises and politics; however, rarely do people realize that PR spans far beyond major issues such as the environment and politics In fact, there are at least seven distinguishable types of PR campaigns: employee relations, community relations, investor relations, consumer relations, media relations, public campaigns, and crisis management (Center, Jackson, Smith, & Stansberry, 2008). In the sections that follow, the campaigns most relevant to the daily lives of college students like you are discussed.

Community Relations

Community relations, or strategies associated with developing positive relationships between an organization and its public, is an increasingly important form of PR nowadays. With the rise in corporate scandals and crises, as well as social media, it's no wonder that community relations is an important persuasive factor in how we judge an organization. Practitioners striving to develop positive community relations use strategies that focus on informing the public of events happening within an organization, making information that is relevant to the public available to them, donating resources where needed within the community, maintaining a good reputation, volunteering, advertising, and participating in the community on a regular basis. This is one of the most important types of PR campaigns, as all organizations require positive community relations to remain trusted entities. Thus, whether you realize it or not, you're taking in messages specifically crafted by organizations for this purpose as you accept scholarships, attend festivals, and "like" companies on Facebook.

An exemplar of the importance of community relations is a situation with a CITGO refinery in Corpus Christi, Texas. This particular refining company has a record of strong community relations through recognizing and providing scholarships to young academic achievers, sponsoring various community nonprofit organizations, and even donating a fire truck to a local high school/college dual-credit Fire Science Academy program (Sausley, 2010). In 2009, however, CITGO was faced with a terrible event when a plant explosion caused an employee to suffer from lung damage, burns on his body, and the loss of part of his left arm (KIIITV News, 2009). While the public was initially angry at the refining company, they have quickly forgiven it and accepted the notion that this was merely an accident that CITGO has done its best to prevent from happening again. The difference between CITGO and British Petroleum is, in part, the fact that CITGO had a strong record of community relations *before* an accident happened and, therefore, appears to care more about the well-being of the community and its employees.

Consumer Relations

Imagine that you ordered a gift for a loved one using a company's website. You have never purchased anything from this particular company online or otherwise, and you are disappointed to learn that it will take 7 to 14 days for the gift to be delivered since the occasion is only 2 days away. The day after you place the order, a representative contacts you by telephone to mention that he saw the event date engraved on the gift and to offer a shipping option that will allow the gift to arrive on the day of the event. You might not only be surprised that a company representative would go out of his way to help you when you did not request that the gift make it in time, but be so impressed that you would tell others about the company and purchase additional items from its website.

The example above exemplifies the duty of the consumer relations practitioner and the persuasive power that can be achieved through positive customer service. In PR, **consumer relations** deals with an organization's ability to satisfy and create a positive experience for its consumers. This is especially important in a free market, where there are many organizations

Ethical Connection

Make a connection between public relations and ethics. What examples related to consumer, employee, and community relations come to mind in terms of unethical persuasive strategies?

competing for the same target audience of consumers. As earlier chapters in this textbook have mentioned, not all persuasion is negative, and consumer relations is definitely a form of persuasion that can be viewed as positive for both the organization and the consumer. As organizations compete to satisfy consumers, their customers are usually presented with positive attitudes, quality service, and discounts or free products. This type of persuasive campaign fits well with our definition of PR that emphasizes two-way communication and mutual benefit.

Employee Relations

How many times have you come home from work, vowing that you were going to search for work elsewhere and quit your job as soon as you were financially stable? Have you ever felt like your boss does not care about your feelings or needs? Have you ever learned information about changes being made at your workplace from someone other than your supervisors? Many of us have experienced these types of issues in our professional lives without realizing that they fall under the umbrella of PR, specifically, **employee relations,** or attempts to develop positive relationships between employers and employees.

Organizations with employees can benefit from a PR practitioner's support in many areas of communication, such as recruiting, training, working conditions, mediation, grievances, rewards, recognition, information dissemination, satisfaction, layoffs, termination, and transition. In this sense, the practitioner serves as the main source of persuasion for the employer, in hopes that employees develop a sense of trust in, loyalty to, and satisfaction with the organization. Center, Jackson, Smith, and Stansberry (2008) identified five rules to practice effective employee relations: Tell employees information that affects them and their jobs first; tell the employees the bad news along with the good news; be sure that employees receive information about them and their jobs in a timely manner; inform employees about subjects that they identify as being important; and use the media that employees trust, which is often face-to-face communication (pp. 25–26). Each of these tips can be viewed as a strategy for effectively influencing the opinions of employees while simultaneously creating positive relationships with them. If employees are happy with the organization, they will do good work for it. This, in turn, results in customers becoming happy with the organization as they sense the cohesion among employees and employers. This can be a powerful form of persuasion.

A popular example dealing with employee relations belongs to Wal-Mart, an international grocer and retailer. Over the years, many employees have launched formal complaints against Wal-Mart regarding issues pertaining to employee relations, such as wages, working conditions, and health insurance. Many critics have noted the average pay for employees is around $13,800 per year, with the poverty line being at $14,600 per year (Bianco & Zellner, 2003). This criticism has been worsened by Wal-Mart founder Sam Walton's response, as reported by *Frontline*: "I pay low wages. I can take advantage of that. We're going to be successful, but the basis is a very low-wage, low-benefit model of employment" (PBS.org). Because of Wal-Mart's size and relative ease in finding individuals who need employment in today's economy, the criticism has had little noticeable impact; however, many individuals stand by their refusal to work or shop at Wal-Mart, and it is well known that Wal-Mart is lacking in the area of employee relations.

Public Issues

In 2009, the future of a well-known building in Corpus Christi, Texas, was at stake. The building, Memorial Coliseum, was built in 1954 and was dedicated to 400 men and women who lost their lives in World War II. Memorial Coliseum's rich history included surviving hurricanes and tropical storms and hosting high school and college graduation ceremonies and live concerts from legendary musicians such as Elvis and Selena. Unfortunately, the Memorial Coliseum had not been kept up and had become an eyesore and a health hazard rather than the architecturally and culturally significant building it once was. The decisions as to what should be done with the coliseum divided the community, as younger idealists saw the opportunity for economic and aesthetic development and elder individuals saw the historical significance of a building dedicated to those who had lost their lives in war. Representatives from both sides of the issue launched PR campaigns in hopes that their cause would prevail. On June 30, 2010, the coliseum was demolished.

The above example illustrates the importance of effective public issues campaigns, as well as the ways that these campaigns can create significant changes in daily life. A **public issues** campaign occurs when people from two or more opposing sides of an argument have emotional convictions about a decision that has the power to impact their lives. In situations like this, the practitioners are in competition with each other in creating an effective campaign that can win over the **general public,** or those who are neutral, or do not feel strongly in favor of or opposed to the issue. The planning phase of PR is of particular interest in this type of campaign. In the example of the Memorial Coliseum, the historical significance of the building was not as powerful an argument as the aesthetic and economic significance of the property. Those in favor of tearing down the coliseum compiled research from community leaders and college students and were

community relations	strategies associated with developing positive relationships between an organization and its public
consumer relations	organization's ability to satisfy and create a positive experience for its consumers
employee relations	attempts to develop positive relationships between employers and employees
pubic issues	decisions about which people from two or more opposing sides have emotional convictions and that have the power to impact their lives
general public	those who are neutral, or do not feel strongly in favor of or opposed to an issue

able to include plans for a "better" memorial in their arguments. They also paid attention to the types of media that individuals trusted most and used social networking, face-to-face forums, and fun events to get the public's attention. In this case, as well as most other public issues cases, the campaign with the most attention to public opinion was the most persuasive.

CRISIS MANAGEMENT

A final type of PR that we encounter in our daily lives is the crisis management campaign. Due to its popularity, this type of PR is discussed in detail, warranting its own section in this chapter. **Crisis management** includes proactively planning a response strategy, implementing that strategy in the event of a crisis, evaluating the crisis response, and revising the initial response strategy in an effort to improve for future crises. Due to the amount of crises that have occurred in recent years, this type of PR has quickly become one of the most recognizable.

Types of Crises

In 1999, well-known crisis communication researcher W. Timothy Combs created a crisis typology by synthesizing the various types of crises that have been cited by researchers. These crises include natural disasters, malevolence, technical breakdowns, human breakdowns, challenges, megadamage, organizational misdeeds, workplace violence, and rumors (p. 61). **Natural disasters,** or an organization being damaged as a result of "acts of God," include crises such as Hurricane Katrina or the earthquake in Haiti. **Malevolence,** or outside agents using extreme tactics to harm an organization, includes situations such as the 1982 Tylenol product tampering case, whereby Extra-Strength Tylenol medicine capsules were laced with potassium cyanide, killing seven people. In cases of **technical breakdowns,** an organization's technology fails, causing situations such as the recent Toyota recalls for faulty brakes.

Technology is not the only thing to break down, so to speak. There are also many cases of **human breakdowns,** whereby human error causes harm, such as the incident where a Sea World trainer was killed by a killer whale after being exposed to what OSHA referred to as "hazards that were causing, or likely to cause, death or serious physical harm to employees" (Engle, 2010). **Challenges,** or an organization facing disputes by angry stakeholders, include boycotts and protests, such as those launched against British Petroleum following the Gulf oil spill. In cases like the BP oil spill, **megadamage**—or an accident that causes serious environmental damage—occurs.

Many instances of **organizational misdeeds,** where an organization places profit above values or employee safety, are present in today's society, such as in the cases of Enron and Martha Stewart. Furthermore, when an employee or former employee behaves violently toward coworkers or managers, **workplace violence** occurs. A recent example occurred when a 43-year-old woman reportedly walked into her place of employment (a Kraft plant in Pennsylvania) and shot three people, killing two and critically injuring the other. Finally, **rumors** or false information about an organization, are also considered crises when they cause harm to the organization's reputation or profits. One example of a crisis caused by a rumor is the PR campaign that has been launched by a group called CASPIAN. This group is calling for the boycott of Gillette products, claiming that they include radio frequency identification devices (RFID) that can invade the privacy and take photos of unsuspecting customers. While the truthfulness of this rumor is in doubt, it has an impact on Gillette just as any of the aforementioned types of crises would have on an organization. Thus, the persuasive strategies used by organizations in responding to crises have an immense impact on their longevity and public perception. These strategies are discussed in the following section.

Crisis Response Strategies

The most persuasive aspect of crisis response is the array of strategies used by organizations to protect their identities and convince the public that they should continue to trust them. W. Timothy Coombs (1999) has identified four categories of persuasive crisis communication strategies: nonexistence,

7.4 REMEMBER

crisis management	includes proactively planning a response strategy, implementing that strategy in the event of a crisis, evaluating the crisis response, and revising the initial response strategy in an effort to improve for future crises
natural disasters	"acts of God," including crises such as Hurricane Katrina or the earthquake in Haiti
malevolence	when outside agents use extreme tactics to harm an organization
technical breakdowns	when an organization's technology fails
human breakdowns	when human error causes harm
challenges	when an organization faces disputes with angry stakeholders
megadamage	an accident that causes serious environmental damage
organizational misdeeds	instances where an organization places profit above values or employee safety
workplace violence	when an employee or former employee behaves violently toward coworkers or managers
rumors	false information about an organization

In Your Life

What expectations do you have of corporations and organizations when it comes to apologizing for mistakes? Can you think of some examples of crisis response that persuaded you?

distancing, ingratiation, and mortification (see Figure 7.3). **Nonexistence** strategies, or denial, clarification, intimidation, and attacking the accuser, are typically used with to allow an organization to confront a group, deny the existence of a crisis, and provide an explanation for it. **Distancing** includes offering an excuse, justification, or misrepresentation, minimizing injury, or portraying the victim as deserving. This type of distancing response allows an organization to minimize its responsibility or the perceived damage of the crisis.

In addition to nonexistence and distance strategies, organizations may use **ingratiation** strategies, such as bolstering, transcendence, and praising others. This allows a crisis manager to place the organization's good deeds at the forefront, in turn minimizing the appearance of the crisis. Finally, **mortification**—is a series of strategies consisting of corrective

Strategy	Method	Use
Nonexistence	Denial	Confronting rumors
	Clarification	Denying crisis
	Intimidation	Explaining crisis
	Attacking the accuser	
Distancing	Excuse	Minimizing damage
	Justification	Minimizing responsibility
	Misrepresentation	
	Minimizing injury	
	Deserving victim	
Ingratiation	Bolstering	Maximizing good deeds
	Transcendence	Minimizing damage
	Praising others	
Mortification	Corrective redemption	Taking responsibility
	Repentance	Preventing future crises
	Rectification	Repairing damage

FIGURE 7.3 Persuasive strategies for crisis response

Source: Coombs, W. T. (1999). *Ongoing crisis communication: Planning, managing, and responding.* Thousand Oaks, CA: SAGE.

redemption, repentance, and rectification. These strategies allow organizations to take responsibility for the crisis and repair the damage by taking steps to prevent future crises.

Image Restoration Strategies

Benoit (1997) identified five types of image restoration strategies: denial, evasion of responsibility, reducing the offensiveness, corrective action, and mortification (see Figure 7.4). **Denial** consists of simple denial and shifting the blame, allowing the organization to evade responsibility for a crisis and maintain or restore its image. **Evasion of responsibility** is comprised of provocation (reasonable action taken in response to another offensive act), defeasibility (claiming a lack of information/knowledge), accident, and good intentions. This strategy is an organization's way of lessening the severity of the crisis and/or minimizing its responsibility. **Reducing the offensiveness** is a way for organizations to repair the image by contributing to a lessened perceived offensiveness of the event. Strategies in this category include bolstering, minimization, differentiation, transcendence (talking about organizational history of excellence/superiority), attacking one's accuser, and compensation. Two final strategies include **corrective action,** or taking responsibility for a crisis and planning ways to solve the problem and prevent

Strategy	Method	Use
Denial	Simple denial Shifting the blame	Refusing responsibility Stating that crisis did not occur
Evasion of Responsibility	Provocation Defeasibility Accident Good intentions	Lessening severity of crisis Minimizing responsibility
Reducing the Offensiveness	Bolstering Minimization Differentiation Transcendence Attacking the accuser Compensation	Maximizing good deeds Minimizing damage Minimizing crisis Accepting responsibility Shifting responsibility
Corrective Action	Repair Corrective action	Accepting responsibility Preventing future crises Repairing damage
Mortification	Confession Apology	Accepting responsibility

FIGURE 7.4 Persuasive strategies for image restoration

Source: Benoit, W. L. (1997). Image restoration discourse and crisis communication. In D. P. Millar & R. L. Heath (Eds.), *Responding to crisis: A rhetorical approach to crisis communication* (pp. 263–280). Mahwah, NJ: Lawrence Erlbaum Associates.

future crises, and **mortification,** or confessing responsibility and asking for forgiveness. In both of these strategies, organizations hope that the public will forgive them based on their perceived sincerity (Benoit, 1997).

Apologia

When faced with a crisis, many organizations opt to communicate a response involving strategies that allow the organization to quickly recover from the incident. This type of response (see Figure 7.5), as discussed by Hearit (1994), is known as apologia. **Apologia** is a character-based defense whose success largely depends on the persona of the spokesperson and is comprised of denial, counterattack, differentiation, apology, and legal strategies (Hearit, 1994). In apologia, organizations typically have no choice other than to apologize and claim that they regret the incident's occurrence. Alternative strategies to apologia are for organizations to sidestep liability, remain silent, argue that the crisis was unintentional, challenge the ethics or knowledge of dissenters, and/or utilize a scapegoat.

Regardless of the type of crisis and crisis response, image restoration, or apologia strategies used by an organization, persuasion remains the

Remember: You can use your knowledge of persuasion to engage real-life situations. Consider the scenario below and think about what you would do as you apply the material in this chapter.

Your friend called you and asked if you could watch her nephew for a few hours while she runs a few errands around town. You didn't have any plans at the moment and so you decided to be a good friend and help her out. As you are going to the fridge to get the two of you some snacks, you are caught off guard by a commercial that your friend's nephew is currently witnessing. A naked woman comes on the screen, covering only the "bad parts," and suggests that viewers try a new brand of condoms that promises ultimate pleasure. Although you try to find the remote to change the channel, you are unable to do so in time and your friend's nephew is full of questions now. This commercial left you feeling very offended and worried about what the young child just saw. You decide that you wish to take action and you contact the public relations department of the company advertising the condoms. Using your knowledge gained from this chapter, how would you carefully address the issue at hand without yelling or being forceful over the phone? What would you do?

In Your Life

What does it take for you to be persuaded by an apology? In your view, what are the persuasive qualities of a good apology?

common denominator. In all crises, organizations are at risk of having a tarnished image and losing public support and profits. Therefore, all crisis management communications are carefully constructed with the purpose of persuasion. Studying the types of strategies used by PR practitioners following a crisis makes it easier to recognize when these messages are used. This is becoming increasingly important as new media change the shape of PR, allowing it to be much more natural and implicit. This argument is further discussed in the following section.

Strategy	Method	Use
Apologia	Denial	Wanting to recover quickly
	Counterattack	Attempting to avoid liability
	Differentiation	Denying responsibility
	Apology	Shifting responsibility
	Legal	Apologizing
		Remaining silent

FIGURE 7.5 Persuasive strategies for apologia

Source: Hearit, K. M. (1994). Apologies and public relations crises at Chrysler, Toshiba, and Volvo. *Public Relations Review, 20*(2), 113–125.

NEW MEDIA AND PERSUASIVE PUBLIC CAMPAIGNS

A chapter on persuasive public campaigns would not be complete without a discussion of the ways that the persuasive landscape has been changed by **new media,** or the convergence of traditional media (such as film, music, language, images, and text) with the interactive ability of computer technology. The rise of new media has allowed the mission of persuasive campaigns to be accomplished better and easier than ever before. While advertising campaigns have typically been viewed as a one-way communication process, both Barack Obama's 2008 presidential campaign and the NOH8 campaign referenced earlier in this chapter show how new media have shifted advertising closer to two-way communication. Coincidentally, new media have had a similar impact on public relations. Because of the degree to which new media have "reinvented" the practice of PR, Solis and Breakenridge (2009) have termed this shift "PR 2.0." **PR 2.0** consists of refocusing public relations efforts by placing the public at the forefront via democratic and participatory media. While this idea is termed PR 2.0, it is also applicable to other persuasive campaigns. According to Solis and Breakenridge, new media allow (1) more emphasis on two-way communication, (2) a larger focus on building relationships, (3) more far-reaching strategies, and (4) less cost associated with producing effective persuasive messages. Each of these changes is discussed in some detail in the sections that follow.

Social Media in Your Life: Have You Seen This?

Go to YouTube and enter the following keywords: BP, oil spill, birds

This clip displays the results of a disaster caused by the BP oil spill. What's your reaction?

Two-Way Communication

If you return to the original discussion of advertising and public relations, you will remember that two-way communication has long been viewed as a hallmark of PR that sets it apart from marketing, advertising, and other related fields. More recently, however, public relations and advertising have begun to look more similar as many people fail to make a distinction between the two fields. While this may be seen as a weakness of practitioners involved in both areas, it may also be seen as the result of new media's impact on campaigning. The beauty of new media is that they allow organizations, companies, individuals, advertisers, and PR practitioners to speak directly with the public at any time of day or night. Where traditional tactics limit the practitioner to a key set of individuals (a target audience) and strategies (surveys, focus groups, or interviews), new media keep the public's views at the forefront—they are free, accessible, and do not require a practitioner to solicit participants for public opinion studies.

Relationship-Building

With the added interest in and ease of access to constant two-way communication, the relationship between the organization and its public improves vastly. By responding to and engaging in conversations with the public through new media (such as social networking on a Facebook page), organizations are demonstrating that they are listening and that they care about public opinion. By hiring a few representatives to manage their online presence by responding to customer questions, complaints, or compliments, the organization is ultimately saving money and gaining a positive image at the same time. A customer for example, recently experienced difficulty in making a purchase online at a popular retailer. She immediately logged in to Facebook, visited the company's page, and left a comment about her difficulties. Within five minutes, the page owner responded with an apology, a suggestion for another attempt, and an email address to write to if the problem persisted. This quick response not only eliminated what could have become an angry phone call to a customer service agent, but also improved the customer's perception of the company while minimizing the frustration associated with the difficulty.

Far-Reaching Strategies

Not only do new media improve relationships, they also have far-reaching effects. As Solis and Breakenridge (2009) claim, "companies lost 100% control of their communications a long time ago. People are discussing their brands, products, and services right now, across multiple forums of Social Media, with or without them" (p. xix). Thus, it is of great benefit for advertisers and PR practitioners to recognize the persuasive influence that others have on their practice and to embrace it by participating in and contributing to this shift. By building trust and positive relationships via new media, organizations retain a positive influence across sites—especially those sites over which they have no control. For instance, returning to the previous example, the customer has applauded the efforts of the company on other related Facebook pages. While the company may not have knowledge of this, the influence of positive word of mouth is far-reaching enough for the company to feel its impact and constitutes an advertising campaign on its own.

Cost-Effective Persuasion

An additional benefit of new media is that they are cost-effective—as a matter of fact, they are free for the most part. Gone are the days where organizations had to spend money producing a commercial, buying airtime during slots when their target audience would be tuning in to television, buying radio spots to play audio commercials, and relying on the news media to photograph and report their events. With social media, people and organizations can create videos and distribute them on the Internet, where multiple audiences may view them at any time of the day or week, thus broadening the scope of influence. Furthermore, the nature of new media embraces and readily trusts "amateur" photos and short messages, such as the 140-character-or-less posts required on Twitter. This change creates many additional opportunities for persuasion that are no longer limited by budgets and the targeting of specific audiences.

7.5 REMEMBER

nonexistence	denial, clarification, intimidation, and attacking the accuser
distancing	tactics including excuse, justification, misrepresentation, minimizing injury, and deserving victim that allow an organization to minimize its responsibility or the perceived damage of a crisis
ingratiation	bolstering, transcendence, and praising others
mortification	strategies consisting of corrective redemption, repentance, and rectification
denial	simple denial and shifting of blame
evasion of responsibility	provocation, defeasibility, accident, and good intentions
reducing the offensiveness	bolstering, minimization, differentiation, transcendence, attacking the accuser, and compensation
corrective action	taking responsibility for a crisis and planning ways to solve the problem and prevent future crises
mortification	confessing responsibility and asking for forgiveness
apologia	character-based defense whose success largely depends on the persona of the spokesperson, comprised of denial, counterattack, differentiation, apology, and legal strategies
new media	the convergence of traditional media (such as film, music, language, images, and text) with the interactive ability of computer technology
PR 2.0	refocusing public relations efforts by placing the public at the forefront via democratic and participatory media

SUMMARY

As you conclude your study of persuasion in public relations, the daily occurrence of these influential messages cannot be emphasized enough. Regardless of whether you are scanning the Internet at work, watching television, reading a fan page on Facebook, or enjoying a community event, you are likely consuming a carefully constructed campaign aimed at changing your attitudes or beliefs about something. While this may sound a bit scary, you must also remember that not all persuasion is negative, especially where public relations is concerned. PR is focused on building positive relationships between an organization and its public through the use of ethical means. Thus, have confidence in knowing that the vast amount of PR messages you receive are truthful and to your benefit. With the rise in new media allowing both advertising and PR to become more relationship oriented, we have an increasing impact on organizations and the strategies that they use to influence us. However, all things considered, it is beneficial to be able to recognize when these persuasive attempts come from an organization that may not be operating under ethical standards. By understanding the definition, foundations, process, and types of advertising and public relations campaigns, as well as the influence that new media have had on advertising and public relations, we can accomplish this goal.

DISCUSSION QUESTIONS

Public Campaigns

1. Recall one advertising campaign that you believe was effective and one that you believe was ineffective. What persuasive appeals were used in these campaigns? What made them effective or ineffective?

2. What do you think are the most important elements of the definition of public relations? Is there anything that you believe should be added or removed from this definition?

3. Have you been knowingly influenced by a public relations campaign lately? What type of public relations did this campaign represent (community, consumer, etc.)?

4. Think of the various types of new media that you consume. Do you believe that one is more trustworthy or persuasive than another?

5. How might an organization benefit from using social media such as Facebook and Twitter in its advertising efforts? Its crisis response efforts?

Persuasion and Personal Relationships

8

Narissra Punyanunt-Carter

YOUR OBJECTIVES

After studying this chapter, you should be able to:

1. Explain the use of power and persuasion in interpersonal relationships.
2. Identify six principles of power.
3. Discuss ways to influence goals and engage in persuasive interpersonal relationships.
4. Identify and explain verbal and nonverbal interpersonal persuasion behaviors.
5. Apply persuasive behaviors in your interpersonal relationships.

CHAPTER OUTLINE

Interpersonal

Alyssa and Gavin have been dating for 3 years now. Alyssa recently got a job offer near her parents' home. Gavin would like to pursue a graduate degree. They both do not want to have a long-distance relationship. At the same time, they both would like to get married and have children some day. However, they are unsure what to do in this situation. Alyssa is afraid that if she takes the job, Gavin might leave her for another woman. Gavin is afraid that if he doesn't pursue his education now, he won't ever have the time in the future.

In every interpersonal relationship, there comes a time when one person may need and/or want something from the other. **Interpersonal relationships** are our relations and interactions with other people. As illustrated in the example with Gavin and Alyssa, many relationships encounter power struggles. Each person may want to persuade the other to do something that the other may not necessarily want to do. Every day, individuals use all sorts of persuasive techniques to get what they want. These techniques may include humor, threats, praise, comfort, and others. In each of these circumstances, persuasion in an interpersonal context is very specific.

In this chapter, you will study the different interpersonal communicative influences that are used to achieve objectives. When the speaker has the objective of influencing the receiver's opinions, beliefs, or attitudes, this is persuasion in an interpersonal context. The way the speaker communicates this to the other person is through power. Power will be defined in more detail later in this chapter, when you study the six principles of power. You will also examine influence goals and learn about nonverbal and verbal interpersonal persuasion behaviors.

The ways in which people use power vary depending on what they want in the relationship. For instance, someone has to persuade another person to give money, acceptance, love, affection, sex, help with chores, and the like. Power and persuasion in the interpersonal context take place in romantic and platonic relationships. Think about times where you have used power or persuasion to get a friend to help you move or get someone to go on a date with you.

POWER DEFINED

Berger (1985) defined **power** as a person's ability to influence others. Individuals often exert power by using resources (Guerrero, Andersen, & Afifi, 2011). In interpersonal relationships, people manage resources by giving them to or taking them away from others. These resources may take many forms, such as sex, money, time, or rewards. For instance, Alyssa may give Gavin more affection when he displays positive behaviors towards her. Berger (1985) noted that power influences relationship partners' feelings, behaviors, and actions toward each other. If Gavin perceives himself to be more powerful in the relationship with Alyssa, do you think that might influence the amount of positive behavior he gives to her?

Power is a basic aspect in a relationship because most people have the ability to choose how they will use it. It is said that individuals have free will. In other words, we are free agents and we have **agency,** the ability to control our behaviors and actions with others. In interpersonal relationships, people typically will make decisions in

interpersonal relationships	our relations and interactions with other people
power	a person's ability to influence others
agency	the ability to control our behaviors and actions with others

In Your Life

What types of power can you think of that have influenced you in your relationships? Which ones do you think are most influential for men and women?

a fair manner. However, people can also use power for **dominance,** or overuse of power through abusive behaviors. Dominance can impact relationships in a negative manner, sometimes leading to harassment or submission (Guerrero et al., 2011). Dominance is usually used to terminate relationships and/or create more dissatisfying relationships. Have you ever had a boss who used his dominance in the relationship to foster a negative attitude in the workplace?

Dominance can be a part of **social influence,** which is when people change another person's thoughts, feelings, and or behaviors. Social influence can be direct or indirect. In most cases, social influence can be very strategic (Guerrero et al., 2011). From an apple on the teacher's desk to a nice dinner cooked for a loved one, there are countless instances where we use strategy to gain social approval or favor.

SIX PRINCIPLES OF POWER

The first principle of power is that it is based on **perception**—how we interpret others' verbal and nonverbal communication (Guerrero et al., 2011). People can influence each other through a variety of means. Oftentimes, these means are based on the perception that a person is influential in some fashion, such as wealth or status. Most students perceive their professors, as well as police officers and public officials, as figures of power. Do you attribute the same power over your actions to your professor that you would to a police officer?

The second principle of power is that power is a **relational concept.** That is, power is part of the relational dynamic. If one person is submissive, then the other is usually dominant. Romantic relationships have power balances. For instance, Alyssa might have financial power, whereas Gavin might have expert power in handling money. Research has shown that the most satisfying relationships are the ones where both partners have an equal balance of power. Married couples have an influence on each other.

Usually the actions of one person have an impact on the other person. If Gavin does decide to continue on with graduate school, it will clearly have an impact on Alyssa and their entire relationship.

The third principle is that power is based on **resources.** The scarcer a resource, the more intense the power struggle will become. People enter a relationship with many different resources. These resources may include money, status, attractiveness, communication skills, affection, love, sexual rewards, and support. The **scarcity hypothesis** states that people have the most control or power when their partner perceives that they have resources considered valuable and/or hard to attain. For example, if Alyssa has the financial power, as stated earlier, she might be better able to coerce Gavin into doing something for her if she threatens to take away her financial support. However, if Gavin does not perceive her financial support as essential, then the threat will likely have no effect on him.

The fourth principle is that the individual who has less to lose in the relationship possesses more power. Sometimes people have something called **dependence power,** which occurs when the individual has other choices, such as another love interest, another job opportunity, and/or another friend. There is also a concept called the **principle of least interest,** which states that if there is a difference between the perceptions of happiness between partners, then the person who is happiest possesses the most power. For instance, if Alyssa feels more love toward Gavin than he does for her, Gavin has more power in this relationship. When there is an imbalance in the relationship, the person who is not as committed or interested in the relationship can make more demands because he is not as vested in the relationship and doesn't care as much about the future of the relationship. Can you think of a relationship you have had where you had dependence power? How about the opposite—a time when the other person had little or nothing to lose?

The fifth principle is that power can be either disabling or enabling in a relationship. It has been shown that people can use *persuasive power* to gain accomplishments. At the same time, unnecessary or extreme power can also cause people to terminate their relationships. Research has shown that disproportionate power in a relationship can cause problems. Men are more likely to have power issues and to have them affect their romantic relationships. If men and women have increased power needs, they are also less likely to have close friendships with others (McAdams, 1985). Do you know anyone who needs to constantly have control in her relationships, whether they are romantic, platonic, or professional? How do friends, family, and coworkers perceive this person?

The sixth principle is that the more powerful person in the relationship has the ability to create and dissolve rules. This is also known as the **prerogative principle,** that powerful people have the ability to defy

Social Media in Your Life: Have You Seen This?

Go to YouTube and enter the following keywords: eharmony, be yourself, what if, if it's love, if you're ready

This clip demonstrates one way social media can affect your personal life. How do you feel about building relationships through online dating sites?

In Your Life

Can you give examples of each of these six principles in your relationship(s)? Do you feel that these principles are accurate? Why or why not?

rules in their interactions with others without many of the negative consequences. For instance, Alyssa may be likely to get away with more at her engineering firm because she is the only female in an all-male firm. However, this scenario can become a double-edged sword. Would Alyssa always have the prerogative power, or could she face increased scrutiny in an all-male workforce?

INFLUENCE GOALS IN INTERPERSONAL RELATIONSHIPS

When you think of communication, you think of influence. Couples are always trying to get their partners to do something, such as take out the trash, avoid overeating, or make a major decision. Think about relationships you have been in, whether romantic or platonic. Have you ever had someone ask you to make a change in lifestyle? Has anyone ever asked you to change a habit? All relationships carry some semblance of influence between partners. Most of the influences fall into the following seven dimensions (Dillard, 1989):

1. **Making Lifestyle Changes**   Oftentimes in intimate relationships there are times when one person provides suggestions concerning his partner's lifestyle. Some examples of lifestyle changes may be persuading your partner to quit smoking or to get a divorce. Dillard (1989) noted that lifestyle requests are typically direct and logical. Has a friend or loved one ever asked you to make a change in your lifestyle, like exercising more or eating healthier? How did you respond to this request?

2. **Getting Assistance**   Another type of interpersonal influence goal is to get help from another. For instance, you may need some assistance writing a book report, moving items from one location to another, or paying off debt. These requests may not be as important as a lifestyle request, but they may be very important in the relationship. Oftentimes these requests are not explicit. Hence, the person making the request might say, "I'm thirsty" rather than "I would like you to get me a drink." If Alyssa has the financial power in the relationship with Gavin, how might Gavin implicitly ask her for help with his bills?

3. **Sharing Activities**   In order to maintain relationships, individuals will engage in shared activities. These activities may include doing things to increase intimacy, such as sharing hobbies, spending time together, and partaking in common interests. It has been shown that males are more likely to increase intimacy in their male friendships by doing activities together, because males do not typically self-disclose to each other. Males will usually compete in sports, party, or exercise

In Your Life

Think about a current
or previous romantic
relationship that you
had. What types of
interpersonal goals did
you try to persuade your
partner to accept? Were
these requests justified?
Why or why not? Do you
think these were accept-
able and appropriate
requests? What was the
outcome?

with their friends. Relationships are more likely to intensify with more shared activities, because they increase intimacy and closeness with the other person. Romantic partners will frequently spend a large amount of time together. Persuasive requests for shared activities are usually more emotional in nature than logical (Dillard, 1989). Do you agree that these requests are generally emotional? What could be some logical reasons Alyssa would ask Gavin to see a movie with her?

4. **Having Sex** In intimate relationships, a common persuasive goal is engaging in sexual behaviors. Females are less likely to initiate sex compared to males, although it has been shown that females are more likely to suggest sex in a marital relationship. Having sex, using pro-tection, and requesting more sex are all persuasive goals that romantic partners may have. Think about some of the other uses for persuasion you have already explored. If Alyssa helped Gavin to quit smoking (life-style change) or helped him out with his bills (getting assistance), do you think this would aid her in persuading Gavin to have sex with her?

5. **Changing Politics** Another interpersonal persuasive goal deals with politics and changing political opinions. Trying to get someone involved with politics, asking others to vote for a particular candidate, or requesting that someone support a cause are all examples of shared political activities. If your friends and family support your political beliefs, it can increase satisfaction in your relationship with them. Dillard (1989) noted that partners will often use indirect attempts to change political attitudes. Political tendencies tend to be very sensi-tive topics, even among intimate couples. How have you reacted when someone has asked you to rethink your political affiliations?

6. **Promoting Health** In our relationships with others, we may want to improve their mental and physical well-being. For instance, we may encourage our parents to see a doctor when they are ill, our kids to get a flu shot to prevent illness, or our partners to exercise so that they remain healthy. If her health suggestions are taken and followed, the persuader may feel that she made a difference. However, if the receiver of the message perceives that the suggestions are unwarranted, then he might experience **psychological reactance**, which means that he perceives the persuader as too demanding and insistent. Consequently, the receiver may even engage in more unhealthy behaviors. It has been shown that wives who nag their husbands about their health problems may make things worse physically and emotionally. Dillard (1989) dis-covered that health messages are best when they are reasonable and concise. However, it is very easy to offend someone when talking about mental or physical health. Do you think a direct or indirect request would work better in these types of situations?

dominance	the overuse of power through abusive behaviors; can impact relationships in a negative manner, sometimes leading to harassment or submission
social influence	when people change another person's thoughts, feelings, and/or behaviors
perception	how we interpret others' verbal and nonverbal communication
relational concept	power is part of the relational dynamic
resources	physical or abstract concepts that a person may possess in a relationship, such as love and support
scarcity hypothesis	states that people have the most control or power when their partner perceives that they have resources considered valuable and/or hard to attain
dependence power	power that occurs when an individual has other choices, such as another love interest, job opportunity, and/or friend
principle of least interest	idea that, if there is a difference between the perceptions of happiness between partners, then the person who is happiest possesses the most power
prerogative principle	concept that powerful people have the ability to defy rules in their interactions with others without many of the negative consequences
psychological reactance	when a receiver perceives the persuader to be too challenging and controlling

7. **Offering Relationship Advice** The last type of interpersonal goal is offering relationship advice. Examples include telling your significant other that you need a separation or telling your best friend to terminate a relationship with an abusive lover. Giving advice about relationships can be difficult because sometimes people are unwilling to accept what you have to say. For instance, if you found out that your best friend's husband was cheating on her, would you tell her or would you let her find out by herself? If you didn't say anything, she might

be hurt because you kept information from her. However, if you did say something, she might side with her husband and criticize you for being jealous. Dillard (1989) stated that people will communicate their opinions about relationships in a more direct way. In addition, they are more likely to be positive and use rational, valid appeals. Do you agree with Dillard? Think of a time when you discussed relationships with a friend or loved one. Did you use a rational and valid argument? Did the other person react in a rational way?

VERBAL POWER PLAYS

Most people think that persuasion in interpersonal relationships is strictly verbal (Guerrero et al., 2011), but it can be nonverbal as well. You will learn about nonverbal aspects of power later in this chapter; however, in this section you will review some of the verbal power plays people use when interacting with others.

Studies in persuasion have shown that individuals use a variety of strategies to get their partners to do something (Guerrero, 1996). Do you do a friend a favor in the hopes that he can return it later? Or do you simply come out and ask him to do something for you? These are known as **compliance-gaining strategies**. Competent communicators have many methods for obtaining compliance. You might be thinking, how can I gain compliance from others? Let's take a look at a few methods.

Direct Requests

A very obvious way that you can get others to comply is to simply ask for their compliance, or use a **direct request**. Direct requests are used by men and women equally. Typically, the person who feels more support and power in the relationship will use a direct request. Asking a person for a ride to the airport is an example of a direct request. Studies have shown that satisfying romantic relationships use more direct requests than unsatisfying relationships. Do you think married couples use more direct requests in their relationships compared to dating couples? When might a direct request be improper or not well received?

Bargaining

Another verbal ploy that people use is bargaining. **Bargaining** is consenting to do something in exchange for something else. For instance, you may be more likely to give up taking a dream job at another location so that you can stay closer to loved ones. Individuals who use this technique will often bring up past favors and/or debts in order to get what they want. Research has shown that more powerful individuals are less likely to use this ploy. Would Alyssa asking Gavin to do the dishes in exchange for a nice dinner be considered bargaining?

Aversive Stimulation

In **aversive stimulation,** individuals cry, complain, sulk, or pout in order to get what they want (Infante, Chandler, & Rudd, 1989). Individuals who use this attempt believe that the receiver will be more likely to give in to stop the annoying behavior. Small children tend to use this behavior, because they have not mastered the other strategies. This strategy is often irritating and unpleasant, but it's generally quite effective. It is not limited to small children however. Have you had a friend, sibling, or loved one use this strategy on you? Was it effective, or was it unattractive to you?

Ingratiation

When people "kiss up" to others to get what they want, they are using **ingratiation.** For instance, you may be more likely to bend over backwards for your boss so that you will get a raise. Another example is being really nice to a friend so that she will do something for you in return. There are times when partners may use **illicit ingratiation,** which is just acting nice, but not being sincere, so that the other person will comply. This strategy is effective only if the other person perceives the act as genuine (Huston, Surra, Fitzgerald, & Cate, 1981). Do you think this is effective in the workplace? If Gavin began to flirt with his female boss to get the vacation time he wanted, would this be an example of illicit ingratiation?

Indirect Requests

Indirect requests are sometimes classified as *hinting*, because the request maker does not directly let the other person know what she wants (McAdams, 1985). Rather, her goal will be implied. For instance, Alyssa might tell Gavin she is really hungry rather than suggesting that they go out for dinner. This strategy is considered polite. However, sometimes it is not very effective because it assumes that the receiver will be able to interpret the implication. How have indirect requests worked for you in current and previous relationships?

Moral Appeals

Moral appeals are attempts to imply that a righteous or moral person would comply with the request. Parents often use this strategy to reinforce positive behavior with their children. However, "goodness" is based on the receiver's perception. This strategy can lead to conflict, because the receiver may feel like the attempt is a personal attack (Sabourin & Stamp,

1995). If a friend asked you to go to his church under the guise of it being good for you, how would you perceive his request?

Manipulation

Manipulation is using strategies that make the other person feel negatively, such as shame, jealousy, or guilt. For instance, Alyssa may go on a romantic date with someone else in order to make Gavin jealous. These strategies may be ineffective, because receivers typically do not respond well to manipulation (Babcock, Waltz, Jacobson, & Gottman, 1993). Manipulation can often make matters worse. Hence, Gavin could possibly break up with Alyssa because he may feel that she doesn't value their current relationship. Can you think of any examples where manipulation can be beneficial to a relationship?

Deception

Ethical Connection

What if you found out that a friend of yours was lying to her significant other about a pregnancy in order to get married? What would you do?

Sometimes people may lie just, or use **deception,** to get what they want (Cupach & Spitzberg, 1994). For instance, Gavin might tell Alyssa that their anniversary gift is very special and needs extra time to be shipped rather than telling her he forgot to get a gift. There are some ethical issues with this strategy. On one hand, the deception might keep Alyssa from having her feelings hurt. On the other hand, if Alyssa finds out about the deception, it can create problems of trust in their relationship. Have you ever deceived someone you were in a relationship with to spare his or her feelings?

Distributive Communication

Distributive communication includes strategies that insult, hurt, or blame the partner in order to gain compliance (Sagrestano, Heavey, & Christensen, 1999). Research has shown that both men and women engage in these behaviors. However, these behaviors are also likely to result in conflict. Suppose Gavin reminds Alyssa about the time she forgot to eat dinner with him at his parents' house, and then asks her to help buy a gift for them. While this strategy might work, it could also make Alyssa feel resentful towards Gavin for bringing up the earlier incident. Always be careful when using distributive communication with a relational partner.

Threats

Threats are strategies to bully and/or terrorize others in order to make them comply. People use threats when they believe the other person is less

PERSUASION RESEARCH SNAPSHOT

Interpersonal communication covers a wide variety of topics, but dating and relationships are a unique aspect of communication where we tend to be more persuasive than normal. Think about this: Would you consider dating someone you met online? Although this is an off-putting subject for many people, online dating has become increasingly popular in recent years. Seventeen percent of couples who married last year met online, and the online dating business is now worth over $4 billion worldwide. Why have online dating sites like eHarmony® become so popular? Or, maybe more importantly, why have they become so effective?

Online communication has surged in popularity over recent years thanks to the rise of social networking sites such as Facebook. More than ever, computer-mediated communication (CMC) is an effective communication tool, both for socializing and dating. But how do we use CMC to persuade someone to date us? Any relationship, whether it starts online or offline, begins by reducing uncertainty about the other person and self-disclosing information. Previous research indicates that it is easier to disclose information about yourself in an online setting compared to face-to-face interactions. Does this make it easier to meet prospective dating partners online?

In a recent study, researchers Jennifer Gibbs, Nicole Ellison, and Chih-Hui Lai looked at uncertainty reduction strategies and self-disclosure in online dating. The researchers used uncertainty reduction theory (URT) to frame the study. Basically, URT focuses on how we self-disclose personal information to reduce uncertainty about another individual in an attempt to increase social attraction. The authors wanted to investigate online relationships and the issues of privacy concerns, uncertainty reduction behaviors, and self-disclosure. They gave a survey to 592 participants who were all active subscribers to at least one dating site. The type of information disclosed and the degree of uncertainty reduction were analyzed from the findings.

The research showed that different uncertainty reduction strategies were used based on three different online dating concerns: personal security, misrepresentation, and recognition. Basically, these three concerns framed the way participants went about disclosing information about themselves. The more concerned participants were about these issues, the less likely they were willing to disclose personal information to another person. In addition, participants were generally more likely to ask questions about thoughts and feelings as a way to reduce uncertainty, as opposed to giving information about their house or job. In this way participants were able to reduce uncertainty without giving away critical information that could embarrass or harm them.

Do you find it easier to talk about personal information online compared to face-to-face? Sometimes the degree of anonymity CMC offers us

(continued)

makes it easier to talk about things we would rather not in a physical setting. Think about this and relate it to the dramatic increase in online dating over recent years. Do you see this as a passing trend or a new way to begin relationships in our society?

Do you want to know more about this study? If so, read: Gibbs, J. L., Ellison, N. B., & Lai, C. (2011). First comes love, then comes Google: An investigation of uncertainty reduction strategies and self-disclosure in online dating. *Communication Research, 38*(1), 70–100.

powerful. Men and women use threats equally. Threats by one individual can lead to threats by the other as well. If Alyssa threatens Gavin by withholding sex from him, and Gavin responds by threatening to terminate the relationship, does it seem possible that either person will receive what he or she wants?

8.3 REMEMBER

compliance-gaining	strategies to get others to do what we want
direct request	simply asking for something in a straightforward manner
bargaining	consenting to do something in exchange for something else
aversive stimulation	when individuals cry, complain, sulk, or pout in order to get what they want
ingratiation	"kissing up" to others to get what you want
illicit ingratiation	being nice, but not sincere, just to get what you want
indirect request	hinting
moral appeal	implying that a moral person would comply with your request
manipulation	making the other person feel ashamed, jealous, or guilty
deception	lying
distributive communication	insulting, hurting, or blaming others
threats	bullying others

NONVERBAL BEHAVIORS THAT INCREASE POWER

Even though individuals may use verbal ploys in order to get what they want, it has been shown that **nonverbal messages**—communication other than written or spoken language that creates meaning for someone—are also quite powerful (Guerrero et al., 2011; Ivy & Wahl, 2009). Think about animals; they do not have a universal verbal code. Animals have nonverbal displays to let other animals know that they might engage in conflict. There are many ways in which power can be communicated nonverbally. Have you ever had a romantic partner give you the "cold shoulder"? What are some other nonverbal cues that people use to portray their feelings?

Physical Appearance

Research has shown that attractive people are more persuasive than less attractive people. Attractive people are more likely to be forgiven and be seen as more powerful. Formal dress (i.e., suit and tie for men, tailored suit for women) also tends to give a more powerful perception; there are studies that show expensive shoes give the impression of more power (Andersen, 2008). Dress can affect how men and women are perceived. In the business and professional arenas, there tend to be more standards for how men should dress than for women. However, if a woman dresses too provocatively, then there is a decrease in perceptions of power. Does this double standard apply in all situations, or can you think of some exceptions?

Andersen noted that muscular, fit body types have been linked to perceptions of power. Guerrero and Floyd (2006) defined **principle of elevation** as how a person's height can affect perceptions of power. Think about how the taller presidential candidate usually wins. Also, think about how court judges will typically be elevated to show more power. Do you perceive tall people to be more threatening, commanding, or confident when you first meet them? It is important to note that perceptions of power are usually critical only at the beginning of a relationship. The effects of physical appearance on power will change once the individuals interact more with each other.

Spatial Behavior

Another nonverbal factor that has an impact on power is the way that we use space in interpersonal relationships. Most people will interact at an appropriate distance from each other. However, we are more likely to invade another person's space if we want to show dominance or more power. Two examples would be a parent who wants to talk to his child about troublesome behavior or a boss who wants to reprimand her employee. On the other hand, allowing more distance between yourself and someone else could indicate that you do not want to increase contact with that person. It may appear rude, but at the same time, it also might make that person perceive you as more powerful. Space can also communicate affection or disinterest. If Alyssa and Gavin are sitting knee-to-knee, would you assume that they are very affectionate towards each other?

Eye Behavior

People in our culture value eye contact. Studies have indicated that we are more likely to perceive people as more powerful if they provide more eye contact while speaking. This principle is called **visual centrality**. In other words, you increase perceptions of power when you increase the amount of eye contact you give while talking. However, direct eye contact can often be viewed as dominating and threatening. Hence, there must be a balance in terms of how much eye contact you give someone. This is known as the **visual dominance ratio,** which is a mathematical calculation of speaking time with eye contact divided over listening time with eye contact. If the score is high, it suggests dominance; if the score is low, it indicates submissiveness or weakness. When Alyssa talks with her boss, do you think her eye contact will be different with him than it will be with Gavin? What is she communicating to her boss if she uses significant eye contact?

Body Movements

Some body movements can convey higher status and more power. For instance, hands placed on the hips can indicate a very dominant position. Powerful people tend to have a more relaxed nonverbal style (Andersen,

8.4 REMEMBER

nonverbal messages	communication other than written or spoken language that creates meaning for someone
principle of elevation	idea that height influences perception of power
visual centrality	increasing perceptions of power by providing more eye contact
visual dominance ratio	ratio of speaking time with eye contact divided by listening time with eye contact

2008). Moreover, the way individuals use gestures can show confidence, which increases perceptions of power. Facial expressions can also communicate power. Smiles are seen as friendly but do not necessarily suggest power. Rather, frowns and sneers are viewed as expressions that powerful people use in their interactions. Think about any time you have talked to a police officer or a judge. Did you feel he had less power if he smiled and behaved informally with you?

Touch

Touch can be a very affectionate type of behavior. However, it can be a gesture of power, because usually a person who touches another has more authority and/or power. Beware of inappropriate touching, which can be perceived as sexual harassment or assault. Even if the toucher has good intentions, if the receiver of the touch views it negatively, then it can be classified as harassment. Touch in interpersonal relationships has been associated with relationship satisfaction, conflict, and quality. Hence, we must be aware of how touch is perceived by others. The type of touch you give a lover will be perceived differently when used on a coworker.

Voice

Research has indicated that more powerful people speak with better diction and articulation (Andersen, 2008). Moreover, they tend to use fewer vocal fillers and pauses. Male voices are seen as more powerful than female voices due to pitch differences. Also, people who speak faster are seen as more powerful, because people often associate speech rate with cognitive ability rate. Confidence and power can be perceived in how we use our voices and vocal tones with other people. Have you ever had a professor who stuttered or spoke in a low, mumbling voice? Did you find him less convincing and credible than some of your other professors?

In Your Life
Do you think verbal power ploys are better than nonverbal displays of power? Why or why not? Can you think of some recent power ploys that others have used on you? Were they successful? What made these requests successful—the verbal or nonverbal aspects?

Artifacts

Items that powerful people possess usually speak volumes. When we see a person with a fancy car or mansion, we assume that she must have money, and at the same time, power. These status symbols may take the form of larger offices or better parking places. Giving valuable artifacts to others can denote power as well. If Alyssa gave Gavin a very expensive watch for his birthday, do you think that might affect Gavin's perception of Alyssa's power?

PERSUASION AND POWER ACROSS INTERPERSONAL RELATIONSHIPS

Think of your interpersonal relationships. Oftentimes, power is an integral part of these relationships. Sometimes one person has more power than the other person. These power plays exist in our family relationships, romantic relationships, and our friendships with others. Remember that the balance of power can always change. As you get older, your parents' power over you can diminish. On the other hand, a lover's power can grow as you become more intimate with each other. It is vital to keep these power changes in mind as you navigate your different relationships.

Family

In a family, parents will usually have more power than their children. Parents are responsible for making decisions about their children and typically have a great deal of control over them. Parents may use a variety of incentives to influence their child's behavior, such as money, guilt, or punishment. While there are many different incentives or punishments that parents can use, their use of incentives or punishments typically falls into the three categories discussed below.

Baumrind (1971, 1991) explained that there are three main perspectives to parenting: authoritative, permissive, and authoritarian. First, **authoritative** parents are the happy medium between being too strict and too lenient. They set rules, but also allow for some flexibility. Second, **permissive** parents allow their children to do what they want. They are nondirective and undemanding with their children and are more likely to be a buddy to their child. Third, **authoritarian** parents are demanding and nonresponsive. They have set codes of conduct and do not believe that children should be allowed to question their parents.

When children get older, they deal with a phase called **separation and individuation,** which is when the child, usually a teen, tries to create some boundaries for his or her own identity separate from the ones developed by the parents (Baxter, Braithwaite, & Nicholson, 1999). During this period in the child's life, there may be more tension and power struggles in the relationship. The best parent-child relationships are ones where power among all members becomes more supported. In other words, the child respects the parents (and vice versa), which creates a more loving climate. Can you think of times growing up where you ran into conflict with your parents regarding your independence or privileges?

Marriage

Power struggles not only exist in families but in marriages as well (Guerrero et al., 2011). It has been shown that when there is mutual respect and a perception of equality, there are higher levels of satisfaction. This is especially true for dating relationships and friendships (Duck & Wood, 1995). However, satisfaction may be harder to achieve in marriages, where people have to share finances, children, and tasks. According to Fitzpatrick (1988) there are three marriage types: traditional, independents, and separates. First, **traditional** marriages are those in which the male is the breadwinner of the family. The wife usually stays home with the children and does not make major decisions for the family. It has been shown that these marriages have lower levels of conflict. Second, **independents** have nonconventional beliefs about marriage. They are psychologically close, but not physically close. They do not avoid conflict because they share everything. Third, **separates** have a higher need for autonomy. They tend to have large amounts of physical and psychological distance. In turn, they tend to avoid conflict. Overall, the different marital types have different conflict and persuasive behaviors in their relationships (Graham, 1997). Given what we know about Alyssa and Gavin, what type of marital relationship do you think they would have?

Power and persuasion are evident in interpersonal relationships. Just as in our example of Gavin and Alyssa, we have to make decisions that may impact our relationships with others. Persuasion and power are also based on other people's perceptions. These perceptions can be achieved through verbal and nonverbal means.

8.5 REMEMBER

authoritative	a combination of authoritarian and permissive
permissive	nondirective and undemanding
authoritarian	demanding and nonresponsive
separation and individuation	when a child, usually a teen, tries to create some boundaries for his or her own identity separate from the ones developed by the parents
traditionals	couples with a traditional view of marriage
independents	couples who have nonconventional beliefs about marriage
separates	couples who have a higher need for autonomy

Remember: You can use your knowledge of persuasion to engage real-life situations. Consider the scenario below and think about what you would do as you apply your study of the persuasive dimensions of interpersonal communication.

You're fresh out of college and in the market for employment. Upon completing several interviews with multiple employers, you decide to accept an offer as an account manager at a reputable company in a larger city. The first person you meet is your boss who shows immediate interest in you, and you receive a promotion within 2 months. Many of your colleagues begin treating you differently, and it's rumored that you are sleeping with the boss and this is the only reason for your success. You schedule a meeting with your boss to discuss these issues. During the meeting, your boss makes a pass at you and confesses feelings for you. You wish to keep this job—you changed your whole life for this opportunity. How might you use persuasion and what you've learned in this chapter to maintain and improve the interpersonal relationships you hold with your colleagues as well as your boss? What would you do?

SUMMARY

This chapter has connected interpersonal communication to your study of persuasion. After reading this chapter, you should be mindful of how to evaluate your power in your relationships and the influence of both verbal and nonverbal communication. The example of Gavin and Alyssa shows us that married couples, partners, and friends use persuasion in relationships. Hopefully this chapter prompted you to think about your own relationships. How do you use persuasion in your own relationships? What are the topics? What are your techniques?

DISCUSSION QUESTIONS

Interpersonal

1. What are some tactics people use to exert interpersonal influence on friends and loved ones when it comes to interpersonal issues?
2. What are interpersonal power principles?
3. How does a relationship concept relate to power?
4. What are verbal influence strategies? Which ones are most effective?
5. What are nonverbal influence strategies? Which ones are most effective?

Persuasive Dimensions of Nonverbal Communication 9

YOUR OBJECTIVES

After studying this chapter, you should be able to:

1. Define nonverbal communication and connect it to your study of persuasion.
2. Explain how the nonverbal code of environment can be persuasive.
3. Understand Sheldon's Body Types.
4. Evaluate facial and eye behavior, for they connect to your study of persuasion.
5. Apply the nonverbal dimensions of persuasion to real-life situations.

Nonverbal

Imagine this: You just walked into your friend Jake's house in the middle of July. You see food all over the grimy kitchen counters and observe that the thermostat reads 81 degrees and there are dirty clothes scattered about the rooms amongst plastic cups and empty pizza boxes. You hear Jake belch and yell out from the other room to grab him a soda. When you walk into Jake's room, you see him standing in the corner with unwashed hair, wearing a holey shirt and grungy sweatpants. He reaches out to give you a one-armed hug as he grabs the soda can out of your hand and slouches down into his chair.

NONVERBAL COMMUNICATION AS PERSUASION

The nonverbal cues you are presented with in Jake's house provide a variety of ways you can choose to interpret or be persuaded by your interaction. **Nonverbal communication** includes all the ways to communicate without using words. What you wear and how you look, move, and gesture and your facial and eye expressions are all included in these kinds of messages. Therefore, the persuasive power of nonverbal communication is important to study. As you focus on the persuasive dimensions of nonverbal communication in this chapter, keep the following questions in mind: How can nonverbal cues persuade others? What counts as nonverbal communication and how can that impact persuasion and influence? What are the specific codes (categories) of nonverbal communication connected to the study of persuasion?

Nonverbal messages are persuasive because they communicate feelings and attitudes. When looking at old photos or videotapes of people in different moods and situations, the simplest nonverbal actions can be quite revealing. Perhaps you are reviewing a store video camera after there has been a robbery. The only way the shoplifter can be identified is through nonverbal cues such as reaching out to grab something and hiding it in a jacket or looking around to make sure that no one is watching. When looking at photo albums of family reunions, you can usually tell that the people who are smiling and have their arms around each other are happy to be there; however, a child with his arms crossed, staring off into the distance, would display that he was not enjoying himself and would rather be somewhere else.

Nonverbal messages are persuasive because they're more believable than verbal messages. Perhaps you're a receptionist for a big financial company. Job interviews are being held for a new vice president position in your office, and you are signing everyone in. The first person comes to the interview in what looks like an uncomfortable suit, sweating and tapping his foot annoyingly, with his eyes glued to the clock. You tell him not to be nervous and he replies, "Oh, I'm not nervous at all." In this instance, the nonverbal cues would be much more powerful than the verbal message given to you. Would you be persuaded that this job candidate is not nervous? This situation embodies the famous quote, "Actions speak louder than words."

There is an extensive list of ways in which you can present ideas or actions in an influential and persuasive way. This chapter explores nonverbal persuasive messages that are communicated through nonverbal codes (e.g., environments and surroundings, use of space, physical appearance, body movements and gestures, facial and eye expressions, touch). Before you begin exploring the persuasive power of environment, take a moment to review the Persuasion Research Snapshot to connect your study of persuasion to nonverbal communication.

 PERSUASION RESEARCH SNAPSHOT

Think about it. Have you ever felt connected to a speaker when she was delivering a message but you were not paying full attention to her words? Instead, did you focus on her physical appearance, how she smelled, or her hand gestures? Was the persuader's message made even more effective through nonverbal communication?

Indeed, nonverbal communication plays a major role in how we interpret a persuader's message. When you listen to a speech as an audience member, you tune into many aspects that influence your perception of the speaker and whether or not you are persuaded. For instance, speech rate is critical in determining how confident the speaker seems. If she speaks too slowly, this might be seen as a lack of self-assurance. On the other hand, if the persuader speaks at a faster, firmer rate, you would see them as more confident and maybe even more knowledgeable. Think about what initially impacts you as an audience member. Did the speaker's straight posture catch your eye and make you feel that she was credible and therefore worthy of your time?

In a 2008 study, researchers Joseph Cesario and E. Tory Higgins looked at whether nonverbal cues affected the effectiveness of a message and whether they could be used as a persuasion technique. To better understand their findings, they used regulatory-fit theory as a framework. This theory focuses on the receiver's discernment of an activity and his or her place in that activity. Different behavioral strategies are observed to learn which are most beneficial to the activity. The researchers wanted to find out: Can the persuader use nonverbal communication as a tool to connect with the audience in a way that makes the receivers find a "fit" with the intended message? The key here is to think about the speaker trying to make the audience connect with the message through nonverbal cues. Participants were seated in a room in which they watched two videos of the same teacher delivering a speech on implementing an after-school program for children. In one video,

(continued)

the teacher was eager and excited when presenting his argument, which was evident mainly through his hand gestures and rate of speech. In the second video, the teacher was more laid-back and relaxed.

This study revealed that an eager style of message delivery had a positive impact on message effectiveness. It also supported the regulatory-fit theory that message effectiveness is increased when the audience members feel like they connect with the message. It is best to think of the findings of this study in two parts. First, nonverbal cues enhanced the receivers' understanding and the effectiveness of the speaker's message. Second, when the audience members felt the message was effective, they had an increased emotion of feeling of identifying with the message.

Making a connection and fitting it to what is being said is essential to everyday persuasion. Next time you listen to someone deliver a speech, be aware of other ways that he is communicating to you. Does an immense amount of pauses reflect his nervousness? Does his long hair make him seem more liberal? What speaks most to you?

Do you want to know more about this study? If so, read: Cesario, J., & Higgins, E. (2008). Making message recipients "feel right": How nonverbal cues can increase persuasion. *Psychological Science, 19*, 415–420.

ENVIRONMENT

Think back to the example of Jake's house. How did the different environmental factors persuade your opinion? Upon entering the house, you might automatically form an idea about Jake. The **environment**—the built or natural surroundings that serve as the context in which people interact—created by Jake might persuade you that he is not a clean person or would not be a good roommate. Environments lead to **impression management,** the formation of an impression, perception, or view of another (Goffman, 1971; Harris & Sachau, 2005). The choices you make about the environment that you live or work in reveal a good deal about who you are and aid in creating your impression management. Also, your nonverbal communication is altered by the environment in which you find yourself. Your nonverbal messages, for example, would most likely be different while you're in Jake's house talking about last night's game than they would be if you were at your parents' house, having dinner and talking about the game.

This is not to suggest that people with messy offices or houses are bad people. In fact, some of your best professors probably have messy offices. On the other hand, many professors' offices are extremely comfortable, warm, and inviting. The point is that the environments created in offices, homes, and so on establish comfortable or uncomfortable communication contexts

Social Media in Your Life: Have You Seen This?

Go to YouTube and enter the following keywords: hoarders, hoarding

This video clip demonstrates the nonverbal code of environment. What does the living environment of the people featured in the show tell you about them?

that influence our perceptions of safety and comfort, as well as of the attitude and character of the persons inhabiting the space (Bowen & Kilmann, 1975; Holley & Steiner, 2005; McCroskey & McVetta, 1978). These attributes could have a profound impact on the persuasiveness of an environment.

Formality

We as communicators usually use words like "stuffy" and "serious" or "relaxed" and "casual" to explain our perception of the formality of an environment. Think of where you like to go eat. Why do you go there? Is it only for the food? Or do the energy, server uniforms, and music persuade you to go there? Places like sports bars and nightclubs usually offer a "loud" environment to give the impression of being fun, laid-back places. In this way, they are trying to persuade you to buy into the lifestyle of the establishment. How about the types of clothes you wear? Do you wear nice denim jeans and a polo shirt most of the time? Or do you prefer an old T-shirt and some cutoff shorts with flip-flops? You choose your clothing to indicate similarity with others, because perceived similarity persuades others that you are like them and therefore likeable and trustworthy.

Think of the different kinds of bars in your college town. In some bars, you would wear cowboy boots, jeans, and a button-up shirt and expect to be two-stepping to loud country music all night long. At a different bar up the street, you might see people wearing gothic makeup and baggy black clothes and listening to metal music. On the corner could be a lounge with an older crowd sipping wine and smoking cigars while listening to soft jazz. There is a different level of formality to each one of these places, which would persuade you to dress a certain way or expect a certain thing when going to one rather than the other.

Color

Researchers have generally categorized colors as being either warm (e.g., red, orange, yellow) or cool (e.g., blue, green). They have found that warm colors are more arousing and, in some cases, more stressful, than cool colors, which are viewed as relaxing and less stressful (Bellizzi, Crowley, & Hasty, 1983). The color—including the hue, saturation, and brightness—of a certain place, magazine ad, or outfit is usually intentionally chosen to persuade people to feel a certain way. Think about why red is such a common theme in bars and restaurants. Behavioral studies have suggested that seeing the color red leads to a heightened sense of awareness and makes us more likely to act on impulses and be more aggressive. The color persuades you to be more aggressive in spending your money, and it has also been shown to persuade people to leave earlier. In places like restaurants, where customer turnover is an important factor, this makes the color red very appealing. On the other hand, many customer service areas in retail stores are accented with solid blue colors. The color blue has been shown to have a calming effect on people, which would be useful to businesses dealing with potentially irate customers. Blue backgrounds can persuade customers to be more calm and cooperative when dealing with refunds and returns.

Lighting

Lighting also shapes your perceptions of an environment, which influence how you communicate and how you are persuaded in that environment. Have you ever been pulled over by a police officer at night? If you have, chances are you had a very bright flashlight shining into your eyes. Officers use this tactic much in the same way police interrogators use bright lights when questioning people. The bright light makes you uncomfortable and less likely to focus on elaborate lies or other details. Pleasant or not, the light persuades you to be honest.

Sound

Noise impacts environment by influencing the way you feel, what you say, and your desire to stay or leave. Think of being at a dance club on a hot summer weekend night. You have two groups of friends there and you've decided to go meet up with both of them. One group is sitting right next to the stage with the live band's speaker pointed directly at the table. The other group of friends is sitting closer to the back, far away from the dance floor and stage. The band that evening plays a lot of country music, which you can't stand. Chances are, your dislike for that music is going to persuade you to sit with your friends who are farther away from the stage. Many bars and clubs use sound to persuade a certain demographic to go there. There are country-themed bars, metal-themed bars, and hip-hop-themed nightclubs. Another good example of persuasive noise is a spa. Spas generally play slower-paced music to help you relax. How would you feel going into a massage if the masseuse had heavy metal playing in the background?

Let's turn to another example. Chelsea and Brandon are a newly married couple searching for their first home, and they've narrowed it down to two choices. The first choice, Chelsea's favorite, is across the street from an elementary school. Chelsea, being an elementary school teacher, finds the house to be conveniently located and extremely comfortable. Brandon, who works at home, would prefer not to live there because of the screams and yells coming from the children across the street before and after school and

In Your Life

Can you think of a time when an environment's smell impacted your ideas or perceptions of a person or a place? Did the smell persuade you to stay or to leave, to find the person less credible or more interesting?

during recess. The second house, Brandon's favorite, is located behind a country music venue. Brandon enjoys the idea of this house because he can walk across the street during the evening after a day of working at home and enjoy listening to his favorite bands with friends. Chelsea isn't too fond of this house because she has to wake up early every morning and go to work. It's hard for her to sleep with country music blaring through her bedroom wall each night. The sounds associated with these houses influence Chelsea and Brandon in different ways.

Smell

A pleasant smell is something that many of us spend a good part of our day maintaining. Each day, Americans take baths and showers, deodorize, brush, floss, gargle, wipe, sanitize, and freshen to cover up natural body odors. If smell wasn't important, people wouldn't buy so many toiletry products and go through all of these activities.

Imagine this: Lauren and Jordan have been hanging out for a couple weeks. They've been on a few dates and talk on the phone every night. Jordan finally asks Lauren if she wants to come over to his house to watch a movie. Lauren anxiously gets ready by putting on her makeup, fixing her hair, and spraying her favorite perfume on her neck and wrists. When Jordan comes to pick up Lauren at her house, she notices that he smells amazing. She gets into his truck and smells the same smell of cologne and car air freshener. Throughout their blooming relationship, Jordan has told Lauren about his dogs and how much he loves them. It isn't until they open up the door to Jordan's house that Lauren realizes just how much he loves them. She is automatically overwhelmed by the smell of pet odor. Although the house looks fairly clean and free from dust and trash, the smell makes it seem filthy. The smell of the house impacts Lauren's opinion of Jordan, whether consciously or unconsciously. She might choose to continue dating him only if he only comes to her house or insist that he keep his animals outside and steam-clean the carpets.

On a more positive note, consider all of the perfume advertisements placed in magazines. You might find up to three different pages of advertisements for different perfumes and colognes throughout a magazine, each with its own little flap for your smelling pleasure. Why do companies pay so much to place these alluring ads in magazines? The smells coming from these pages impact your ideas about their product and form associations about its smell. Perhaps these advertisements are paired with pictures of beautiful young adults in order to convey the message that you will feel more sexy or attractive if you use the product.

Temperature

Factors that help create temperatures, such as weather, climate, barometric pressure, and seasons, all have an effect on us (Anderson & Anderson, 1984; Baron, 1972; Griffit, 1970). How does temperature influence your behavior and thoughts? Think about a job that requires you to move around a great deal. Warm environments can make people feel lethargic or physically drained. If your employer kept your workplace temperature a little too cold for comfort, it would most likely persuade you to move around more and work harder. Temperature is something you feel, regardless of persuasion. However, it is possible to manipulate temperature to gain a desired effect in some people. The cold workplace is one example; how could your professors be using temperature to influence the classroom?

Researchers have given specific attention to temperature and climate and have generated the following list of related behavioral changes (Knapp & Hall, 2006):

1. During the summer, people spend more time with friends.
2. During the summer, assault and rape crimes increase.
3. From July to November, people tend to report less happiness but more activity and less boredom.
4. People use the phone less in the summer than in the winter.

All of the environmental attributes you've studied contribute to the way a certain context can persuade you to feel. Each has a different way of influencing your emotions and feelings. The next section explains ways that spatial distance can impact your thoughts and mind-set in any given situation.

PROXEMICS

"You're in my bubble!"

"Get out of my face."

"He was all up on me."

When you think about these statements, do you imagine someone violating your personal space? All of these statements relate to the proxemic aspect of nonverbal communication. **Proxemics** is defined as the way that distance and space play a communicative role in our everyday life, or how we use physical space and spatial zones. Proxemics is an important nonverbal communication cue because your preferences regarding distance and space reveal a good deal about who you are as a person. Both your verbal and nonverbal messages are impacted by distance and space, and you use metaphors of distance and space to talk about your interpersonal relationships.

Anthropologist Edwin T. Hall (1959, 1968, 1983) has helped us understand proxemics by providing a classification of spatial zones, sometimes referred to as *conversational distances*. Hall's first zone is **intimate space**. This zone measures zero to 1½ feet between communicators and is usually reserved for those emotionally close to us, such as spouses, sexual partners, or dear friends. Intimate space might be used by a close friend whispering to another about a man sitting in front of them at the movie theater. This distance is also used in romantic relationships, when partners whisper about private matters not intended for others to hear. These messages usually aren't questioned; therefore, persuasion may not occur.

The second zone is **personal space**—from 1½ to 4 feet of space between communicators. Personal space can be used in relaxed situations among friends, family, or colleagues. The matter of discussion is usually not private and the conversation and interaction are less structured. Communication at this distance does not allow for either person to give a speech or for the conversation to be one-sided. Hall's third zone, **social space,** is 4 to 12 feet of distance between communicators. Social space is used in most formal situations, such as in professional life and in most educational contexts. Persuaders aren't overfriendly in conversations; however, they are not opposed to feedback or interaction. An interview or business meeting is an example of a situation that might involve social space. The fourth and final zone is **public space**—12 feet and beyond. The type of persuasion used in public space must be formal, as there is little interaction with or room for response from the audience.

Why do you stand a certain distance from people in conversation? Are you perfectly comfortable in the middle seat in an airplane, with a stranger on either side of you? Why might you cozy up to one person, but keep your distance from another? Why do some people get too close in conversation, while others seem to stay farther away than you're used to? According to research, certain factors influence how you manage your own personal space and how you use proxemics when you relate to other people in everyday life (Sommer, 2002).

Cultural Background

Cultural background is a key factor that contributes to our understanding of nonverbal cues. Let's consider two appealing studies to help illustrate this point. One line of research examined the use of space in Japan, which

Intimate Space
1½ feet between communicators

Personal Space
1½ to 4 feet between communicators

Social Space
4 to 12 feet between communicators

Public Space
12 feet and beyond

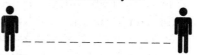

FIGURE 9.1 Hall's Zones of Space

9.1 REMEMBER

nonverbal communication	all the ways to communicate without words
environment	the built or natural surroundings that serve as the context in which people interact
impression management	the formation of an impression, perception, or view of another
proxemics	the way that distance and space play a communicative role in our everyday lives, or how we use our physical space and spatial zones
intimate space	zone measuring zero to 1½ feet between communicators
personal space	zone measuring 1½ to 4 feet between communicators
social space	zone measuring 4 to 12 feet between communicators
public space	zone between communicators measuring 12 feet and beyond

contains dense urban areas in which space is at a premium (Altman, 1975). In Japanese culture, specific types of spaces are given specific meanings because of the value placed on space. For example, street intersections are named rather than streets, because intersections are more important in Japanese daily life than streets. Rooms are identified according to their function, with structures built to enhance a room's functionality, such as movable walls and room dividers that can transform a space. The research also examined the Japanese people's tendency to miniaturize objects, producing such things as bonsai plants, because of their cultural sense of space. As a second example, Hall (1966) observed Arab cultures for their use of proxemics, noting significant differences between how Arabs and Westerners view public space and conversational distance. Arabs do not seek privacy in public space, preferring to converse intimately in public and viewing less-than-intimate conversations as rude behavior. The intimate behaviors include close distances between people, direct and continuous eye contact, and frequent touch.

Think about how these cultural distances can impact persuasion. In a Japanese-American business deal, can accommodating a Japanese business-man's idea of personal space have a positive impact on the negotiation? What about the Middle East peace process? How could lack of understanding of proxemics send an aggressive or destructive message to Arab diplomats?

Think about your cultural background and how it impacts persuasion in your life. Perhaps you and your best friend come from different cultural backgrounds. How do you use space differently to persuade each other? When you are trying to convince him to go with you to your family reunion, do you stand close and whisper in his ear? Or do you act as if it is a normal, everyday conversation and stand at a social distance while asking him? Is your persuasion style associated with your cultural background?

Sex and Sexual Orientation

Sex and sexual orientation can also have an effect on communication style and use of proxemics. Think about the difference between women and men in the amount of space between them that is acceptable. It seems to be socially appropriate in U.S. culture for women to sit next to each other at a movie theater, bar, or restaurant. With men, however, some social force seems to exist that tells them it's less than appropriate to sit right next to each other (Ivy & Wahl, 2009). Men can and do sit this way, but it may cause some discomfort or lead men to feel that they have to joke their way through the behavior. Why is it that if a group of men go to see a movie together, they usually sit with at least one seat between them?

The primary explanation for men's spatial behavior relates to homophobia—a fear of being perceived as or labeled gay. Most women

In Your Life

People from different cultures often have different nonverbal ways of greeting one another. What examples have you personally experienced? Do these different ways of greeting have an impact on how you feel about people from these different cultures?

don't have to deal with this perception, because the scope of acceptance about women's behavior tends to be wider than about men's. If two women sit close together in a public setting, even moving more closely to whisper to each other, most people don't observe this behavior and think, "They must be lesbians." But many men are concerned that their nonverbal behavior will persuade people to perceive them as gay. Proxemics is one of the most prominent codes that factors into such perceptions.

Status

A person's status within society also affects proxemic behavior. This happens in two ways: (1) A high-status person's use of space tends to differ from that of people with lower status, and (2) others manage space differently in a high-status person's presence. In their review of this topic, nonverbal scholars Judee Burgoon and Norah Dunbar (2006) explain:

> Powerful people have access to more space, larger territories, and more private territories, which also afford their occupants or owners great insulation from intrusion by others and more space in which to display other visible indications of their status and power. They may display more territorial markers, have easy access to others, and may have others' access regulated by gatekeepers—people such as receptionists who can prevent intrusions. In addition to access to space, dominance may also be expressed by taking up more physical space (i.e., a combination of enlarging one's size and occupying more space). (p. 289)

Would a person's status influence the way you were persuaded by her?

Higher-status people tend to operate in larger "bubbles" of personal space than lower-status people and to invade others' space more readily (Carney, Hall, & Smith LeBeau, 2005; Remland, 1981). Think about any time you have had a confrontation with bosses or authority figures. Chances are you gave them a respectable personal space when interacting with them. However, the same rules do not necessarily apply to them. A boss can invade your personal space as a gesture of dominance in an effort to persuade you to work the way she wants you to. So who seems to have the most impact and persuasive power over regular, low-status individuals? Those who hold the power and have higher statuses and bigger personal spaces most influence us.

KINESICS

Have you ever been behind your desk at work and heard footsteps coming down the hall? What went through your head? *Is that my boss? Is that a coworker? Should I stop messing around on Facebook and pull up my assignment?*

Could you tell if the person was in a good mood or bad mood? In a hurry or not? Footsteps are only one nonverbal cue within the larger category of body motion, which is one element within the larger category of nonverbal behavior known as *kinesics*. **Kinesics** is the study of human movement, gestures, and posture (Birdwhistell, 1960). The way our body moves; the way we gesture with our hands, arms, shoulders, and, occasionally, with our torso, legs, and feet; as well as how we walk, stand, and carry ourselves all provide a great deal of information about who we are. The range, intensity, or amount of body movement we have can vary and create different perceptions and persuasive messages.

When considering kinesics, we must look at a person's entire body. When people stand tall with shoulders back and chin up, they tend to exude power, strength, and dominance. When people stand closed off, with arms crossed, shoulders hunched over, and eyes on the ground, they make you believe that they probably don't want to be approached or talked to. Other examples of body language giving off nonverbal clues include cocking our head when we're confused, nodding our head when we're in agreement (or shaking our head in opposition), or putting our hands on our waist when we're fed up or annoyed.

Posture, Dominance, and Status

Let's think about posture. What can your posture say about you? What kinds of persuasive messages can be conveyed through your posture and how will people perceive you? In American culture as well as many other cultures abroad, an upright yet relaxed body posture is attached to many attractive attributes, such as confidence, positivity, and high self-esteem (Guerrero & Floyd, 2006). Perhaps in order to be a more influential persuader, you should always stand in this way. Posture can be persuasive to the extent that it includes or excludes one person relative to other people, that two people face each other directly rather than stand side to side, or that they mirror or imitate each other's behavior (Ivy & Wahl, 2009).

The relationship between posture, dominance, and status has also been the subject of much research (Aries, Gold, & Weigel, 1983; Burgoon, 1991; Carney, Hall, & Lebeau, 2005). Those with dominance and high status might puff up their chest, stiffen their back, thrust their chin forward, and lean toward others in a way that attempts to convince others of their power. As an example, imagine working for a newspaper. You are a feature writer and you have a story due today. Not only did you show up 15 minutes late to work, but you also left your notes sitting on your nightstand. Your editor won't let you go home, considering you live 20 miles away. The deadline was 10 minutes ago and you have nothing to turn in. When your boss calls you into his office to talk, what kind of stance and approach do you think he'll take?

One position that illustrates a relaxed yet dominant style and that conveys self-confidence is called the "cape and crown," which simply means lifting up the arms and placing the hands on the back of the head, sometimes in conjunction with a hip tilt. People can enact this kinesic behavior in a seated position, perhaps leaning back in a chair or with their feet elevated. The position is considered more of a male than a female behavior; however, it is quite common among female celebrities such as Beyoncé, because it conveys an "I'm in charge; I'm royalty" message (Soll, 2007, p. 18).

Walk

How you walk is also a very important nonverbal communicative act that you use to get a message across. It is also one of the most personal and long-lasting elements within your nonverbal repertoire, but it's often one of the most overlooked (Ivy & Wahl, 2009). How do you walk? Some people walk with slumped shoulders, heads down and feet close to the ground, almost shuffling. What does this kind of walk tell you about them? Some people walk with a bounce, while others seem to glide as if they were on ice. Some move their arms intensely; others don't seem to be attached to their legs at all. What about people who are pigeon-toed? Bowlegged? Knock-kneed? All of these different walking styles enable you to form certain perceptions of people. Of course, a person's culture has an effect on walking behavior. An upright carriage, with the head held high, shoulders squared, and a wide stride and a quick pace conveys confidence and positivity in American culture, but in some Asian cultures this style of walking may convey arrogance, a lack of politeness and respect for others, and lower status.

Some generalizations have been made about the sexes and their ways of walking, to the extent that some believe a person's sex can be determined by simply observing their walk. Andersen (2004) suggests that men's bodies are somewhat motionless while walking, with the hips and torso facing frontward, the feet moving about 1 foot apart in stride, and the arms swinging significantly. In contrast, Andersen explains that "women add motion to their locomotion," in that they have more swing or side-to-side motion in their walks (p. 92). Women's hips move more than men's, mostly due to the fact that women tend to put one foot in front of the other when walking, which engages the hip action.

The pace at which you walk can also portray a huge nonverbal message. For example, Heather worked her way through college by working at a restaurant. She started out as a server and was automatically a standout. She was constantly on the move, with a fast and determined walk. She eventually worked her way up to become a manager, where her duties were much less physically intense. Heather always walked with a fast pace, even if it was just in circles (which it often was), and made everyone believe that she was the hardest-working woman in the building. By moving fast, she always kept others on their toes and motivated to work just as hard as she. With this behavior, the higher-status person calls the nonverbal shots; lower-status people are expected to adapt their nonverbal communication to parallel or remain subordinate to the higher-status person's.

Gestures

Ekman and Friesen (1969) classified some nonverbal gestures that influence perceptions according to how they function in human interaction. These five categories are emblems, illustrators, affect displays, regulators, and adaptors.

Emblems, such as the American flag in the United States, have specific, widely understood meanings in a given culture and may actually substitute for a word or phrase. One gesture that has become emblematic over time is the index and middle finger up in the air, palm facing out, which could be interpreted as the number 2, as a symbol for peace, or as a V for victory. Another example of gestures that could become emblematic for a co-culture (a subgroup within a larger culture) are those made with hand and arm signals in conjunction with a college mascot or athletic team. Some of these include the "Gig 'em Aggies" gesture at Texas A&M University, the "Hook 'em Horns" gesture at the University of Texas, and the "Get your guns up" gesture made by students attending Texas Tech University. All of these gestures have other meanings than those related to their university's athletic teams.

Illustrators can complement, contradict, or accent a verbal message (Beattie & Shovelton, 1999; Streeck, 1993). Sometimes they can substitute for a verbal message, but they are usually used to aid in getting a message across. When giving someone directions, we often use our hands to aid in our description of where to go. When we tell people we are full, we often rub our bellies while doing so. These illustrators complement verbal messages. A contradictory illustrator might be yawning but telling someone we aren't tired. How many times have you seen a friend cry, but when you ask what's the matter, she says, "Nothing"? These kinds of illustrators contradict verbal messages. Ekman and Friesen's third category, **affect displays,** includes nonverbal gestures, postures, and facial expressions that communicate emotion (Ivy & Wahl, 2009). Our face tends to express which kind of emotion we're feeling, while our body reveals the intensity of the emotion we're feeling. If we're happy, for example, our face may telegraph our joy to others. The movement of our hands, the openness of our posture, and the speed with which we move tell others just how happy we are. Likewise, if we're depressed, our face likely reveals our sadness or dejection, unless we're very practiced at masking our emotions. Our slumped shoulders and lowered head indicate the intensity of our despair.

Regulators control the interaction or flow of communication between people. When we're eager to respond to a message, we're likely to make eye contact, raise our eyebrows, open our mouth, take in a breath, and lean forward slightly. When we do not want to be part of the conversation, we do the opposite: We tend to avert our eyes, close our mouth, cross our arms, and lean back in our seats or away from the verbal action.

Adaptors, the last category, help us to satisfy a personal need, cope with emotions, and adapt to the immediate situation. Think about sitting in the pew at Sunday morning church service. Perhaps the service is nearing a close and you have just finished singing a hymn. When the preacher directs you to be seated again, you sit, noticing a small vibration in the pew. You look down the row and see a man shaking his thigh vigorously, bouncing his leg up and down very quickly. There are a lot of thigh shakers out there who never even realize they do it. This helps them adapt to their current situation and fulfills their personal needs at the moment.

TOUCH

Touch is accomplished when one person's body comes into contact with another person's body. It is the only nonverbal cue in this chapter that involves physical contact. Other cues can involve physical contact, but they do not have to. Touch is the most powerful of all the codes of nonverbal

9.2 REMEMBER

kinesics	the study of human movement, gestures, and posture
emblems	widely understood meanings in a given culture that may actually substitute for a word or phrase
illustrators	complement, contradict, or accent a verbal message
affect displays	nonverbal gestures, postures, and facial expressions that communicate emotion
regulators	control the interaction or flow of communication between people
adaptors	help satisfy a personal need, cope with emotions, and adapt to the immediate situation

communication, but it is also the most misunderstood in that the sender's meaning may not correspond with the receiver's interpretation of the touch. This kind of incongruence happens frequently, in all kinds of settings and within all kinds of relationships. Sometimes a misunderstanding is small and of relatively minor consequence. Think about being on an airplane with a friend sitting to the left of you and a stranger to the right. Perhaps you've noticed the touchiness of the stranger sitting next to you. Maybe he slaps your knee or nudges your elbow in order to convey friendliness or playfulness. This could come off as offensive if you are not expecting that kind of interaction. Perhaps, while getting off the airplane, your friend playfully slaps you on the behind. To you and your friend, this might be a normal everyday thing; however, in a different situation it could come across as offensive not only to the person being touched, but also to observers.

Different areas of the body and the characteristics of the communicators' relationship can create different levels of persuasion. For example, pretend you're on a date with your boyfriend or girlfriend. You walk into a restaurant and are greeted by the host. As she motions for you to follow her, your date gently places a hand on the small of your back and directs you in front of him or her. How does this touch make you feel? What if your date had grabbed the top of your arm instead? Would you have felt differently about that touch if it had come from the host?

Types of Touch

Social psychologist Richard Heslin (1974) helps us categorize types of touch and touch behavior. He created categories that range from distant and impersonal to close and intimate types of touches. The first kind of touch, the *functional/professional* touch, serves a specific function, usually within the context of a professional relationship, and is usually low in intimacy. Social/polite touches are associated with cultural norms. These touches include handshakes, hugs, and kisses as greeting and departure rituals. These touches indicate fairly low intimacy within a relationship. Touches that are used for *friendship/warmth* are used when people show their nonromantic emotion and affection toward one another. These kinds of touches are used to show liking and connection between two people and have an impact on their relationship. They portray affection and friendship and are enacted differently across cultures. *Love/intimacy* touches are highly personal and intimate and are used to communicate strong feelings of affection toward one another. This type of touch is especially important to persuasion and influence. Hugs may last longer than normal and kisses may be on the lips rather than on the cheeks. While typically thought of as occurring in romantic relationships, these touches can also be used in other loving relationships, such as between family members. The last type of touch is for *sexual arousal*. These touches are extremely intimate and target sexual zones and regions of the body specifically for the purpose of sexual arousal. If people engaged in this kind of touching also love each other, then touches in the love/intimacy category could overlap with this category.

Persuasive messages are easily communicated through touch. Imagine this scenario: Mona and Kristy are best friends. Kristy has been begging Mona to go to a party with her tonight, but Mona knows she has a test in the morning and should just spend the night at home studying. Kristy talked to Mona on the phone all day, but Mona just won't give in. Kristy decides to go to Mona's house to try to convince her face-to-face. When Kristy walks in, Mona puts her head down and shakes it back and forth. Kristy then walks over to Mona, grabs her arm, and attempts to pull her toward the door. Mona gives in, grabs her purse, and walks arm-in-arm with Kristy to the car. By demonstrating how much she wanted Mona to go by physically going to see her and "dragging" her to the door, Kristy persuaded Mona that attending the party would be worth it.

Appropriateness

Touch can be negative when it violates our expectations. Each person has different opinions on what is appropriate and inappropriate in relation to location, duration, and intensity of touch. Location includes where on the body contact is made, as well as the setting or context within which the touch occurs. Duration means how long a touch lasts. Touches can be fleeting or long-lasting, but each individual has rules about that as well. The intensity of a touch can also demonstrate many different kinds of communicative messages. For example, if your significant other places a hand on your shoulder while standing beside you, it could mean many different things. If that hand is just resting on your shoulder, it could help you to become more comfortable or relaxed. If the hand is gripping your shoulder in a forceful manner, the touch is likely to impact you in a different way. Touch is very important in different aspects of all types of relationships, offering comfort within friendships, conveying intimacy within marriages, signaling differences between genders, and demonstrating power and status between students and teachers.

PHYSICAL APPEARANCE

Kaitlyn: "Did you see the new guy we hired?"
Samantha: "No, is he cute?"
Kaitlyn: "Yes! He's tall, blonde, and tan."
Samantha: "Well, that's great! He'll make great tips."
Kaitlyn: "Even if he wasn't a good server, I'd still tip him good for being so cute!"

Have you ever tipped a server simply because he or she was good-looking? Through this example, Kaitlyn and Samantha emphasize the importance of physical appearance in regard to persuasive messages. Our **physical appearance** is the way our bodies and overall appearance nonverbally communicate to others and impact our view of ourselves in everyday life. Think about how much time a day you spend "getting ready." *Does my hair look okay? Do these shoes match my outfit? Should I tuck in my shirt or leave it out? Is this perfume too strong?* Why do we care so much about our body image? It is because everything about our physical appearance impacts our ability to persuade and to influence other people's perceptions.

Your physical appearance is related to your nonverbal communication because the decisions you make to maintain or alter your physical appearance reveal a great deal about who you are. Similarly, the physical appearance of other people impacts your perceptions of them, how you communicate with them, how approachable they seem, how attractive or unattractive they appear, and more.

Attraction refers to how you are drawn toward other people interpersonally, spiritually, emotionally, physically, and/or sexually for possible friendship, dating, love, partnership, and marriage (Mulvey, 2006). Attraction might play a big role in how you develop relationships from a psychological standpoint; however, physical attractiveness involves more obvious perceptions of beauty and how you are drawn to others. **Physical attractiveness** is a culturally derived perception of beauty, formed by features of our appearance such as height, weight, size, shape, and so on. In other words, we form a mental picture of physical appearance that dictates what *is* and *is not* attractive. The distinction between the two is this: You may be attracted to someone you believe to be physically attractive, *or not.* Some people are *attractive*, but you're not *attracted* to them.

Perhaps you are looking to buy a new car. You have been to three different car lots to look at the same type of car. At the first lot, you were greeted by a short woman with thick-rimmed glasses and frizzy hair. She showed you the car you wanted for a decent price, but you decided to continue shopping. At the second car lot, an overweight, balding man greeted you and showed you a cheaper version of the car you saw at the first lot. The man sort of gave you the creeps, so you decided to keep looking. The third car salesman was a tall, slender, dark-haired woman wearing designer shoes. She presented you with the same car as the other two; however, the price was higher. Would the woman at the third car lot be able to persuade you easier than the other two, simply based on the fact that she was attractive?

In Your Life

Think about how online or mediated communication relies on nonverbal messages (e.g., emoticons, text response time). What aspects of nonverbal communication are most complicated to you when you're trying to persuade someone online?

Body Types

The appearance of our body helps others form perceptions and stereotypes, as well as make decisions about how to communicate with us (Bodenhausen & Macrae, 1998; Forbes, Adams-Curtis, Rade, & Jaberg, 2001). Usually, body types can be classified into three different categories: (a) ectomorphs, (b) mesomorphs, and (c) endomorphs. According to Sheldon's (1940) theory, each body type has a corresponding psychological type. Endomorphs, like Santa Claus and Danny DeVito, typically have body types that are rounded or oval and are usually heavyset or stocky, but not necessarily obese. For endomorphs, the corresponding psychological type is called **viscerotonic,** described as slow, sociable, emotional, forgiving, and relaxed. Mesomorphs generally have triangular-shaped bodies, with broad shoulders and narrower hips. They are muscular and athletic, with a good balance between height and weight. David Beckham, Jessica Biel, and Michael Phelps are good examples of mesomorphs. The personality associated with these body types is considered **somatonic,** meaning such people show characteristics of dominance, confidence, energy, enthusiasm, competitiveness, and optimistic attitudes. Ectomorphs, such as Abraham Lincoln and Sacha Baron Cohen, are tall, skinny, and fragile-looking, with flat chests and limited muscular development. They have **cerebrotonic** psychological attributes, such as often being tense, awkward, careful, polite, and detached. Do these body types and corresponding psychological types describe you? Do they ring true in how you perceive and are influenced by people with different body types?

A good example of how physical appearance relates to persuasion can be found in many men's magazines. If you flip through *Maxim* or *GQ*, you will probably see an advertisement for shoes with raised soles that add an extra 3 to 4 inches to your height. Why would somebody be interested in this product? Height has a great deal to do with persuasion, as taller people can be perceived as more intimidating than shorter ones. Also, taller people are statistically more likely to make more money than shorter people. Raised-insole shoes are just one example of products people can buy to alter their appearance. What other products can you think of that relate to physical persuasion?

Hair

People's hair can also impact the way you perceive them and the way you choose to approach them. Think of your ideal partner. When someone asks you to describe the type of man or woman you are typically attracted to, you usually respond with some sort of physical characteristics, most of the time including hair color or type. Do you like long hair? Short hair? Do you like blondes, brunettes, or redheads? Oftentimes blonde women are made fun of for being dumb and ditzy. Why is that? When you talk to a blonde, are you less

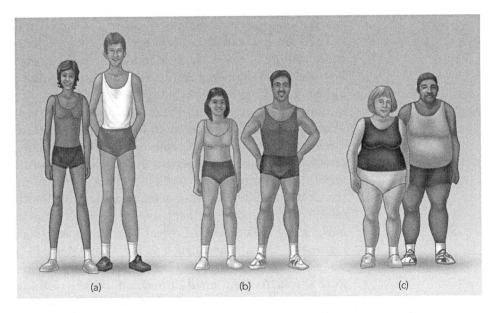

FIGURE 9.2 Sheldon's Body Types

Source: Figure from *Psychology: From Inquiry to Understanding,* 1st Edition, by Scott O. Lilienfeld, Steven J. Lynn, Laura L. Namy and Nancy J. Woolf. Copyright © 2009 by Pearson Education, Inc. Printed and Electronically reproduced by permission of Pearson Education, Inc., Upper Saddle River, New Jersey.

likely to be persuaded by what she says, simply because of her hair color? In addition to our perception of other people's attractiveness, we tend to evaluate personality and intelligence based on hair color. Blondes are labeled dumb, while people with red hair are perceived as hot tempered or filled with anger (Ivy & Wahl, 2009). What about when women and men dye their hair to keep the gray from showing? With this action, they are consciously or unconsciously trying to persuade you to think or feel a certain way about them. Does it work?

When you consider hair length, what do you find most attractive? Women with long hair are said to have more sex appeal, while those with shorter, crisper cuts are considered more professional and "put together." Men with Mohawks or mullets are portrayed to be less responsible and less professional. What if you saw a girl with a Mohawk or shaved head? Would you assume she was a lesbian? Would her haircut persuade you to believe certain things about her?

Clothing

According to communication scholars Knapp and Hall (2006), attire provides the following functions: decoration, protection, sexual attraction, concealment, group identification, display of status, and persuasion. How can clothing persuade people? Researchers have studied the impact of clothing on persuading others to comply (e.g., follow directions, fundraise, pick up garbage, deposit money in parking meters) (Lawrence & Watson, 1991). Research results indicate that a police officer in uniform directing traffic is more likely to get people to comply than someone not in uniform (Young, 1999). We're also more persuaded to donate money when approached by someone in uniform than someone not in uniform. Firefighters, police officers, and members of the military are highly successful fundraisers for special causes; their uniforms symbolize their service and communicate credibility, both of which are very persuasive (Ivy & Wahl, 2009). Another good example would be the uniforms of car salespeople. Car companies that generally sell economically priced cars might allow their workers to wear polo shirts and khaki pants. However, higher-end car companies such as BMW and Mercedes require their sales force to wear suits to work, because their target market wears suits to work as well. As mentioned earlier, similarity in clothing increases perceptions of similarity between individuals, which makes them appear more likable and more open to persuasion.

Jewelry

In addition to clothing, jewelry can also be a temporary aspect of physical adornment that provides clues about personalities, attitudes, and behaviors that nonverbally communicate something about us to other people (Tiggemann & Golder, 2006). How many of us are wearing rings, bracelets, anklets, watches, necklaces, earrings, nose rings, belly button rings, or any other type of jewelry right now? Why do we wear this jewelry? What kind of nonverbal messages are you sending and what are you trying to get across? If you are single and out with some friends, what is one of the first things you do when you spot an attractive man or woman? Glancing down to look at someone's ring finger is a normal and acceptable gesture. Depending on whether or not that person is wearing a ring, you will be persuaded to approach or not approach him or her. You must also consider how jewelry can communicate professionalism in the workplace. Why do most restaurants have strict dress codes and restrictions on visible tattoos and jewelry? Many want to make sure their employees have the "brand image" that they are trying to cultivate in order to persuade you to eat there. Imagine yourself going to a nice, expensive restaurant for dinner one evening. When your server approaches, he has piercings in his lips, nose, eyebrows, and tongue. Would this influence your feelings about eating there?

Ethical Connection

The advertising field relies heavily on physical attractiveness to persuade consumers. Some groups feel that this can lead to unethical practices (such as excessive photo editing) and create unrealistic role models. At what point does the use of physical attractiveness in advertising become ethically questionable?

FACE AND EYES

The human face plays a very important role in communication. Your face is connected to your public identity, or how you present yourself in everyday encounters. Facial expressions are key to persuasion and to influencing other's perceptions. Perhaps you're at a local pub with a friend and the bartender asks what you would like to drink. You ask for suggestions, and he says to shout something out and he'll give you his thoughts on the drink. When you mention the name of the first beer, he wrinkles his forehead, winces, and shakes his head. Without saying a word, he is telling you that the beer isn't tasty. You shout out the name of a cocktail and he cocks his head to the side, purses his lips, and looks up at the ceiling. By these facial expressions, he is persuading you to choose something else. Next, you unintentionally yell out the name of his favorite drink and he nods his head in excitement and opens his eyes wide. Just by his facial expressions, the bartender persuaded you to choose the last one.

Facial expressions are easily noticed. The smallest things, like the blinking of eyes or the wrinkling of the nose, can convey a message. Some of the most recognizable emotions can be conveyed purely through facial expressions. Happiness can be shown by a big smile or raising of the eyebrows. Sadness is shown through relaxed eyes and a frown. Surprise can be shown with an open mouth and wide-open eyes. When people are fearful, they tend to have wide eyes and to draw their head backward. Anger can be conveyed through scrunched eyes and pursed lips, while disgust can be shown with a slightly open mouth and a turn of the head.

Facial Action Coding System (FACS)

How does one go about locating and evaluating facial expressions? Ekman and Friesen (1969) designed a process called the Facial Action Coding System (FACS) that separates the face into three regions: eyebrows and forehead; eyes and eyelids; and lower face, including the cheeks, nose, and mouth. Using Ekman's six primary emotions (sadness, anger, disgust, fear, happiness, and surprise), researchers have learned to classify particular emotions in terms of where they emerge on the face (Atkinson, Tipples, Burt, & Young, 2005; Mendolia, 2007). Facial expressions have a huge impact on the message being delivered and have the ability to persuade easily, without words. Using the eyebrow and forehead region can communicate a variety of different messages. For example, cocked eyebrows can be a sign of question or confusion; knitted eyebrows can signal pain, illness, or frustration; and flashing eyebrows can demonstrate flirtation or a friendly greeting. Our eyes and eyelids are used not only for vision and protection from environmental factors, but they can also communicate our feelings and emotions. For example, winking is an easy way to communicate to someone using your eyes only. Depending on the situation, winking can mean a number of things. What is your reaction when someone you don't know winks at you across a room? What if your granddad winks at you during a family dinner? How do you feel when someone winks at you in a professional situation? Moving lower down the face, cheeks can also communicate messages, willingly or unwillingly. Most of us know a friend or loved one who often blushes when feeling embarrassed, ashamed, or self-conscious. Perhaps this happens to you after a receiving a compliment from an attractive person. The shape and size of a person's nose can also communicate something to people. Some people have a perky, "button" nose, often conveying youthfulness; others have a large, bulbous nose that may send a different kind of signal to an onlooker. Plus, the bridge of the nose is integral to facial expression; it's a primary area for conveying the emotion of disgust, as we typically wrinkle the bridge of the nose when we confront a disgusting stimulus. The human mouth, also used for talking and eating, is a primary displayer of emotions on the face. It displays smiling, laughing, frowning, screaming, singing, and so on. The human mouth is one of the most active body parts and expresses a variety of emotions.

Eye Behavior

The study of eye behavior, **oculesics,** examines eye contact, eye movement, and other functions of the eye. Particularly in U.S. culture, people feel connected to others if eye contact is established, believing that the eyes truly are "the windows to the soul." That's why eye behavior is emphasized in basic communication courses and has been a central topic within the study of nonverbal communication for many years (Argyle & Dean, 1965; Guerrero & Floyd, 2006; Manusov & Patterson, 2006).

Eye behavior can stimulate arousal by creating a positive or negative response to another person. We all experience some sort of arousal, positive or negative, when we see someone else. If it is a friend or loved one we like or haven't seen in a while, eye behavior will stimulate positive arousal. On the other hand, if we see someone we aren't too fond of, we will experience negative arousal. Another influence of eye behavior relates to salience, meaning that what we do with our eyes is more noticeable than other actions of the face and body. Our eyes are important in developing relationships with others and managing our everyday communication. Think about being at the grocery store and all of the different people you make eye contact with. You can convince someone to move, apologize for being in the way, and let someone know you need to get by his cart all with the

In Your Life

Have you ever been accused of rolling your eyes or "staring off into space" during a conversation? Did you consciously realize that you were doing it? How did this behavior affect the rest of the conversation you had? Do you have any examples of how eye behavior has positively influenced a communication exchange?

physical appearance	the way our bodies and overall appearance nonverbally communicate to others and impact our view of ourselves in everyday life
attraction	how we are drawn toward other people interpersonally, spiritually, emotionally, physically, and/or sexually for possible friendship, dating, love, partnership, and marriage
physical attractiveness	culturally derived perception of beauty, formed by features of our appearance
viscerotonic	slow, sociable, emotional, forgiving, and relaxed
somatonic	dominant, confident, energetic, enthusiastic, competitive, and optimistic
cerebrotonic	often tense, awkward, careful, polite, and detached
oculesics	the study of eye behavior

use of eye contact. Eye contact can be used to communicate whether at the grocery store, home, work, school, or a sporting event. The third influence of eye behavior is involvement—the need to interact with another person, even if it's a simple visual acknowledgment or head nod. A good example is when we pass by a stranger on campus. There is always some sort of connection between strangers who are walking past each other outside of the library on a college campus. Even if they do not know each other at all, the awkward involvement sometimes leads us to have brief eye contact, exchange a quick and mumbled "hi," or give each other a short head nod. You can choose not to involve yourself in this interaction, but if the other person is obviously trying to make eye contact, you will most likely be persuaded to react.

In addition to influences of eye behavior, researchers have also explored its various purposes (Kendon, 1967). Eye behavior can be used to recognize others, scan the environment and situation, think and recall memories, decrease physical and psychological distance, regulate interaction, establish and define relationships, display power, express emotions, exclude others, and monitor feedback. Gazing, one-sided looks, and pupil dilation can influence different eye behaviors and communicate different persuasive and deceptive messages.

Remember: You can use your knowledge of persuasion to engage real-life situations. Consider the scenario below and think about what you would do as you apply your study of nonverbal communication and persuasion in your life.

It's your big day: You applied for an executive position at a hospital, and you got it! The corner office is yours, and as you walk in you see nothing but bare walls and an empty desk. The space is rather large and you begin to brainstorm about the ways you could decorate this empty room. As a part of your new job, you must meet with other employees to discuss their performance each month. The person who had this position before you had a reputation for making these meetings a nightmare for the employees. They described his office as a "prison cell." In what ways could you construct the environment of your new office to help nonverbally persuade employees to relax and be comfortable as you meet with them to review their progress over the past month? What would you do?

SUMMARY

This chapter explored how the codes of nonverbal communication (e.g., environment, space, face, eyes, posture, motion) connect to the study of persuasion. When considering the persuasiveness of messages, it's important to include the power of nonverbal communication. How you perceive the environment around you has a huge impact on how you interpret and create messages. Whether it is the lighting, the temperature, or the color of the paint on the wall, nonverbal communication will impact the persuasiveness of the message.

DISCUSSION QUESTIONS

Nonverbal

1. What is the most persuasive nonverbal communication code in your life? Why?
2. What factors in your environment make you want to linger longer or leave sooner?
3. Are you easily persuaded by touch (handshakes, hugs, pats on the back)? Do these forms of touch impact you in positive or negative ways?
4. How do you use nonverbal communication in your life to persuade others?
5. How can face and eye behavior be persuasive?

Persuasive Dimensions of Health Communication 10

Juliann Scholl

YOUR OBJECTIVES

After studying this chapter, you should be able to:

1. Explain the terms *health* and *health communication*.
2. Identify the instances in which health-related persuasion plays a role in interpersonal relationships.
3. Discuss the ways in which patients and providers engage in persuasion during the medical encounter.
4. Explain direct-to-consumer advertising and understand the theoretical explanations underlying the persuasive tactics used.
5. Discuss the assumptions of current theories that are applied to health campaign messages.

CHAPTER OUTLINE

I learned that I am a client of my doctor; I am an equal person in my medical decisions. I am not a patient; I am capable of making decisions about my health with the help of my doctor. You have to talk with your doctor as if [he or she] were a partner. [He or she] cannot talk down to you or make decisions for you without your consent.

Media literacy, specifically that of healthcare, needs to be taught widespread. If the majority of the American public had the ability to logically and analytically break down advertising and media messages, then they would have the power to radically change the American media for the better. Pharmaceutical companies would be forced to employ different, perhaps more straightforward, methods to sell their products or services.

Health

These statements are two of the many journal entries taken from a health communication course at the university level. In their journals, students discuss their role as patients, how much power they want to exert or give up in the doctor's office, and how they want their doctors to view them. They also have opinions about health messages they see on television and the Internet, the amount of trust or distrust they have of major pharmaceutical companies, and the kinds of messages that motivate them to adopt healthy behaviors as well as change harmful ones. All of these issues, more or less, relate to the use of persuasion in health care.

This chapter encourages you to think about how persuasion plays out in your health and in the health care system in which you take part, as well as how you talk about your health with others close to you. As you probably have already learned, persuasion—both subtle and large-scale—is ubiquitous in life, and one of its most influential roles is in matters of your health. People can be swayed by television or Internet messages they receive as well as the influence of their peers and social networks. For instance, after seeing repeated advertisements for a prescription allergy medication, you may decide to mention it to your doctor the next time you go in for a checkup. Or, at the prodding of your roommate, you may decide to go to the campus health center to investigate your sore throat after putting it off for weeks.

As you may imagine, persuasion can have a significant impact on your health decisions—for better or for worse. You can increase your communication effectiveness in the doctor's office and at home partly by understanding how persuasion comes into play. Du Pré (2010) points out:

> Our personal health is shaped in part by the choices we make as individuals. Communication—be it through news stories, PSAs, entertainment programming, or conversations with health professionals, neighbors, friends, or family members—often has an impact on whether we smoke, exercise, drink and drive, get enough sleep, take part in health screenings, and so on. Consequently, persuasion theories...are of paramount interest in people interested in public health, health education, and health promotion. Persuasion is also important at community and societal levels as we negotiate issues of social equity, justice, community resources, and the environment. (pp. 9–10)

When talking about persuasion and health, you will consider the concept of health and what it means to have health, as well as define the term *health communication* in ways that relate to persuasion. Next, you will explore interpersonal issues of health, particularly the persuasion that takes place during doctor visits and interactions with other health care professionals. These interpersonal issues will also include self-efficacy, locus of control, and sensitive conversations about safer sex. Finally, you will discover the persuasive implications of pharmaceutical advertisements and health campaigns to which you are exposed several times a day.

DEFINING HEALTH AND HEALTH COMMUNICATION

What does it mean to be healthy, or to be in good health? Good health is one of those things many people count among their blessings. When you've suffered loss or disappointment, you may have thought, "Well, at least I have my health." When talking about what health means, we have to acknowledge that it goes well beyond how we feel physically, or being free of illness or injury. Since 1948, the World Health Organization (WHO) has defined **health** as "a state of complete physical, mental and social well-being and not merely the absence of disease or infirmity" (p. 100). The WHO later expanded this definition to include spiritual, intellectual, and environmental health. Working off of this definition for the purposes of this chapter, health is a state of physical, emotional, mental, and spiritual well-being, which is more than the mere absence of illness or injury.

Good health allows you to engage in the activities you desire, helps you maintain a good mood, promotes your happiness, and enables—not hinders—your relationships with other people. Your state of health and your overall perceptions of health are at the core of life. How you feel at a given moment can color your mood, impact how well you perform a task, and influence your general outlook on life. For many of you, being healthy means being happy, and the pursuit of happiness is a significant

In Your Life

How would you respond if a friend asked, "Would you consider yourself healthy?" How would you explain your health status to this friend? How might your answer be considered persuasive?

motivation that many persuaders play on when getting you to adopt a behavior or buy a prescription drug.

Many of the researchers who explore these issues of health engage in the study of **health communication,** defined as (a) the construction and sharing of meanings about the provision of health care delivery and (b) the promotion of public health through mediated channels. As early as the 1960s, health communication emerged as a distinct area of study, and was developed mainly by scholars in persuasion, medicine, sociology, and psychology (Kreps, Query, & Bonaguro, 2008). Health communication scholars study a variety of subjects: how couples talk to each other about illness, the communication that occurs in hospitals and in interdisciplinary health teams, how health campaigns are constructed, how to talk to children about illness, and so on. Health communication scholars particularly interested in persuasion might look at the motivations people have for adopting positive or harmful health behaviors, as well as the influence social networks have on our daily health-related practices.

Examining health from a persuasive angle in this chapter means understanding how you talk about your health to your doctors. There's much persuasion that goes on in the doctor's office, between both patient and health care provider. On the one hand, patients may be concerned with coming across as knowledgeable and competent in front of the doctor; on the other hand, the doctor may try to engage in persuasion to get the patient to comply with her medical instructions or to take the medicine as properly directed. While much of the health communication research has focused on *doctor*-patient interactions, we communicate with a variety of professionals—triage nurses, nutritionists, lab technicians, and emergency personnel, among others. That being said, the term **health care provider** is used here to refer to these and other individuals who are trained to administer a variety of health services to the public.

But doctors and other health professionals are not the only people involved in your interpersonal interactions. For instance, when you are experiencing unusual physical symptoms or are concerned about a pain that won't go away, who is the first person you talk to about it? That person will not likely be your doctor, but perhaps your best friend, romantic partner, or a parent. Even if you put off going to the doctor or find a way to shrug off the pain, your friend or loved one may encourage you—or persuade you—to make a doctor's appointment to get it checked out.

In addition to the persuasion that occurs in our interpersonal interactions, persuasive health communication also accounts for the messages that are delivered to various audiences through a variety of channels (e.g., TV, Internet, and print media). This next section will review the delivery of health messages to the public. The study of persuasion helps

10.1 REMEMBER

health	more than the absence of illness or injury, a state of physical, emotional, mental, and spiritual well-being
health communication	the construction and sharing of meanings about the provision of health care delivery and the promotion of public health through mediated channels
health care provider	a professional (e.g., doctor, nurse, therapist) who is trained to provide a health care service to the public

you find meaning in the many health-related messages to which you are exposed. Much is asked about the level of impact mediated messages have on your behaviors and attitudes related to health. Indeed, health messages (for example, about the harms of smoking, risks of unprotected sex, and effects of a high-fat diet) can help or impede the positive health decisions you make.

As you can see, the study of persuasion can not only shed light on the kinds of health-related decisions you make, but perhaps help you make better ones. The rest of this chapter will first discuss the interpersonal issues of health and how persuasion plays a role, not only in the patient-doctor interaction, but in other aspects of our relational life. Second, you will look at persuasion and its role in health messages mediated through the media and through campaigns.

INTERPERSONAL ISSUES OF HEALTH

Our states of health—and how people talk about health—are an important component of our interpersonal relationships and everyday interactions. More specifically, conversations about health are a prevalent part of how you build and maintain your most important relationships. One of the characteristics of interpersonal relationships is the idea of control—using your messages and nonverbal cues to exert influence over others in your lives. As you may already be aware, people use power strategies to get others to comply with their wishes. Such power tactics include the ability to reward, punish, promote expertise, pull rank, or make references to desirable images or models (French & Raven, 1960). Some of these wishes have to do with your desire to see your friends and loved ones take good care of themselves. When exerting power in your relationships, you sometimes attempt to influence the health decisions of others. For example, if you want a friend to join you for a bike ride, you might tell her that you will be

Remember: You can use your knowledge of persuasion to engage real-life situations. Consider the scenario below and think about what you would do as you apply your study of the persuasive dimensions of health in your life.

Your best friend confides in you, revealing that he has been told by his family physician that he has an STD. Later that evening, the two of you go to a local fraternity party, where your friend has a few too many drinks and says that he would like to go home with a young woman he met that evening. As his best friend, you have a decision to make. In what way can you use persuasion and your knowledge of the potential risks involving STDs to encourage your friend to make the right decision? What would you do?

spending more time together (reward) and that you know firsthand how cycling will increase your endurance (expert power).

Talking about Health to Others

Your most important interpersonal relationships—with your families, friends, teachers, and others—are marked by **socialization** processes. Socialization occurs when you are taught what is appropriate and inappropriate in a given situation. People are taught all the time what to do, say, and expect in a variety of communication situations. More specifically, important others help to socialize you about your health, your perceptions of doctors, and your understanding of the health care system. This socialization is perhaps the most common form of persuasion in your everyday lives because this process often teaches you how to behave and how you should expect to be treated as patients (Wright, Sparks, & O'Hair, 2008). As a kid, Jazmin's parents told her that the doctor was her friend, was smart, and that she should listen to what he had to say. Jazmin was also advised not to ask too many questions because the doctor had many other patients to see. Since then, Jazmin has been mindful of her parents' words of advice and how they have helped—and hindered—her ability to seek adequate health care in her adulthood. These memories have reminded Jazmin that she took a submissive role during the doctor's visit to avoid being labeled a "bad patient." Socialization can also happen in your adult years when you're guided as to whether a health issue is minor or serious. We can be socialized every time someone says, "You've been in pain for three weeks?!! You better get that checked out."

Much of your socialization comes in the form of **social support**. Social support is defined here as enabling, empowering, and facilitating another person's ability to meet his or her emotional, informational, and/or instrumental needs. **Emotional support** is the kind with which most of us are familiar—listening to and empathizing with a person's difficult situation, or giving much-needed reassurance. In addition to providing a sympathetic listening ear, you can provide **information support** consisting of facts, statistics, stories, or resources that enable a person to be more informed about his health situation. This can occur when you refer a newly diagnosed diabetic to a website with valuable information. Finally, you can offer **instrumental support,** physical or tangible assistance with daily or mundane tasks, such as giving a friend a ride to her monthly medical checkup. Overall, giving social support means helping others cope with stressful situations in a variety of ways.

Social support can be a subtle, but influential, form of interpersonal persuasion. Many of us take it upon ourselves to use social support as a way to convince a friend or loved one to take action or to make better health decisions. Consider Jayna's friend, Chuck, who was severely obese and in danger of developing diabetes. Jayna was very concerned about her friend's health and wanted to offer some social support. On occasion she would invite Chuck to go bike riding with her. If Chuck complained that his bike had a flat tire, Jayna would offer to come over and change the tire, which was a form of instrumental support. She even shared with him various facts about the physical benefits of bike riding (informational support), and when he did accompany her on a ride, she shouted out phrases of encouragement, such as "Wow, you're getting faster each time we ride" (emotional support). Jayna really believed that all of her efforts at social support would motivate and persuade him to make some positive changes in his diet and exercise routine.

Unfortunately, simply offering social support may not be enough. It certainly didn't work in Jayna's case. Chuck apparently didn't have enough self-efficacy to respond to her attempts at social support and to make the needed changes in his lifestyle. Bandura (1986) defines **self-efficacy** as the belief one has in his or her ability to do certain things. In other words, as much as Chuck wanted to lose weight and get healthier, he simply did not believe in his ability to do so. He sometimes told Jayna, "Obesity runs in my family, so I probably won't ever be skinny" and "I just don't have the time to exercise like I should." It stands to reason that Chuck did not believe he could make the needed changes in his lifestyle, and this affected his ability to cope. Self-efficacy can influence how people cope with various health issues (du Pré 2010). If you believe you have the resources and ability to manage your health, you are more likely to do it, and you will be more influenced by those interpersonal messages you get from family and friends about eating healthy, practicing safer sex, avoiding unhealthy relationships, and other physical and emotional issues. On the other hand, low levels of self-efficacy can negatively influence our eating and exercise habits, as well as our emotional outlook on life. Such a low self-efficacy has been associated with lack of knowledge about health issues as well as poor lifestyle habits, such as eating too much and not exercising (Fry & Prentice-Dunn, 2005). With Chuck's low self-efficacy in the way, Jayna was not able to have the persuasive impact on him that she would have liked.

Self-efficacy also can be understood in terms of *locus of control* (Rotter & Mulry, 1965). An **internal locus of control** reflects the belief that you control the results you achieve. In other words, you may ask yourself, "What did I do to bring about this outcome?" or "What can I do to get the result I want?" People with an internal locus of control are more motivated to take action, become more informed about relevant health conditions, and feel more confident about guarding themselves from potential health threats, such as illness or injury (Fry & Prentice-Dunn, 2005). In contrast, an **external locus of control** means that you perceive the cause of events to be beyond your control, mostly due to outside forces such as heredity or a higher spiritual power. An external locus of control might cause you to take a fatalistic stance on a health issue, as did Chuck, who believed that diabetes and obesity had just happened to him and there was very little he could do about it.

Self-efficacy and locus of control have interpersonal persuasive consequences because they can influence how we respond to attempts by others to influence our beliefs, attitudes, assumptions, and behaviors related to health. A friend might tell you, "I'm really concerned about you. You look tired and your face looks sunken in. Are you okay?" If you have an internal locus, you may decide to take a closer look at your eating and sleeping habits or investigate the causes of fatigue to see if you have a reason to go to the doctor. You may also decide to reexamine your daily routine to see if you can fit in more time to relax. On the contrary, if you were external in locus of control, you might respond differently, and instead dismiss your friend's comment and decide that you're just busy and that there's nothing you can do about changing your health situation, or that it's out of your hands. This difference in self-efficacy can have profound impacts on the way you respond to others' interpersonal messages, for better or worse. In addition, the next time you want to talk to a friend or loved one about a health issue she's dealing with, consider what you know about her level of self-efficacy and the impact your communication might have on her.

A lot of interpersonal persuasion takes place between couples, especially when health matters are involved. One prevalent area of research is the discussion of safer sex and condom use. With HIV and other sexually transmitted infections on the rise (Amason & Webb, in press), discussions of sexual health are important. Many young adults are hesitant to discuss safer sex, much less practice it. This topic is often difficult for young people to talk about because of its sensitive nature, the communication styles of the individuals involved, and feelings of embarrassment or the fear of offending the other with the request to use a condom.

Amason and Webb (in press) propose effective **health protective sexual communication (HPSC)** as a persuasive way to introduce the topic of safer sex, engage in interpersonal influence, and thus explore ways couples can protect themselves against possible infection. This concept can be viewed as a form of interpersonal persuasion because one of the best ways to combat the spread of infection is a productive social exchange between sexual partners and among members of peer groups. Because of the potential embarrassment and fear associated with condoms and sexually transmitted infections, romantic partners may find that the use of persuasive tactics can both protect them as well as maintain relational quality and satisfaction. When attempting to persuade a partner that the couple should use a condom, Amason and Webb suggest a number of approaches. These include:

» Benefit to the persuader. ("It will give me peace of mind knowing that we're playing it safe.")

» Benefit to the persuaded. ("You won't have to worry about getting sick.")

» Focus on the activity. ("Without worrying about getting sick, we can enjoy it a lot more.")

» Mutual benefit. ("This will bring us closer together as a couple.")

» Discussion of sexual history, which often leads to increased likelihood of condom use, according to the authors.

In Your Life

When you are concerned about health-related issues, with whom are you most likely to first discuss your feelings and symptoms? Do the types of symptoms affect with whom you talk? What influences you to talk with these specific people? How do these discussions affect your decision to seek treatment?

Amason and Webb acknowledge other strategies, such as threat of punishment and deception. But threats and deception could erode trust within the relationship and possibly lead to resentment. Nonetheless, making the condom request an issue of health—rather than distrust of the partner—might yield a more positive response and greater compliance.

Being in an interpersonal relationship implies the use of persuasion from time to time. It helps you maintain a sense of control and provides you with an idea of where you stand. Health is one of the most important things you can discuss in your relationships, and you attempt to influence the attitudes, beliefs, and behaviors of those close to you mostly because you care about their well-being. Let's move to another

socialization	the process that occurs when we are taught what is appropriate and inappropriate in a given communication situation—what to do, say, or expect from others
social support	enabling, empowering, and facilitating another person's ability to meet his or her physical, emotional, and/or informational needs
emotional support	listening to and empathizing with a person's difficult situation, or giving much-needed reassurance
informational support	facts, statistics, stories, or resources that enable people to be more informed about their health situation
instrumental support	providing physical or tangible assistance with daily or mundane tasks
self-efficacy	the belief one has in his or her ability to do certain things
internal locus of control	the belief that you control the results you achieve
external locus of control	the belief that the cause of events is beyond your control, that they are mostly attributed to outside forces such as heredity or a higher spiritual power
health protective sexual communication (HPSC)	a set of persuasive strategies used to introduce the topic of safer sex

type of interpersonal persuasion in health care, that between the patient and the health care provider.

Persuasion in the Patient-Provider Interaction

Persuasive communication is the most valuable tool that medical providers have at their disposal. Scholars who first began to explore health communication realized that communication is not just a tool doctors and caregivers use to prescribe medicine and offer recommendations; it is a form of treatment in itself. "[E]ven when the goal is physical care, communication is the vehicle by which people (both professionals and patients) learn about health and reach agreement about what is wrong and what should be done" (du Pré, 2010, p. 9). Through communication, providers provide their best treatment recommendations and offer encouragement; patients use communication to indicate their agreement with such treatments as well as how they wish to be treated by their providers. Moreover, communication is increasingly a point of interest for those in psychology and medicine, and paying attention to persuasion in the doctor's office can help us understand the choices people make and the behaviors in which they engage.

In other chapters, you may have read about how the environment can be used for persuasive purposes. The doctor's office is no exception. Walking into a medical clinic can set the tone for the remainder of a patient's medical visit. The environment can convey a variety of feelings—it can feel professional, friendly, intimidating, sterile, or indifferent. Providers who are aware of the effect of environment are likely to put some thought and planning into the colors, lighting, furniture, and layout of their physical settings. Bouchard (1993) found that altering some key environmental components, such as eliminating disinfectant odors and enhancing patient physical privacy, has been linked with increased patient satisfaction. Environmental cues may seem subtle and unnoticeable, but they can serve as important factors in gaining patient trust and acceptance.

Persuasion also manifests itself as dominance or control of the conversation between patient and provider. Patients vary in the extent to which they expect their doctors to be dominant or controlling. Older patients tend to take a more submissive role with the doctor and expect that doctor to be in charge of the interaction (Adelman, Greene, & Charon, 1991). Younger patients, on the other hand, may not like a doctor who is paternalistic or who dominates the conversation. Regardless of age, sex, or other demographic characteristics, some patients might adopt a view of **paternalism,** which implies a belief that the doctor knows best, that one should defer to the doctor, and that the patient is the one who obeys and cooperates with the provider. This abdication of power can make it easier for the provider to persuade the patient on a number of levels, whether getting him to be more forthcoming about the reason for the visit or convincing him to take a prescription as instructed.

However, it is increasingly the case that patients might not see a prescription or medical advice as something to follow without question. This becomes an issue of **patient compliance,** which refers to the patient's adherence to a doctor's advice, recommendation, or medical prescription. Patient compliance—or noncompliance—is always an important topic to providers, as noncompliance is often viewed as a widespread problem (Klingle, 1993). Patient noncompliance has been associated with increased hospital stays (McDonnel & Jacobs, 2002), as well as up to a 20% increase in unintentional pregnancies (Rosenberg, Waugh, & Long, 1995).

Some patients may see the medical recommendation or prescription as an "option" that can be chosen or disregarded (Stevenson, Britten, Barry, Bradley, & Barber, 2002). Whereas doctors see noncompliance as deviance, some patients merely see it as reasoned decision making and the exercise of choice. In some cases of noncompliance, for example, patients who are prescribed a 7-day drug prescription may not take the drug all 7 days if symptoms start to improve. Also, patients who are warned to improve their diet because of a recent diabetes diagnosis may still find it hard to cut down on sweets. People who don't follow medical advice aren't necessarily lazy or indifferent about their health. Rather, such patients have at least one or more concerns. For instance, a patient may sincerely want to take the prescription but be unable to afford it. Even if she could afford it, the patient might not have the kind of daily schedule that would allow her to take the medicine at the prescribed intervals or times of day. Second, if a prescribed medicine seems to be working or reducing symptoms, a patient may decide to stop taking it; this might also be the case if the medicine appears to be having no effect (Forrest, Shadmi, Nutting, & Starfield, 2007). Other factors include unpleasant side effects of the medicine and not agreeing with a diagnosis that threatens the patient's self-image (e.g., obesity, depression, hearing loss).

It is easy to put blame solely on the patient for not following medical advice. However, it is arguable that caregivers share some of the responsibility for patient adherence to treatment (du Pré, 2010). The lack of patient-provider cooperation can lead to harmful outcomes, such as diabetes-related complications, deaths due to asthma, or increased hospitalization because of heart disease. Doctors who are under managed care systems may even be denied their medical privileges if their treatment outcomes are below performance standards. In addition, doctors' reputations among their patients may suffer as well. So, as you may imagine, doctors and caregivers have a lot to gain (or lose) in terms of their ability to seek compliance from their patients.

To combat patient noncompliance, health providers have to engage in their own form of audience analysis by getting information about the noncompliance factors their patients deal with. Addressing these factors in a nonthreatening way can persuade patients to be more compliant with their treatments and recommendations. One such method of persuasion is **motivated interviewing,** a concept proposed by Stephen Rollnick and William Miller (1995). This method is patient centered in that providers don't tell patients what to do. Rather, the patient is told of a number of medical and behavioral options, and the provider asks a series of questions to guide the patient to the most appropriate decision. The notion here is that although the provider is the expert on the medicine, the patient is the expert on his own body and lifestyle. With that in mind, the provider

Ethical Connection

When a person's life is in question, ethical issues are very likely to arise. When might care provider persuasion go beyond the best interest of the patient and become unethical? How might care providers present persuasive information without having ethical questions raised?

can use subtle and friendly persuasion to encourage the patient to make healthy decisions. Specific strategies include asking questions, listening, conveying a respectful tone, focusing on gradual behavioral changes, and tailoring any recommendations to the patient's physical, emotional, and lifestyle needs.

It may be the provider's responsibility to facilitate a cooperative and encouraging medical interaction, but patients have some persuasion tools at their disposal, too. Patients need to be aware of the preexisting beliefs providers have of them (e.g., "good" vs. "bad" patient) and how these beliefs influence the interpersonal treatment they receive (Geist & Hardesty, 1990). These beliefs are often bolstered by the verbal and nonverbal cues patients communicate, such as smiling, making eye contact, rolling their eyes, and other such cues. These behaviors are often interpreted by providers and can help or hurt the immediacy that develops between patient and provider. **Immediacy** is the psychological closeness or connectedness you have with someone. The behaviors that enhance immediacy include smiling, leaning forward, making eye contact, and nodding to show involvement in the conversation (Burgoon & Hale, 1988). Geist and Hardesty have found that providers are trained to rely heavily on patient cues for information when evaluating their health problems. Their study's findings also reveal that physicians' interpretations of patient cues influence their communication with the patients as well as the medical treatment they employ. The behaviors that enhance interpersonal immediacy may serve to brand one as a "good patient," whereas cues that get someone labeled a "bad patient" may be complaining, arguing, or challenging the doctor's authority (Wright et al., 2008). This isn't to say that patients shouldn't ask questions or make

10.3 REMEMBER

paternalism	the belief that the doctor knows best, that one should defer to the doctor, and that the patient is the one who obeys and cooperates with the provider
patient compliance	refers to the patient's adherence to a doctor's advice, recommendation, or medical prescription
motivated interviewing	a method used by providers to ask questions in a nonthreatening way to guide patients to the most appropriate medical and behavioral decisions; a form of persuasion to gain compliance from the patient
immediacy	psychological closeness or connectedness between interactants

complaints. However, doing these things in an interpersonally immediate way can have a very persuasive impact on the communication outcome of the interaction.

MEDIATED PERSUASION IN ADVERTISING AND HEALTH CAMPAIGNS

When it comes to public service announcements and health campaigns, very few have led to substantial changes in health behaviors among the U.S. population. For the most part, people in general do know about what makes a healthy diet, that smoking is associated with a host of negative health problems, and so on. But even with the best health-oriented intentions, there seem to be a host of factors that keep us from making the best choices for our health (du Pré, 2010). These factors include the strong persuasive messages (i.e., late-night burger and pizza ads seen on TV) that somehow encourage us to disregard our healthy eating or to take unnecessary risks In addition, the pro–social health campaigns that encourage people to practice safer sex or to get the exercise they need often fall short of making a healthy impact. This section deals with the advertising and health campaigns with which you are bombarded on a daily basis. More specifically, you will explore the use of advertising to consumers (often called direct-to-consumer advertising), pro–social health campaigns, the theories that explain the impact of these persuasive messages, and how these campaigns and messages should be evaluated.

Direct-to-Consumer Advertising

One of the most interesting claims students make goes something like this: "I know that advertising is out there and I'm exposed to it every day, but I don't think it affects me." What is amusing about this claim is that while they boast of their immunity to such advertisements, they're holding their iPhones and wearing Abercrombie & Fitch T-shirts. The reality is that the media affect us all to varying degrees; otherwise, these companies wouldn't be spending the massive amounts of money they do to design and disseminate those campaigns (see Photo 10.1). Every day people are exposed to massive amounts of advertising that tries to convince them to give up their time, effort, and money. And increasingly large amounts of this advertising come from drug companies.

Much of our hard-earned money is targeted by pharmaceutical companies who have medicines and equipment that promise to enhance the quality of our health and lives. The purpose here is not to demonize these companies. It goes without saying that the pharmaceutical industry has developed and provided some of the most advanced medicines ever seen, and these drugs have done wonders to enhance the quality and quantity

PHOTO 10.1 Drug companies use a variety of advertising strategies to promote brand recognition and product sales. As illustrated in this photo, ads for the popular acid reflux drug Prilosec can be seen on the sides of buses and it has been a major corporate sponsor of large music events and concert series.

of life. For instance, asthma drugs can help asthma sufferers lead active and fulfilling lives. But let's face it—pharmaceutical companies are businesses, and along with enhancing the health of their patients, they want to increase their profits as much as they can. As consumers, a little information can go a long way in understanding how they appeal to our desires and needs, and how we can intelligently evaluate their messages so that we can make the best decisions for our health.

One of the most innovative ways these companies have marketed their products is through **direct-to-consumer (DTC) advertising,** by which pharmaceutical companies use their advertising dollars to bypass the physician and disseminate information about prescription drugs directly to the consumer. Since the late 1990s, when the Food and Drug Administration released guidelines for their use, these advertisements have appeared as commercials on television, on YouTube, and as video streams on commercial websites; we also come across such print ads in popular magazines. Through careful crafting, these ads present colorful animated characters and convey messages that appeal to a variety of consumers' needs (e.g., safety, happiness, sex, companionship). Moreover, these ads seem to tap into many consumers' outlook on their personal lives. One ad campaign in particular is the one for Prilosec OTC, a drug designed to combat heartburn, a common symptom of acid reflux disease. As you study a couple of Prilosec video advertisements, you'll explore two persuasion theories—cultivation theory and social comparison theory—that can be used to explain the message techniques used in these commercials, as well as their potential impacts.

Cultivation theory (Gerbner, Gross, Morgan, & Signorielli, 1994) is based largely on the relationship between television viewing and individuals' perceptions of reality. According to cultivation theory, people develop notions about themselves and the world at large through messages and images they encounter in the media. While the media's influence is not static or unchanging, certain mediated messages can have profound impacts if (1) the images portrayed are highly consistent, (2) people are exposed to large amounts of media, and (3) viewers have little to no criteria or experience in evaluating the messages they are exposed to.

Let's examine how cultivation theory can explain the potential impact of the Prilosec commercials. The Prilosec campaign is fairly consistent in its organization of television spots. In one, we are introduced to an animated character in the shape of a fireball. He calls himself "Burnie" and he is about to interrupt a young woman's fun night at the dance club with a severe episode of heartburn. Soon, however, the woman tells the viewer that she took Prilosec, so nothing is going to get in the way of her good time. She continues to dance the night away, forgetting about her close brush with heartburn. In another spot, a modestly dressed woman appears to be suffering from acid reflux. She holds her chest and has a distressed look on her face. The background in the commercial is dark and gloomy, and there is a grandfather clock next to her ticking away the minutes since she first experienced symptoms. But when the voice-over exclaims, "It's Prilosec time!" the grandfather clock shatters, the sun appears, and now we see the woman in a more festive, colorful dress, looking jubilant, arms thrown in the air. Recall that one component of cultivation theory is the consistency in the messages. In both commercials, you see the repeated hint of the disruptive threat of heartburn, followed by the quick liberation from this disruptive condition. Other consistent components of the message include directives to "ask one's your doctor for more information," as well as a very quick disclaimer about potential side effects at the commercials' end.

According to cultivation theory, other factors that may enhance this campaign's effectiveness are large amounts of exposure to the medium and the lack of knowledge or experience needed to evaluate the claims effectively. Prilosec ads had appeared on television, on YouTube, and as video streams on various medical and health-related websites. Thus it can be argued that Prilosec is attempting to convey its messages to the same audience in as many ways and as many times as possible. It is also possible that the same TV commercial can be aired multiple times in the same evening, allowing for repeated exposures to the same ad.

As for assessing the message's credibility, many television viewers may not possess the skills needed to assess the medical terminology or claims put forth by the ad. Some viewers have low levels of **health literacy**—the ability to understand medical education literature, instructions on prescription drug bottles, a doctor's instructions, and consent forms for medical procedures (National Network of Libraries of Medicine, 2010). Low health literacy may hinder some individuals' capacity for identifying the weaknesses of the ad campaign (such as limited discussion of side effects and how drug trials are reported), and they may end up accepting the core message at face value. Another factor inhibiting ability to evaluate a claim is the lack of life experience, which would in this case mean not ever having had acid reflux disease or much practice reading prescription drug labels.

In addition to the previous factors, "heavy [media] viewers will be more likely to perceive the real world in ways that reflect the most stable and recurrent patterns of portrayals in the television world" (Signorielli & Morgan, 1990, p. 10). Heavy viewers of television may believe the reality that is shown on TV, despite how different it may be from their own experience. Therefore, people who frequently watch television and see multiple ads for Prilosec may conclude that the painful and inconvenient symptoms of acid reflux disease may be wiped out simply by taking a little purple pill.

What they may not be considering are complications of acid reflux disease in addition to heartburn (e.g., narrowing of the esophagus, bloody vomiting, unexplained weight loss), which may not be treated so easily by Prilosec. They also might overlook the long-term effects of taking this medication every day, which is what the ads recommend.

Whereas cultivation theory explains the impact of advertising on heavy television viewers, **social comparison theory** (Festinger, 1957) might help you understand why you sometimes want to be like the figures or models seen in the media. Social comparison theory argues that you often compare yourself to others, whether they are real people in your lives or the people seen on television or elsewhere. If you want to get a sense of how attractive, strong, wealthy, or healthy you are, then social comparison theory claims that you'll likely take a look at others around you to see how well you compare. If you are constantly bombarded by size 0 models on television and you happen to be a size 10, you may conclude that you might need to lose weight; if you see people popping a purple pill and dancing the night away, then you may assume that you need to visit your doctor to tell him about that heartburn you experienced after your recent late-night pizza binge. It is not entirely a bad thing to compare ourselves to others, especially if we associate with individuals who possess good lifestyle habits; comparing ourselves to these individuals can serve as a positive motivator. However, the danger comes when we compare ourselves to an unreal or unattainable standard (du Pré, 2010). This motivation to make social comparisons and to conform to the often-unrealistic standard is what makes some messages very persuasive and appealing.

Let's return to "Burnie," the meddlesome fireball in one of the Prilosec ads previously mentioned. Burnie is the malicious little guy who shows up at the wrong time, wants nothing more than to disrupt our good time at the nightclub, and is a dangerous force that robs us of our social life. He is soon interrupted by the dancing woman who brags about ridding herself of her frequent heartburn with the pill. What we don't hear about is how long the pill takes to start working, what side effects she may be experiencing, as well as how costly it is. What we see and hear about instead is the quick cure. Like the dancing woman, many of us may want that carefree life in which we can do what we want without being interrupted by illness or injury. And when we do get sick, we want to get over it quickly. Unfortunately, for some people who do suffer frequent heartburn, this fast-acting scenario is unrealistic. The pill may not work for them, or they may experience more serious complications that merely accompany the heartburn.

The implication of this and other such ads is that unrealistic images or standards can have serious consequences on our mental and physical health. Advertising that encourages us to compare ourselves to other people or images should be viewed with caution. If we cannot achieve the kind of life and experience portrayed in the commercial, we may become dissatisfied with our own experience. In this particular case, the inability to wipe out heartburn in just a few seconds can be discouraging, if not detrimental, to one's healthy self-image or sense of hope in combating a chronic condition.

When considering the messages portrayed in commercial advertisements for drugs and other health products, you can take small but important steps to be a conscientious and intelligent media consumer. Whether you are watching television commercials for prescription drugs or browsing a pharmaceutical website, you can follow these suggestions offered by du Pré (2010):

» Question the information if you cannot find an author or source. This should also be the case if the source is not well known.

» When researching a medical condition or health issue on the Internet, seek another source if the website is trying to sell a product or service. Credible websites (usually with the domain .org or .gov) normally offer reliable information that is free to the public.

» Check the date the website was last updated. Also, are the references missing? Do the references seem questionable?

» With health claims on television or the web, look for red-flag terms, such as "miraculous cure" or "secret formula." Legitimate health professionals want the public to have free access to information; therefore, touting a "secret formula" would be unethical and unprofessional.

» Be wary of commercials that report "actual" case studies of satisfied customers. Such anecdotal cases cannot replace years of clinical trials designed to test drugs and procedures. Also, these case studies may not even be from actual customers. Do your own research. Ask health professionals for their opinions or advice, and learn how to read a medical journal article.

» Contact the Better Business Bureau or the Federal Trade Commission if you have suspicions about any health claims made.

Pro-Social Health Messages and Health Campaigns

In addition to the commercial advertisements that are a part of your everyday life, you also encounter many pro-social health messages, often in the form of television and radio public service announcements (PSAs), educational pamphlets or literature, websites devoted to a health issue

direct-to-consumer (DTC) advertising	advertising designed for and disseminated to patients and consumers, thus bypassing the health care providers
cultivation theory	explains the impact of television viewing and media consumption on viewers' perceptions of reality and the world around them
health literacy	the ability to understand medical education literature, instructions on prescription drug bottles, a doctor's instructions, and consent forms for medical procedures
social comparison theory	argues that people tend to make self-assessments by comparing themselves to others

In Your Life

What type of mediated message is most likely to influence you? In your opinion, what is the biggest health risk currently affecting the human population? Why do you feel this way? Have you seen any mediated messages recently? How have they persuaded you that this health risk is more important than other risks?

or cause, and other types of materials. **Pro-social health messages** are designed not to sell a product or service, but to educate and persuade the public on various health issues. Another term for a pro-social message is the **health campaign,** which Wright et al. (2008) define as "a systematic effort to change health behaviors (or attitudes and beliefs about health and/or social and environmental conditions that mediate health behaviors) within a target population of people who are at risk for a health problem or problems" (p. 232).

Many health issues, such as HIV/AIDS, the spread of the swine flu and other infections, and the epidemics of diabetes and obesity pose real threats to individuals and to societies at large. In order to make a real impact on people's health and to reduce the impact of these and other health threats, health educators and promoters have to tap into the strongest motivations within us—motivations that encourage us to make healthy choices as well as change more harmful behaviors. There are other motivations that persuaders need to address, which are those that entice you to engage in behaviors that you know carry risks. In reality, most people know the dangers of smoking, having unprotected sex, and consuming a diet consisting mostly of fatty foods. Sometimes, however, the seemingly unhealthy behavior is still appealing because it's fun, convenient, or socially rewarding. Persuasion scholars have the heavy challenge of combating such influences.

The Real Impact of Persuasive Mediated Messages

Unfortunately, the research on health campaigns is somewhat discouraging. That's because very little is known about how to design messages that impact long-term behavioral change. Most successful campaigns do tend to increase our awareness of certain health issues (e.g., smoking cessation, safer sex, healthy eating). But even when some campaigns appear to change our behavior in the short term, they do little more than merely influence our *intent* to change our behavior—not the actual behavior itself. This shows that raising awareness is not enough. Pro-social health campaigns are unlikely to have significant impacts on behavioral change unless they are aligned with targets' beliefs and the beliefs supported by their social networks. For example, sexually active teenagers can be given the most comprehensive information on safer sex and the human reproductive system, but if their peers don't buy into the messages promoting safer sex, or if they do not believe the threats of disease or unplanned pregnancy are relevant to them, then it shouldn't be assumed that simply conveying this message to teenagers will be enough. According to du Pré (2010), "the promoter must know the audience, and he or she must consider, not just why audience members should act in recommended ways, but also why they find it difficult to do so" (p. 341).

In 2010, du Pré pointed out that the most successful health campaigns address an audience's diverse motivations. For instance, a particular target audience may want to be able to understand the cause and nature of a particular chronic illness, so they might want detailed explanations, definitions of terms, current research findings, or current information on policy issues. Other message targets might rather hear about the same chronic illness from an emotional standpoint; they may be aware of the technical explanations but may need be pushed emotionally (e.g., through fear) to act on the message or feel personally involved with it.

It would be a mistake to assume that message targets will do something if we simply tell them to do it. A health message urging targets to quit smoking may be compelling, but it will not be effective unless targets are given worthwhile reasons to quit. Such reasons are explained by the **health belief model** (Rosenstock, 1960; Stretcher & Rosenstock, 1997), which argues that people base their reactions to a message on certain considerations. Put another way, people will change a health-related behavior if (1) they will be negatively affected if they maintain their current behavior; (2) the negative effects of the current behavior are substantial; (3) the behavior change will bring about a desired result; (4) the time, money, and effort needed for a person to change are worthwhile; and (5) they are exposed to a novel or eye-opening occurrence, such as a brush with danger, a scary image, or an attractive enticement. This fifth element is called a *cue to action*.

To put the health belief model into perspective, suppose you are exposed to a PSA about dangerous drinking and driving while intoxicated, a serious issue among the university student population (Zhang, Wang, Scholl & Buchanan, 2008). Because it can be seen by some college students as desirable and acceptable to drink heavily in social situations, targets of this particular campaign would need compelling reasons to change their binge-drinking behavior. To apply the health belief model, a message discouraging dangerous drinking would, first, have to convince students of their personal susceptibility to the negative effects of drinking and driving. To satisfy this criterion, students might be given statistics about the high incidence of drunk driving among their age group. Second, they would have to be persuaded of the serious consequences of dangerous drinking and driving, which include not only being at odds with the law, but also being exposed to the increased risk of injury or assault. Third, the benefits of behavioral change (e.g., not worrying about getting arrested for intoxicated driving, increased safety) would need to appear substantial enough to cut down on binge drinking. Fourth, the target would need to be able to justify the perceived costs associated with changing the behavior (e.g., less time spent at parties or with peers). Finally, the message would need to contain an element that is novel or compelling enough to be memorable and attention-getting.

It is the fifth tenet of the health belief model that deserves some attention. As previously stated, this cue to action has to grab the recipient's attention. According to Murray-Johnson and Witte (2003), cues to action allow targets to make an assessment of their own resources in order to determine if they can act on the message. More specifically, these cues to action can be internal or external. **Internal cues to action** materialize from within the individual, or are internally motivated. For instance, you might decide to start an exercise program because, when you look in the mirror lately, you don't like how your body looks. You decide to make a change because of your reasons, not because someone else in your social network told you to do it. Message designers might draw upon such internal cues by showing images of excessive body fat or other startling images. There are also **external cues to action,** which come from outside the person in the form of peer pressure or testimonials by famous actors or athletes. For instance, you may recall when Magic Johnson announced to the world that he was HIV positive. At that time, very few celebrities were brave enough to "come out" about their HIV status, and it was a time when AIDS was thought to be a disease plaguing only the homosexual community. Johnson's announcement was very shocking at the time to much of the public, but it arguably had a long-term impact on increasing awareness of the HIV/AIDS epidemic and making it more relevant to wider audiences. What makes it an external cue to action is that it motivated many people to practice safer sex and to get tested, not because of a personal reason, but because of another person's situation.

As previously stated, target audiences need to be motivated in order to make desired behavioral changes. One significant motivator is fear, and it's been used at length to get people to adopt healthy behaviors as well as change unhealthy ones. While it may be tempting to design a message that scares an audience with gruesome or shocking images, fear appeals should be used with caution when it comes to health messages. Eliciting excessive amounts of fear in target audiences can backfire, causing them either to dismiss the message as silly or to avoid the message altogether out of extreme fear. Excessive amounts of fear might be elicited through extreme details, as with Morman's (2000) study investigating the use of graphic diagrams in messages promoting testicular self-exams to detect cancer in men. When tested for their attitudes and intentions to perform self-exams, the men in Morman's study exhibited the most favorable reactions to the message when there was *no* diagram accompanying it, suggesting that the men receiving the diagram may have experienced greater levels of fear than those who received no diagram. Whether the fear is too mild or too severe, targets can become too preoccupied to think intelligently about a threat and how to protect themselves against it. More specifically, if the elicited fear is too mild, targets will not likely take the message seriously. On the other hand, an intense fear appeal can distract targets from their perceived ability to cope with the threat.

Witte (1992) addresses the use of fear in her **extended parallel process model (EPPM)**. According to the EPPM, people assess threatening messages on two levels. First, they determine whether they are personally at risk for the negative health consequence being discussed in the message. Witte calls this **danger control**. For example, targets exposed to a message about protecting themselves from the swine flu will likely determine how severe the threat of swine flu really is. Second, message targets decide whether they have the ability to prevent the negative outcome; this is called **fear control**, which also involves deciding how well they can cope with the emotional reaction to the threat. To illustrate, a man considering the threat of swine flu will assess his ability to prevent becoming infected with the virus, as well as his ability to cope with getting sick. EPPM claims that both types of control have to be high for a message to be effective, which was found to be the case in messages about performing testicular self-exams to detect cancer. In his study of fear appeals and masculinity, Morman (2000) found that men's intentions to perform the self-exam increased when both the perception of threat and coping ability were high. With this particular sample of men, however, the behavioral intention was upheld only when strong masculine beliefs were endorsed in the messages used in the study.

The distinction between assessing the threat and assessing one's reaction to it is an important one. If targets perceive a severe enough risk but don't feel they can avoid the outcome, the overall fear appeal will not work to elicit behavioral change. Imagine that you have a friend who has diabetes. She knows that diabetes is an important health issue that can cause irreversible damage if left untreated. But she may claim that diabetes runs in her family, so she's likely to get it anyway. Given this perceived likelihood of developing diabetes, not only is she likely to maintain her poor health habits, but she is likely to avoid paying attention to any diabetes health messages because of her lack of fear control.

Fear is one of the strongest motivators a message designer can use (Murray-Johnson & Witte, 2003). Yet fear is just one emotion that many message designers elicit. Other types of motivation appeals include pity and guilt, humor, and sex (Gass & Seiter, 1999). All these motivations are inducements that work to increase a target's desire to do or believe something. The trick is not to design messages that elicit emotions that could contradict each other, such as one that uses both sex appeals and appeals to guilt. Using fear or other types of motivations effectively and ethically implies consideration of the confidence of target audience members that they can cope with the very emotion or motivation being elicited (Wright et al., 2008).

Evaluating Mediated Health Messages

Not all pro-social health campaigns are created equally. Regardless of the health topic, or the theory driving the persuasive message, the most successful campaigns have some common characteristics. One important component is audience analysis, an issue that is always at the forefront of persuasion. Message designers want to understand the demographic and attitudinal characteristics of their target audiences. More specifically, they often conduct surveys and focus group interviews to get at the strongest attitudes and beliefs held by these individuals. Other questions of audience analysis have to do with reasons for targets' current behaviors, as well as financial or economic factors that prevent them from making important behavioral changes (e.g., perceived limited income that prevents buying healthy food to prevent diabetes). Besides audience analysis, another key component of a successful campaign is being able to create an awareness of the health problem and its solutions. As with the cues to action from the health belief model, awareness means grabbing and keeping the audience's attention for a lasting impact. Awareness also

PERSUASION RESEARCH SNAPSHOT

Nutrition and obesity have become ever-growing concerns in America for all ages. As you have read in this chapter, persuasion through media is especially prevalent. When you check your Facebook page, do the ads on the side entice you to purchase the product or to learn more? Do the pop-ups on Netflix.com, like "free 30 day trial of Hydroxy Cut," compel you to act now while supplies last? If instances like these are ones that you can relate to, then you know how advertising has the power to inform and persuade audiences.

Most of us are constantly consuming products, following our own brand preferences. Prior to purchasing these artifacts, we view numerous online advertisements in which spokespeople persuade us to do so. Children are just as easily influenced by these professionals, but through different means. In a recent study, researchers sought to see the effects of advertising to children through online games.

Advergames are games accessed through the Internet in which children can engage in entertainment as well as be informed by persuaders about specific brands. For example, M&Ms chocolate candies had a game that resembled PacMan. The yellow and red M&Ms, as seen on television, guided the children through the maze as they competed to get as many points as possible. While they did so, the M&M brand name and logo were integrated throughout all the images. In addition, these types of games are seen to have educational functions. They inform children about how to follow healthy eating habits, explain why ingredients included in the product are good for them, and teach kids about other subject areas such as math or science. The current study specifically focused on strategies that were most successful in persuading children.

The websites of such companies as Kellogg Company, Sour Patch Kids, and Oscar Mayer were more successful in reaching children through games than through any other application. Results of this study found that active game components were the main source of getting attention from their audiences. Of these components, brand logo was most identified, followed by the product package, the brand food item, and the spokescharacter for the brand. Very few of the advergames educated children on maintaining healthy eating habits. Many of the brands promoted candy and other products that were full of sugar, calories, and carbohydrates. Other studies support the contention that advergames promote consumption of brand products that lead to unhealthy eating habits. These unhealthy eating habits lead to obesity, which is even a bigger concern. The key component of concern is the cause of this problem. So, what is worse, the advertisers trying to sell their product or the consumption that results in obesity? Is it good health ultimately the consumer's responsibility or the persuaders'?

When you graze through a product's website, are you looking for nutritional facts or the overall appeal of the merchandise? Does the polar bear on Coca-Cola's website enhance your preference for its soda over Pepsi?

(continued)

As consumers, we must be critical of the brands companies try to sell us. Is their concern enhancing our health and informing us about how their product can improve it? Or are they promoting falsified promises through fun media such as advergames that lead us to believe that their product can truly make us healthier? Once again, the ball is in our court: We must decide which brands best suit our needs. Which brands will you choose?

Do you want to know more about this study? If, so read: Lee, M., Choi, Y., Quilliam, E. T., & Cole, R. (2009). Playing with food: Content analysis of food advergames. *Journal of Consumer Affairs, 43,* 129–154.

10.5 REMEMBER

pro-social health messages	messages designed not to sell a product or service, but to educate and persuade the public on various health issues
health campaigns	mediated messages designed to change or reinforce health behaviors, attitudes, or beliefs held by a target population
health belief model	argues that people will change a health-related behavior if they feel negatively affected by it, the negative effects of the current behavior are substantial, the behavioral change will bring about a desired result, the effort needed for them to change is worthwhile, and they are exposed to a novel or eye-opening occurrence within the message
internal cues to action	cues within a persuasive message that address motivations within the individual
external cues to action	cues within a persuasive message that address motivations derived from outside the individual, such as peer pressure or environmental factors
extended parallel process model (EPPM)	states that when people are exposed to a fear appeal, they assess their vulnerability to the perceived threat as well as their ability to cope with the threat in order to minimize its impact
danger control	determining whether you are personally at risk for the negative health consequence being discussed in the message
fear control	deciding whether you have the ability to prevent the negative outcome and deciding how you well you can cope with the emotional reaction to threat

means creating a sense of urgency so that targets assess the health issue as serious, understand how it affects them personally, and feel motivated enough to take action.

Successful messages don't just stop at creating awareness. Facilitating long-term behavioral change requires some instruction on how to enact the new, healthier behavior. Messages need to point to the means with which targets can adopt the message and perform the desired behaviors, such as specifying to heart disease patients what specific foods are low in cholesterol and where to purchase healthier foods. Finally, when using persuasive tactics, the source of the message needs to have credibility with the audience. Such a credible source can be a well-known expert or a likable celebrity who appears to be connected to the health issue. Another persuasive tactic is using the right kind and amount of emotional appeal. As stated earlier, fear appeals can be compelling, but they should be used with caution. And emotional appeals should not stand on their own; they only provide support for the content of the message, which needs to have a strong logical appeal as well.

SUMMARY

In this chapter, you studied the role persuasion plays in your health and health care, both from an interpersonal standpoint and with regard to advertisements and health campaigns. In interpersonal contexts, people use persuasion to effect change in those they relate with and care about, especially in the form of social support. In interactions between health care providers and patients, persuasion manifests itself in the way providers attempt to gain information from patients to promote their compliance with medical treatment, as well as to enhance their own credibility. Patients are persuasive, too, in that many find ways to exert their own influence in the medical conversation and avoid being labeled "bad patients."

In addition to interpersonal relationships, you also looked at persuasion as it is used in pharmaceutical advertisements and pro-social health campaigns. Direct-to-consumer advertising has swelled in the past 10 years, and you learned to understand its impact through the application of cultivation theory and social comparison theory. You have also learned about the strengths and limitations of pro-social health campaigns through an examination of the health belief model and the extended parallel process model. Finally, the most effective health campaigns possess certain characteristics: They analyze the target audience, create awareness, provide instructions and directives, and enhance source credibility.

DISCUSSION QUESTIONS

Health

1. What is *health communication* and how do scholars study persuasion in the context of health?

2. Why are some patients noncompliant with medical treatment or doctors' recommendations? How can providers use persuasion to increase patient compliance?

3. What is direct-to-consumer advertising? What are the implications of advertising directly to the consumer instead of targeting medical doctors?

4. What are the core assumptions of cultivation theory and social comparison theory? How can these theories be used to explain the effectiveness of direct-to-consumer advertising of pharmaceuticals?

5. What is the purpose of a pro-social health campaign? How effective have they been in the past when attempting to elicit changes in health-related attitudes or behaviors in their targets?

Persuasion in Business and Professional Contexts

11

YOUR OBJECTIVES

After studying this chapter, you should be able to:

1. Understand the importance of persuasion in business and professional life.
2. Distinguish between direct and indirect persuasive communication in business and professional life.
3. Understand the persuasive power of email and social networking sites.
5. Apply your study of persuasion to on-the-job situations.
6. Describe the persuasive essentials of leadership.

CHAPTER OUTLINE

Caleb works as a client relations representative for a large cell phone company—his first job since graduating from college with a major in communication. Caleb's professional goal is to work his way up into management; he's confident that his degree and track record will fast-track him to higher positions. He feels that things are going well at work, but here's the problem: Caleb's perception of himself differs from perceptions most everyone else has about him. He's not the most sensitive communicator, nor is he particularly open to feedback, so Caleb's view of himself and his potential may not be grounded in reality. He wonders what he can do to persuade his employer that he's a perfect fit for the management track.

PERSUASION IN BUSINESS AND PROFESSIONAL CONTEXTS

In this chapter, you will explore persuasion that occurs in business and professional settings. These are settings in which persuasion is important in getting a job as well as succeeding in that job. In addition, the role of persuasion in developing leadership abilities is examined. Does this sound complicated? Indeed, it can be overwhelming to think about getting a job after college. However, your study of persuasion is incomplete without considering business and professional contexts.

You've probably been asked the question, "What are you going to do after you graduate?" While it's sometimes difficult to predict the future, it's important to focus on communication skills, especially persuasive techniques, as you approach any professional context. One of the first situations in which you can use your persuasive communication skills is the job search process. Many people make the mistake of approaching their job search with too much confidence. After all, they have their degree and should be competitive in the job market, right?

Yet many people who have college degrees and professional training still struggle to find a job. We wonder, "Why can't Sarah get a job? She's so talented." Sure, Sarah *is* talented, but she may have no awareness of how she comes across in job interviews. What information does she need to succeed? How does persuasion apply to this situation? Sarah can take a look at some persuasive communication skills that are important in any professional setting.

USING PERSUASION TO GET THE JOB

In Your Life

Think about your current or future career: What strategies would you use to be persuasive during a job search or interview? As you read this chapter, be aware of both direct and indirect persuasion in your business and professional life.

Persuasive communication is critical to job applicants in any hiring situation (Quintanilla & Wahl, 2011). You may think that persuasion related to the hiring process only occurs face-to-face or in a direct manner. However, persuasion in a job search is both direct and indirect, in terms of the impression established in professional situations and the impact of these communicative decisions on the hiring process. **Direct persuasion** refers to what you do during a live interview with a hiring committee, manager, or business owner, whether it's accomplished through face-to-face interaction, telephone communication, or perhaps even an online interview via videoconference or Skype. In contrast, indirect persuasion refers to those job interviewing decisions or actions that tend not to occur face-to-face. In other words, indirect persuasion comes before or after the actual interview, but it's just as important as direct persuasion. Both of these persuasive forms are explored in the sections that follow.

Direct Persuasion

Direct persuasion can be best understood by applying many of the persuasive dimensions of the nonverbal communication codes you studied in Chapter 9 to the job interview context. One primary code is **physical appearance**—the way your body and overall appearance communicate to others and impact your view of yourself in everyday life. Physical appearance has a direct impact because it communicates something about you to people in hiring positions (Ivy & Wahl, 2009; Quintanilla & Wahl, 2011). With an increasing emphasis on communicating a professional image in the job search process, more employers are searching for people who have "the look" that will build business.

Physical appearance as direct persuasion in a job interview is important for two reasons: (1) Your physical appearance as well as the decisions you make to maintain or alter your physical appearance communicate persuasive signals to other people; and (2) the physical appearance of other people impacts your perceptions of them (and, in this case, the organization with which you interview), how you communicate with them, how approachable they seem, and the like. Your coworkers' and bosses' physical appearance directly informs you about such things as workplace culture, what clothing or uniform to wear, and what types of people work there (Ivy & Wahl, 2009).

A central component of physical appearance is clothing. Keep in mind that clothing communicates something to people, so it's no surprise that it's a critical persuasive signal in a job interview. Before going further, it's important for you to consider something that students ask about when this topic comes up in class: Students often believe that, because people who work at a certain business or organization dress casually, applicants should also dress casually for job interviews. They think that doing so will show they've done an "audience analysis," meaning they've researched the company and are dressed casually for the interview so they'll be perceived as "fitting in." This viewpoint is not accurate, so remember this: An applicant for a job is on the outside, looking in and wanting in. Job candidates don't work at the business or for the organization yet, but are selling themselves to land a position. It's not a good idea to try to match workers' style of dress until you land the job, because *you aren't yet one of them.* You need to look like you want the job, that you're competing for the job, and that you care enough about getting the job to go out of your way to look impressive.

In terms of apparel, clues such as "business casual," "professional attire," or "dressing down" give us a sense of what's expected, but you don't always get those clues provided to you prior to a job interview. Can clothing help you get a job? Nonverbal communication research reveals the persuasive cues potential employers look for. Note that this information mainly applies to career-type job interviews, not as much to interviews for part-time summer jobs or other kinds of opportunities (Ivy & Wahl, 2009):

1. In general, go for a conservative look: Remember, even if the company is a casual place, don't dress casually until you get the job. Going conservative for men means a dark suit, white shirt, and nice, serious tie (no stains, no cartoon characters), dark socks (that match the color of the suit), and dress shoes (polished and clean). For women, a dark suit with a skirt is still preferable, although pantsuits are now more acceptable than they used to be. (Watch the hemlines of the skirts, and sit down in them before you purchase them; some skirts don't work well or show more than you want when you sit.) A light-colored blouse under the suit works best; avoid bright colors. Hose and nice dress shoes (clean and polished, with a low heel) are still expected.

2. Pay attention to artifacts (e.g., jewelry, piercings, fingernail polish, makeup, briefcases) so that you don't wear or carry too much of anything that might be distracting to an interviewer. Nice leather or microfiber accessories (portfolios, briefcases) make a good impression.

3. The best guideline is to find out ahead of the interview what is standard or typical dress at the organization you're interviewing with, and go one step higher or more professional than that. You can tone it down once you get the job.

Hair length is another persuasive factor to consider related to physical appearance. Young men who want to be viewed in job interviews as more mature and seasoned are often advised by stylists to let their hair grow out to a traditional length in order to avoid the look of a "baby face" (Masip, Garrido, & Herrero, 2004). Men with longer hair (below the collar) are advised to cut or trim their hair for interviews so that they will be viewed as professional, serious, and credible. Keep in mind that hair length and style may not be important in certain industries, so you can do what you want with your hair *once you land a job*. But when you're *seeking* the job, your best bet is to go conservative. If you are male and have long hair, at least pull it back for the interview. What about men's facial hair? Job interviewers' perceptions of facial hair vary, so whether facial hair will work for or against you in an interview can depend on the situation. The most conservative look is clean-shaven.

Body smell during a job interview is another form of direct persuasion. Communication scholars use the term **olfaction** to refer to the role of smell in human interaction (Andersen, 2004). For both women and men, it's a balancing act in terms of how much scent, body powder, or cologne to use, since smell is closely connected to our overall appearance. Nonverbal communication scholar Robert Baron (1983) studied artificial scents and the evaluation of job applicants. Male interviewers in his study struggled when they tried to ignore applicants' smell, more so than female interviewers. Male interviewers rated applicants who wore cologne less favorably than those who did not, while female interviewers rated applicants wearing cologne more favorably. You might think that cologne would be a good thing to wear at an interview, since it could help create a positive impression. The opposite is actually true: Avoid wearing any cologne when interviewing for a job because nervous perspiration can activate and enhance the strength of a scent. You could overwhelm an interviewer and lose a job opportunity, all because your cologne was too strong.

What other aspects of direct persuasion do you need to be aware of when trying to get a job? In addition to physical appearance, your **kinesics** (defined as human movement, gestures, and posture), in particular your

In Your Life

Considering the research on the persuasive dimensions of smell in interview situations, what decision would you make? Would you choose to wear cologne or perfume?

body posture, serves as direct nonverbal persuasion since posture is attached to many attractive attributes in U.S. culture, such as confidence, positivity, and high self-esteem (Guerrero & Floyd, 2006). People make personality judgments based on something as subjective as posture, so it's worth thinking about. How aware are you of your posture? Do you tend to stand in a dominant position, or does your stance typically give off signs of weakness, timidity, or low self-esteem? In a job interview, an interviewer tends to be much more relaxed than an applicant, who is putting herself or himself on the line to get hired. So even if the interviewer looks relaxed, maintain your professional, erect body posture. The level of relaxation or tension you feel will tend to show up in body posture and movement, which can be clues to potential employers (Ivy & Wahl, 2009).

Ever thought about the persuasiveness of your voice during an interview? Remember that when you study how people express themselves through their voices, you're studying **vocalics,** sometimes referred to as *paralanguage*. Besides being able to identify someone from his or her voice, you can also come to detect physical, emotional, and attitudinal states through **tone of voice,** which is a nontechnical term for all the elements that the human voice can produce and manipulate. Think about the direct impact your tone of voice can have in an interview setting. What does your voice say about you to potential employers? Vocalics are particularly critical in telephone interviews, which these days are often precursors to face-to-face interviews. Phone interviews save employers money and time, and they're often a weeding-out tool.

One very important aspect of direct persuasion to consider within the category of **haptics** (or touch) is the **professional handshake,** which can be distinguished from the social handshake (Hiemstra, 1999). In professional settings in the United States, the handshake is critical to making a good first impression. In the professional handshake, here's what needs to happen: The hands need to meet fully, firmly, and equally (meaning palm-to-palm; locked or hooked around the space between the thumb and forefinger; and with no turn of the hands, i.e., hands stay straight up and down) and definite but brief shaking. Social handshakes don't usually turn out this way; they often aren't equal, meaning that people may only take the time to grab part of the hand or a few fingers. They're often accomplished with a quick touch and no shake, and this may or may not create a negative impression. However, giving a social handshake when a professional one is expected will not serve you well.

Your communication classes are not a bad place to practice shaking hands with others. Read over the explanation of a good professional handshake above, and see if you can extend this kind of shake to classmates and they to you. Are certain handshakes better than others? Why?

Do some handshakes creep you out? Why? Here a few handshake types to avoid (Ivy & Wahl, 2009):

1. **The Crusher** A person can give you a painful experience by squeezing your hand too tightly. Some men exhibit this behavior, as though handshaking were a precursor to arm wrestling or some other form of competition.
2. **The Pumper** A person who shakes too long can leave you rattled—physically and emotionally. Too much shaking can be a nonverbal sign that you're overeager.
3. **The Taker** A person who takes your hand to shake it before you've even extended it can send aggressive signals. Most often, this is a nonverbal dominance move.
4. **The Frenchie** No international stereotypes intended, but some men (French as well as American) have seen too many old movies in which a man took a woman's hand, turned it palm down, raised it, and kissed it. You know this form of greeting is unprofessional, but you may run into this kind of shaker socially.
5. **The Gapper** One handshake that tends to give people a creepy or empty, unfulfilled feeling occurs when they can't feel the palm of the other person. The credibility of a handshake lies mostly in the palms. If you extend your hand straight out to people and they cup their hand instead of responding with a flat palm, it creates a hollow in the handshake and tends to give people negative impressions. People may deem you weak, untrustworthy, or insecure if you give them a "gapped" handshake.

In Your Life

Have you experienced any of these handshakes? What was your reaction or impression of the person? Your handshake may not come immediately to mind as an important direct persuasive tool when approaching the professional interview, but it's something to think about and work on.

One final form of direct persuasive communication critical to successful job interviewing is **eye gaze** (commonly referred to as eye contact), defined as looking at the general eye area of other people. Eye gaze is extremely important in U.S. culture, because people make all kinds of judgments about others—particularly about their trustworthiness and sincerity—on the basis of whether they make or avoid eye contact. In fact, research has found that of all the nonverbal cues, eye contact is the most critical to judgments of credibility (Beebe, 1974). So if you want to be persuasive within the first few seconds of meeting a potential employer, you will stand with good posture and extend your hand to give a firm, professional handshake while at the same time making good eye contact.

The next section gives attention to indirect persuasion, or the more subtle cues that impact getting a job.

direct persuasion	persuasive cues related to telephone, face-to-face, or online communication, as in a live interview with a hiring committee, manager, or business owner
physical appearance	how our bodies and appearance persuade others and impact our view of ourselves
olfaction	role of smell in human interaction
kinesics	human movement, gestures, and posture
vocalics	how people express themselves through their voice
tone of voice	elements that the human voice can produce and manipulate
haptics	human touch
professional handshake	full, firm, and equal handshake that makes a good and professional first impression
eye gaze (contact)	looking at the general eye area of other people

Indirect Persuasion

As established in the previous sections, the direct power of nonverbal communication is persuasive. What about more subtle, *indirect* persuasion? Realize that indirect persuasion can make all the difference when it comes to standing out among other applicants. As a reminder, **indirect persuasion** refers to decisions or actions that tend not to occur face-to-face; these are the subtle cues that speak volumes about you before or after the actual interview, and they're just as important as the direct cues.

Let's begin with the **cover letter** (letter of introduction to a potential employer) and **resume** (a document that details your educational and professional experience). You've probably not thought of it this way before, but cover letters and resumes serve as nonverbal reflections of who you are and what you have to offer. Many job application processes today are conducted entirely online, but some companies and organizations still prefer receiving hard copies of documents. Plus it's wise to take hard-copy backups of documents with you to interviews, so that if your interviewer misplaced your materials, you have extras to provide.

When introducing yourself, expressing your interest in the job, listing your education, career goals, experience, references, and so on, think about what your documents communicate nonverbally about you. Given that a cover letter and resume are a bunch of words on pieces of paper, how can they persuade employers to hire you or not? Here are some aspects of cover letters and resumes that you need to consider if you hope to present yourself to potential employers in the best manner possible.

1. **Paper Quality**   People who submit cover letters and resumes on traditional white (cheap) printer paper run the risk of having their documents look like everyone else's. In contrast, documents printed on high-quality beige or gray paper say something about the applicant's interest in establishing a positive first impression. This trend can vary year to year; if everyone is using light-colored paper, use white paper to make your documents stand out.

2. **Print Quality, Font, and Ink Color**   In addition to the quality of your cover letter and resume paper, it's also important to consider print quality, font, and color. Poorly printed documents can send a message that an applicant is sloppy or doesn't care about details. The font you choose to use communicates nonverbal signals as well and conveys your words in a manner that shapes people's impressions of you (Bringhurst, 2004). Think also about ink color for your cover letter and resume. It's unwise to try to squeeze out the last bit of ink from a cartridge to print job interview documents; if your typeface is too faint to be easily read, your papers will most likely end up in the trash, so make sure your print is dark and readable. While most of us print important documents in traditional black, some people print resumes in blue, red, or even pink ink! What kind of signal does ink color send? Some employers may see the use of ink colors other than black as creative or distinct, while others will see it negatively, deciding you're "off the wall." A good rule of thumb is to stick with traditional black because of the potential indirect message other colors might send.

3. **Typos and Misspellings**   **Typos** (mistakes in typing) and **misspellings** (mistakes in spelling) can certainly influence employers' perceptions of you in a negative way. These are probably the most common mistakes students make with their cover letters and resumes. Resumes with even a single typo can immediately land in the garbage can. People *do* make mistakes, but the job interview process is a critical time in your life to be extra careful with communication. Misspellings, typos, and wrong addresses are indirect forms of nonverbal persuasion that can prevent you from getting an interview or proceeding beyond the first level. Don't rely solely on a computer spell-check program; get a second set of eyes to proofread your resume before copying it and certainly before sending it out.

Social Media in Your Life: Have You Seen This?

Go to YouTube and enter the following keywords: That Guy: Interview

This clip illustrates what not to do in a business and professional situation. See if you can find other clips related to the persuasive and not so persuasive dimensions of business and professional communication.

4. **Length**   The general rule used to be, and still is to a great extent, to keep your cover letter short and sweet and your resume to a single page. However, for some of us who have years of experience, a one-page resume is hard to manage and doesn't really sell us in the best way. You may encounter a reason to produce a more extended resume, but just realize that some potential employers will hurl your resume in the trash heap without reading it simply because it's longer than one page.

Email

What are some other factors that serve as indirect persuasion? Since so much pre-interview communication takes place via email, it's important to think about the influence of email exchanges. For starters, have you ever thought about how your email address communicates such things as your personality, interests, occupation, and even your deviances from the norm? Granted, the address itself is verbal, but the image it communicates makes it a nonverbal cue. The typical email address for a professor might look like this: <richard.prof@university.edu>. The first part of the email address designates the owner's or recipient's name; the last part points to the server or location where the recipient can be found.

As email has become more commonly utilized, people have begun to move away from providing their real name in their email address in order to protect their identity (Ivy & Wahl, 2009; Quintanilla & Wahl, 2011). Instead, now many people select something about themselves to include, so that they communicate a more creative email address. For example, Rachel is on the swim team and her athletic participation is a defining factor in her sense of self. Instead of using <rachel.garcia@email.com>, Rachel can have some fun by creating a different email address, such as <swimmingdolphin@email.com>. Reflect on your email address for just a moment. Does it contain your real name or a made-up name? Perhaps you set up your email account years ago. Does your email address still reflect who you are and is it appropriate for the business world? Further, make sure that you review every email to ensure that you've included appropriate content (see Figure 11.1).

While there is a sense of play or freedom when setting up an email address, it's important to think about the impressions others will form about us based on such a simple thing as our email address (Ivy & Wahl, 2009). Remember to take a critical look at your email addresses when applying for jobs or graduate programs. Think about the reaction a job recruiter or graduate director might have when receiving an email message from <funnybunny@university.edu> or <readyforanyone@hotmail.com> versus

✓ Uses spell-check to fix mechanical and grammatical errors

✓ Is free from jokes

✓ Doesn't contain harassing, negative, or aggressive language

✓ Illustrates professional excellence

✓ Is free of racist, sexist, or discriminatory language

✓ Is free of sexual language, violence, and pornographic images

FIGURE 11.1 Checklist for Appropriate Email Content

Source: Flynn, N. (2008). *The e-policy handbook: Rules and best practices to safely manage your company's email, blogs, social networking, and other electronic communication tools.* Broadway, NY: AMACOM Books.

<stacy.student@university.edu>. Which address implies more credibility and communicates a more positive first impression, professionally speaking? In addition to your actual email address, remember to think about how others might perceive you based on your email style. Take a look at Figure 11.2 and think critically about the content of your email before you hit Send.

Bully	verbally aggressive and usually insulting
Impersonal Comedian/ Watchdog	forwards material such as jokes, funny stories, and warnings about computer viruses and scams to people's address books
Inspirational Speaker	forwards messages about medical tribute months, fundraisers, and good causes; also known to send religious information and prayer requests
Jack Rabbit	responds to email messages immediately but hurriedly; often uses incomplete sentences, abbreviations (such as "bc" for "because" and "LOL" for "laugh out loud"), no caps, and no punctuation
Non-Responder	refuses to respond to email messages even when questions are raised
Over-Talker (AKA, "It's All about Me")	sends lengthy, self-oriented email messages, often containing vivid, personal self-disclosure, accompanied by numerous recent photos; expects an immediate reply as to what you think about her/him, the disclosure, and the photos
Sniper	passive/aggressive style; uses brief, one-word replies; too busy to write in complete sentences
Trainee	first-time user lacking confidence; usually sends the same message two or three times; neglects or forgets to attach pictures and documents
Turtle	takes 2 to 3 weeks to respond to email messages; original message is forgotten by the time the reply is received

FIGURE 11.2 Email Styles

Source: Figure adapted and reproduced with permission of: Ivy, D. K., & Wahl, S. T. (2009). The *nonverbal self: Communication for a lifetime.* Boston, MA: Allyn & Bacon.

Ethical Connection

What do you think about an employer or job recruiter conducting an online search about you? Do you think this practice is ethical? Why? Why not?

Social Networking: The Facebook Factor

Have you ever attended a business etiquette dinner? Panelists from major corporations give students tips for landing a job in their company and presenting themselves in the job market. Students often ask: "Is it true that many companies are now looking at applicants' Facebook accounts and running Google searches to see what comes up?" Indeed, representatives from various companies will likely respond that they have, in fact, run Internet searches on potential applicants. Many recruiters are especially interested in how potential applicants represent themselves online. So, in addition to the email address you use in your job search process, it's also important to be mindful about what you post on the web related to your personal life.

In addition to pre-interview persuasive communication (e.g., your resume paper, print details, email addresses), think about post-interview decisions that can send nonverbal signals. Business etiquette specialists and personal effectiveness consultants advise people always to send a thank-you note after such encounters as job interviews (Post & Post, 2005). If you have a group of people interviewing you, the suggestion is to thank each person individually, not just the chair or head of the group. But will an email message of thanks suffice? Email has evolved into a norm for our everyday communication, especially in professional contexts. Many people have gotten away from sending handwritten thank-you notes via traditional mail since email is faster and cheaper. After all, isn't an email message sent hours or the day after a job interview more impressive than a handwritten card received days or weeks later? While sending a thank-you email is indeed faster, it doesn't take much time or effort, and employers know that (because they use email a lot, too). What nonverbal signal

11.2 REMEMBER

indirect persuasion	decisions or actions that tend not to occur face to face, but before or after a job interview
cover letter	letter of introduction to a potential employer
resume	a document that details a job applicant's educational and professional experience
typos	mistakes in typing
misspellings	mistakes in spelling

about you and your professionalism is conveyed when a potential employer receives a nice-looking, handwritten thank-you note within a few days of your interview? Such attention to detail and the care involved can communicate many positive things about you.

PERSUASION ON THE JOB

You've been fortunate enough to impress the hiring committee and/or manager, and now they're bringing you in as part of their team. So, what do you do *now*? What can you expect on the job? Whom are you going to talk to? Are you going to get along with your clients? Are your customers or coworkers going to be nice? These are important questions to think about. This section of the chapter focuses on the important role of persuasive communication with the customers or clients you're expected to impress. After all, your successful use of persuasion to get the job is what got you here in the first place!

Persuading Customers and Clients

Nonverbal communication is critical to successfully interacting with customers, clients, or potential business contacts. As you make this connection between persuasion and business and professional contexts, always consider the persuasive power of nonverbal communication. **Customer relations,** also known as customer service, is the interaction between employees or representatives of an organization or business and the people the organization sells to or serves. Retail centers, restaurants, banks, insurance companies, movie theaters, and so on are but a few examples of locations in which we experience service. Nonverbal communication helps professionals fine-tune their relations with customers, who expect and demand excellent service. In today's competitive business environment, consumers expect to be served by competent professionals knowledgeable about their products and services and who communicate with dignity, respect, and courtesy. Unfortunately, many times that's not the case.

Let's explore some basic persuasive functions of nonverbal cues, relating them to customer service. Nonverbal cues can work independently or in tandem with verbal language to convey meaning. First, nonverbal cues can *substitute* for verbal messages. Imagine you're at a basketball game and see a guy going up and down the aisles of the arena, selling cotton candy. He gets near your row and your hunger kicks in, but you know he can't hear you way down the row. You simply call on your nonverbal powers, wave to get his attention, make eye contact, and hold up one or two fingers, depending how hungry you are. These kinesic and eye behaviors substitute when verbal communication won't do the trick. In customer relations,

In Your Life

As you think about your role as a customer across industries (e.g., travel, dining, shopping), what are the persuasive qualities of someone you view as professional? In addition, what would you do as a professional to persuade your clients and/or customers about the product or service you're representing?

nonverbal cues often substitute for verbal messages; that's why it's important for customer service reps to work to develop and improve their nonverbal sending and receiving abilities.

Nonverbal cues are used in connection with words, to *complement* your communication or to clarify or extend the meaning of your words. This complementary function allows you to convey more information, leading to a more accurate interpretation by receivers of your communication. Complementary cues also help color your expressed emotions and attitudes. For example, a long, heavy sigh may reveal how tired or bored you are—something to avoid if you work in customer relations. You've likely placed an order at a fast-food restaurant and heard the voice of an employee sigh, "Whenever you're ready..." The likely downward pitch and sigh accompanying the speech act to cue you as to the emotional (bored) state of the employee.

On occasion, your nonverbal cues *contradict* rather than complement your verbal cues. Have you ever dealt with someone behind a counter when you have a real problem with something you bought that now won't work? While the employee's verbal communication might be acceptable, his nonverbal facial expressions, body posture, vocalic indications of exasperation, and other cues contradict the verbal message. Sometimes customer service reps get frustrated or sick of dealing with complainers all day, but that doesn't mean their behavior as professionals shouldn't be at its best. Those of you who work in customer relations, either part time while in college or as a career, need to remember that you need to coordinate your nonverbal and verbal communication so as to represent your organization professionally.

Nonverbal behaviors may also serve a *repeating* function. Say you're working as a flight attendant and the airline you work for allows passengers to bring only one carry-on item onto the plane. A passenger has violated the carry-on rule, made it past the ticket counter workers, and now wants to stow all of her stuff. The first time you speak to her, you (the customer service rep) explain that she needs to gate-check extra bags. When you realize that the passenger is too far away from you or too wrapped up in the "stowing" activity to hear you, you hold up baggage claim tickets and point to the excessive bags. In this example, your verbal communication comes first, followed by a nonverbal signal that repeats the message, thus clarifying the communication that's exchanged between the two of you. Customer service personnel often use this repeating function, because many times customers won't understand or accept a verbal message alone.

One of the more fascinating persuasive functions of nonverbal communication in customer relations is its ability to *regulate* conversation (Ekman, 1965). Most conversations occur in a series of turns at talk by the interactants, and this is true of the customer service rep/customer exchange as well. Those turns are negotiated by a series of regulator cues. For example, the customer service rep may lean toward the customer, make eye contact, raise his eyebrows, and take in a breath—all before uttering a word. These nonverbal cues are important, because when customers perceive positive conversational regulators—bodily, facial, and vocal cues of patience and concern—the entire exchange is affected and likely to move in the right direction. Similarly, when customers are frustrated or aggressive, their negative nonverbal conversational regulators may rouse the same kind of behavior in the employee. The whole point of the exchange is likely to be defeated as a result.

Finally, nonverbal behaviors in customer relations often *accent* or emphasize a verbal message. Customer relations professionals have to be very careful on this point, because certain accenting cues can be perceived negatively and can make a bad encounter with a member of the public worse. For example, if an angry or frustrated customer slams down a receipt on a counter, yelling "Just give me my money back!" a customer service rep shouldn't follow suit or the exchange will escalate, possibly causing other disgruntled customers to become involved. Many customer relations personnel work entirely over the phone. Nonverbal vocalic accents—like raising the pitch or volume of the voice—are tricky, too, because such cues typically intensify a bad situation. Telephone service reps need to be trained in how to use their voices to calm and reassure customers, but not patronize or appease them.

Communicating effectively with customers is essential in professional contexts. If you work in customer service, take responsibility for the excellent service you're expected to provide. Customers and clients want to do business with organizations and professionals who employ effective verbal and nonverbal communication skills—those who are empathetic and responsive to their concerns. **Unresponsive behavior**—verbally and nonverbally communicating an apathetic or uncaring attitude–is deadly in customer service. Many of us have experienced bad service from unresponsive agents; they give off that blank stare that tells us they could care less and hate their jobs. They've seen enough crabby people all day, and we're just the next person in a very long line. As people, they may not be aggressive or rude, but as employees, their facial expressions, lack of eye contact, and flat vocal tone make us feel unimportant or, worse, like a nuisance.

So in sum, customer relations professionals should employ nonverbal communication behaviors such as smiling, making eye contact, and exhibiting a positive attitude through tone of voice. For instance, consider the work of professional communication consultants who use their expertise as communication scholars to assist in the design and delivery of customer service trainings, orientation programs, and leadership seminars. One of the most requested workshop topics—from professionals in the health care industry to real estate—is customer service, because companies know the value of excellent customer service for new and repeat business. Some of the most highly trained professionals in industries of all kinds need a reminder that their communication skills, especially their nonverbal skills, are crucial in fostering a work environment in which people treat others with respect.

Ever thought about how to empathize with someone who is frustrated? Better yet, how would you train others to communicate empathy to others, especially in business and professional settings? Researchers have examined the process of training employees in persuasive techniques, as the Persuasion Research Snapshot describes.

 PERSUASION RESEARCH SNAPSHOT

As students, many of you are unfamiliar with professional work settings and environments. However, after graduation your interactions in these settings are going to become a critical part of your professional career. Persuading customers and other businesses is important in virtually every communication field. Think about it: What types of persuasion are the most effective in a business setting? Convincing a friend to help you move requires slightly different persuasive skills than convincing another company to buy your product. How do you know what persuasive strategies are the most effective?

Persuasion is a vital skill in every aspect of life, but special emphasis is placed on professional persuasion because it is through this communication that you will make a living. Today's marketplace is becoming increasingly more competitive at the business-to-business level, and companies are keen to improve communications with potential customers. Sales training in the current workplace focuses on improving not only verbal communication, but nonverbal as well. With that in mind, using empathy (mentally placing yourself in the position of another person) and mirroring (imitating the speech and nonverbal communication of another person) are uniquely important in business persuasion.

In a recent study, researchers Robin Peterson and Yam Limbu looked at the empathy and mirroring strategies to see how effective each was in an exploratory study. Both mirroring theory and empathy theory were used to better frame the researchers' findings. The researchers asked the question: If three separate groups are specifically trained in either empathy or mirroring strategies (or both), which group will have more effective salespeople? Twelve separate classes were divided into four groups; one group was specifically trained in empathy strategies, one group in mirroring strategies, one group in both, and the last group received no training, thereby becoming the control group. After the training was completed, each student made a sales call to a small retailer in an attempt to convince him or her to attend a free sales techniques seminar on campus.

The study showed that there was no significant difference in the effectiveness of empathy or mirroring training when taken by themselves. However, when mirroring and empathy training were combined, there was a significant increase in positive response from the retailers. The control group scored lowest in all categories, leading researchers to propose that some training is more effective than none at all.

Think about what this means for businesses today. There is no definite "best" strategy to use in business persuasion. Rather, combining persuasive techniques seems to be the best course of action. Does this change how you would go about communicating to a target customer? Why would being able to empathize with customers and mirror their communication work so well together? Adapting your communication to others is an important skill, especially in the art of persuasion. Think about how you accommodate others during your interactions throughout the day, and consider how it helps your ability to persuade.

Do you want to know more about this study? If so, read: Peterson, R. T., & Limbu, Y. (2009). The convergence of mirroring and empathy: Communications training in business-to-business personal selling persuasion efforts. *Journal of Business-to-Business Marketing, 16*(3), 193–219.

The Persuasive Essentials of Leadership

Leadership is "a dynamic relationship based on mutual influence and common purpose between leaders and collaborators in which both are moved to higher levels of motivation and moral development as they affect real, intended change" (Freiberg & Freiberg, 1996, p. 298). As you study this definition, the role of persuasion in leadership should be clear to you. According to this definition, *change* is dependent on a dynamic relationship, mutual influence, and a common purpose. You can't have a *dynamic*

11.3 REMEMBER

customer relations	also known as customer service—the interaction between employees or representatives of an organization or business and the people the organization sells to or serves
unresponsive behavior	verbal and nonverbal communication of an apathetic or uncaring attitude
leadership	a dynamic relationship based on mutual influence and common purpose between leaders and collaborators in which both are moved to higher levels of motivation and moral development as they affect real, intended change

relationship without effective communication. In addition, *mutual influence* and *common purpose* both rely on two-way communication. Furthermore, having leaders and *collaborators*, as opposed to leaders and followers, again implies the need for effective communication. By examining this and other definitions of leadership, the role of persuasion is clear.

So far, this chapter has applied persuasion to important professional situations—persuading to get a job and functioning on the job. This discussion brings your next point of study—persuasion and leadership. No doubt, many readers of this textbook are currently in leadership positions in their educational, professional, social, or personal lives. Many of you will emerge into leadership as you finish school and pursue your career interests. No matter where you are in the process of developing leadership, attention to nonverbal communication will only enhance what you can achieve. One of the most important facets of being persuasive as a leader is mastering nonverbal communication.

Scholars have long studied the topic of leadership and communication, providing typologies of leadership styles, strategies, and approaches. Here are some questions to get you started: Do you join clubs as a college student and remain just a member, or do you tend to become a leader of those clubs? If you admire leadership as a quality in people, but you don't view yourself as a leader, why is that? What are some persuasive qualities and nonverbal communication skills of good leaders?

Many people make the mistake of viewing leadership as a title. Once they're promoted or elected into a particular position of leadership, they think that's it—*job over, I've arrived.* Leadership is a skill, one that needs to be developed and fostered throughout life. Think about the qualities of leaders who are successful at what they do. What makes them great? How are they persuasive in their communication?

Impression Management   One of the essential leadership abilities is **impression management,** controlling the impression, perception, or view others have of you. Effective leaders work on creating a desired impression so that others perceive them as they want to be perceived. They also recognize others' efforts at impression management. Communication scholars Crane and Crane (2002) provide specific impression management strategies for leaders:

1. Effective leaders should recognize a variety of factors that lead to the use of impression management strategies by employees. In other words, leaders should be effective receivers and interpreters of the verbal and nonverbal cues their employees, coworkers, superiors, and customers/clients give off as they attempt to affect others' perceptions of them.

2. Some level of impression management is always going to be present in professional settings. Leaders should differentiate between honest versus manipulative strategies used by employees to shape perception.

3. Effective leaders should become keenly aware of the image they wish to project to their audience, and work to actually project the desired image, staying open to feedback about their image. (That audience includes customers/clients, subordinates, fellow leaders, superiors, and rivals.)

4. Before using an impression management strategy, it's important for leaders to know their audience, the situation, and the goal of any encounter.

5. Leaders should lead through honest performance. The best impression a leader can make is to be a high performer.

6. Leaders should present their real selves and not a false front to their various audiences; reality makes the best impression.

Dress to Impress   Another essential for leaders is to wear clothing and use accessories (artifacts) that signal to others that they're leaders. Many of the tips provided for appropriate interview attire apply to leaders as well. However, leaders may need to strategically "dress down" when a situation calls for it, such as when they're expected to build rapport with clients or employees or informally celebrate an organization's accomplishments.

Business and Social Etiquette   Leaders should strive to enact the following business and social etiquette skills:

1. Know how to make an entrance and work a room.

2. Be well versed in first-meeting (initial interaction) strategies (e.g., professional handshakes).

3. Practice making business and social introductions with confidence and poise.

4. Pay attention to others' nonverbal cues, as well as the related emotions and attitudes driving those cues.

5. Make use of the skill of perception checking. That is, check your perceptions of others with people you trust.

Utilizing Power in Leadership   True leadership is about power. Both professional and personal relationships have a power dimension. So, in order to better understand the role of power in your relationships and the resulting communication, let's look at the five types of power as defined by John French and Bertram Raven (1968): legitimate power, coercive power, reward power, expert power, referent power, and connection power.

Legitimate power is based on a position of authority. The manager has legitimate power over the department budget and employee schedules. While a position/job title may give someone legitimate power, it doesn't mean he or she will exercise that power (Quintanilla & Wahl, 2011).

Coercive power refers to the ability to control another person's behavior with negative reinforcement, while **reward power** describes control over another person's behavior through positive reinforcement. Clearly, a person with legitimate power has both coercive and reward power over subordinates. For example, a manager could reward an employee with a paid vacation and a raise or punish the employee with an undesirable schedule and no raise. But people with legitimate power are not the only ones with coercive and reward power. Anyone who can offer positive or negative reinforcements has power. So, the staff member who can process your paperwork quickly versus slowly and the administrative assistant who can choose to squeeze you in or make you wait for a meeting with the boss both have coercive and reward power (Quintanilla & Wahl, 2011).

Expert power is based on one's superior expertise in a specific field. In our fast-paced, increasingly specialized world, it should be no surprise that experts are given power. Consider the *Saturday Night Live* skit on expert power. The skit begins with a song: "Nick Burns, your company's computer guy. He's gonna fix your computer and then he's gonna make fun of you." Why would Nick Burns make fun of his coworkers? He finds their lack of knowledge about computers irritating. The coworkers put up with the abuse because they need him. Without Nick's knowledge, they can't do their jobs. He has expertise that gives him power over them.

You give **referent power** to someone because you want that person to like you. You may feel a connection to that person or you may wish to be like that person—either way, it gives him or her power over you. High school peer pressure is a form of referent power. Sasha has been a partner at the law firm for years. She's organized, highly knowledgeable, and excellent with clients. Sasha has a very positive attitude about life and has found a healthy balance between work life and home life. While she has never taken a leadership title, many of the young attorneys look to her as a role model. They follow her lead and seek her advice because they have granted her referent power.

Connection power is based on the old expression: It's not what you know but who you know. Having a connection to people in positions of power or having a strong support system definitely acts as a source of power. If the CEO's son works in the mailroom, chances are he will be treated very differently than the other members of the mailroom staff.

Examining types of power reveals a critical difference between managers and leaders. "Manager" is a title, which brings with it legitimate power. **Managerial functions** include important duties like being in charge of and responsible for various goals and functions in an organization. They also involve supervising subordinates. Leaders may be managers and they may have legitimate power, but neither is a requirement for leadership. **Leadership functions** include influencing and guiding followers as opposed to subordinates, as well as being innovative and creating a vision for future direction. Leaders often have multiple types of power, with referent power likely to be in the mix (Quintanilla & Wahl, 2011).

11.4 REMEMBER

impression management	controlling the impression, perception, or view others have of you
legitimate power	power based on a position of authority
coercive power	the ability to control another person's behavior with negative reinforcement
reward power	control over another person's behavior through positive reinforcement
expert power	power based on one's superior expertise in a specified field
referent power	power you give to another when you want him or her to like you
connection power	power derived from having a connection to people in positions of power or having a strong support system
managerial functions	important duties such as being in charge and responsible for various goals and functions in an organization
leadership functions	influencing and guiding followers as opposed to subordinates, as well as being innovative and creating a vision for future direction

Remember: You can use your knowledge of persuasion to engage real-life situations. Consider the scenario below and think about what you would do as you apply your study of persuasion to business and professional life.

You have become extremely close with four of your coworkers. After work, you often go out for drinks with them, and you have even babysat twice for two of them. Needless to say, trust is not an issue among the five of you; you are all the best of friends. Monday morning rolls around, and as you sit down at your desk you notice that there is an opportunity for a promotion within your company. You are extremely interested in this opportunity. That day at lunch, you and this group of friends are sitting around the table at your regular café of choice when you find that the four of them plan to apply for this position as well. As it comes time for interviews, you are selected to interview last. When you walk into the office and sit in front of your boss's desk, she asks you one simple question: "Why should I pick you instead of the other four who are applying for this promotion?" Immediately you realize that you and your best friends are the only ones who applied. Without degrading your friends or reporting any of their misbehaviors, how do you persuade your boss that you are "better" and more deserving than your best friends? What would you do?

SUMMARY

This chapter explored the application of persuasion to a key context in your life: business and professional settings. Remember the importance of direct and indirect persuasive communication in trying to get a job and the impact of direct persuasion during job interviews (e.g., physical appearance, clothing, hair length, body smell, professional handshake). Be aware of the more subtle, indirect forms of persuasion before and after an interview (e.g., your resume, hand-written thank-you notes, email addresses, web postings).

Next you reviewed the persuasive dimensions of leadership. Factors such as impression management and being aware of one's own and others' verbal and nonverbal communication are essential to leadership. Effective leaders pay attention to their own nonverbal communication. Further, effective leaders understand the different types of power and are able to make important distinctions between managerial and leadership functions.

DISCUSSION QUESTIONS

Business

1. What forms of direct persuasion do you think are most important when trying to get a job? What indirect nonverbal strategies are most important?

2. Do you think that a professional handshake is an important skill for you to work on, or do you have this nonverbal cue down?

3. Think about your current social networking accounts in terms of what's available to the public. Will you remove information posted on the web about yourself once you're job hunting?

4. Are you going to change your email address for business and professional contexts or keep the same one you've had as a college student? Why or why not?

5. Review how leadership is connected to persuasion. Make a list of people you look up to for their leadership skills. What makes them persuasive? Which qualities of theirs do you find motivating?

Persuasive Presentations

Eric Jenkins and Chad Edwards

12

YOUR OBJECTIVES

After studying this chapter, you should be able to:

1. Understand the questions of policy, value, and fact and apply them to your study of persuasion presentations.
2. List and describe the organizational patterns for persuasive presentations.
3. Identify and describe the types of arguments.
4. Identify and describe the standards for arguments.
5. Recognize common fallacies used in persuasive presentations.

CHAPTER OUTLINE

Presentations

I'm going to speak in favor of the city smoking ordinance.

My specific purpose is to persuade the audience not to text and drive.

I need to persuade the audience to engage their community through volunteering.

Kids shouldn't play video games because they promote violence.

Freedom is America's most valuable contribution to the world because freedom reduces suffering.

Social Media in Your Life: Have You Seen This?

Go to YouTube and enter the following keywords: the office, presentation clip

This clip contains an example of a presentation. How effective were the presenter's methods of presenting?

PERSUASIVE PRESENTATIONS IN YOUR LIFE

The statements above should make you think: Are there any topics in your life that you might want to persuade others about? In this chapter, you will review the importance of persuasive presentations in your life. Presenting persuasive arguments and information is vitally important in the world today. Whether you're discussing a city smoking ordinance or speaking in favor of a day care program on your college campus, you're engaged in the creation of a persuasive argument. With the emergence of new technologies (e.g., videoconferences, Skype), you can no longer expect a persuasive presentation to be seen only by those in the room. Instead, your persuasive presentations can be disseminated across the world, using a vast array of technology. Therefore, you need to prepare for future careers in which your persuasive presentations may need to persuade larger, more global audiences. This chapter will address how you can create organized and effective persuasive presentations and familiarize you with the different types of argument. Additionally, this chapter will help you support your claims and arguments and show you how to organize your information in order to persuade others.

DETERMINING YOUR PERSUASIVE PURPOSE

You first need to decide on the purpose of your persuasive presentation. This important step will allow you to plan how and what to research, how to organize, and how to best format your argument in your persuasive speech. In the following section, you will read about various types of topics and purpose statements.

Topic

The **topic** is the general idea of your persuasive presentation. Take, for example, a workplace situation. Your boss needs you to present a persuasive appeal to the sales force that the company should start targeting older adults as customers. The general topic for this persuasive appeal would be "The Older Adult Demographic and Shopping Preferences." At first glance, you might be thinking that this is a large topic to cover in a small presentation. You are right. The next step is to narrow this topic down.

General Purpose Statement

General purpose statements are statements about the reason for the speech. Basically, the general purpose statement expresses the overall goal of the appeal. Your general purpose will be either *to inform* or *to persuade*. The general purpose is usually decided for you. In this case, your boss wants you to persuade. Your local service club might want you to deliver a presentation informing the club about an issue of local importance. Most presentations contain elements of each type of general purpose. However, if the overall goal is informing, then the general purpose is *to inform*. If the overall goal is persuading, then the general purpose is *to persuade*. In this chapter, you will learn specifically about persuading.

Specific Purpose Statement

Specific purpose statements are the exact goals of the presentation. Specific purpose statements contain both the general topic and the general purpose. Put simply, the specific purpose is a narrowing of your general persuasive topic. Imagine you asked to give a presentation on increasing community engagement initiatives on your college campus. The topic of this presentation would be something like "Increasing Community Engagement Initiatives on Campus." The general purpose would be *to persuade* because your goal is to have these initiatives implemented. The specific purpose statement is a more focused sentence using the overall topic and the general purpose for guidance. For this example, your specific purpose statement might be, "I will persuade my audience that certain community engagement initiatives should be implemented on campus." Do you see how this example includes the topic and general purpose but addresses them in a more focused way?

When developing your specific purpose statement, it is important to follow a couple of guidelines. First, your specific purpose statement should be a declarative sentence and not a question; for example, "I will persuade my audience that Skype is an effective means for conducting business communication." Second, a specific purpose statement should focus on one idea instead of several; for example, "I will persuade my audience that the city should ban smoking in all public places." In this example, there is only one idea: the ban on smoking. Third, the specific purpose statement should be as specific as possible; for example, "I will persuade my audience that the local school board should increase funding for the speech and debate program in high school." Notice how the specific purpose statement is targeted to the speech and debate program and not all high school activities. By taking the time to develop and write a strong specific purpose statement, you will start off with guidance on developing your persuasive speech.

Persuasive Presentations

In Your Life

Make a list of situations in your life where you might be required to make a persuasive argument. What factors related to designing a persuasive presentation concern you the most?

Persuasive presentations seek to shift or change your audience's attitudes, beliefs, or values. Additionally, you may use persuasive presentations to help reinforce existing ideas that your audience might hold. Persuasive topics can be divided into three questions: questions of policy, value, or fact. **Questions of policy** include persuading an audience to change an existing policy or law or create a new policy or law: "The local city council should adopt a higher tax on downtown businesses." **Questions of value** involve persuading an audience on the merits of a particular position—that it is good or bad, just or unjust, moral or immoral, etc.: "The U.S. invasion of Iraq was immoral." When persuading on **questions of fact,** you are arguing whether an idea is true or false: "NASA did land men on the moon." As you formulate your arguments, the particular type of question will guide you.

- What are the goals of the persuasive presentation? Are you trying to completely change the audience's view or reinforce existing beliefs? Know what you are trying to accomplish with the presentation.
- Use a diverse array of sources to enhance the credibility of your message.
- If your persuasive presentation calls for it, propose a strong, workable solution to the problem. Most of the time, the solution needs to be feasible and make logical sense at first glance.
- In the conclusion, you need to leave the audience with a clear and concise call to action. What can the audience member do immediately to help solve the problem?

FIGURE 12.1 Tips for Persuasive Presentations

CONSIDER THE AUDIENCE

Taking an inventory of the audience's attitudes and beliefs is a critical process as you develop persuasive presentations. Two important terms to be familiar with as you think about persuasive presentations are *attitudes* and *beliefs*. First, **attitudes** are learned ways of thinking that influence behavior and general likes and dislikes of messages (Fishbein & Ajzen, 1975). Put simply, we all form positive or negative attitudes about a variety of people, ideas, and the like. The audience's attitudes will give you a sense of how your topic might be viewed. However, persuasive presentations designed and delivered based on careful consideration of the audience can lead to attitude change (see Photo 12.1).

Second, **beliefs** are ideas typically categorized as true or false by members of the audience. Take a moment to think about your own beliefs. What factors serve as the foundation of your beliefs? Clearly, your life

12.1 REMEMBER

topic	the general subject of your presentation
general purpose statement	large framing statement about the reason for the speech
specific purpose statement	statement listing the exact goals of the persuasive presentation
persuasive presentations	presentations that seek to change, alter, or modify an audience's attitudes, beliefs, values, or outlook about a topic
questions of policy	involve persuading an audience to change an existing law, plan, or policy or create a new policy
questions of value	involve persuading an audience as to the relative merits of a position
questions of fact	involve persuading an audience whether something is true or not
attitudes	learned thought processes that guide our behavior and thinking and represent our likes or dislikes
beliefs	ideas we hold about what is true or false; formed from experiences in the world, attitudes, and significant relationships

PHOTO 12.1 First Lady Michelle Obama uses persuasive presentations in the process of fundraising, political campaigning, and making arguments for or against legislation.

experiences, family, personal relationships, culture, attitudes, and more all drive your beliefs. If you're wondering if it's more difficult to change beliefs than attitudes, you're correct. For instance, you might have the attitude that Red Bull is an awesome energy drink. You might have the belief that all U.S. cities should ban smoking in restaurants or that all college campuses should implement recycling programs.

Ethical Connection
How does considering the audience of a persuasive presentation connect to ethics?

Pay attention to the difference between attitude and belief in the previous examples. As you consider the audience, remember that attitudes can usually be changed easily, while changing beliefs requires time and solid persuasive evidence. So if you're trying to change a belief rather than an attitude, you will need stronger arguments. Put your own attitudes and beliefs to the test. Can you think of one of your own beliefs (versus attitudes) that would be hard for a persuader to change? As you engage in an analysis of the audience, try to get a sense of their beliefs—this will help you to select more convincing evidence to support your persuasive presentation. Consider acknowledging the audience's beliefs, and invite them to consider your message. More than likely, an audience's beliefs will not change in response to your one persuasive presentation. Yet, you might be able to open the door to expose them to more persuasion in the future. Put simply, changing beliefs can be complicated and can take time.

ORGANIZING YOUR PERSUASIVE PRESENTATION

An **organizational pattern** provides a structure to your persuasive presentation and helps the audience process information. Regardless of the communication context, organization is a key component to any persuasive presentation. Take a moment to think about your own experiences with presentations. As an audience member, you're likely to easily "check out" of the presentation if it's not organized. In fact, many of you will probably agree that there are few things worse than a sloppy presentation. Why would anyone be persuaded by information that's not organized in a way that makes sense? Your topic selection will often determine the best organizational pattern for you to use. If you're wondering what options you have in terms of organizing persuasive presentations, the next few sections review the most common organizational patterns.

Cause-and-Effect Pattern

A **cause-and-effect pattern** of organization addresses a topic in terms of the cause-and-effect relationship. For instance, getting the audience to consider the cause of a problem and examining the effects on society might be the best way to organize your persuasive presentation for some types of topics. This pattern is used with a variety of issues such as health care, the environment, the economy, and more. Remember to use the words "cause" and "effect" in your persuasive presentation in order for the audience to focus on the issue. You want your audience to see the connection in your argument. In other words, you need to consciously connect the cause to the effect for your audience. For example, you could use this pattern when discussing the need to decrease fast-food diets in United States:

I. Why people eat fast food (cause)
II. The effects of eating fast food (effect)

Problem-Solution Pattern

A **problem-solution pattern** of organization involves taking on a problem and presenting a solution. Organizing a presentation with a problem-solution pattern might be compared to talking to a close friend about a problem in your relationship and trying to come up with a solution. The problem-solution pattern is based on two simple parts: identifying a problem and proposing a solution. While this pattern might seem like a great choice due to its simplicity, it requires that you persuade the audience that your proposed solution is the best way to solve the problem. You must also be able to persuade your audience that the problem is indeed a problem worthy of a solution. You could organize a speech about the need for a child care center on campus using this pattern:

1. The lack of a child care center on campus is a serious issue because students with children can't afford options off campus. (problem)
2. This problem can be solved by building a child care center on campus. (solution)

Monroe's Motivated Sequence

Monroe's Motivated Sequence is a common organizational pattern used in the design and delivery of persuasive presentations. It includes the following five components:

1. Attention: In the early introductory portion of your persuasive presentation, be sure to capture the audience's attention. In this step of the sequence, consider using a meaningful narrative or a powerful statistic, providing an example or a quotation, or asking a question that connects the audience to your topic.
2. Need: In your first main point, make the audience aware of a significant problem that needs to be addressed with some sort of action.
3. Satisfaction: In your second main point, set up an action plan that addresses/satisfies the problem. Be sure to provide specific information about the plan that will make sense to the audience.

4. Visualization: In your last main point, explain the advantages of the plan and help the audience visualize how the plan will solve the problem. Try to point out to the audience the negative consequences if the plan is not adopted.

5. Call to Action: The call to action serves as the conclusion of your persuasive presentation. This is where you ask the audience to take action by implementing your plan.

Review the outline that follows to see how Monroe's Motivated Sequence can be used in persuasive presentations.

Sample Persuasive Outline

Child Abuse and Neglect

Specific Purpose: To persuade my audience about getting involved to reduce child abuse and neglect.

Thesis Statement: We need to act now to help prevent child abuse and neglect.

Organizational Pattern: Monroe's Motivated Sequence

Introduction (Attention)

I. Attention-Getting Device—Close to 500,000 children have been subjected to abuse and neglect in our state alone!

II. Introduce Your Topic—The problems of child abuse and neglect and ways to help.

III. Demonstrating the Importance—This problem is only growing and becoming more complex, and it impacts all of us.

IV. Preview of Main Points—Today, I will discuss the problems of child abuse and neglect, ways we can help, and the impact of our help on our local community.

Body

I. **Need:** Child abuse and neglect are large and growing problems.

   A. In our county, the number of children abused and neglected is increasing.

      1. There has been a 120% increase in abuse and neglect in the last 3 years.

         a. Many of these children have been involved in previous incidents reported to the state system.

         b. It seems like this problem will only continue because of lack of state funding for prevention programs.

2. There is a general lack of knowledge about this problem in our community.

    a. Most people don't know the signs of child abuse and neglect.

    b. People don't know how or where to report suspected abuse or neglect to authorities.

B. Child abuse and neglect can cause tremendous problems:

    1. Increased anxiety for these children

    2. Increased chances of substance dependence later on in life

    3. Deceased chances of graduating from high school

    Transition: Clearly this issue needs to be addressed by our community. Fortunately, there are many things we can do to help.

II. **Satisfaction:** By spreading the word about the problem of child abuse and neglect, we can educate others to be aware of this issue.

A. Help children at an early age understand child abuse and neglect.

    1. Teach children about appropriate behavior.

    2. Strongly encourage children to talk to their teachers about these kinds of issues.

B. Get involved.

    1. We all can volunteer at the local school for the abuse prevention program.

    2. Spread the word on social media (e.g., Facebook, Twitter) about April being child abuse and neglect awareness month.

    3. Donate to the local homeless shelter's program for abuse and neglect.

    4. Write to our local and state representatives asking them to sponsor the current legislation that increases state funding for prevention programs.

    Transition: Now that I have talked about specific ways in which we could help, I will discuss some of the benefits of taking action.

III. **Visualization:** Getting involved will benefit these children and the larger community.

A. We will have a better community and safer environment for our children.

    1. Educating children on child abuse and neglect in elementary school will help them to understand what is appropriate and inappropriate behavior.

2. Encouraging children who have been abused or neglected to tell a trusted adult will help them get the necessary assistance.

3. More community awareness will potentially increase access to prevention programs.

B. **Call to Action:** Donations will help ensure that our local nonprofit organizations have the resources to promote awareness and provide assistance to children in need.

C. Writing to our local politicians will help spread awareness of this horrible situation and put pressure on them to increase funding for prevention programs.

Transition: With our efforts, we can help reduce child abuse and neglect in our local community.

Conclusion

I. Restate Thesis and Main Points—Today, I discussed the problems of child abuse and neglect, provided ways we can immediately get involved to help, and talked about the benefits of helping.

II. Concluding Device—You never know when you might see a child in need one day.

A. I encourage you all to get involved in this issue.

1. I am passing around handouts listing local organizations where you could volunteer or donate your time and money.

2. On this handout are also the email addresses for our community's politicians. Please write to them asking them to support the current bill to increase funding for prevention programs.

B. We all need to do our part to help protect the children in our community and help those who already have been impacted by child abuse and neglect.

---

1. Cause-and-Effect—This organizational pattern shows the cause of your topic and its effect.

2. Problem-Solution—This pattern can help you demonstrate the problem and provide a solution.

3. Monroe's Motivated Sequence—Monroe's pattern allows you to design your persuasive presentation based on the following features: attention, need, satisfaction, visualization, and call for action.

FIGURE 12.2 Organizing Your Persuasive Presentation

In Your Life

As you think about situations in your life that might require you to design and deliver a persuasive presentation, what organizational pattern in this chapter makes the most sense to you?

 REMEMBER

organizational pattern	structure for a persuasive presentation that helps the audience process information
cause-and-effect pattern	organizational pattern that addresses a topic in terms of a cause-and-effect relationship
problem-solution pattern	pattern of organization that involves taking on a problem and presenting a solution
Monroe's Motivated Sequence	persuasive organizational pattern popular with many speakers that consists of five parts: attention, need, satisfaction, visualization, call to action

PERSUASION RESEARCH SNAPSHOT

As you study persuasive presentations in this chapter, think about how you use persuasive presentations in your classes. Chances are you use PowerPoint very often. Do you think PowerPoint is an effective tool to use for persuasion? There is a great deal of literature that argues against the use of PowerPoint. Among the criticism leveled against it, PowerPoint has been accused of being a novelty that distracts from relevant information and classroom interaction. Do you think PowerPoint detracts from learning? How much attention do you pay to PowerPoint presentations?

As you have learned, persuasive presentations play an important role in a variety of communication contexts. They help people decide to buy a certain car, enroll in a certain class, or join a specific cause. How these presentations lay out information for you is critical to their persuasiveness, and PowerPoint (PPT) is the most universal presentation method students see on college campuses. Have you ever seen a PPT presentation that caught your attention and helped you learn information? Or do you zone out when you see your professor fire up the projector?

Researchers Lisa Burke and Karen James conducted a study to investigate how students perceive PPT novelty and effectiveness. While previous research into the effectiveness of PPT has generally been positive, these studies are relatively dated and may not apply to students in the Facebook and Twitter era. The researchers wanted to gauge whether students find PPT to be an effective learning tool or a novelty gimmick that is outdated. Undergraduate students in business departments were surveyed about their attitudes on PPT and how effective a learning tool they thought it was.

The results showed that only 27% of respondents still consider PPT to be interesting and fresh in their classes; this minority indicated greater satisfaction with the format compared to other respondents. This shows a significant decline in satisfaction over the last 10 years. The authors propose that these findings have a troubling implication for PPT: The effectiveness of PPT as a teaching school may continue to decline as time passes. If this is the case, then teachers will need to find a new presentation format that results in greater student satisfaction and effectiveness.

Think about how the PPT problem relates to persuasive presentations. While you might not think a classroom PPT presentation is persuasive, its purpose is to influence you to process and learn knowledge. In essence, the presentation is "persuading" you to accept new knowledge. What can educators do to present information in a more appealing format? Would you be more interested in a Facebook-themed presentation style? These are questions you may have to answer as you continue your college education and career.

Do you want to know more about this study? If so, read: Burke, L. A., & James, K. E. (2008). PowerPoint-based lectures in business education: An empirical investigation of student-perceived novelty and effectiveness. *Business Communication Quarterly, 71*(3), 277–296.

TYPES OF ARGUMENTS

One useful way to classify arguments is according to the type of data they employ. Based on the type of data, different questions can be raised and different standards used to evaluate the strength of the argument. In other words, being able to classify the types of arguments will help you test the persuasiveness of the argument. Many of the following types of argument are borrowed from Thomas A. Hollihan and Kevin T. Baaske's *Arguments and Arguing: The Products and Process of Human Decision Making* (1998). In each section, you will find an explanation of each type of argument, an example, and some critical questions that can be raised against each it as a test of its strength. If warrants are the foundations on which arguments are built, the data provides the building blocks for the construction. Being able to identify and question the types of building blocks will help make your own arguments more persuasive and strengthen your understanding of other persuasive messages.

Argument by Example

An **argument by example** uses examples as the main source of data. It is generally a form of inductive reasoning where a specific example is used to support a broader claim. In the private sphere, an instance of argument by example is "I am bad at relationships (claim). My last relationship ended quickly (data)." In the technical sphere, an instance of argument by example is "All things that go up must come down (claim) because the apple fell from the tree (data)." In the public sphere, an instance of argument by example is "The United States is bad at nation-building (claim). Iraq has become a quagmire (data)." In all of these instances, one example (the last relationship, the apple, Iraq) is used to support the general claim. In all spheres, arguments by example are frequently encountered.

What kinds of questions might be raised against arguments by example? First, you might question whether the example is relevant to the claim. For instance, the United States did not enter the Iraq war with the intention of nation-building, so perhaps this example does not really demonstrate the country's effectiveness at it. Additionally, the speed with which a relationship ends is not necessarily relevant to whether someone is good or bad at relationships. Other factors might be more important, such as the lack of shared interests, a lack of mutual attraction, or bad timing. Although it seems obvious that an example needs to be relevant to the claim, there are many instances when people provide irrelevant examples that should not be persuasive.

Second, you might ask whether the example is sufficient to prove the claim. Oftentimes, providing only one example is not enough evidence to support the broader claim. One relationship ending quickly is probably not enough to draw a general conclusion about a person's ability to have a good relationship. The same goes for one apple falling or one failed attempt at nation-building. There are many other instances of nation-building, relationships, and falling objects that need to be considered. These examples add some evidence to the claim but do not in and of themselves provide sufficient evidence for the claim.

What kind of example might be enough evidence to support a general claim? Only an example that is significant and typical, or what some call *representative*, can sufficiently justify a claim. This presents a third question you might ask of an argument by example: Is the example typical or representative? If someone uses an outlandish or extreme example to support the claim, you might challenge that this extreme or outlandish situation is not representative of the broader claim. Such arguments by example that draw a general conclusion from an atypical or unrepresentative example are called **hasty generalizations**. So, if someone has only had one relationship and it ended quickly, we might call this a hasty generalization. Often, a teenager whose first relationship has just ended will make such a hasty generalization ("Nobody loves me," or "I am bad at relationships") without enough evidence to draw the general conclusion. On the other hand, the apple falling seems to be a typical and representative example. The apple is a representative object in this example; typically, any object that goes up into the air will come back down.

Finally, you might question an argument by example if there are counterexamples that work against the conclusion. If someone has had other relationships that were happy and long lasting, then relying on the most recent relationship as the primary example is probably not very convincing. There are also some counterexamples to the Iraq argument. The United States had some significant success helping rebuild Germany and Japan after World War II, and more recently has been somewhat successful in Bosnia and Kosovo. A counterexample directly questions the typicality and sufficiency of an argument by example, so it is often a preferred response when it comes to these types of argument.

Argument by Definition

An **argument by definition** uses the definition of a concept as the data to illustrate that a specific case falls under that category. An argument by definition contends that a certain instance does or does not meet the definition of a more general category. Therefore, argument by definition is generally a form of deductive reasoning, working from the general definition to make an argument about the specific case. An example of argument by definition in the private sphere might be "Paul is a bad friend (claim) because friends stand by you in bad times as well as good times (data)." In the public sphere, arguments over abortion, pornography, or sexual harassment often contain arguments by definition. For instance, someone might argue that abortion is murder because life begins at conception. Someone might contend, in opposition, that abortion is not murder because life is defined by self-sufficiency (the being must be able to survive on its own to be considered alive). Indeed, the abortion debate, as in both of these examples, often turns on the definition of life. The same is true for pornography and the question of indecency. Someone who defines indecency as sex will conclude that pornography is indecency. Finally, the perception of sexual harassment often depends upon the definition. Someone might claim that coworkers who continually make sexual jokes are guilty of sexual harassment because the definition of sexual harassment includes creating an unfriendly or uncomfortable work environment. Others might contend that sexual jokes are not sexual harassment because sexual harassment is only direct touching or explicit coercion (what is called *quid pro quo*, demands that someone perform a sexual favor to keep his or her job or to get a raise).

What questions might be raised against arguments by definition? First, there is always the question of relevance. Is the definition really relevant to the case being presented? For instance, is the definition of indecency relevant to the debate over pornography since pornography is something watched in private and indecency is about actions that take place in public? Second, you can ask whether the definition is accurate. In the example of abortion above, someone might challenge the definition of life that assumes life begins at conception. Or in the instance of sexual harassment, most laws include the creation of an unfriendly work environment as sexual harassment, so someone who insists sexual harassment is only quid pro quo might be relying on an inaccurate definition. Remember that definitions might exclude important cases or might be biased towards a particular interest, so there is no reason to accept the definition as given. Definitions can be more or less accurate, more or less inclusive, and more or less biased, and therefore should not be taken at face value.

We might also ask if there are counter-definitions. The debate over abortion often pivots on the different definitions of life. Someone who sees life as beginning at conception will likely see abortion as murder. Someone who sees life as self-sufficiency will likely see abortion as the woman's choice. The sexual harassment examples above also feature two competing definitions (an unfriendly environment versus quid pro quo). Even the example of the definition of friend might be countered with another definition or with an alteration to the initial definition. Perhaps Paul will say he is a friend, but not your best friend. He could define friendship as the sharing of good times together; only the best friend is required to stand by you in good times and in bad times.

Argument by Analogy

An **argument by analogy** looks for similarities between different examples to draw a conclusion. It uses an analogy (an extended comparison) as the main form of data. The analogy can be literal, making a direct connection between two cases, or figurative, making an indirect or metaphorical connection between cases. An example of literal analogies is "Iraq is like Vietnam. It is an intervention against an intractable regime in a regional hot spot that has become a bloody quagmire." Or, "Parenting is like driving. They are both serious life responsibilities that should require a license." Or, "Police have realized the value of profiling to catch drug offenders. The CIA should use profiling to catch terrorists." An example of figurative analogies is "Iraq is like a hornet's nest. The more we poke and prod, the angrier they get." Or, "Jill is such a baby. She just cries when she does not get her way."

When asking questions about arguments by analogy, the issues of relevance and sufficiency are again at the forefront. For relevance, you might ask: "Are the compared cases really alike?" Is parenting really like driving? Is Iraq really a hornet's nest? Parents do not directly put the lives of others at risk, and requiring a license before anyone gets pregnant would be difficult to enforce. Iraqis are people, not insects. They have a vast diversity of opinions and feelings. Some Iraqis who were oppressed under Saddam Hussein even support the U.S. intervention and therefore our presence has not made them angrier.

The issue of sufficiency raises the question, "Are there other factors which may not make the analogy translate to the new case?" In other words, are the cases sufficiently similar to compare? Parenting and driving might seem similar at first glance, but when you consider the difficulties of enforcing a parenting license and the issues of freedom and privacy, the case becomes more complicated. Does everyone have to have a license before they have sexual intercourse, even if they do not plan on having children and they use birth control? What happens then when there are accidents? Also, doesn't the U.S. Constitution provide for the right to privacy and the right to control your own body? How then would a license to have children be constitutional? Indeed, such a requirement seems like something more appropriate for an authoritarian country than democratic America. There are also other factors that make profiling, from drug offenders to terrorists, more problematic. Profiling drug users is based upon the actions of the offender, such as acting erratically and having symptoms such as inappropriately dilated eyes. Profiling terrorists would probably be based more upon racial characteristics, such as profiling any Arabic person. Within the United States, such racial profiling raises equal protection issues under the Constitution, which requires that the government treat all races equally. Abroad, racial profiling seems largely ineffective. If CIA operatives are working in the Middle East, do they search everyone since practically everyone is Arabic and hence "looks" like a terrorist? When many factors between the two compared cases differ, argument scholars call the claim a **false analogy.**

Finally, ask whether the compared cases are described accurately. The war in Vietnam, for instance, was quite a different situation than the Iraq war. Even though both can be described as U.S. intervention against intractable regimes in regional hot spots, this description is inaccurate because Iraq was not a hot spot when the United States intervened (there was no ongoing war). The very term *hot spot* comes from the Cold War, and the Cold War played a major role in making Vietnam such a protracted conflict since the North Vietnamese were supported by the USSR and China. In Iraq, the previously existing government had no such support and was quickly toppled. The problem in Iraq was not an intractable regime but many splinter groups who resisted U.S. occupation. The opposition is less unified and less formal than in Vietnam, so the original description is inaccurate in numerous ways.

Argument by Cause

Arguments by cause are arguments about causes and effects. Generally, the claim is backed by data that suggests there is a direct connection between a factor and an outcome. Hollihan and Baaske (1998) delineate two kinds of arguments by cause. First, an argument from causal correlation is a type of inductive reasoning. They describe an argument from causal correlation as one that "examines specific cases, classes of cases, or both, in order to identify an actual relationship or correlation between them" (p. 78). In other words, arguments from causal correlation suggest that there is a correlation between a factor and an outcome, or a cause and an effect. You have already been exposed to an argument by causal correlation with the video game argument in the introduction. The claim "Kids should not play video games" is supported by data of a causal correlation ("Video games encourage violent behavior.") This is a causal correlation because it asserts a link between one factor (playing violent video games) and an outcome (violent behavior). A couple of other examples of argument by causal correlation follow:

» Eating at McDonalds regularly results in obesity because the food is high in fat.

» U.S. military action creates more terrorists because violence begets violence.

» Diets high in fruits and vegetables fight cancer because they contain many antioxidants.

As the last example shows, much scientific reasoning is based on causal correlation. Scientists examine various factors and construct experiments to determine their effects. So they have been able to demonstrate a high correlation between, for instance, your diet and your prospects for good health or between smoking and various types of cancer. This type of argument, like most scientific thinking, is a form of inductive reasoning because it starts with specifics (eating at McDonalds, U.S. military action, playing violent video games) rather than general principles in order to reason about their effects.

Many questions can be asked of arguments by causal correlation. First, you might ask, "Is there a regular and consistent relationship between cause and effect?" This is really a question of sufficiency. Is there sufficient reason to believe the cause will produce the effect? Does frequently eating at McDonalds regularly and consistently create obesity? Does playing violent video games regularly and consistently produce violent behavior? For the video games argument, we might say there is not a regular and consistent cause-effect relationship because many children play violent video games without going on to be violent in their daily lives. In fact, young boys have played violent games for centuries, and most turn into respectable citizens and loving fathers or brothers. Many other factors influence whether someone will become violent, such as his economic status, the care and attention of his parents, his educational level, his social friendships and relationships, his personality, and other habits.

A second question you can ask of arguments by causal correlation is, "Is there a strong correlation between the cause and effect?" To take the McDonalds example, does frequently eating at McDonalds usually produce obesity? There is certainly a well-established correlation between diets high in fat and obesity, but here again many other factors may come into play, such as how much the person snacks between meals, what she eats for other meals, how much she exercises, her general body type and metabolism, and even what she eats at McDonalds. McDonalds has recently responded to criticism of the high sugar and fat content of its food by providing more healthy options, such as salads and fruit cups. A person who eats at McDonalds frequently could still possibly find ways to eat mostly healthy foods and avoid obesity. Yet much of McDonald's food is still high in fat and sugar, so the correlation here remains a strong one in most instances.

Finally, you might ask a question of relevance about arguments by causal correlation. Is the causal correlation relevant and reasonable? Many superstitions are based on arguments from causal correlation that fail this test of relevance. Stepping on a crack does not have any relevance to whether your mom breaks her back. Basic laws of physics and biology suggest that there is probably another cause of your mom's ailing back (perhaps too much housework to clean up after you!). The same is true for black cats and bad luck. Do not kick the cat and blame it for your misfortune. Misfortune is usually caused by our own failures or the failures of others. If you look closely at your bad luck, there is usually a much more relevant and reasonable explanation than that cat you saw the other day. Think of a casino. Many people moan about their bad luck in gambling, but when you think about it rationally, the entire game is set up for players to fail. The odds are always against you, so it's not really bad luck that the dice did not hit your number. It is the typical and expected outcome. Some people look to the stars, or the voices in their head, or angels and demons, or fate for causes and effects. Almost always, however, there is a more relevant, reasonable, and certainly mundane reason that can be uncovered with just a little digging.

Hollihan and Baaske's second type of argument by cause is argument from causal generalization, which "argues deductively from some general principles that are assumed to be true, to judgments about specific cases under consideration" (1998, p. 82). In other words, arguments from causal generalization start with a generally accepted or acknowledged cause to reason about a specific case. These arguments follow deductive reasoning and in a sense are the inverse of the arguments by causal correlation. A few examples of arguments by casual generalization follow:

» Sunburns are caused by too much exposure to the sun. Jane's red face tells me she must have stayed out in the sun too long.

» Health care costs are the number one cause of bankruptcy in the United States. Bob must have declared bankruptcy due to his illness.

» People who always talk about themselves have a hard time making friends. That is why Jules is such a loner.

» Confidence is attractive to women. Erion's success with the ladies is because of his confidence.

» Serial killers typically exhibit some form of mental illness. It must have been his schizophrenia that drove Ted Bundy to mass murder.

In each of these examples, the argument starts with a general cause and then applies it to the specific case. This is why arguments from causal generalization are a form of deductive reasoning and why they are distinct from arguments by causal correlation. Arguments by causal correlation move from specifics to specifics. Here the argument moves from generalization to a specific instance. Although they are different, these two types of arguments are classified together because they each reason about causes and effects. The major claim is backed up either by a general cause-effect relationship or by a specific cause-effect correlation.

Given the similarities, many of the questions you might ask of arguments by causal generalization are similar to those you would ask about arguments by causal correlation. In fact, you have probably already started to question some of the above examples. This is precisely why it is so valuable to be able to recognize different types of arguments. Being able to do so will help you to best understand and question various persuasive messages you encounter in your daily life. So what are some of the questions you started to ask about the above examples? They probably follow a similar pattern to all of the types of arguments we have analyzed so far. They probably question the sufficiency, the relevance, and the reasonability of the claims and data.

For instance, you can always ask if there is sufficient evidence to support the claim. Is the cause sufficient to produce the effect? Is too much sun sufficient to produce a sunburn? Surely. What about bankruptcies? Are health care costs sufficient to cause bankruptcy? In some instances such as severe disease or injury, health care costs can certainly cause bankruptcy. But what if Bob had only a common cold? Then you might wonder about the sufficiency of this argument. Another even more questionable example is the confidence argument. Is confidence sufficient to ensure success with dating? Probably not. Although confidence plays a role, confidence alone without charm, wit, good looks, and good opportunities will probably fall short. Furthermore, many schizophrenics do not commit mass murder, so Bundy's mental illness is not sufficient to prove what caused his horrible actions.

Second, you can always question the relevance of an argument by cause. Is talking about oneself really relevant to how many friends one has? Maybe yes, but also maybe not. Some people are very self-centered and yet still have many friends. This also may or may not be relevant to Jules's situation. Maybe she prefers being a loner, or maybe she suffers from social anxiety disorder. Or take the sunburn example. Perhaps you have mistaken Jane's red face for a sunburn when in actuality she is embarrassed at the moment or extremely hot. Then the cause of sunburns is not relevant to Jane's red face, and our argument does not seem very persuasive anymore.

Finally, you can question whether the cause is reasonable or whether it might actually result in very different effects. Are confident people typically attractive to the other sex? Perhaps, but their confidence might also scare off some people who are not confident, or it might be read as a sign of conceitedness. Schizophrenia or other mental illnesses like depression might make people more caring and understanding of the pain of others, rather than driving them to want to hurt people. People who always talk about themselves might be seen as outgoing and friendly, causing them to have more friends rather than fewer. This is one of the major limitations of arguments by causal generalization. It is very hard to prove that any cause always has the same effect, except when we are talking about laws of nature or other unchanging conditions. When it comes to humans and their social and political lives, any factor can have many different effects for different people at different times in different places. A hard upbringing might make one person strong and another person weak. Success can make some people strive for more and other people become content. Winning the lottery causes some people to be happy and brings others misery because the people around them all become greedy (it happens all the time—look it up if you don't believe me!). There are very few causes that have a direct and definite effect each and every time because every person and every situation is different. So many factors are at play that arguments by causal generalization often tend to overgeneralize.

In Your Life

When you are trying to persuade someone in your life, which style of argument are you most likely to use? Which do you feel makes you more convincing? As you continue reading about the different types of argument, consider that you are trying to convince a friend to go to a concert with you. Your friend does not particularly like the kind of music that the band plays. Which types of argument might be the most successful in getting your friend to join you?

Argument by Sign

Arguments by sign use signs as their form of data. These arguments by sign contend that certain factors, examples, materials, or instances are signs of the broader claim. We as communicators often reference them in our daily lives when we say that something that happened was a sign of something else (like a sign of good or bad fortune). Arguments by sign are a form of deductive reasoning because they use features of a specific instance to argue that a general claim is true. An example of an argument by sign in the private sphere might be, "She is losing interest in me because she did not call me back." Or, "My low grades are proof that I have too heavy a class load." An example of an argument by sign in the public sphere might be, "The continued violence in Iraq, the low voter participation, and statements from opposition groups prove that the American presence is not welcome." Or, "Akeem was imprisoned without trial due to a search-and-seizure warrant. He must be a victim of the Patriot Act." "All of the protests are a sign that people are not happy with their government" is one final example in the public sphere.

Once again, you can raise questions about arguments by sign in relation to their sufficiency, relevance, and reasonableness. For sufficiency, you can always ask if there are enough signs presented to illustrate the claim. So, for instance, is one failure to return a phone call enough of a sign to signal disinterest? Or, have there been enough protests to illustrate that people are generally unhappy with their government? Finally, is being arrested on a search-and-seizure warrant a strong enough sign to prove that Akeem was a victim of the Patriot Act? There is no set standard for how many signs are sufficient to prove the claim. It will be up to listeners to determine whether they agree the cited signs are enough to justify the claim. However, as with all issues of sufficiency, the more signs someone provides as data, generally, the stronger the argument. So the Iraq example above seems more persuasive than the other examples because the arguer has listed numerous signs to illustrate that America's presence is unwanted, including low voter turnout, continued violence, and statements from opposition groups.

Of course, an arguer might present a large number of signs but still not be very persuasive if the signs are not relevant to the claim. If search-and-seizure warrants were legal before the Patriot Act, then this sign does nothing to prove the claim that Akeem was a victim of the act. If Akeem was arrested for drug trafficking and not suspicion of terrorism, then the relevance to the Patriot Act is questionable as well. Maybe the student complaining about his grades always had low grades, even before he took a heavy class load. In that case, the low grades are more likely a sign of amount of work effort or academic aptitude. Finally, protests might not be a relevant sign of dissatisfaction with the government if the protests are not aimed at the government but are instead directed at a corporation or another institution. As always with issues of relevance, the presence of other factors can reduce the relevance of the sign. In the phone call example, perhaps the reason she did not call back was because her phone died or she was asleep, not because she is no longer interested. It can be risky to jump too quickly from one sign to a general conclusion, so always ask if the sign is really relevant and if other factors may explain the sign.

Sometimes these other factors might even lead to a question about the reasonableness of the signs in general. What if there are other, contradictory signs? For instance, she may not have called back, but she may have texted you with an explanation and an apology. Maybe she asked you out on another date, sending a clear sign that contradicts the lack of a phone call. Or perhaps the continued violence is a sign that people in Iraq are fighting back against insurgent groups rather than fighting against the American military. There are also signs such as the smooth running of an election, the declining *rate* of violence, and the presence of American flags in the windows of homes that counter the claim that America's presence is unwanted. Polls that show people are happy on balance with their lives can be used as a counter-sign to the recent rise in protests. Perhaps the protests are signs that people have a renewed faith in their government's ability to actually listen to their demands. After all, why would people protest if they did not think the government would ever respond? The relevance and sufficiency of the signs as well as the existence of contradictory signs are all potential issues that you should raise when someone uses an argument by sign as a means of persuasion.

Argument by Statistic

Many times, people will use statistical data in order to support their claims. You typically find arguments by statistics in the technical and public spheres, although they occasionally make their way into the private sphere as well. **Arguments by statistic** can be used for deductive or inductive reasoning, depending on whether the argument moves from specific statistics to a more general claim or from general statistics to a more specific claim. Statistics lend an air of credibility and certainty to an argument, but there are many questions that must be raised about statistics. Indeed, while you might think that statistics are simply facts and hence not part of an argument, the meaning and significance of statistics are often up for debate. Therefore, in most instances statistics should be seen as arguments and not as a simple reporting of facts. Any quick look at statistical data will reveal that there are competing and even contradictory statistical estimates for the same issue. Furthermore, the same statistic can be used as data for completely contradictory arguments. For example, the statistical fact that the United States spends $500 million a year on aid to Africa can be used to support the claim that "the United States spends too much on foreign aid" (since $500 million seems like a lot to most people) or to support the claim that "the United States doesn't spend enough on foreign aid" (since $500 million is a drop in the bucket, less than 1% of the total federal budget). Despite the appearance of factuality and neutrality, statistics should be considered part of a larger argument and evaluated in that context.

It is particularly important to raise questions about arguments by statistics because of their apparent neutrality and credibility. As always, you can raise questions about the relevance and sufficiency of the statistics. For instance, using the number of homeless people to support arguments about the unemployment rate or the general state of the economy may not be relevant. Homelessness is not the same as unemployment, since there are many people who are unemployed but have a home. Further, homelessness is not a very accurate indicator of the general economy since some homeless people may be homeless not due to economic factors but due to personal or social factors such as mental illness, drug use, or personal preference (they may be drifters who choose to be homeless).

Sufficiency is an even more important question to raise about arguments by statistics. Statistical research methods can only examine a small sample of the given category since it is too time and resource intensive to gather data about every person or thing that fits the category. Take statistics on homelessness again. Those studies cannot find and catalog every homeless person because of the sheer numbers of people and sheer size of the country. So the studies will sample the homeless population from certain cities and certain places (perhaps by recording the number of homeless people in New York City who go to shelters). From there, they will estimate what percentage of homeless people go to shelters and what percentage do not. Based on those numbers, they will estimate how many homeless people there are in the entire country. Thus, one study may conservatively estimate the percentage of homeless people in shelters while another study may arrive at a very liberal estimate. The fact that statistical methods must take a sample and estimate the broader numbers does not necessarily make them inaccurate. But it does mean that questions of sufficiency should always be asked of statistical arguments. Sufficiency is a question of the *sample size* of the statistical study. The **sample size** is the number of people or study objects surveyed in order to draw the numerical conclusions. A smaller sample size (from a study that surveys fewer objects or people) raises more questions as to its sufficiency.

Another issue with arguments by statistics is related to the method used to gather the statistics and the possible existence of counter-statistics or counter-methods. You saw in the homelessness example that one method might estimate a high percentage of homeless people in shelters while another might estimate a low percentage. This is a crucial consideration since the final numbers will vary widely dependent on the method used. Which approach is more reasonable? If there is reason to believe that many homeless do not go to shelters, then there is probably a strong reason to question the studies that estimate a high percentage go to shelters. Furthermore, the method used to gather the numbers might raise some doubt about the statistics. For instance, many opinion polls are based on randomly selected phone calls to houses listed in the phone book. The problem with such a method for gathering data is that it leaves out people who do not spend much time at home and people who have only cell phones. In fact, studies show that young adults tend to have only cell phones, not home phones. So, these polls tend to leave out the youth, a very large part of the voting demographic. Some pollers even claim that this cell-phone effect explains why Barack Obama won the 2008 election by a larger margin than many of the polls leading up to the election had predicted. Statistical measurements must use methods of gathering data that are limited and methods of estimating that are inexact and potentially problematic. Therefore, questioning the methods of statistical gathering is an important element of critically examining attempts to persuade you.

Finally, statistical methods raise the important issue of credibility (discussed more extensively below). Perhaps you have heard the saying that one can find statistics to support any point of view. This is a common saying because there is an element of truth to it and because manipulating the method can allow two studies to reach widely different conclusions. In political debates, you often hear politicians quoting two drastically different statistics on the same issue, one saying her plan will save millions with another claiming it will cost millions. So does this mean you should throw out all arguments by statistics, insisting that they can be used to prove anything and are therefore useless? Not necessarily. But it does mean you should pay careful attention to the source of the statistic. Ask questions about the credibility of that source. Does the source have an incentive to inflate or deflate the numbers? Will the source gain money, political power, new group members, or prestige if its statistic is accepted? Does the statistic come from a partisan or special-interest group? If you can answer yes to any of these questions, you should be particularly suspicious of the source and the statistic. Try, instead, to look for statistics from non-partisan and scholarly sources. These sources have no special interest or bias in relation to the statistics. Especially with scholarly sources, publications are usually peer-reviewed by other scholars. Peer review helps ensure the accuracy of the method and helps decrease the likelihood of overt bias. Arguments by statistic can be a useful tool for helping us quantify the significance of a social or political trend. Sometimes coming up with numbers is the only way to demonstrate the extent of a problem. However, you should always be careful to ensure that statistics are relevant, sufficient, accurate, and credible, since statistics can be found to support almost any point of view.

Argument by Principle or Value

According to Gregg B. Walker and Malcolm O. Sillars (1990), "When people argue, attempting to gain adherence from an audience, they appeal to, employ, and interpret values" (p. 135). As a form of persuasion, argumentation attempts to gain audience adherence. Since this adherence takes place in the context of multiple choices, argumentation frequently takes the form of **argumentation by principles or values**. Why an audience might adhere to one choice over another often comes down to how well the argument links to their previously existing values or principles. Take the foreign aid argument above. If someone values humanitarianism, she is likely to see U.S. foreign aid as a drop in the bucket. If someone values fiscal conservatism, he is likely to see foreign aid as an unnecessary waste of money. Walker and Sillars point out that values play a crucial role in every aspect of argumentation since values can be used as a claim, data, backing, and especially warrants. We had an example of values being the claim of an argument in the "Freedom is America's most valuable contribution to the world" argument. This argument also features a warrant based on values that says "reducing suffering is a valuable contribution to the world." This section will focus on using values or principles as either data or backing. Examples of argument by value include the following:

» The death penalty should be abolished because it violates the constitutional principle against cruel and unusual punishment.

» Abortion should remain legal because it is a woman's right to choose what happens with her body.

» Environmental regulations violate the primary American value of free enterprise.

» Racism must be struggled against because it is a moral affront to equality and justice.

In each of these instances, certain values or principles are invoked as data to support the claim. Here the values include justice, privacy, free enterprise, and equality. Additionally, the constitutional principle against cruel and unusual punishment is used as data against the death penalty. As always, we can question the relevance or sufficiency of these values or principles. Perhaps free enterprise is not really relevant to the issue of environmental regulation, or perhaps cruel and unusual punishment is not the issue when it comes to the death penalty since lethal injection is said to be quick and painless. Yet the questions of relevance and sufficiency are not as important as some other issues related to the degree of acceptance of the value and the hierarchy of values to which an audience adheres.

Values vary widely from culture to culture and even person to person. So whether a value is accepted as legitimate data will often vary as well. Basically, you can ask whether this is a value you share or one that might only apply in a particular place or time. Most of the values invoked in the examples above are American values such as equality, Constitutional principles, privacy, and free enterprise. In other cultures, equality is not as highly valued, so those cultures might be more willing to accept some forms of racism. Or perhaps another culture does not value free enterprise, and therefore the audience will not accept this value as a reason to reject environmental protections. Walker and Sillars (1990) distinguish between universal values such as beauty, truthfulness, and justice and specific values such as equality, privacy, and free enterprise that are relative from culture to culture. Values such as justice are universal in the sense that they are shared widely from culture to culture. The important point here from a persuasion standpoint is that you should consider which values your audience might share in order to be the most persuasive. If you cannot isolate the specific values of the audience, relying on more universal values may be your best bet.

Even more important than the universality of the value is the value hierarchy. Reading the examples above, many of you probably noticed that there were counter-values that might respond to the primary claims. For instance, you might value free enterprise but do you do so at the expense of your value for nature? Or some people might value privacy and choice, but not as much as they do their religious principles, which condemn abortion. In fact, much of the debate over abortion boils down to competing values. Values do not exist in a vacuum. They relate to other values and are often ordered according to varying hierarchies. Whether we adhere to the argument often depends on how we rank those values in a hierarchy. As Walker and Sillars (1990) state, "Value hierarchies provide a key to analyzing salient values and value conflicts in the predispositions of their audiences" (p. 141). The persuasiveness of arguments by value or principle will thus depend on the different cultural beliefs of the audience as well as the various hierarchies through which the audience ranks values.

REMEMBER

argument by example	a form of inductive reasoning where a specific example is used to support a broader claim
hasty generalization	arguments by example that draw a general conclusion from an atypical or unrepresentative example
argument by definition	argument that uses the definition of a concept as the data to illustrate that a specific case falls under that category
argument by analogy	argument that looks for similarities between different examples to draw a conclusion
false analogy	when many factors are different between two compared cases in an argument
arguments by cause	arguments about causes and effects
arguments by sign	arguments contending that certain factors, examples, materials, or instances are signs of the broader claim
arguments by statistic	arguments supported by statistical data, used in deductive or inductive reasoning
sample size	the number of people or study objects surveyed in order to draw numerical conclusions
argument by principles or values	an argument that attempts to gain audience adherence by appealing to their previously existing principles or values

STANDARDS FOR ARGUMENT

Hopefully after the last section you are able to see how different types of arguments can be more or less persuasive. This section includes the standards for strong and persuasive arguments that were used throughout the previous section. This will help serve as a summary and reminder as well as provide you with some standards you can apply to any type of argument you encounter in your daily life. Basically, the three primary standards are relevance, sufficiency, and credibility of the argument. After outlining these basic standards, the following sections illustrate them by naming a few common argumentative fallacies (or flaws in reason) you will frequently hear.

Relevance

Relevance may seem like an obvious standard for a persuasive argument. The data and warrants used should be related and relevant to the major claim. The basic question you can ask is: "Do the data and warrant directly connect to the claim?" While this may seem obvious, the careful listener or reader will encounter numerous examples of irrelevant arguments. There are even names for many of these common irrelevant arguments. As a general category, these fallacies of relevance are often called *red herrings*. An example of a red herring might be, "Why should we fix education when there is such a crisis in parenting?" While parenting might influence education and at first glance seem relevant, the crisis in parenting does not mean we should not try to fix education. The relevance of this claim is suspect. Oftentimes the red herring argument will rely on emotionally loaded data to distract attention from the question at hand. For instance, someone might argue, "Why should we help Haiti after the earthquake when we have so many problems with hunger and poverty in the United States?" The problems of hunger and poverty are severe and do pack an emotional punch, but they are not relevant to whether or not we should help Haiti recover from the devastating earthquake.

Fallacies of relevance include the **ad hominem** fallacy, the **ad populum** fallacy, and the **non sequitur** fallacy. An ad hominem fallacy attacks the arguer rather than the argument itself. An ad hominem fallacy is usually an insult directed at the source of the argument that is irrelevant to the truthfulness of the claim. For instance, someone might say that "Al Gore is wrong about global warming because he is a crazy tree-hugger." Whether or not Gore hugs trees is not relevant to the question of global warming. Therefore this is flawed reasoning and should be an unpersuasive argument. An ad populum fallacy is one that asserts something must be true because many people believe it. For instance, "Most people believe the stimulus bill has not created jobs. The bill must be failing." What most people believe is not relevant to whether the bill created jobs or not. For the ad populum fallacy, I like to think of that famous parental question, "If your friends jumped off a bridge, would you?" Just because an idea is popular does not make it correct. Finally, a non sequitur is an argument that incorrectly assumes one thing is the cause of another. So, the examples of superstition covered above are examples of non sequitur. Crossing the path of that black cat did not cause you to fail that test, no matter how much you would like to believe it.

In Your Life

Can you think of some examples of ad hominem, ad populum, or non sequitur fallacies that you've experienced in your life?

Sufficiency

Sufficiency is an important standard for argument. Basically, **sufficiency** asks if there is enough evidence to support the claim. One example, one expert, or a statistic with a small sample size may not be enough evidence to draw the general conclusion. Once again, there are some common names for various fallacies of sufficiency. These include the *correlation not causation fallacy*, *circular reasoning* or *begging the question*, and the *testimonial*.

The **correlation not causation fallacy** asserts that because one thing follows another or because two things often are found together, one must cause the other. For instance, imagine your friend says, "I got a flu shot and then got sick. Obviously, the shot caused me to get sick." The flu shot came before she got sick, but this does not prove that it caused her to get sick. There is not sufficient evidence here to prove it was the shot that caused the sickness. **Begging the question/circular reasoning** is a form of argument where the conclusion is drawn based on the premises of the argument. In other words, the data refers circularly back to the claim, without either having sufficient backing. For instance, "I know God exists because the Bible was written by God." Here, the data presumes that God exists and that data is used to prove that God exists. Another example might be, "All of humankind is capable of reason because the definition of humankind is the animal-that-reasons." Again, the reasoning moves in a circle from human as reasoning animal to the conclusion that humans are reasoning animals. These arguments may or may not be true, but there is not sufficient evidence to prove them. In fact, there is no real evidence offered, since the evidence is based on the same assumption as the claim.

Finally, a **testimonial** is an argument where the testimony of one user or witness is offered as data for a claim. This type of reasoning is frequently seen in advertisements. "I use this soap and it makes my clothes soft. It will make your clothes soft, too." This argument seems reasonable on first glance, but there is not sufficient evidence to prove the general claim, especially when you consider that the person who offered the testimonial was probably paid to do so. Perhaps a better example is as follows: "I can't believe you are saying Jack has anger problems. He has never been angry with me." Once again, Jack's lack of anger with one person is not sufficient to prove that he does not have anger problems. Or take the famous defense against racism, "I cannot be racist because I have a black friend." Here, not only is a black friend insufficient proof of an absence of racism but the data is also not very relevant, since feelings about one friend might not indicate how a person feels about a whole class of people.

Credibility

Credibility (ethos) is such a crucial part of argument and persuasion that Aristotle made ethos one of the three components of persuasion (see Photo 12.2). Any time someone makes an argument, you should consider his credibility, since his biases and interests are probably

PHOTO 12.2 Despite book tours and persuasive presentations, credibility is sometimes difficult to establish and maintain for politicians like Sarah Palin.

influencing both what he is saying and why he is trying to persuade you. Furthermore, any time someone cites a source for data or relies on an authoritative warrant, the issue of credibility should be front and center. The standard of credibility asks whether the source is trustworthy and believable or has a bias or self-interest that causes her to slant the argument in a particular way. This is a difficult question to answer because every arguer will have certain biases and certain perspectives. Indeed, any time someone is trying to persuade you, they are necessarily bringing some level of bias into the argument. So when should you trust the source and when should you not?

To answer this question, ignore arguments in the private sphere since the issue of credibility there will often turn on personal decisions about the arguer's trustworthiness, personality, and track record. We all develop different reasons for believing or not believing people in our private lives. So who can we trust in the public and technical spheres? First, try to find sources or arguers who do not stand to directly gain something from the success or failure of the argument. You should trust the used car salesperson trying to sell you a car less than you trust a student advisor at your university who recommends a class. The advisor does not stand to gain or lose anything from her recommendation, whereas the used car salesman will make money if he persuades you. This is also true for sources such as special-interest groups. Always prefer scholarly and nonpartisan sources to those engaged in outright political organizing and lobbying. These special-interest groups gain donations and political prestige by persuading members, so they have an incentive to slant the arguments in their direction. This warning applies as well to the news media. Today, the larger their audience, the more money the news media stand to make, so they have an incentive to sensationalize and exaggerate the news. This is why it may seem like our country is in a constant state of crisis if you regularly watch the evening news. The same is true for Internet sources, which often make advertising revenues by attracting page views. The extreme and dramatic will bring surfers to their websites, so they have an incentive to exaggerate and rant rather than rationally deliberate.

Why are scholarly and nonpartisan sources more likely to lack bias? First, scholarly and nonpartisan sources do not directly stand to gain from the outcome of the argument. A scholar or nonpartisan group is not paid by lobbying organizations or other institutions directly interested in the outcome. A scholar might gain prestige or tenure from publishing, but she will accrue that benefit no matter what her conclusions. Second, scholars and nonpartisan groups have systems for double-checking their conclusions. As mentioned earlier, scholarly publications undergo peer review, where other experts check to make sure their facts are supported and an inappropriate bias does not enter into their arguments. A similar process happens with many nonpartisan groups since they often publish findings from a diverse panel representing different parties and ideological beliefs. This process of ensuring all sides are represented works like peer review to ensure that the more biased and extreme conclusions are filtered out of the final product.

How can you recognize scholarly and nonpartisan sources? First, look for the qualifications of your sources and suspect anyone who does not cite those qualifications. With a quick Internet search, you can find out whether the source has scholarly qualifications and is receiving funding from some other, more biased sources. Sometimes groups will name themselves something that sounds completely nonpartisan and innocent, so doing a little research is a great way to double-check and make sure they are scholarly and nonpartisan. Second, look for sources published in government or scholarly publications. Government sources such as the Congressional Research Center and Congressional Budget Office are made up of respected nonpartisan researchers who take many steps to ensure fair and unbiased findings. Publications of scholars in peer-reviewed journals are also less likely to exhibit bias than something from a popular magazine or a random blog or website. Scholarly publications can usually be recognized by the frequent use of citations in footnotes or endnotes and by the list of scholarly editors often found on their inside cover.

Finally, remember that just because a source is scholarly and nonpartisan does not mean it is not opinionated or controversial. Sometimes scholarly and nonpartisan arguments will run counter to popular opinion or seem very opinionated. This does not invalidate their credibility, since all arguments require some controversy and some opinion. What guarantees that these sources are superior is, instead, the double-checking that goes on and the lack of direct gain or loss from their expression of an opinion. In today's information age, there are so many sources out there that you can easily feel overwhelmed. People throw statistics and testimony around on all sides of an argument, making it difficult to discern whom to trust. Because of this flood of sources, it is easy to be misled by biased and shoddy sources (of which there are plenty on the Internet). The best way

12.4 REMEMBER

relevance	idea that the data and warrants used in an argument should be related and relevant to the major claim
ad hominem	fallacy that attacks the arguer rather than the argument itself
ad populum	fallacy that asserts something must be true because many people believe it
non sequitur	argument that incorrectly assumes one thing is the cause of another
sufficiency	asks if there is enough evidence to support the claim
correlation not causation fallacy	fallacy that because one thing follows another or because two things often are found together, one must cause the other
begging the question/circular reasoning	form of argument where the conclusion is drawn based on the premises of the argument
testimonial	argument where the testimony of one user or witness is offered as data for a claim
credibility (ethos)	crucial part of argument and persuasion—one of the three components of persuasion, according to Aristotle

Remember: You can use your knowledge of persuasion to engage real-life situations. Consider the scenario below and think about what you would do as you study persuasive presentations.

You take a job as a salesperson who works strictly for commission. You've looked around and you feel like this is the only job you can get right now with no work experience. The company sets up meetings for you to present its products and sell them to those present. You are selling kitchen cleaning products that have a high chemical content and are guaranteed to work. The company you work for gives you an electronic presentation that shows how the products work. Many of the presentations you've done so far have not gone well, and those present say that your presentation looks outdated and unbelievable. How would you use persuasion to convince your company that it needs a new presentation method? Also, how would you model the presentation to persuade your audience if your company asked you to do so? What would you do?

to make sure you do not fall for some biased persuasion, then, is to check your sources. Do a little research on the sources. Make sure they are scholarly and nonpartisan. If you do this, then you will be in the best position to determine your own, well-informed opinion on the subject. And then maybe you can begin to persuade someone else through the essential and enduring human practice of argumentation.

SUMMARY

This chapter reviewed the principles of persuasive presentations. Having a specific purpose grounded in persuasion is important as you face a variety of situations in your life that require persuasive presentations. After reading this chapter, you should be mindful of how to organize a persuasive presentation. In addition, remember to evaluate the types of arguments. Hopefully you're now able to see how the different types of arguments can be more or less persuasive. Remember the standards for strong and persuasive arguments that were reviewed in the last sections. You can apply these standards to any type of argument across communication contexts. Consider everything that you read in this chapter as you create and evaluate persuasive presentations in your life.

SAMPLE PERSUASIVE SPEECH

Prosecution Deferred Is Justice Denied

Hope Stallings, Berry College

What do Morgan Stanley, Wachovia, Fannie Mae, Merrill Lynch, and AIG all have in common? You might say that they all contributed to the credit crisis in September, and according to the *Washington Post* of March 25, 2009, the ensuing $787 billion government bailout of big business. And you'd be right—partially. You see, these corporations have something else in common. In the past five years, each has been indicted on criminal charges like fraud. Never heard about the trial or verdict? That's because in spite of their fraudulent behavior, these corporations never went to court. They avoided media spotlight, investor scrutiny, and public outrage by entering into deferred prosecution agreements. The *Record* of July 21, 2008, explains that deferred prosecution agreements allow corporations to avoid criminal convictions by paying a small fine out of court. In other words, these companies paid our government to ensure that we remain ignorant, and we have, right up to the collapse of our economy and our personal financial security.

> Hope begins her speech with a rhetorical question to get her listeners' attention.

In their current form deferred prosecution agreements, or DPAs, are unethical, unjust, and flat out wrong. In this new day, we must work together with our new administration and new Congress to reform madness and reclaim justice. To become a part of this reformation of DPAs, we first need to understand the details of deferred prosecution agreements; we'll then consider causes, and finally formulate solutions.

According to the *Mondaq News Alert* of April 22, 2008, a deferred prosecution agreement occurs when a prosecutor files an indictment for a company that has committed a crime, and that indictment is put on hold in exchange for a commitment by that company to reform and pay a fine. If the company meets the obligations listed in the agreement, the prosecutor, also called a corporate monitor, asks the judge to dismiss the indictment, and the company gets away without a criminal conviction. In a DPA, the government collects fines and then appoints a corporate monitor to impose internal changes with little to no Department of Justice guidelines. American Banker of December 12, 2008, reports that DPAs are becoming unfortunately more common, as our now frail banking system means that banks and corporations that formerly might have been a target of criminal charges may now face the lighter load of a DPA. And the numbers agree. The *Corporate Crime Reporter* revealed on January 29, 2009, that between 2003 and 2009, there were 112 reported corporate DPAs, compared to only 11 between 1992 and 2001.

> Because her audience is likely supportive of her persuasive goal, she explicitly provides an overview of her message, signaling that she will identify causes of the problem and then present solutions.

One hundred twelve might not seem like many, but consider the devastating impact that just one of these ineffective DPAs can have on our economy. The *Wall Street Journal* of March 27, 2009, reports that in 2004, insurance giant AIG avoided criminal charges for fraud by entering into a deferred prosecution agreement. AIG paid a $126 million fine and was appointed a corporate monitor, but in 2008, found

> Here, Hope provides statistics to support her argument that the problem has recently gotten worse.

Source: From *Winning Orations*, 2009, Mankato, MN: Interstate Oratorical Association, 2009. Reprinted by permission.

itself under another federal investigation for the same thing; the *Wall Street Journal* says that this time, AIG's fraud contributed to its downfall in September's credit crisis. And AIG is not alone. Even household names such as American Express, Monster.com, Chevron, AmSouth Bank, KPMG, and Countrywide Financial have all avoided criminal convictions by entering into DPAs. Or consider the case of Powers Fasteners, which entered into a DPA to avoid a manslaughter charge after the Boston Big Dig tunnel collapse. According to the Washington Post of December 18, 2008, Powers Fasteners agreed to pay $16 million and recall the faulty epoxy that caused the collapse. But that's cold consolation to the family of Milena De-Valle, who was killed after being crushed by 26 tons of ceiling panels as a result of the epoxy. DPAs are allowing corporations to get away with murder. Literally.

Deferred prosecution agreements clearly run counter to our ideals of justice and fairness. We therefore need to understand why they occur, namely corporate corruption, government collusion, and public delusion.

The first cause of this problem is that corporations have abandoned ethical behavior in search of profit. The *Associated Press* reported on March 10, 2008, that though deferred prosecution agreements were originally designed to allow individuals such as juveniles and first-time drug offenders to reform without the stigma of a conviction, corporations started entering into DPAs about fifteen years ago for the same reasons: to avoid thescandal and revenue decrease associated with criminal charges. And if the corporation's executives pull the right strings, it will even get to choose its own corporate monitor in the DPA. According to the previously cited *Mondaq News Alert,* the corporate monitor is either appointed by the U.S. Department of Justice or selected by the corporation itself. Because this monitor acts as a prosecutor, judge, and jury for the corporation with few guidelines, choosing a former employee, friend, or political ally for a corporate monitor often results in no internal changes and the indictment still being dropped.

The second cause is that the government is in collusion with Corporate America. The October 2008 issue of the *Metropolitan Corporate Counsel* reported that the postindictment collapse of Arthur Andersen prompted U.S. Attorney General Larry Thompson to release the Thompson Memorandum, which made it easier for corporations to enter into DPAs. By encouraging corporations to enter into DPAs, the Department of Justice sought to save the economy from the results of another fraud scandal while cleaning out the court docket and staying friendly with big business. *Time* Magazine of March 30, 2009, states that Washington simply looked the other way in regards to corporate crime, allowing corporations to break rules without serious repercussions in order to make friends.

The final cause is public delusion. Since the collapse of Enron, we've been deluded into thinking that we've got it all covered. The events of the last few months have made it tragically and abundantly clear that we do not. According to the *Associated Press* of April 7, 2009, deferred prosecution agreements didn't draw any attention until 2008 after it was disclosed that John Ashcroft had been secretly selected as a corporate monitor. With the Ashcroft assignment, DPAs

Hope provides a clear transition from her description of the problem to her listing of the causes of the problem.

She uses clear signposts to enumerate the number of specific causes of the problem that she is presenting.

finally made the news. But because it's difficult to explain deferred prosecution agreements without using legal or financial jargon, DPAs have not been widely discussed by the mainstream media that seeks to write on a fourth-grade reading level. Additionally, the U.S. House of Representatives documents revealed on May 22, 2008, that some DPAs are never made public at all, and even Congress and the Department of Justice have difficulties counting just how many have occurred covertly in recent years.

Now that we understand the catastrophic impact of DPAs on our economy and personal economic well-being, we should be sufficiently angry to do something about it. I wish I could say that solutions come on three levels: corporate, governmental, and individual, but I can't. The fact is, we've hoped for too long that corporations could monitor themselves, and we've all felt the results of their failure to do so. Now is the time for the government to step in with the support of the people and change the current state of DPAs.

Though banishing corporate deferred prosecution agreements completely is a longterm solution, it is more practical for Congress to pass legislation altering DPAs and mandating that they be made public. Representatives Bill Pascrell and Steve Cohen are attempting to do just that through the Accountability in Deferred Prosecution Act. *The States News Service* of April 2, 2009, reveals that the Accountability in Deferred Prosecution Act of 2009 will regulate corporate deferred prosecution agreements in federal criminal cases. The bill will set guidelines ensuring an open and public process, and will prevent corporations from choosing their own corporate monitor, which brings us to personal solutions.

We must become active in this fight for justice, through political activism and encouraging awareness. Contact your congressional representatives in support of the Accountability in Deferred Prosecution Act of 2009. Without encouragement from us, the bill may not gain enough votes to pass the House and Senate. Second, though it sounds cliché, we must spread awareness of this issue. Because the cause of public delusion can only be solved by awareness, and as long as we're apathetic about awareness of DPAs, the problems will continue. I challenge you to take two minutes—just two minutes—today to talk to someone else at this tournament about DPAs. Mention it to your friends or coworkers back home; contact your local media. I have compiled a fact sheet to help you do just that; please take one after the round. Also visit my Web site www.dangersofdpas.org, on which you can find the latest news about DPAs, examples of real-life DPAs, and links to contact your representatives in support of the Accountability in Deferred Prosecution Act. By taking small steps toward awareness now, we can ignite change.

So today, by understanding the problems, causes and solutions of corporate deferred prosecution agreements, we've learned how to become a part of the reformation. We cannot let these corporate wrongdoings continue. AIG, Fannie Mae, and Merrill Lynch are institutions that we've trusted with our financial investments, and until the trust between institution and individual can be reestablished, we must invest in reforms that will end this shameful, unethical, and unjust practice of corporate deferred prosecution agreements once and for all.

Here, she uses transition phrases to summarize her analysis and then point her audience toward the solutions she will suggest.

Hope encourages her listeners to take a specific action step to address the problem she has documented.

In her conclusion, Hope provides a brief summary statement of the problem and offers a final motivational message to encourage her listeners to join her in taking action to solve the problem.

DISCUSSION QUESTIONS

Presentations

1 What is the difference between a general purpose statement and a specific purpose statement?

2 What are the three types of questions used in developing a persuasive presentation?

3 Can you come up with an example of each type of argument?

4 Can you identify which question might be the best to raise about each of your examples?

5 What are some ways that you go about identifying credible sources for persuasive presentations?

Persuasive Humor

13

George Pacheco Jr. and John Meyer

YOUR OBJECTIVES

After studying this chapter, you should be able to:

1. Understand the role humor plays in persuasion.
2. Evaluate humorous messages for persuasiveness.
3. Understand how persuaders use humor to reach audiences.

SAC Federal Credit Union
Bellevue Branch

03 Jan 2018 11:36 AM

Teller Number: 1223
Branch: 5
Seq.#: 1412

Check $255.04
$255.04   Avail Date:01-03-18

Acct#: *****4973
Essolakina T. Nador
Value
Deposit
Amt:$255.04
Current Balance: $803.64
Available Balance: $803.64

ww.sacfcu.com
Member Service: 402-292-8000

Humor

As you begin studying the role humor plays in persuasion, it's important to note that the role of humor in today's world is complex. In its early form, humor was viewed by many as nothing more than foolish behavior. Kings and members of royal families mocked the court jester, for only someone laughable would conduct himself in such foolish ways. Only the court jester could get away with a lot of behavior considered unacceptable, allowing for social discipline through humor. Plato and other early scholars believed laughter was no more than the loss of control and that only those who lacked self-control would dare laugh publicly. Through the progression of time, people have come to learn and understand much more about humor as a phenomenon. Scholars discuss humor's various communicative, physiological, psychological, and sociological aspects. For the purposes of this chapter, let's focus on the communicative aspects of humor, more specifically, how it persuades.

Humor, as a communicated message, has the power to persuade. Message creators use humor in a variety of different situations and in very specific ways. Advertisers, public relations firms, politicians, educators, and salespersons all use humor as a method of establishing a rapport with their audience, followed by systematic persuasion via their messages. This chapter explores specific persuasive tactics meant to persuade the audience through humor. By making sense of these humor uses, the audience begins to understand the messages and develops a deeper, more nuanced view of "what is being said" versus "what is seen or heard." With such a wide range of vehicles carrying humor messages to audiences, it is important to understand the powerful messages communicated through humor.

The explosion of humor in popular culture has been dramatized recently by "news" shows such as Jon Stewart's *The Daily Show* and Stephen Colbert's *The Colbert Report*, as well as a variety of socially conscious comedians like George Lopez, Carlos Mencia, Chris Rock, and Ralphie May and popular animated television shows including *South Park, Family Guy*, and *The Boondocks*. Audiences are continually faced with humorous messages created with a specific intent to influence their thoughts. These humor messages are often rhetorical in nature and indirect in delivery. Audiences are forced to make connections in order to understand the hidden messages, thus requiring a kind of deep analysis in order to "get it." In order to uncover the persuasive messages found in humor, we must look beyond the obvious message to understand the intended message; in doing so, we make critical distinctions between an obvious message and a more subtle message that creates the humor and may be the subtle source of persuasion.

WHAT IS HUMOR?

So what is **humor**? How can you begin to define something so diverse, yet so personal, as humor? Freud (1905) argued that humor releases submerged urges from the subconscious. Morreall (1983) described humor as a pleasant psychological shift and Veatch (1998) called it the simultaneous presence in the mind of a normal pattern and a violation of that same pattern. With so many varying definitions of humor, it is important to note that universally, humor itself is caused by a psychological reaction to a visual or verbal stimulant. Something must cause the laughter. To that end, it is also important to note that humor requires an understanding of a pattern. As you will explore later in the chapter, the audience must make an enthymematic connection with the message if its persuasive intent is to be effective.

We as communicators use humor in a variety of different functions. When we meet people for the first time, humor can serve as an ice breaker. We often find a great deal of stress in these situations, and humor works to lessen that stress. Communicators also often use humor to break through divisive social barriers. There are a variety of topics society deems to be taboo and the use of humor in these situations effectively breaks that taboo barrier prohibiting comments about a topic, thus allowing for a discussion to take place. Educators often use humor in the classroom. Research shows that humor in the classroom makes subject material more memorable, making it more likely to be retained and thus more effective. Politicians and speechwriters understand the effectiveness of humor in publicly communicated messages, and often create humorous messages specifically to reach their audiences.

Regardless of the reasons for the use of humor in any situation, the desired result leaves the audience reacting in laughter or feeling pleasure, and thus open to further communication. This positive reaction is what makes humor such a powerful tool. People like laughter; they enjoy feeling good, and when a message does that, it affects the thought process, causing them to consider alternative perspectives or even reinforcing an existing thought. This is seen in political humor. During Ronald Reagan's 1976 and 1980 presidential campaigns, he used humor masterfully to deconstruct his opponents' credibility while constructing his own. Meyer (1990) noted that Reagan used humor as a weapon to ridicule political stances of the opposition while telling friendly and memorable stories identifying with his audiences.

Humor has long been a tool for dealing with taboo issues, social injustices, and potentially offensive subject matter. At different times during our country's history, "Benjamin Franklin used quips and humorous drawings to urge colonists to form a national identity, Samuel Langhorn Clemens poked fun at social customs. Humor has exposed social problems and forced us to confront taboo subjects" (Rybacki & Rybacki, 1991, p. 308). Aristotle, for example, "felt that we must laugh when we see painless deformity" (Schaeffer, 1981, p. 4). Humor not only presents itself as a powerful tool for persuasion, it creates an environment where discussion of taboo topics can be approached publicly. Failing to recognize this persuasive power humor has over audiences means failing to acknowledge one of the most effective vehicles of persuasion. By deconstructing these samples

In Your Life

Think about humor in your own life. Are you persuaded by humorous messages? Have you ever used humor as a persuasive technique?

of humor, one gains insight into the process of persuasive humor and develops a critical understanding of the messages being sent to audiences, thus understanding how humor influences our beliefs and choices. To understand the background of the use of humor in persuasion, three primary theories of humor identified by researchers deserve exploration.

THREE THEORIES OF HUMOR

Humor is communicated, interpreted, and understood through the lenses of three primary theories. Meyer (2000) argued that "communication is a key factor in nearly all theories of humor because of its resulting from a message or interaction perceived by someone" (p. 311). **Superiority theory** offers the explanation that humor is found in feeling above or better than the subject being laughed at. The **relief theory** of humor makes the argument that humor is sparked in situations where a feeling of tension is relieved, allowing for the humor to present itself, and **incongruity theory** holds that humor is a result of a break from an expected pattern or norm (Morreall, 1983). Superiority, relief, and incongruity theories of humor each offer insight as to why people find certain communicated messages funny and how those messages can affect persuasive messages.

Superiority Theory

Feelings of superiority are not unfamiliar to those who appreciate humor. "The oldest and probably still the most widespread theory of laughter is that laughter is an expression of a person's feelings of superiority over other people" (Morreall, 1983, p. 4). Some of the earliest accounts of this idea can be traced all the way back to Plato, who argued that "what makes a person laughable...is self-ignorance" (cited in Morreall, 1983, p. 4). This idea of humor being an issue of self-ignorance is not as common in modern superiority theory research. Current research focuses on the use of superiority theory as a sense of being more successful than whatever is causing the laughter. Self-ignorance is only a small part of the picture. "Superiority theory bases itself in the idea that we are ready to laugh at others who we deem not as smart, good looking, wealthy, or educated as ourselves. These feelings of superiority are what creates the humor for us even at the expense of others' well-being" (Pacheco, 2008, p. 20). These feelings of superiority lead to reactions of humor and often the physical manifestation, laughter. O'Donnell (2003) added that "laughing at ignorance, hostile laughter, and laughing at the follies of children can all best be explained from this perspective" (p. 10).

Superiority theory can be a useful tool for examining humor in various situations such as interpersonal relationships, political speeches, and organized debates.

To extend the notion set forth by Plato's argument of humor and laughter being no more than "self-ignorance," Gruner (1997) argued that even when we laugh at ourselves, we are using the superiority theory of humor. Each time we make a mistake, we blame our ignorance of that particular subject matter or situation; by laughing at such a mistake, we laugh at our own self-ignorance. Although different from Plato's original notion that a serious man should not laugh because it shows him to be ignorant, this laughter is based in self-ignorance. Take, for example, a person who is running late for work who does not realize that, rather than adding sugar to her coffee, she added flour. Her discovery of this mistake creates a strong feeling of superiority because she knows that, if she hadn't been running late, she never would have made such a mistake. The resulting reaction is often laughter.

Following is an excerpt of the speech delivered by Sarah Palin at the 2008 Republican National Convention (*New York Times*, 2008). Examine this text for the uses of humor. Does Palin employ a sense of superiority over the opposition? Is her use of humor self-deprecating? How so?

> I had the privilege of living most of my life in a small town. I was just your average hockey mom and signed up for the PTA.
> (APPLAUSE)
>
> I love those hockey moms. You know what they say the difference is between a hockey mom and a pit bull? Lipstick.
> (APPLAUSE)
>
> So I signed up for the PTA because I wanted to make my kids' public education even better. And when I ran for city council, I didn't need focus groups and voter profiles because I knew those voters, and I knew their families, too.
>
> Before I became governor of the great state of Alaska...
> (APPLAUSE)
>
> ...I was mayor of my hometown. And since our opponents in this presidential election seem to look down on that experience, let me explain to them what the job involved.
> (APPLAUSE)
>
> I guess—I guess a small-town mayor is sort of like a community organizer, except that you have actual responsibilities.
> (APPLAUSE)

Sarah Palin's overall goal was to persuade her audience to support her bid for vice president of the United States. Consider the following questions.

1. How does Palin use humor in this brief excerpt?
2. What message is she trying to convey to her audience?
3. Is her use of humor effective?

Relief Theory

Relief theory argues that people experience humor based on some form of relief in stressful situations or stressful events (Herring & Meggert, 1994; Meyer, 2000; Morreall, 1983). People laugh after a stressful situation has been resolved, tensions have deflated, and the danger has passed. This creates a sense of relief within, and the nervous energy exits the body in the form of laughter. "Often tension results from dissonance people experience after making a decision or sensing the approach of incompatible and undesirable thoughts or actions" (Meyer, 2000, p. 312). By expressing and experiencing humor in these situations, people begin the process of moving past the stress. Often, these stressful situations are the result of some choices made, thus enhancing the relief when those situations subside. Ultimately, the reason for the stress is not as important as the feeling of relief beyond the stress. Regardless of the cause of the stress, humor and laughter are the result.

A specific application of the relief theory can be understood in the context of a person who is changing a flat tire. During this process, imagine that he leans against the car and the car falls off the jack that was holding it up. The relief that he feels from knowing that he could have been under the car when that happened could lead to laughter. Instead of being in a potentially serious situation, he is safe, and his next actions are manageable, leading to feelings of stress relief, expressed through laughter.

In Your Life

What is your view of humor as a way to release stress? How does relief theory connect to persuasion?

Incongruity Theory

In the third theory of humor, laughter results from a violation of an expected norm. Incongruity theory suggests that people laugh at these perceived violations because they are unexpected, unconventional, and often uncomfortable. Morreall (1983) also suggested that people do not perceive an instance of humor unless the element of surprise is present. Although a surprising incongruence is often a fact in the presence of humor, it is not a requirement. Often, people do laugh at these situations where the expected norm is violated, but surprise is not a necessary component of the humor itself. In order to understand this better, let's examine Morreall's (1983) definition of incongruity, which, importantly, focuses on a "violation of a pattern in someone's picture of how things should be" (pp. 60–61). Take, for example, the use of stereotypes in our culture. These ideas are generally not welcome in open forum discussions. Public decorum requires people to treat each other with respect. However, a joke teller is free to employ these same stereotypes in a joke. For example, if two colleagues at the office are sitting and having a friendly conversation, one colleague may tell a joke that he would never tell in an open forum with others present. Both may laugh and enjoy the experience, but both also know that in public, that kind of off-color joke would be unwelcome. This situation is common, and the resulting expression of laughter is acceptable as long as neither party feels attacked or violated.

But why would something be okay in private but not in public? Take this idea a step further by thinking of a popular comedian like Dave Chappelle or Larry the Cable Guy. These are characters who make a living by saying things in public that most people could not get away with saying. Comedians take these stereotypes and make them the center of a comedic joke, and this experience violates the expected norm of nondiscussion (Pacheco, 2008). Incongruity theory attributes humor to laughing at an occurrence resulting from an unexpected, perhaps out of the ordinary, nonthreatening surprise (Berger, 1976; Deckers & Devine, 1981; McGhee, 1979). This use of incongruity can certainly apply to presenting an alternative perspective for a persuasive use of humor. Friends telling jokes, comedians telling jokes, and jokes forwarded through email all work to create a space where the taboo can become an open forum. There is safety in the idea: "Oh, well, it was only a joke." However, though seemingly lightweight in nature, humor is a significant vehicle for transforming otherwise taboo issues and creating a public dialogue.

With humor as incongruity, because the violation of a social norm is so strong and so sudden, people often laugh first, and then begin the process of thinking about the issues at hand. "Rather than focusing on the physiological or emotional effects of humor, the incongruity theory emphasizes cognition. Individuals must have rationally come to understand normal patterns of reality before they can notice differences" (Meyer, 2000, p. 313). It is from these differences that the element of incongruity works to create humor, and the process of using humor to persuade builds.

Below you will find an expert example from the stand-up routine of comedian George Lopez. Examine the text and the questions that follow.

And let me tell you this, people don't want us here; that is insane.
That is the most insane thing to not want Latinos in the United States.
We do all the jobs that no one in America wants to do. That's what we

Social Media in Your Life: Have You Seen This?

Go to YouTube and enter the following keywords: George Lopez, stand up

This clip contains humorous material. Does this clip persuade you to change your feelings about the subject at hand?

do! Who do you think is rebuilding New Orleans? Guess! (Mariachi music and grito). You know who? FEMA, that's who, Find Every Mexican Available! FEMA! That's right, us, like it or not. At 5:30 in the morning, we are working; we are not at Starbucks playing SUDOKU (Rickenbaugh & Miller, 2005).

1. How does Lopez use humor to reach his audience?
2. Should his message be taken verbatim?
3. What makes this joke incongruent?

PERSUASIVE EFFECTS OF HUMOR

The widespread use of humor suggests that it does have some desirable persuasive effects. Research has shown humor's capacity to promote objectivity, audience interest, and speaker credibility, which are its three major benefits in the realm of persuasion. These effects show that humor cannot persuade by itself, but it is an active and effective ingredient in the persuasion mix. Some kind of evidence must be introduced with the humor, and claims must be made (even if enthymematically, as explained below).

Appreciating humor requires—and perhaps engenders—a sense of objectivity about an issue (Grimes, 1955). Incongruity from humor helps an audience see a new perspective on the topic, as they examine the one they were surprised by as well as the one they had been attached to. Thus, using humor with an audience successfully opens up other perspectives on an issue, facilitating persuasion. Rationality and objectivity go hand in hand, and promoting more objectivity through laughing at an issue may promote persuasion through rational appeals. Individuals who are in a good mood will less likely disagree with a persuasive message. By manipulating concepts incongruously for the sake of humor, persuaders provide a building up and release of tension, creating audience relief and mood enhancement (Maase, Fink, & Kaplowitz, 1984). Playing with concepts in a persuasive talk can, through humor, get people thinking and perhaps even persuade them.

Humor in a presentation clearly increases an audience's interest (Duncan & Nelson, 1985), which enhances persuasion. Some humor can serve to gain attention and express opinions in memorable ways. Humor use memorably encapsulates speakers' views and ingratiates them in the eyes of audiences. Humor can dramatize the clash of views that occurs in political rhetoric, and successful and popular politicians have shown effective uses of humor. Humor can also show a politician's ability to relate to and establish a rapport with an audience. Self-deprecatory humor can be used sparingly to

In Your Life

Think of some examples in your life where humor has had a persuasive impact.

effectively enhance a powerful politician's credibility, as presidents Gerald Ford and Ronald Reagan often did (Chapel, 1978; Meyer, 1990).

Humor in speeches adds credibility and aids information retention, but only to a certain point (Gruner, 1967), as too much humor can "boomerang" and actually damage a persuader's credibility (Taylor, 1974). The sense humor gives of "being on the same page" also suggests that, if we share something humorous with someone, we are more persuadable by that someone. A sense of familiarity results that seems to lower people's usual defenses against persuasion. A sense of common understanding through humor can unite speakers with audiences. Relevant humor shows an audience that they are appreciated by the speaker and gets them involved. Humor in a persuasive message may also serve as a distraction, creating less mental counterarguing and increasing levels of acceptance (Osterhouse & Brock, 1970).

 PERSUASION RESEARCH SNAPSHOT

Think about how you use and perceive humor in your life. Do you find yourself more socially attracted to people who have a great sense of humor? Humor has always been used as an icebreaker, but you might be surprised at how humor can be used to persuade you. Think about some of your favorite Super Bowl commercials. Advertisers put a great deal of effort and money into creating a commercial that people will remember, and many people will argue that the funniest take place on Super Bowl Sunday. Can humor influence you to like or buy a certain product? Also, can humor be used to make you think a certain way about political and social issues?

Indeed, humor plays a powerful role in persuasion. Using effective humor builds rapport, increases likability, and increases staying power in the mind. This can be a double-edged sword, though. Using offensive or irrelevant humor can have the opposite effect on a person. Therefore, it is important to study and understand how humor can be perceived and how it can be used in a positive way. Have you ever had a professor who made the class crack up on a regular basis? Think about how you perceived that professor and how it affected your attention in the class. Humor can either enhance your concentration or distract you from important information in the lecture.

Recently researchers Robin Nabi, Emily Moyer-Guseé, and Sahara Byrne conducted a study to analyze the effect of humor on social issue messages. They drew from several cognitive response theories of persuasion to frame their research. Traditional research in this field has concluded that although humor can be attributed to closer information processing and source-liking, there is a greater chance that observers will discount the message than when humor is not used. Basically, while you may like a comedian and think about

(continued)

his message, you are less likely to take it seriously because it's just part of the act. The researchers wanted to find out if this assertion is still valid. Two separate research groups were presented with four monologues from popular comedians. Group 1 read monologues by political comedian Bill Maher, while group 2 read monologues from comedian Chris Rock. Participants then filled out a survey detailing their impressions of the comic, his perceived humor, his credibility, and their message discounting related to his social commentary.

The results largely reinforced previous findings in this field. The use of humor resulted in greater source-liking (of the comedian), closer information processing, and reduced counterargument. However, there was also greater message discounting as a result. The findings were largely replicated in both studies, giving more validity to the argument. This led the researchers to assert that although humorous messages may be processed carefully, they are not processed critically.

Think about what this study means to the big picture. While humor is useful for persuasion and likability, it can also prevent you from being taken seriously. What are some instances when using humor can be appropriate and effective for you? Is it a good idea to use humor to impress your friends at a bar? How about using humor in a research presentation?

Do you want to know more about this study? If so, read: Nabi, R. L., Moyer-Guseé, E., & Byrne, S. (2007). All joking aside: A serious investigation into the persuasive effect of funny social issue messages. *Communication Monographs, 74*(1), 29–54.

PERSUASIVE USES OF HUMOR

Humor is the result of a communicated message and therefore can be used to create persuasive messages. Looking back at the three primary theories of humor, in each one, a communicated message (whether understood or misunderstood) is a necessary component. Because of the endless ways in which humor can be generated, it has potentially vast effectiveness as an argument or tool of persuasion. Early researchers revealed that humor could be an effective tool for persuading others (Goffman, 1967). Because research also shows humor aids one's memory recall and makes things more appealing, uses of humor have been integrated into much of our daily existence. Each time you turn on the television, log in to your email, surf the web, or drive down a highway, you are inundated with humorous messages. Advertisers regularly use humor in their attempts to persuade audiences to choose their products. "First, advertisers know that if they can get you to laugh with them, you will like them better. And if you like them better you are more open to their ideas. But there's another reason for using humor that advertisers love: humor makes messages memorable" (Danbom, 2005, p. 669). By creating messages with humor, advertisers are relying on that humor to function as a persuasive message.

Beyond the world of advertising, educators and corporate trainers adopt the use of humor in their classes and training sessions because it not only enhances the experience of the audience, but it makes things more memorable. By using humor, trainers are better able to maintain their audience's attention, help them understand the subject matter more clearly, and work to make the information more applicable (Pacheco, 2008). Teachers also find humor helpful. "In an educational setting, the use of humor is a strategy that educators can use in facilitating and enhancing the learning process" (Dziegielewski et al., p. 77). Humor use in classrooms can also be linked to students' success. Research shows that teachers who use humor in the classroom help students retain more information, and humor helps students and teachers build stronger relationships (Korobkin, 1988). These stronger relationships make the classroom environment more controllable and a more fertile learning environment. "Studies have reported that humor is effective in the college classroom to promote comprehension, create a positive environment, encourage student involvement, hold students' attention, foster cognitive development, and manage desirable behavior" (Punyanunt, 2000, p. 32). This mutually beneficial use of humor works to help create a livelier and more active classroom, while developing a method that helps students retain and recall information.

Health officials argue that humor has a positive effect on a person's physical health as well. "Humor is good for your heart and circulatory system. Twenty seconds of laughter gives the heart the same workout as three minutes of strenuous exercise" (Danbom, 2005, p. 669). Research shows that the good feeling that results from humor really does enhance health. So including humor in your persuasive efforts can actually help others feel good and improve their health.

Politicians seek to capitalize on these good feelings, and through the years they have attempted to use humor to put audiences in a positive frame of mind for persuasion. President Ronald Reagan generated enough humor that authors collected funny stories and quips from his speeches. Humor seemed quite an effective part of his rhetoric. He could persuade about many controversial topics while maintaining a notably high level of goodwill from the public. He was well thought of even by many who disagreed with him. His use of humor was an essential reason. His humor could keep people entertained on one level, and perhaps persuade them at another level. Reagan would find a way to tell a story or tell a joke about himself that would reach out to his audiences and show them that he could relate to their lives. Through adding this element of entertainment

In Your Life

What is your impression of the use of humor in educational and health contexts?

for audiences, Reagan successfully bolstered his credibility. In addition, however, Reagan would find a way to mock "inferior" politicians who favored what were, to him, all sorts of ridiculous measures, persuasively uniting his audience with him in opposition to "them." He once noted that "bureaucracy has a built-in instinct for preservation and reproduction of its own kind. A federal program, once started, is the nearest thing to eternal life you'll ever see on this earth" (Reagan, 1976). He would also tell humorous stories to memorably make campaign points.

These types of real-life applications make the study of humor viable and also reveal the usefulness of humor as a tool of persuasion. Advertisers, corporate trainers, educators, politicians, and health care workers all use humor and its positive effects to persuade their audiences to take some action. By examining the roles humor plays in each of these fields, we see that humor has the power to alter people's actions, thus resulting in persuasion.

Connecting with the Audience

Humor has also been found to create and strengthen communicative messages. Booth-Butterfield and Booth-Butterfield (1991) argue that "humor is typically perceived as a positive communication attribute, one that generates support, approval and goal attainment" (p. 206). Communicators who use humor do so to maintain audiences' attention and present their messages to the audience in a more memorable way. This use of humor seems unintentional to audience members, "yet the invocation of humor is so commonplace among public speakers that the study of how humor works and what it works for is enlightening for those who wish to know why it is used so much" (Meyer, 1990, p. 76). The presence of humor in a message is shown to increase the value of the message; researching and understanding why this is true allows others to create more effective messages using humor. By using humor, communicators are able to develop arguments and relay them to audiences without leaving the audience feeling attacked or offended. Humor's usefulness carries over into persuasive acts. Communicators are looking to create messages to persuade audiences through humor, as in the instances when "the theories of humor suggest ways in which Reagan could and did use humor as an effective rhetorical appeal, while at the same time entertaining or ingratiating his audience" (Meyer, 1990, p. 76). This duality enhances the use of humor's persuasiveness, thus making the audience more likely to support not only Reagan's political positions, but also his personal character. Through the humor, he becomes more persuasive and more likable.

Ethical Connection

Connect persuasive humor to an ethical perspective. Can you think of some examples where the use of humor to persuade might be viewed as unethical?

Making the Enthymematic Connection

Finding incongruities to appreciate humor requires audience members to use what Aristotle called the **enthymeme**. In an effort to make their experiences known and clear, many African American comedians have used social commentary about stereotypical experiences during their routines (Martineau, 1972). By using humor as social commentary, the comedian is creating an argument in the humor. "The communicator develops arguments in an attempt to persuade the audience to share her or his reasoning" (Shultz & Germeroth, 1998, p. 23). In other words, the comedian develops arguments intending to persuade the audience to agree with his or her reasoning. By allowing themselves to be persuaded in such circumstances, often without argument claims forthrightly stated, the audience members are enacting what Aristotle called the *enthymeme*. "The enthymeme is a kind of rhetorical deduction based on audience-accepted warrants that yield probable conclusions" (Sillars & Gronbeck, 2001, p. 118). These conclusions are the punch line. Making this enthymematic connection is an essential component of humor's power in persuasion. If the receiver of the message does not understand the message, no persuasion will occur.

According to Aristotle, an argument is made when the audience has some type of working knowledge about the subject matter. The enthymeme shows that the audience has some kind of authoritative take on the argument's claim. For example, "This leader has accepted invitations to lavish entertainments at the homes of the wealthy and therefore we must beware of him, for he is planning to pervert justice in their favor (suppressed here is the premise that those who accept expensive attentions are planning favoritism)" (Bizzell & Herzberg, 2001, p. 172). In order for an enthymematic conclusion to be drawn here, the audience members must have some prior knowledge of a similar situation that causes them to conclude that because the invitations were accepted, favors will be asked and honored. This enthymematic conclusion is based on the experiences of the audience members. Aristotle also argued that "the best enthymemes will be based on knowledge specific to one's subject, such as politics or physics" (Bizzell & Herzberg, 2001, p. 176). Because messages are often evaluated based on personal frames of reference, the better you understand the subject matter, the more likely you are to uncover the hidden meaning. This familiarity with the subject allows you to hear and understand, not only what is literally being said, but what is inferred.

Carlos Mencia is one of the most controversial comedians working today. Mencia has an entirely different approach to humor, both in delivery and style. While much of his material focuses on Hispanic/Latino stereotypes, he furthers it by making light of many cultures and issues both in the news and in society in general. After a show in Tucson, Arizona, Mencia was heavily criticized for joking about Mexican immigrants who refuse to honor the American way of life: "Let me tell you why white America is mad at you. You come to this country because it's better, then you wave a flag for the country you came from like it's better" (Burch, 2006). Mencia attributed this type of attitude toward immigration and racial issues in the United States to experiences from his own life as an immigrant.

The brashness of Mencia's comedy style has become the focus of both his fans and his critics. Focusing on race, sexual orientation, politics, religion, and social class structures, Mencia goes out of his way to violate what are considered socially or politically correct topic or commentary boundaries. Critics argue that Mencia uses these jokes for cheap laughs; however, Mencia argues that he attacks all races and religions equally in an effort to encourage his audiences to think about what is going on in the world around them. This no-barrier approach to comedy catapulted Mencia into the spotlight. During an interview, Mencia noted, "I do an interesting job of balancing a stereotype with how to use the stereotype. These guys want to be American. They work really hard. They're good at what they do. It has many layers. And it causes this weird thing where you want to get mad, but you're not sure. And that's what I like" (Deggans, 2006, p. 30). In the use of subject matter and jokes, Mencia is relying on the audience to make that enthymematic connection in order to laugh. Critics of his work would argue that these jokes simply are not funny, they are instead offensive; however, through the enthymeme, audiences are able to uncover the intended, persuasive message.

13.1 REMEMBER

humor	laughter caused by a psychological reaction to a visual or verbal stimulant
superiority theory	theory that humor is found in feeling above or better than the subject being laughed at
relief theory	theory that humor is sparked in situations where a feeling of tension is relieved, allowing for the humor to present itself
incongruity theory	theory that humor is a result of a break from an expected pattern or norm
enthymeme	rhetorical deduction based on audience-accepted warrants that yield probable conclusions

LIMITATIONS OF HUMOR IN PERSUASION

Politicians have long used narrative to scorn through satire, and put down through buffoonery, those they oppose. President Abraham Lincoln developed comic storytelling into a major source of argument and evidence (Schutz, 1977). He could use ridicule as a powerful rhetorical weapon as he delighted in pointing out the ignorance of the consequences of their arguments of his pro-slavery opponents. Even a hint of disagreement with a power structure or authority expressed through humor may arouse interest in an audience through potential conflict. A danger of using satire, however, is that it often primarily reinforces the views of those who already agree rather than changing anyone's mind (Bloom & Bloom, 1979). People either choose to be entertained by the satire, or take it literally and thus need to be corrected with a forthright telling of the persuasive claim advocated. This spoils the entertaining effects of the humor of satire.

The American Legacy Foundation was formed under the terms of the Master Settlement Agreement after the Big Tobacco trials in 1998. This settlement required that settlement money fund national public education on the harmful effects of smoking. A direct result is the Truth.com campaign. This campaign has launched a series of commercials designed to inform and persuade audiences about the harmful effects of smoking. More specifically, Truth.com launched another campaign called ShardsOglass.com. Rather than focusing on the harmful effects of smoking, this series of television commercials focuses on the tobacco industry's deceptive campaign practices. Read the following dialogue taken from one of the ShardsOglass television commercials. See if you can decipher what the intended message is versus the actual message:

> At Shard O Glass Freeze Pops, we want you to know where we stand on important glass freeze-pop issues. We now agree, there is no such thing as a safe glass freeze-pop. The only proven way to reduce health risks from our glass pops is to not eat them. To learn more, visit our website. And remember, Shard O Glass Freeze-Pops are for adults only.

Now consider the following questions:

1. What is the message?
2. Is the commercial really talking about frozen desserts laden with tiny pieces of glass? Of course not; the message is a satirical look at the tobacco industry's continued promotion of its products despite the well-documented harmful effects on smokers' health.

Remember: You can use your knowledge of persuasion to engage real-life situations. Consider the scenario below and think about what you would do as you apply your study of persuasive humor.

You've had enough of your coworkers making comments about you behind your back. You've asked them to stop several times and feel as though you cannot take any more of this treatment. You schedule a meeting with your boss to see if there is anything that you can do to move desks or otherwise escape this situation. As you walk into your boss's office, you realize that he is on the phone with a friend and laughing hysterically. Your boss finally puts down the phone and asks what you need to talk about. As you begin to explain your crisis, your boss makes your issue seem lighter than it is by joking and attempting to humor you. This makes you feel as though you aren't being taken seriously. You really need this job and you don't want to be disrespectful. What would you do?

SUMMARY

By using humor as social commentary, the joke teller creates a persuasive message. "The communicator develops arguments in an attempt to persuade the audience to share her or his reasoning" (Shultz & Germeroth, 1998, p. 23). So the joke teller, along with entertaining, develops arguments intentionally designed to persuade. "Comedians as rhetors use the humor in their messages to influence what the audience believes by creating arguments for those beliefs. Humor as an argument is a persuasive tool, not only because it aids in memory and retention of information, but because in the comedic setting it allows for an open discussion" (Pacheco, 2008, p. 151). Telling jokes that deal with taboo topics is not acceptable in common society, but through the use of humor, the taboo nature of a subject is greatly diminished. Because of this, humor is a necessary tool for developing and confronting needed social discussion about these taboo ideas. Humor is the vehicle that allows these ideas to be brought to light and discussed openly.

Hauser (1986) defined argument as "reasoned appeals based on evidence of fact and opinion that led to a conclusion" (p. 46). The idea that an argument contains both facts and opinions creates a solid foundation for the practice of using humor in efforts to persuade because it acknowledges both truths that are known and those that are perceived. "By incorporating what is known as truth based on factual evidence, and what is perceived as truth based on opinion or assumption, the joke teller creates arguments that reflect a notion of reality" (Pacheco, 2008, p. 152). Hauser (1986) furthered this idea by noting "through arguments, rhetors attempt to provide an audience with a solid basis for holding a belief and coordinating its actions with its beliefs" (p. 46). As a persuasive device, humor uses rational thought to achieve the intended connection with the audience. To be persuasive, it also needs to incorporate reasoned appeals. To make a rational claim, the joke must possess some factual truths or assumed opinions. Without these facts and opinions, a joke is just a joke.

DISCUSSION QUESTIONS

1. Why is it important to study humor as a communicative persuasive tool?
2. With humor permeating so many aspects of our daily lives, is it an effective persuasive tactic?
3. How does humor work to strengthen existing beliefs?
4. Think of an advertising campaign that made you laugh. Were you persuaded to try that product? Why?
5. Can you think of a personal example where you used or someone used humor to persuade others?

References

Chapter 1

Edwards, A., Edwards, C., Wahl, S. T., & Myers, S. (2013). *The communication age: Connecting and engaging.* Thousand Oaks, CA: Sage.

Fiske, J. (1989). *Understanding popular culture.* Boston: Unwin Hyman.

Frey, L. R., & Carragee, K. M. (Eds.). (2007). *Communication activism: Volume 1. Communication for social change.* Cresskill, NJ: Hampton Press.

Habermas, J. (1979). *Communication and the evolution of society.* Boston, MA: Beacon Press.

Japp, P. M., Meister, M., & Japp, D. K. (2005). *Communication ethics, media, & popular culture.* New York: Peter Lang.

Johannesen, R. L., Valde, K. S., & Whedbee, K. E. (2008). *Ethics in human communication* (6th ed). Prospect Heights, IL: Waveland Press.

Langan, E. J. (1999). Environmental features in theme restaurants. In L. K. Guerrero, J. A. DeVito, & M. L. Hecht (Eds.), *The nonverbal communication reader: Classic and contemporary readings* (2nd ed., pp. 255–263). Prospect Heights, IL: Waveland.

Chapter 2

Johannesen, R. L., Valde, K. S., & Whedbee, K. E. (2008). *Ethics in human communication* (6th ed.). Prospect Heights, IL: Waveland Press.

Quintanilla, K. M., & Wahl, S. T. (2011). *Business and professional communication: Keys for workplace excellence.* Thousand Oaks, CA: Sage.

Wellman, C. (1988). *Morals and ethics.* Upper Saddle River, NJ: Prentice Hall.

Chapter 3

Bandura, A. (1977). *Social learning theory.* New York: General Learning Press.

Blumler, J. (1979). The role of theory in uses and gratifications studies. *Communication Research, 6,* 9–34.

Festinger, L. (1962) *A theory of cognitive dissonance.* Stanford, CA: Stanford University Press.

Fisher, W. R. (1984). Narration as a human communication paradigm: The case of public moral argument. *Communication Monographs, 51,* 1–22.

Heider, F. (1946). Attitudes and cognitive organization. *Journal of Psychology, 21,* 107–112.

Heider, F. (1958). *The psychology of interpersonal relations.* New York: Wiley.

Newcomb, T. M. (1953). An approach to the study of communicative acts. *Psychological Review, 60,* 393–404.

Petty, R. E., & Cacioppo, J. T. (1996). *Attitudes and persuasion: Classic and contemporary approaches.* Boulder, CO: Westview Press.

Rank, H. (1976). Teaching about public persuasion. In D. Dieterich (Ed.), *Teaching and doublespeak*. Urbana, IL: National Council of Teachers of English.

Sherif, C. W., Sherif, M., & Nebergall, R. E. (1965). *Attitude and attitude change: The social judgment-involvement approach*. Philadelphia: Saunders.

Chapter 4

Brockeride, W. (1972). Arguers as lovers. *Philosophy and Rhetoric, 5*(1), 1–11.

Goodnight, T. G. (1982). The personal, technical, and public spheres of argument: A speculative inquiry into the art of public deliberation. *Journal of the American Forensic Association, 18*, 214–227.

Hart, R. (1970). *Philosophical commonality and speech types.* (Unpublished doctoral dissertation). Pennsylvania State University.

Perelman, C., & Olbrechts-Tyteca, L. (1969). *The new rhetoric: A treatise on argumentation*. Notre Dame, IN: University of Notre Dame Press.

Tannen, D. (1998). *The argument culture: Stopping America's war of words*. New York: Ballantine Books.

Toulmin, S. (1958). *The uses of argument*. New York, NY: Cambridge University Press.

Zarefsky, D. (1994). Argumentation in the tradition of speech communication studies. *Proceedings of the keynote presentation at the third international conference of argumentation* (pp. 1–27). Amsterdam, The Netherlands: University of Amsterdam, The Netherlands.

Chapter 5

Blair, J. A. (1996). The possibility and actuality of visual argument. *Argumentation and Advocacy, 33*(1), 23–39.

Edwards, J. L., & Winkler, C. K. (1997). Representative form and the visual ideograph: The Iwo Jima image in editorial cartoons. *Quarterly Journal of Speech, 83*, 289–310.

Engstrom, E. (2007, January). Selling with sex in Sin City: The case of the Hard Rock Hotel Casino. *Journal of Promotion Management, 13*, 169. Retrieved August 5, 2009. doi:10.1300/J057v13n0111

Fisher, W. R. (1984). Narration as human communication paradigm: The case of public moral argument. *Communication Monographs, 51*, 1–22.

Fleming, D. (1996). Can pictures be arguments? *Argumentation & Advocacy, 33*(1), 11–22. Retrieved April 17, 2010, from Ebsco Communication and Mass Media Complete.

Foss, S. K. (2004). Framing the study of visual rhetoric: Toward a transformation of rhetorical theory. In C. A. Hill & M. Helmers (Eds.), *Defining visual rhetorics* (pp. 303–314). Mahwah, NJ: Lawrence Erlbaum Associates.

Hatfield, K. L., Hinck, A., & Birkholt, M. J. (2007). Seeing the visual in argumentation: A rhetorical analysis of UNICEF Belgium's Smurf PSA as a site of visual argumentation. *Argumentation and Advocacy, 43*, 144–151.

Peters, J. D. (2001). Witnessing. *Media, Culture, & Society, 23*, 707–723.

Vancil, D. L., & Pendell, S. D. (1987). The myth of viewer-listener disagreement in the first Kennedy-Nixon debate. *Central States Speech Journal, 38*, 16–27.

Weaver, R. M. (1953). *The ethics of rhetoric.* Chicago: Henry Regnery. Witte, K. (1992). Putting the fear back into fear appeals: The extended parallel process model. *Communication Monographs, 59*, 329–349.

Chapter 6

Boyd, D. (forthcoming). White flight in networked publics? How race and class shaped American teen engagement with MySpace and Facebook. In L. Nakamura & P. Chow-White (Eds.), *Digital race anthology.* New York, NY: Routledge. Retrieved from http://www.danah.org/papers/2009/WhiteFlightDraft3.pdf

Cialdini, R. B. (2007). *Influence: The psychology of persuasion* (Rev. ed.). New York: Quill.

Diana, A. (2010, June 28). Social media up 230% since 2007. *Information Week.* Retrieved from http://www.informationweek.com/news/software/web_services/showArticle.jhtml?articleID=225701600&subSection=News

Eisenstein, E. L. (1980). *The printing press as an agent of change.* England: Cambridge University Press.

Experian Simmons (2010). Free report: 2010 social networking report. Retrieved from http://www.smrb.com/web/guest/2010-social-media-report

Fisher, W. R. (1984). Narration as human communication paradigm: The case of public moral argument. *Communication Monographs, 51*, 1–22.

Fiske, J. (1989). *Understanding popular culture.* New York, NY: Routledge.

Fogg, B. J. (2008). Mass interpersonal persuasion: An early view of a new phenomenon. In *Proceedings of the Third International Conference on Persuasive Technology,* Persuasive 2008. Berlin: Springer.

Goldman, D. (2009, June 16). MySpace to cut 30% of workforce. CNNMoney.com. Retrieved from http://money.cnn.com/2009/06/16/technology/myspace_layoffs/index.htm

Heussner, K. M. (2010, May 18). New site exposes embarrassing Facebook updates. ABCNews.com. Retrieved from http://abcnews.go.com/Technology/site-exposes-embarrassing-facebook-updates/story?id=10669091

Manovich, L. (2003). New media from Borges to HTML. In N. Wardrip-Fruin & N. Montfort (Eds.), *The new media reader* (pp. 13–25). Cambridge, MA: The MIT Press.

McLuhan, M. (1962). *The Gutenberg galaxy: The making of typographic man* (1st ed.). Canada: University of Toronto Press.

Niedzviecki, H. (2009). *The peep diaries: How we're learning to love watching ourselves and our neighbors.* San Francisco, CA: City Lights Books.

Ong, W. J. (1982). *Orality and literacy: The technologizing of the word.* London: Methuen.

Orwell, G. (1961). *1984.* New York, NY: New American Library.

Smith, J. (2009, February 2). Fastest growing demographic on Facebook: Women over 55. *Insider Facebook.* Retrieved from http://www.insidefacebook.com/2009/02/02/fastest-growing-demographic-on-facebook-women-over-55/

Vansina, J. M. (1985). *Oral tradition as history*. Madison, WI: University of Wisconsin Press.

Wahl, S. T. (2003). Constructions of the public and the private in the Internet Age. *ETD collection for University of Nebraska-Lincoln*. Retrieved from http://digitalcommons.unl.edu/dissertations/AAI3085742

Zuckerberg, M. (2010, February 4). Six years of making connections. The Facebook Blog. Retrieved from http://blog.facebook.com

Chapter 7

Bakhtin, M. M. (1982). *The dialogic imagination: Four essays*. Austin, TX: University of Texas Press Slavic Series.

Benoit, W. L. (1997). Image restoration discourse and crisis communication. In D. P. Millar & R. L. Heath (Eds.), *Responding to crisis: A rhetorical approach to crisis communication* (pp. 263–280). Mahwah, NJ: Lawrence Erlbaum Associates.

Bianco, A., & Zellner, W. (2003, October 6). Is Wal-Mart too powerful? *Bloomberg BusinessWeek*. Retrieved from http://www.businessweek.com/magazine/content/03_40/b3852001_mz001.htm

Binder, L. (1971). *Crisis and sequence in political development*. Princeton, NJ: Princeton University Press.

Blue State Digital (n.d.). Obama for America. Retrieved from http://www.bluestatedigital.com/work/case-studies/barack-obama/

Bobbitt, R., & Sullivan, R. (2009). *Developing the public relations campaign: A team-based approach* . Boston: Pearson/Allyn & Bacon.

Boyd, H. (2011, March 28). Rep. Rangel: Congress should have been consulted on Libya. *Blackvoicenews.com*. Retrieved from http://www.blackvoicenews.com/news/news-wire/45921-rep-rangel-congress-should-have-been-consulted-on-libya.html

Bush, M. (2010, June 2). BP print ads promise to "make this right": Message, however, is undercut by ongoing spill. *Advertising Age*. Retrieved from http://adage.com/article?article_id=144196

Carter, L. (2010). Liberal UCLA college students angry at Obama. *Examiner.com, Los Angeles CA*. Retrieved from http://www.examiner.com/african-american-conservative-in-los-angeles/liberal-ucla-college-students-angry-at-obama

Center, A. H., Jackson, P., Smith, S., & Stansberry, F. (2008). *Public relations practices: Managerial case studies and problems* (7th ed.). Englewood Cliffs, NJ: Prentice Hall.

Collette, C. (2010). Dozens protest at BP gas station as oil continues to leak in Gulf of Mexico. *WTSP*. Retrieved from http://www.wtsp.com/news/mostpop/story.aspx?storyid=133191&provider=top

Coombs, W. T. (1999). *Ongoing crisis communication: Planning, managing, and responding*. Thousand Oaks, CA: Sage.

Dorausch, M. (2007, September 8). Barack Obama presidential campaign website success secrets. *PlanetChiropractic.com*. Retrieved from http://www.planetc1.com/search/barack-obama-presidential-campaign-website-success-secrets.html

Engle, G. (2010, August 23). Sea World fined in trainer death: Park to contest "unfounded allegations." *My Fox Orlando*. Retrieved from http://www.myfoxorlando.com/dpp/news/orange_news/082310-seaworld-fined

Hearit, K. M. (1994). Apologies and public relations crises at Chrysler, Toshiba, and Volvo. *Public Relations Review, 20*(2), 113–125.

KIIITV News (2009, December 9). CITGO employee still recovering from explosion. *KIIITV*. Retrieved from http://www.kiiitv.com/news/local/78914207.html

Kilbourne, J. (1999). *Deadly persuasion: Why women and girls must fight the addictive power of advertising*. New York, NY: The Free Press.

Leiss, W., Kline, S., Jhally, S., & Botterill, J. (2005). *Social communication in advertising: Consumption in the mediated marketplace*. New York, NY: Routledge.

MacAskill, E. (2009, December 2). US liberals express anger over Obama's decision to raise troop levels. *Guardian.co.uk*. Retrieved from http://www.guardian.co.uk/world/2009/dec/02/obama-afghanistan-liberal-backlash

Owen, D. (1981). *Media messages in American presidential campaigns*. Westport, CT: Greenwood Press.

PBS.org (2004, November 16). Is Wal-Mart good for America? *Frontline*. Retrieved from http://www.pbs.org/wgbh/pages/frontline/shows/walmart/view/?utm_campaign=viewpage&utm_medium=viewsearch&utm_source=viewsearch

Plungis, J. (2010, September 1). BP's advertising tripled after oil spill, Waxman says. *Bloomberg BusinessWeek*. Retrieved from http://www.businessweek.com/news/2010-09-01/bp-s-advertising-tripled-after-oil-spill-waxman-says.html.

Robertson, C., & Krauss, C. (2010, August 3). Gulf spill is the largest of its kind, scientists say. *The New York Times*. Retrieved from http://www.nytimes.com/2010/08/03/us/03oilspill.html?_r=1&fta=y

Sausley, L. (2010, June 2). CITGO donates fire truck. *KRISTV*. Retrieved from http://www.kristv.com/news/citgo-donates-fire-truck/

Solis, B., & Breakenridge, D. (2009). *Putting the public back in public relations: How social media is reinventing the aging business of PR*. Upper Saddle River, NJ: FT Press.

Terkel, A. (2010, May 25). BP runs full-page ads in major newspapers defending its oil spill response: "We have taken full responsibility." *Think Progress*. Retrieved from http://thinkprogress.org/2010/05/25/bp-ads/

Turney, M. (2000). Spanning the explanatory and mutual satisfaction phases of public relations: Ivy Lee was decades ahead of his colleagues. *On-line readings in public relations*. Retrieved from http://www.nku.edu/~turney/prclass/readings/3eras2x.html

Welch, W., & Joyner, C. (2010, May 25). Memorial service honors 11 dead oil rig workers. *USA Today*. Retrieved from http://www.usatoday.com/news/nation/2010-05-25-oil-spill-victims-memorial_N.htm.

Yue, L., & Glenn, B. (2007, February 22) Chicago designers create Obama's logo. *Crain's Chicago Business*. Retrieved from http://www.chicagobusiness.com

Chapter 8

Andersen, P. A. (2008). *Nonverbal communication: Forms and functions* (2nd ed.). Prospect Heights: IL: Waveland Press.

Babcock, J. C., Waltz, J., Jacobson, N. S., & Gottman, J. M. (1993). Power and violence: The relationship between communication patterns, power discrepancies, and domestic violence. *Journal of Consulting and Clinical Psychology, 61,* 40–50.

Baumrind, D. (1971). Current patterns of parental authority. *Developmental Psychology Monographs, 4*(1), 1–103.

Baumrind, D. (1991). Parenting styles and adolescent development. In R. M. Leder, A. C. Petersen, & J. Brooks-Gunn (Eds.), *Encyclopedia of adolescence* (Vol. 2, pp. 746–758). New York, NY: Garland.

Baxter, L. A., Braithwaite, D. O., & Nicholson, J. (1999). Turning points in the development of blended family relationships. *Journal of Social and Personal Relationships, 16,* 291–313.

Berger, C. R. (1985). Social power and interpersonal communication. In M. L. Knapp & G. R. Miller (Eds.), *Handbook of interpersonal communication* (pp. 439–499). Beverly Hills, CA: Sage.

Cupach, W. R., & Spitzberg, B. H. (Eds.). (1994). *The dark side of interpersonal communication.* Hillsdale, NJ: Erlbaum.

Dillard, J. P. (1989). Types of influence goals in personal relationships. *Journal of Social and Personal Relationships, 6,* 293–308.

Duck, S., & Wood, J. T. (1995). For better, for worse, for richer, for poorer: The rough and the smooth of relationships. In S. Duck & J. T. Wood (Eds.), *Confronting relationship challenges* (pp. 1–21). Thousand Oaks, CA: Sage.

Fitzpatrick, M. A. (1988). *Between husbands and wives: Communication in marriage.* Newbury Park, CA: Sage.

Graham, E. E. (1997). Turning points and commitment in post-divorce relationships. *Communication Monographs, 64,* 350–367.

Guerrero, L. K. (1996). Attachment-style differences in intimacy and involvement: A test of the four-category model. *Communication Monographs, 63,* 269–292.

Guerrero, L. K., Andersen, P. A., & Afifi, W. A. (2011). *Close encounters: Communication in relationships.* (3rd ed.). Los Angeles, CA: Sage.

Guerrero, L. K., & Floyd, K. (2006). *Nonverbal communication in close relationships.* Mahwah, NJ: Lawrence Erlbaum.

Huston, T. L., Surra, C. A., Fitzgerald, N. M., & Cate, R. M. (1981). From courtship to marriage: Mate selection as an interpersonal process. In S. Duck & R. Gilmour (Eds.), *Personal relationships 2: Developing personal relationships* (pp. 53–90). New York, NY: Academic Press.

Infante, D. A., Chandler, T. A., & Rudd, J. E. (1989). Test of an argumentative skill deficiency model of interspousal violence. *Communication Monographs, 56,* 163–177.

McAdams, D. P. (1985). Motivation and friendship. In S. Duck & D. Perlman (Eds.), *Handbook of personal relationships. Theory, research, and intervention* (pp. 7–22). New York, NY: Wiley.

Sabourin, T. C., & Stamp, G. H. (1995). Communication and the experience of dialectical tensions in family life: An examination of abusive and nonabusive families. *Communication Monographs, 62,* 213–242.

Sagrestano, L. M., Heavey, C. L., & Christensen, A. (1999). Perceived power and physical violence in marital conflict. *Journal of Social Issues, 55,* 65–79.

Chapter 9

Altman, I. (1975). *The environment and social behavior*. Thousand Oaks, CA: Brooks/ Cole.

Andersen, P. A. (2004). *The complete idiot's guide to body language*. New York, NY: Alpha.

Anderson, C. A., & Anderson, D. C. (1984). Ambient temperature and violent crime: Tests of the linear and curvilinear hypotheses. *Journal of Personality and Social Psychology, 46,* 91–97.

Argyle, M., & Dean, J. (1965). Eye contact, distance and addiliation. *Sociometry, 28,* 289–304.

Aries, E. J., Gold, C., & Weigel, R. (1983). Dispositional and situational influences on dominance behavior in small groups. *Journal of Personality and Social Psychology, 44,* 779–786.

Atkinson, A. P., Tipples, J., Burt, D. M., & Young, A. W. (2005). Asymmetric interference between sex and emotion in face perception. *Perception and Psychophysics, 67,* 1199–1213.

Baron, R. A. (1972). Aggression as a function of ambient temperature and prior anger arousal. *Journal of Personality and Social Psychology, 21,* 183–189.

Beattie, G., & Shovelton, J. (1999). Mapping the range of information contained in the iconic hand gestures that accompany spontaneous speech. *Journal of Language and Social Psychology, 18,* 438–462.

Bellizzi, J. A., Crowley, A. E., & Hasty, R. W. (1983). The effects of color in store design. *Journal of Retailing, 59,* 21–45.

Birdwhistell, R. L. (1960). Kinesics and communication. In E. Carpenter & M. McLuhan (Eds.), *Explorations in communication: An anthology* (pp. 54–64). Boston, MA: Beacon.

Bodenhausen, G. V., & Macrae, C. N. (1998). Stereotype activation and inhibition. In J. R. Wyer (Ed.), *Advances in social cognition* (Vol. 11, pp. 1–52). Mahwah, NJ: Erlbaum.

Bowen, D. D., & Kilmann, R. H. (1975). Developing a comparative measure of the learning climate in professional schools. *Journal of Applied Psychology, 60,* 71–79.

Burgoon, J. K. (1991). Relational message interpretations of touch, conversational distance, and posture. *Journal of Nonverbal Behavior, 15,* 233–259.

Burgoon, J. K., & Dunbar, N. E. (2006). Nonverbal expressions of dominance and power in human relationships. In V. Manusov & M. L. Patterson (Eds.), *The Sage handbook of nonverbal communication* (pp. 279–297). Thousand Oaks, CA: Sage.

Carney, D. R., Hall, J. A., & Smith LeBeau, L. (2005). Beliefs about the nonverbal expression of social power. *Journal of Nonverbal Behavior, 29,* 105–123.

Cesario, J., & Higgins, E. (2008). Making message recipients "feel right": How nonverbal cues can increase persuasion. *Psychological Science, 19*, 415–420.

Ekman, P., & Friesen, W. V. (1969). The repertoire of nonverbal behavior: Categories, origins, usage, and coding. *Semiotica, 1*, 49–98.

Forbes, G. B., Adams-Curtis, L. E., Rade, B., & Jaberg, P. (2001). Body dissatisfaction in women and men: The role of gender-typing and self-esteem. *Sex Roles, 44*, 461–484.

Goffman, E. (1971). *Relations in public: Microstudies of the public order.* New York, NY: Harper Colophon Books.

Griffit, W. (1970). Environmental effects on interpersonal affective behavior: Ambient effective temperature and attraction. *Journal of Personality and Social Psychology, 15*, 240–244.

Guerrero, L. L., & Floyd, K. (2006). *Nonverbal communication in close relationships.* Mahwah, NJ: Erlbaum.

Hall, E. T. (1959). *The silent language.* Garden City, NJ: Doubleday.

Hall, E. T. (1966). *The hidden dimension.* Garden City, NJ: Doubleday.

Hall, E. T. (1968). Proxemics. *Current Anthropology, 9*, 83–108.

Hall, E. T. (1983). Proxemics. In A. M. Katz & V. T. Katz (Eds.), *Foundation of nonverbal communication: Readings, exercises, and commentary* (pp. 5–27). Carbondale, IL: Southern Illinois University Press.

Harris, P., & Sachau, D. (2005). Is cleanliness next to godliness? The role of housekeeping in impression formation. *Environment and Behavior, 37*, 81–99.

Heslin, R. (1974). *Steps toward a taxonomy of touching.* Paper presented at the meeting of the Midwestern Psychological Association, Chicago, IL.

Holley, L., & Steiner, S. (2005). Safe space: Student perspectives on classroom environment. *Journal of Social Work Education, 41*, 49–64.

Ivy, D., & Wahl, S. (2009). *The nonverbal self: Communication for a lifetime.* Boston, MA: Allyn & Bacon.

Kendon, A. (1967). Some functions of gaze-direction in social interaction. *Acta Psychologica, 26*, 22–63.

Knapp, M. L., & Hall, J. A. (2006). *Nonverbal communication in human interaction* (6th ed.). Belmont, CA: Thomson/Wadsworth.

Lawrence, S. G., & Watson, M. (1991). Getting others to help: The effectiveness of professional uniforms in charitable fund-raising. *Journal of Applied Communication Research, 19*, 170–185.

Manusov, V., & Patterson, M. L. (2006). *The Sage handbook of nonverbal communication.* Thousand Oaks, CA: Sage.

McCroskey, J. C., & McVetta, W. R. (1978). Classroom seating arrangements: Instructional communication theory versus student preferences. *Communication Education, 27*, 99–110.

Mendolia, M. (2007). Explicit use of categorical and dimensional strategies to decode facial expressions of emotion. *Journal of Nonverbal Behavior, 31*, 57–75.

Mulvey, K. (2006, January 23). Love and the laws of attraction: Express yourself. *The Express*, p. 31.

Remland, M. (1981). Developing leadership skills in nonverbal communication: A situational perspective. *Journal of Business Communication, 18*, 18–31.

Sheldon, W. H. (1940). *The varieties of human physique: An introduction to constitutional psychology*. New York: Harper & Brothers.

Soll, L. (2007, February 9). The best of bad pits. *Entertainment Weekly*, 18.

Sommer, R. (2002). Personal space in a digital age. In R. B. Bechtel and A. Churchman (Eds.), *Handbook of environmental psychology* (pp. 647–660). New York, NY: Wiley.

Streeck, J. (1993). Gesture as communication I: Its coordination with gaze and speech. *Communication Monographs, 60*, 275–299.

Tiggemann, M., & Golder, F. (2006). Tattooing: An expression of uniqueness in the appearance domain. *Body Image, 3*, 309–315.

Young, M. (1999). Dressed to commune, dressed to kill: Changing police imagery in England and Wales. In K. K. Johnson & S. J. Lennon (Eds.), *Appearance and power*. New York, NY: Oxford University Press.

Chapter 10

Adelman, R. D., Greene, M. G., & Charon, R. (1991). Issues in physician-elderly patient interaction. *Aging and Society, 2*, 127–148.

Amason, P., & Webb, L. M. (in press). Interpersonal communication issues in conversations about sexually transmitted diseases. In K. Wright & S. D. Moore (Eds.), *Applications in health communication*. Boston, MA: Allyn & Bacon.

Bandura, A. (1986). *Social foundations of thought and action: A social cognitive approach*. Englewood Cliffs, NJ: Prentice Hall.

Bouchard, L. (1993). Patients' satisfaction with the physical environment of an oncology clinic. *Journal of Psychosocial Oncology, 11*(1), 55–67.

Burgoon, J. K., & Hale, J. L. (1988). Nonverbal expectancy violations: Model elaboration and application to immediacy behaviors. *Communication Monographs, 55*(1), 58–79.

du Pré A. (2010). *Communicating about health: Current issues and perspectives*. New York, NY: Oxford University Press.

Festinger, L. (1957). *A theory of cognitive dissonance*. Stanford, CA: Stanford University Press.

Forrest, C. B., Shadmi, E., Nutting, P. A., & Starfield, B. (2007). Specialty referral completion among primary care patients: Results from the ASPN referral study. *Annals of Family Medicine, 5*(4), 361–367.

French, J. P. R., Jr., & Raven, B. (1960). The bases of social power. In D. Cartwright & A. Zander (Eds.), *Group dynamics* (pp. 607–623). New York, NY: Harper & Row.

Fry, R. B., & Prentice-Dunn, S. (2005). Effects of coping information and value affirmation on responses to a perceived health threat. *Health Communication, 17*(2), 133–147.

Gass, R. H., & Seiter, J. S. (1999). *Persuasion, social influence, and compliance gaining*. Boston, MA: Allyn & Bacon.

Geist, P., & Hardesty, M. (1990). Reliable, silent, hysterical, or assured: Physicians assess patient cues in their medical decision making. *Health Communication, 2*, 69–90.

Gellad, Z. F., & Lyles, K. W. (2007). Direct-to-consumer advertising of pharmaceuticals. *The American Journal of Medicine, 120*(6), 475–180.

Gerbner, G., Gross, L., Morgan, M., & Signorelli, N. (1994). Living with television: The dynamics of the cultivation process. In J. Bryant & D. Zillmann (Eds.), *Perspectives on media effects* (pp. 17–40). Hillsdale, NJ: Lawrence Erlbaum.

Klingle, R. S. (1993). Bringing time into physician compliance-gaining research: Toward a reinforcement expectancy theory of strategy effectiveness. *Health Communication, 6*(1), 85–104.

Kreps, G. L., Query, J. L, Jr., & Bonaguro, E. W. (2008). In L. C. Lederman (Ed.), *Beyond these walls: Readings in health communication* (pp. 3–14). New York, NY: Oxford University Press.

McDonnel, P. J., & Jacobs, M. R. (2002). Hospital admissions resulting from preventable adverse drug reactions. *Annals of Pharmacotherapy, 36*, 1331–1336.

Morman, M. T. (2000). The influence of fear appeals, message design, and masculinity on men's motivation to perform the testicular self-exam. *Journal of Applied Communication Research, 28*(2), 91–116.

Murray-Johnson, L., & Witte, K. (2003). Looking toward the future: Health message design strategies. In T. L. Thompson, A. M. Dorsey, K. I. Miller, & R. Parrott (Eds.), *Handbook of health communication* (pp. 473–495). Mahwah, NJ: Lawrence Erlbaum.

National Network of Libraries of Medicine (2010, January 5). Health literacy. Retrieved from http://nnlm.gov/outreach/consumer/hlthlit.html.

Rollnick, S., & Miller, W. (1995). What is motivational interviewing? *Behavioural and Cognitive Psychotherapy, 23*, 325–334. Reprinted online. Retrieved from http://www.motivationalinterview.org/clinical/whatismi.html

Rosenberg, M., Waugh, M. S., & Long, S. (1995). Unintended pregnancies and misuse and discontinuation of oral contraceptives. *Journal of Reproductive Medicine, 40*, 355–360.

Rosenstock, I. M. (1960). What research in motivation suggests for public health. *American Journal of Public Health, 50*, 295–301.

Rotter, J. B., & Mulry, R. C. (1965). Internal versus external control of reinforcement and decision time. *Journal of Personality and Social Psychology, 2*(4), 598–604.

Signorielli, N., & Morgan, M. (1990). Introduction. In N. Signorielli & M. Morgan (Eds.), *Cultivation analysis: New directions in media effects research* (pp. 1–15). Newbury Park, CA: Sage.

Stevenson, F. A., Britten, N., Barry, C. A., Bradley, C. P., & Barber, N. (2002). Perceptions of legitimacy: The influence on medicine taking and prescribing. *Health: An Interdisciplinary Journal for the Social Study of Health, Illness and Medicine, 6*(1), 85–104.

Stretcher, V. J., & Rosenstock, I. M. (1997). The health belief model. In K. Glanz, F. M. Lewis, & B. K. Rimer (Eds.), *Health behavior and health education* (pp. 41–59). San Francisco, CA: Jossey-Bass.

Witte, K. (1992). Putting fear back into fear appeals: The extended parallel process model. *Communication Monographs, 59*, 329–349.

World Health Organization, Preamble to the Constitution of the World Health Organization as adopted by the International Health Conference, New York,

19–22 June, 1946; signed on 22 July 1946 by the representatives of 61 States (Official Records of the World Health Organization, no. 2, p. 100) and entered into force on 7 April 1948.

Wright, K. B., Sparks, L., & O'Hair, H. D. (2008). *Health communication in the 21st century*. Malden, MA: Blackwell Publishing.

Zhang, Y., Wang, W., Scholl, J. C., & Buchanan, J. (2008). Who are the college students behind the wheel after drinking? *International Electronic Journal of Health Education, 11*, 109–118. Retrieved from http://www.aahperd.org/iejhe/2008/08_Y_Zang.pdf

Chapter 11

Andersen, P. A. (2004). *The complete idiot's guide to body language*. New York, NY: Alpha.

Baron, R. A. (1983). Short note: "Sweet smell of success"? The impact of pleasant artificial scents on the evaluations of job applicants. *Journal of Applied Psychology, 68*, 709–713.

Beebe, S. A. (1974). Eye contact: A nonverbal determinant of speaker credibility. *Speech Teacher, 23*, 21–25.

Bringhurst, R. (2004). *The elements of typographic style* (3rd ed.). New York, NY: Harts and Marks.

Crane, E., & Crane, F. G. (2002). Usage and effectiveness of impression management strategies in organizational settings. *International Journal of Action Methods, 55*, 25–34.

Ekman, P. (1965). Communication through nonverbal behavior: A source of information about an interpersonal relationship. In S. S. Tomkins & C. E. Izard (Eds.), *Affect, cognition, and personality*. New York, NY: Springer.

Freiberg, K., & Freiberg, J. (1996). *NUTS! Southwest Airlines' crazy recipe for business and personal success*. Austin, TX: Bard.

French, R., & Raven, B. (1968). The bases of power. In D. Cartwright & A. Zander (Eds.), *Group dynamics* (pp. 601–623). New York, NY: Harper & Row.

Guerrero, L. K., & Floyd, K. (2006). *Nonverbal communication in close relationships*. Mahwah, NJ: Erlbaum.

Hiemstra, K. M. (1999). Shake my hand: Making the right first impression in business with nonverbal communications. *Business Communication Quarterly, 62*, 71–74.

Ivy, D. K., & Wahl, S. T. (2009). *The nonverbal self: Communication for a lifetime*. Boston, MA: Allyn & Bacon.

Masip, J., Garrido, E., & Herrero, C. (2004). Facial appearance and impressions of credibility: The effects of facial babyishness and age on person perception. *International Journal of Psychology, 39*, 276–289.

Post, P., & Post, P. (2005). *Emily Post's the etiquette advantage in business: Personal skills for professional success* (2nd ed.). New York, NY: Collins.

Quintanilla, K. M., & Wahl, S. T. (2011). *Business and professional communication: Keys for workplace excellence*. Thousand Oaks, CA; Sage.

Chapter 12

Fishbein, M., & Ajzen, I. (1975). *Belief, attitude, intention, and behavior: An introduction to theory and research.* Reading, MA: Addison-Wesley.

Hollihan, T., & Baaske, K. (1998). *Arguments and arguing: The products and process of human decision making.* Prospect Heights, IL: Waveland Press, Inc.

Walker, G., & Sillars, M. O. (1990). Where is argument? Perelman's theory of values. In R. Trapp & J. Shuetz (Eds.), *Perspectives on argumentation: Essays in honor of Wayne Brockeride* (pp. 27–40). Prospect Heights, IL: Waveland Press, Inc.

Chapter 13

Berger, A. A. (1976). Anatomy of the joke. *Journal of Communication, 26*(3), 113–115.

Bizzell, P., & Herzberg, B. (2001). A general introduction. In P. Bizzell & B. Herzberg (Eds.), *The rhetorical tradition: Readings from classical time to the present* (pp. 17–364). Boston, MA: Bedford/St. Martin's.

Bloom, E. A., & Bloom, L. D. (1979). *Satire's persuasive voice.* Ithaca, NY: Cornell.

Booth-Butterfield, M., & Booth-Butterfield, S. (1991). Individual differences in the communication of humorous messages. *Southern Communication Journal, 56,* 32–40.

Burch, C. (2006, February 11). We laugh at Mencia, but we can't laugh him off. *Arizona Daily Star.*

Chapel, G. W. (1978). Humor in the White House: An interview with presidential speechwriter Robert Orben. *Communication Quarterly, 26,* 44–49.

Danbom, D. (2005). Getting serious about humor. *Vital Speeches of the Day, 71*(21), 668–672.

Deckers, L., & Devine, J. (1981). Humor by violating an existing expectancy. *Journal of Psychology, 108,* 107–110.

Deggans, E. (2006). Carlos Mencia can take a joke. *Hispanic, 19*(1), 30–31. Retrieved from the Academic Search Premier database.

Duncan, C. P., & Nelson, J. E. (1985). Effects of humor in a radio advertising experiment. *Journal of Advertising, 14,* 33–40.

Dziegielewski, S. F., Jacinto, A. L., & Rodriguez, L. L. (2004). Humor: An essential communication tool in therapy. *International Journal of Mental Health, 32,* 74–90.

Freud, S. (1905). *Wit and its relation to the unconscious.* New York, NY: Moffat Yard.

Goffman, E. (1967). *Interaction ritual: Essays in face to face behavior.* Chicago, IL: Aldine Publishing Company.

Grimes, W. (1955). The mirth experience in public address. *Speech Monographs, 22,* 243–255.

Gruner, C. R. (1967). Effect of humor on speaker ethos and audience information gain. *Journal of Communication, 17,* 228–233.

Gruner, C. R. (1997). *The game of humor: A comprehensive theory of why we laugh.* New Brunswick, NJ: Transaction Publishers.

Hauser, G. A. (1986). Introduction to rhetorical theory. New York: Harper & Row.

Herring, R., & Meggert, S. (1994). The use of humor as a counselor strategy with Native American Indian children. *Elementary School Guidance & Counseling*, *29*(4), 67–76.

Korobkin, D. (1988). Humor in the classroom: Considerations and strategies. *College Teaching*, *36*, 19–28.

Maase, S. W., Fink, E. K., & Kaplowitz, S. A. (1984). Incongruity in humor: The cognitive dynamics. In R. N. Bostrom & B. H. Westley (Eds.), *Communication Yearbook 8*. Beverly Hills, CA: Sage.

Martineau, W. H. (1972). A model of the social functions of humor. In J. H. Goldstein & P. E. McGhee (Eds.), *The psychology of humor* (pp. 101–128). Chicago, IL: Nelson-Hall.

McGhee, P. E. (1979). *Humor: Its origin and development*. San Francisco, CA: W. H. Freeman.

Meyer, J. (1990). Ronald Reagan and humor: A politician's velvet weapon. *Communication Studies*, *41*(1), 76–88.

Meyer, J. (2000). Humor as a double-edged sword: Four functions of humor in communication. *Communication Theory*, *10*(3), 310–331.

Morreall, J. (1983). *Taking laughter seriously*. Albany, NY: State University of New York Press.

New York Times. Transcript of Palin's Speech at the Republican National Convention. Election Guide 2008 (n.d.). Retrieved from http://elections.nytimes.com/2008/president/conventions/videos/transcripts/20080903_PALIN_SPEECH.html

O'Donnell, D. L. (2003). *The sharing of humor: Sympathetic and empathetic uses of humor* (Unpublished doctoral dissertation). The University of Southern Mississippi, Hattiesburg, MS.

Osterhouse, R., & Brock, T. (1970). Distraction increases yielding to propaganda by inhibiting counterarguing. *Journal of Personality and Social Psychology, 15*, 344–358.

Pacheco, Jr., G. (2008). Rhetoric with humor: An analysis of Hispanic/Latino comedians' uses of humor (Unpublished doctoral dissertation). The University of Southern Mississippi, Hattiesburg, MS.

Punyanunt, N. M. (2000). The effects of humor on perceptions of compliance-gaining in the college classroom. *Communication Research Reports*, *17*(1), 30–38.

Reagan, R. (1976, January 15). [Audiotape transcribed by author.] Campaign appearance in Keane, NH.

Rickenbaugh, K., prod., & Miller, P., dir. *Why You Crying*. Paramount Home Entertainment, 2005. Film.

Rybacki, K., & Rybacki, D. (1991). *Communication criticism: Approaches and genres*. Belmont, CA: Wadsworth.

Schaeffer, N. (1981). *The art of laughter*. New York, NY: Columbia University Press.

Schutz, C. E. (1977). *Political humor*. London: Associated Presses.

ShardsOGlass. (n.d.). Retrieved from http://www.shardsoglass.com/about/ad.cfm

Shultz, K., & Germeroth, D. (1998). Should we laugh or should we cry? John Callahan's humor as a tool to change societal attitudes toward disability. *Howard Journal of Communication, 9,* 229–244.

Sillars, M. O., & Gronbeck, B. E. (2001). *Communication criticism: Rhetoric, social codes, cultural studies.* Prospect Heights, IL: Waveland Press.

Taylor, P. M. (1974). An experimental study of humor and ethos. *Southern Speech Communication Journal, 39,* 359–366.

Veatch, T. C. (1998). A theory of humor. *International Journal of Humor Research, 11,* 161–215.

Credits

Text

Chapter 2: Page 19: "NCA Credo for Ethical Communication" from National Communication Association website, November 1999. Copyright © 1999 by National Communication Association. Reprinted with permission. www.natcom.org

Chapter 11: Page 259: Table from *The Nonverbal Self: Communication for a Lifetime,* 1st Edition, by Diana K. Ivy and Shawn T. Wahl. Copyright © 2009 by Pearson Education, Inc. Printed and Electronically reproduced by permission of Pearson Education, Inc., Upper Saddle River, New Jersey.

Chapter 12: Page 307: "Prosecution Deferred Is Justice Denied" by Hope Stallings, from *Winning Orations,* 2009. Copyright © 2009 by Interstate Oratorical Association. Reprinted with permission of Interstate Oratorical Association, Mankato, MN.

Photos

Chapter 1: Page 4: © Aprescindere | Dreamstime.com; page 5: © Mira Agron | Dreamstime.com; page 8: © Zyron | Dreamstime.com

Chapter 2: Page 29: © Lee Snider | Dreamstime.com

Chapter 3: Page 43 © Skip ODonnell/iStockphoto; page 44: © iofoto/iStockphoto; page 45: © Endrias Zewde | Dreamstime.com

Chapter 4: Page 67: © Micko1986; page 72: © PeopleImages.

Chapter 5: Page 94:© Beth Dixson/Alamy Stock Photo; page 100: © Daneil Raustadt | Dreamstime.com; page 109: Jason Winslow/Splash News/Newscom; page 110: ASSOCIATED PRESS; page 112: NC1 WENN Photos/Newscom

Chapter 7: Page 149: © CHP Newswire/Alamy Stock Photo; page 160: © Paul Mckinnon | Dreamstime.com

Chapter 9: Page 215: Figure from *Psychology: From Inquiry to Understanding,* 1st Edition, by Scott O. Lilienfeld, Steven J. Lynn, Laura L. Namy and Nancy J. Woolf. Copyright © 2009 by Pearson Education, Inc. Printed and Electronically reproduced by permission of Pearson Education, Inc., Upper Saddle River, New Jersey.

Chapter 10: Page 235: Jon Simon Feature Photo Service/Newscom

Chapter 12: Page 278: © Nisarg Lakhmani/Alamy Stock Photo; page 303: © Trevor Walker/Alamy Stock Photo

Index

CPSIA information can be obtained
at www.ICGtesting.com
Printed in the USA
FSOW04n1355110516
20334FS